WE ARE THE INTELLIGENT DESIGNER

DESIGNING THE ANTHROPOCENE

James A Martin

Table of Contents

We Are the Intelligent Designer 1

Introduction..2

Children of the Trees 6

We Evolve Us 9

Nine Billion of Our Closest Relatives 16

This Land is Our Land 24

The Culture of Agronomy 35

Man's Best Friend, and Dinner 43

Sticks & Stones and Nanos...62

We Have the Power 68

The Market for Self-Destruction 82

The Trash Mines of Mumbai 90

Changing the Environment...93

A Sustainable World 108

Evil...123

How to Not Make War 129

The Unnatural Species, Genes, AI, the Synthocene, and Transhuman 134

Homo astro and Homo cosmos..153

The Intelligently Designed Human, *Homo designus*......................................157

Epilogue..163

Bibliography...173

We Are the Intelligent Designer

There are multiple books, stories, and movies on specifics of the Anthropocene's impact. The purpose with this book is show how they interrelate, the synthesis of the Anthropocene's factors on the planet, the life forms, including us, and what it may mean for the future.

All projections of future events are based on the best scientific projections at the time of publication but are subject to outside events. No event is isolated, but all are part of an interrelationship with every other event, and the results will be unknown until they happen. So be it.

Anthropocene (Oxford Languages)

Nouns: *"The current geological age, viewed as the period during which human activity has been the dominant influence on climate and the environment.*

Adjective: *"relating to or denoting the current geological age, viewed as the period during which human activity has been the dominant influence on climate and the environment."*

Intelligent Design

Noun: *the theory that life, or the universe, cannot have arisen by chance and was designed and created by some intelligent entity.*

Design

Noun: *a plan or drawing produced to show the look and function or workings of a building, garment, or another object before it is built or made.*

Verb: decide upon the look and functioning of (a building, garment, or other objects) by making a detailed drawing of it.

Synthocene

Noun: *A future geological age, viewed as the period during which synthetic, robotic, machine intelligence, and AI activity are the dominant influence on climate and the environment.*

Introduction

I am an American, born and raised in the United States and educated as a professional Industrial Designer. This is not to proclaim any special privilege but to establish my perspectives on which this book is centered.

The United States is the largest economy and most culturally impactful country in the world. It's a nation that has done great things but also still working towards the goal first stated in the preamble of the Constitution, "in Order to form a more perfect Union." It's still a work in progress.

As an Industrial Designer, I was curious when I first heard the term "Intelligent Design," often shortened as "ID." We designers thought we were the original IDs who have been intelligently designing things for years, as have our fellow creators of buildings, scripts, spreadsheets, and medical procedures.

Intelligent Designers, Evolution, Artificial Intelligence, Income inequality, Nanos, the Anthropocene, Biodiversity, Transhumanism, and Gene therapy; I am familiar with these terms, but how do they interrelate? So often, I read of these as independent subjects, "siloing."

To understand a design, you must understand each of the factors and how they interrelate. In my work in designing products or teaching technology, I found that if I could make sense of a problem, then the solution would come of itself, and I was able to help students understand. Louis Sullivan first said, "Form follows function." Understand the function, and the form makes sense. I try here to look at the changes in the various functions and limitations and how those changes affected the forms, including us.

I especially looked at the human body (chapter 17). While visually pleasing to our aesthetic senses, there are multiple design faults that are suboptimal to their tasks.

Who are the designers? It's all of us in this world. Our individual planned decisions may be small and often in conflict with the decisions of others, but when combined and interacted, they form the greater design.

So, what have we designed? We have designed our lives, society, and the planet itself. And for that, we control the design. Are we shown to be intelligent designers? Are we making the best design decisions to optimize what we have for our species and the fellow species that share the planet but have no say in the design and the planet itself? Probably not.

A design is not always a single action by a single designer. It's a creation with a thousand designers, often interacting in their own ways without realizing their influence on each other.

We live on the most amazing place in the universe. Telescopes and space probes have shown us many wonders of other worlds, but all of them combined do not match the collection of features that are on the Earth. And we have life, from the simplest bacteria and primitive organisms billions of years old, through plants and animals that have evolved with changing environments to the present rich tapestry that exists on planet Earth today.

Earth's successes have been attributed to being in this *"Goldilocks Zone,"* that perfect location of not too hot or too cold around a perfectly sized star, then built of stardust containing the right materials plus liquid water and mated to a moon sufficiently large enough to stabilize the planet and the Van Allen belt protecting us from the ravages of solar storms as the gas giants (Jupiter, Saturn, and Uranus) cleared a path through the cosmos for this small rock. Less than four billion years ago, the right set of conditions came to be, and here is life that has been able to adapt to almost every condition, features that have allowed for life, including us, features that without which there would be no life and no humans to contemplate the design.

But the planet is not optimized as a designer would make it. The distribution of water is uneven, and weather extremes cause catastrophic losses. Now we humans are taking the tasks to maximize the world to fit our needs. Some of the steps have been planned, and while others are from unintended consequences, all are actions created by humans into a new epoch called the *Anthropocene.*

A design is a synthesis of multiple factors. Whether a product, a script, or a way to accomplish a goal, the design is a plan taken with input from the intention, economic, physical, and social limitations, and awareness, or lack, of consequences. The consequences of carrying out the design may not be the desired result, but it was the design that initiated the action. Design is not only what is but what can be and what could be if it was freed of evolutionary constraints to adapt to new functions drawing from useful but non-evolutionary features. Factors cross influence each other, often in unimaginable ways.

As stated by the original environmentalist John Muir: *"When we try to pick out anything by itself, we find it hitched to everything else in the Universe."* So, it is with the Anthropocene. We have micro goals, but in carrying out actions, we are making macro impacts on the world, our fellow life forms, and ourselves. Planned or unintended, our actions are changing the design. To have a degree of control of the design, we have to look beyond the intended goal and realize the long-term consequences of our actions.

Geologist uses three markers in the evolution of the Anthropocene. They look for changes in artifacts in soil layers (Agricultural Revolution) from planned planting and harvesting of seeds. The second is a layer of coal dust in the 17th century, indicating burning coal for steam engines: control of energy needs (Industrial Revolution). The third is the mid-20th century radiation from atomic tests.

For this, I use three slightly different markers. The *Agricultural Revolution* was the beginning for food control. We took charge of seeds and plants in parallel with the domestication of animals. The second is the *"Age of Expansion,"* from the 15th through 17th century when Western civilizations began to expand the limits of thought (Renaissance and Enlightenment), geography (worldwide exploration), and control of materials and energy (Industrial Revolution and elements).

The Industrial Revolution has itself come in three phases. The first was in the late 17th century, with the steam engine as a reliable power source. The second phase in the 19th century changed with the creation and transmission of electrical power. Electricity could be utilized to where the user was. The third part is the collection and distribution of data.

In the *Age of Expansion,* the Renaissance looked backward to relearn the glories of art, government, and philosophy of the ancient Greek and Roman civilizations. The Enlightenment explored the world as it was through the first applications of the scientific method. They created science. In doing so, they also created contemporary democracy and the rights of individuals. They were able to exchange new ideas by building upon records of existing ideas. Accurate mass idea storage built a foundation for growth, looking to the future that can be more than a cyclical repeat of past actions.

They were designing a new world of the mind.

The navigators were finding new lands. But the lands of the "new worlds" were already inhabited by humans. Some had stable societies at different levels of development. Many had been sustainable to their environment for hundreds of years. They had individual languages, religious values, and trade.

The arrival of the "discovers" brought 16th century European values that perceived the indigenous peoples as primitive who were to be liberated from ignorance (religiously and culturally). As they had different (primitive) values, the Europeans thought that there was a need to educate them.

European economic growth led by rising merchant classes saw the "new lands" as untapped opportunities for resources. Development needed labor which was supplied through human trafficking and forced beginning in the early 16th century, counter to the expansion of individual rights and the importance of scientific inquiry that were central to the Enlightenment.

The third marker of the Anthropocene is the "*Great Acceleration*" beginning from the mid-20th century in the increased production and consumption of energy, data, and products. The third marker layer for future geologists will not be in radioactive dust but in candy wrappers and microchips.

Victor Papanek stated in *Design for the Real World*: "*All men are designers. All that we do, almost all the time, is design, for design is basic to all human activity. The planning and patterning of any act toward a desired foreseeable end constitutes the design process. Design is composing an epic. But design is also pulling an impacted tooth, baking an apple pie…and educating a child. Design is the conscious effort to impose meaningful order.*"

It's easy to get so involved in our own area of expertise that we lose sight of factors that influenced the area and the unaddressed effect of our actions. A design has to cross expertise, acknowledging that each is both a cause and an effect, interlocking functions that produce the form.

Humans are different from all other species. For others, life is; eat, sleep, and reproduce. Humans have a fourth; we think, we imagine. It's the brain that we can't let be idle. We are infoverse.

We *Homo sapiens* (latin: "*wise man*") are generalist in a world of specialists. Where every other life form has survived due to a specialization that fits a specific environmental niche, humans have survived by being adaptable and thereby have prospered in every condition. We have what Dr. Erle C. Ellis calls a "Sociocultural Niche" built as much on our social interactions to a degree beyond any other species, including in non-kin in co-operation through unparalleled communication and cooperation.

As children, we think that we are the center of the world. That made sense for people who seldom travelled beyond what land they could see the land, and therefore they were the center of everything. Myths described how the gods created them as "*the people.*" The Chinese name for their land is *Zhongguo*, literally translated as "Middle Kingdom," "the center of civilization." It wasn't as ego but as a perception of the world they knew. The sun, moon, and stars were centered upon them and their region.

With maturity, each self-centered child becomes an adult that is part of a greater interdependent society. Each of us is an individual within a group, and our individual actions change the environment. We are the center of our universe, and at the same time a minute part of everything.

Further observations and mathematical computations proved that the Earth and a group of bright lights in the sky were recognized as planets. Each revolved around the sun and it, not us, was the center. With further observations, the sun lost its position of center point as it and our solar system was but a part on the fringe of a greater galaxy, the Milky Way. In time recognition that even the Milky Way galaxy was but one in a universe that included billions and billions of galaxies. More recent theories have gone beyond that, and our universe may be but one in a multitude of universes, a multiverse.

Time has equally expanded from our life to our tribal memory. In 1615 AD, Bishop James Usher determined that the earth was created on October 23rd 4,004 BCE (Before Common Era). Contrast that scientists have determined it has been 13.7 billion years from the moment of creation to the present. And that even this might be a mere moment to the multiverse.

Besides changing the shape and makeup of the planet, humans are creating new materials from which it is made. Nature has provided elements and compounds, but humans have combined and reconfigured these into new forms of matter that nature could not create and expanded the basic atomic makeup to new elements. We have helped lives (all life forms) survive by reducing threats of parasites of various forms and will soon be able to reintroduce extinct animals.

Along the way we have reproduced in ways that evolutionary nature could not do. Beginning with bronze, we merged materials into alloys that have properties exceeding anything from nature. While nature grows materials linearly, we created cross-ply, as with plywood, a similar mass but multi times stronger. And nature moves linearly with body parts still connected. We made a new form of action as things can continually rotate as wheels, propellers, and armatures.

For the first time, a sound was not lost as the air vibrations dissipated but was collected by a human created device to be produced and reproduced. Light rays that had always bounced off an object to continue to infinity stimulated a media that could be a permanent record of the passing of those rays, holding them as images to be viewed again, giving immortality to transient energy waves.

Humans began the 20th century by migrating into the third dimension. Our directions before had always been "across," but now they included "down" and "up." With submersibles and airplanes, we entered the realm of fishes and birds and in the last third of the century, expanded to where no Earth life had ever intentionally entered, spaced, or doorway-ed to the universe. Someday we may even take our accomplishments and values to design the cosmos.

Not every issue or example can be covered here. Our knowledge and my understanding is always limited. Central to this story is through the United States. It's the home with which I am most familiar, and it's the most consequential country in the world today and despite resistance, both within and without, leading in areas that will have design impacts on the Anthropocene.

For the first time, a being is not entirely at the mercy of the environment. Rather than being forced to adapt to changes, we are able to design the changes.

We can make the best of this planet in order to bring the best of what humans can be to the cosmos. But we have to take responsibility. We are now the designer and custodian of the world. As Shakespeare wrote through Cassius: "*The fault, dear Brutus, is not in our stars, but in our selves...*" Hopefully, we can prove to do so with wisdom and intelligence.

The form of the Anthropocene is the result of how we have reacted to the changing environmental functions of our species. To understand is to explore how we came to be the dominant species and where this may lead us and the world.

In understanding how our actions cross influence every other action we can truly design the environment to be a sustainable Anthropocene.

"*Our basic common link is that we all inhabit the same small planet. We all breathe the same air. We all cherish our children's future. And we are all mortal.*"

John F Kennedy

Children of the Trees

The best contemporary theory of creation is the Big Bang, which occurred about 13.8 billion years ago (bya). Energy transformed into matter and expanded outward, marking the beginning of time and space. Matter evolved into atoms that grew increasingly complex, forming from dust, gas, and particles. This matter gave rise to stars, serving as focal points for planets, moons, asteroids, comets, and other interstellar bodies.

Around 4.54 bya, near a mid-sized yellow sun, our 'Goldilocks' planet was formed. Over time, it acquired the right conditions including temperature, water, solid land, and an optimal atmosphere comprised of oxygen, nitrogen, CO_2, and other elements crucial for life as we recognize it. A heated central core generates an enhanced magnetic shield, while an ozone layer provides protection against cosmic radiation. Volcanic activity and shifting tectonic plates sustain a continuous recycling of the planet's surface. A collision with a large celestial body tilted the planet, resulting in seasons and the creation of the moon. Earth stands as the most diverse and vibrant world within our observation.

Within a billion years, life emerged and evolution set in motion. Cyanbacteria, a blue-green algae, using photosynthesis, became the first microbes to produce oxygen perhaps as long ago as 3.5 bya and certainly by 2.7 bya in the "Great Oxidation Event."

The design model that evolved into *Homo sapiens* began in the branches during the latter Cretaceous epoch, the last period of dinosaur dominance. Most of the features that are part of all primates and would allow human domination of the planet came about as a result of adapting to the unique conditions of life above the dangerous thunder lizards.

Trees that provided safety from the dominant dinosaurs for over ten million years were a crucial factor in many aspects of primate design. The first recognized pre-primate ancestor the mirorder Primatomorpha mammal group, may have lived as early as 79.6 mya (million years ago).

There were multiple ways that an animal could navigate through the trees, arboreal locomotion. No option offered the dexterity of the primate derived opposed thumb, one of the three most important evolutionary changes in human physiology.

The design of a group of primates called Teilhardina, along with other mammal orders, had skeletal features adapted to living in the three-dimensional world of trees. Brachiate locomotion allows primates to hang and swing between branches. The ankle bones had diagnostic features for mobility that are only present in those of primates and their close relatives today. They had big eye sockets allowing stereoscopic vision that aided in tree jumping rather than the defensive side vision found in other non-predator mammals. The joints, flexible for climbing and clinging to branches, could rotate and adjust accordingly to grab branches while moving through trees. The long limbs were better suited for manipulating fruit or insects. The opposing thumb allowed wrapping around a branch.

Charles Darwin wrote that "Man could not have attained his present dominant position in the world without the use of his hands, which are so admirably adapted to the act of obedience of his will."

The size of the brains and eyes increased even as their snouts reduced, relying more on vision than smell. The foramen magnum moved back towards the center of the skull, suggesting a vertical angle to the spinal cord for a body that is habitually vertical rather than the horizontal orientation

Primarily on a diet of fruits, leaves, and insects, the mandible lower jaw chewed food. Side movement allowed additional movement, later a necessity for speech.

The chest became the dominant feature rather than the back. The anus, used for identification with many horizontal species, was now set upon and so useless for identification. Other means, principally visual and auditory, became dominant. Visual dependence encouraged a group relationship that necessitated communication.

With the warmer African climate, the ancestors of the apes adapted to living along the savannah then diverged about 8-9 mya into two lines that led to gorillas and another that further diverged around 7 mya separating the ancestors of modern chimpanzees and bonobos from the early hominins.

While other primates may momentarily stand and walk, movement across the ground is usually on feet and knuckles. For hominins, verticality became the norm with full bipedal characteristics consistent as early as 4.2 mya,

There are several hypotheses to explain full bipedalism. One theory is that in conjunction with opposing thumbs, males had free hands for tools or weapons, and females could carry children or food while still moving rapidly.

They were in a different environment where vertical orientation proved to be an advantage for survival. They could see over the grasses of the savannah locating potential prey or to avoid predators. With vertical orientation, a smaller amount of the body is exposed to the sun, and more is exposed to cooling winds. Body hair, necessary for cooling, was reduced. The entire skin perspires, giving off retained heat. While not as fast running as other large mammals, exposed skin allowed ongoing heat dissipation for chasing prey until it was forced to slow from exhaustion or overheating, making them easy victims to the hunter group.

Vertical orientation necessitated other changes in the hominin body. The balance system was improved as the femur developed a slightly more angular position moving toward the geometric center of the body. While joints on all four limbs for other primates were of nearly even robustness, bipedal hominins evolved stronger lower joints.

The third major physiological change was in the ability to speak. Two factors were involved; the increased mobility of the tongue and lips and the structure and location of the larynx.

Hominins had a reduced mouth with the change of dental arcade of three types of teeth to parabolic from U-shaped and the development of the chin. Eating meat reduced the need for a large array of grinding molars. Hominins became more day active, putting increased emphasis on sight and hearing. Hominins also gained better control of breathing enabling speaking during breaths. Less constrained by length, facial muscles were able to create more expressions, and as lips became thicker vocal and non-vocal facial communication became more sophisticated.

Through all aspects of hominin evolution, the overriding change was in the increased size of the brain. Like in other advanced primates, the skull of hominins is made of multiple plates that fuse together over time. With a strong jaw for chewing chimpanzee plates are attached to the muscle. As hominin diets changed, the jaw muscle was reduced, allowing for the plates to grow larger before fusing, thereby allowing a greater brain size.

Using the opposing thumb, bipedal stance, and speaking, they began to take control of their fate; defending from and attacking animals, building fires and communities that communicated beyond kindred tribes.

They made tools from weapons to cooking pots and shelters that allowed them to move out of the African cradle into the wider world.

Changing from a scavenger/hunter meat eater to a crop diet led to greater salivary amylase for breaking down starches as teeth became 10% smaller to eat softer foods. The *sapien* jaw has continued to evolve with a decline of size of about 1% every thousand years.

The *Homo sapiens* ancestor became a unique species about 300,000 years ago. They had the body features plus the brain size of contemporary *sapiens* so probably were as smart as we are.

They emigrated out of Africa, probably in multiple waves, about 89,000 years ago, where they encountered tribes of Neanderthals in present day Europe and Denisovans in Asia. As Europe warmed, the glaciers receded, and warmer grassland replaced forests. Speed became more important than strength for hunting.

The evolution of hominins is ongoing through gene mutation to thrive in different environments. In the last 30,000 years, as *sapiens* moved into cooler climates with less sunlight, their skin color lightened. Moving into the present Europe, blue and green eyes became common, and hair varied in color to shades of browns and reds, while eastern movement led to retaining the black color but becoming straight.

We Evolve Us

"Man is an invention produced out of the knowledge(s) he has created as it assigns attributes of knowledge ... inducted into a culture."

Life has changed our planet, and we are but the latest life form that continues to remake the world. But where other changers have done without a plan, humans are changing the world by design, though not always the way we intended, and the first change was to the hominin design.

Hominins built shelters in new areas, allowing hominins to move into territories and environments for which their bodies were not suitable. Mobile shelters provided protection for mobile hominins.

Homo sapiens evolved from the African emigrants. Obvious racial features reflect adaptations to environments different from the African valleys. The Cognitive Genomics Lab estimates that there are 10,000 genetic variations, yet all are still *sapiens*.

As hominin intelligence grew, they were able to use the evolutionary advantages of a larger brain in controlling fire, bipedal, opposable thumb, and superior communication. They began having a greater influence. It was the beginning of "anthropogenic forcing."

Fire and Cooking

The relationship to fire is one of the major differences between hominins and all other animals. All animals react by moving away from it. There is no immunity to fire.

Control of fire brought important changes to hominins. They used fires for heat, keeping predators at bay, and cooking. The fire-side community was encouraged by the light of the fire.

Hominin use of fire may have been as distant as 1.42 mya. Various sites in Kenya show signs of clay shreds among Homo *erectus* artifacts heated to over 400°C.

Hominins were able to move into colder climates with fires for warmth on the colder nights when other mammals became dormant.

Fire changed the diet. Cooked meat was softer to eat with fire acting in a pre-digestive manner, and with heated meats, they were able to consume more for the energy used. Cooked and preserved meat could be eaten days later. Cooking was also effective in killing parasites and pathogens, thereby improving overall health. Cooking allowed the digestion of starchy foods with complex carbohydrates that absorbed more food energy. The addition of fatty acid foods allowed hominins to be able to support a larger brain. With eating cooked food, teeth gradually became smaller, and the jaw shrunk.

By 10,000 BCE, heat-fired clay in fires was made to create permanent containers and pottery. The first metals were shaped two-millennium later through smelting. Gold and copper were the first due to their availability and malleability. In the Chalcolithic period (6,000 to 4,000 BCE), copper was cast into useful items, including weapons. Built upon fire, the human creation of bronze was the first alloy of non-natural sourcing.

Tools

The 20th-century media philosopher Marshall McLuhan stated, "*We shape our tools. And then our tools shape us.*" Our social practices co-evolve with our use of new tools.

Tools are an extension of a being's capability. Hominins using tools about 3.5 mya became *Homo hablis* (skilled man).

Development of tools beyond basic implements required a designer, someone who recognized the potential of materials and synthesized with the useful relationship of multiple items. . Psychiatrist Simon Baron-Cohen believes that there was a genetic change in the *Homo sapien* brain that caused them to look for patterns in casual reasoning, "if-then logic." It is something only humans are capable of. "No other species seems to do this." Humans look for "Why."

The other change was possible by two biological evolutions: a larger brain that was able to relate parts to needs and an opposable thumb to grasp and hold an object for use. One reason is the need; the other implements.

Stone-tipped spears were probably introduced by *Homo heidelbergensis* about 500,000 ya. With the introduction of the atlatl, small spears, and bow powered spears (arrows), hunters were further removed from prey while increasing striking power.

About 350,000 ya more refined tools were created in the Levallois technique that including scrapers, slicers, needles, and flattened needles. Bones were used for tools by Neanderthals about 50,000 BCE. They were superseded by *Homo sapiens* with superior tools.

Domestication

With early tools, hominins were able to have a degree of control over their food supply. Herding goats and sheep and then cattle provided a reliable supply of meat and milk (proteins). Planting and harvesting grains (carbohydrates) and domestication of plants filled out a diet that could be stored and shared. About 11,000 ya domestication led to communities, the first marker of the Anthropocene, the "Agricultural Revolution."

This caused a change of spirituality as the food was less dependent upon "given by the gods" to what they could produce or take down. With the increase in meat availability, the diet became more protein dominant, further enhancing the brain's size and capabilities. Hominins originally followed the herds, taking as needed. Humans prospered with the herds. With success in hunting large mammals, they unknowingly caused a depletion in prey, forcing hunters to go for smaller prey more often obtained by females. At about 5,700 BCE, they gathered sheep and goats into herds that would be led by humans into another stage of human development as herders. With migration, they took their supply of meat and milk with them. About 4,200 BCE, with the assistance of dogs and later grass eating horses, they could live in the prairies that were inhospitable for a hunter-gatherer tribe.

Of the thousands of species of animals, only a few were domesticated to live under human control and with humans. Dr. Jared Diamond proposed six characteristics of domestication:

An animal must be able to exist on a varied diet, including leftovers from humans.

The animal must be able to mature quickly so as not to strain humans until the animal is productive.

Willingness to breed in captivity and kept in pens.

They must be of a gentle disposition to peers and outsiders. They easily fit with the other characteristics and are loyal to their pack.

They must be calm by nature, not always on edge, and ready to flee.

They must be sociable, willing to stay in groups, and follow a leader, eventually being led by a human.

Taming is not the same as *Domesticating*. In the former, the individual animal is forced to subvert natural instincts to comply with human requests. A circus lion is "tamed." A sheepdog is "domesticated."

Domestication provides humans with tools of power and a ready protein supply. It also made humans responsible for the animal's protection and feed. The herd was dependent upon the tribe. Humans had to build defenses, plus diverting water for both planted crops and penned animals alike. Domesticated animals led to the domestication of humans.

The development of agriculture in the Neolithic period, about 12,000 years ago, drastically changed human society and diet. Nomadic life was replaced with villages, and the protein diet was supplemented with a carbohydrate diet from grains. Domesticated grains could be stored, balancing out the producing period with the eating year. With tools for breaking shells and hard husks and with cooking, humans were able to eat all parts of various plants,

Close contact with domestication also had adverse effects. The larger the tight grouping of humans and accompanying animals leads to a higher probability of contamination, infection, and diseases from animals, called "zoonosis." Diseases are passed to humans by parasites like fleas, from the consumption of infected meat, and by release from the decay of dead infected animals.

Agricultural communities gained over their hunter-gather neighbors. With a stable environment, some females were able to shorten the interval between births from over four years to about two out populating nomadic tribes. Farming tribes had a density of ten times that of the nomadic tribes. With an increased food supply, some tribal members were able to become artists, craftsmen, and shamans to organize food distribution or a standing army. Moving along the east/ west Eurasian axis, domesticated animals and plants were spread across a greater area and included a larger variety of species.

There was a price. There were more examples of anemias and vitamin deficiencies, more spinal deformations, and more dental pathologies. Emphasis was placed on maximizing a few crops and animals rather than the diversity of hunter-gatherer life. Foods varied by season, geography, and climate. Unless the body was immersed in physical activities, the excess sugars were stored, creating weight gains.

Communication, Language and Writing

Evolution provided humans with a unique mouth and tongue shaped by muscles that allowed hominins to create a wide variety of sounds and annotations. It's with language and art that ideas and concepts of diverse thoughts are exchanged to design group actions. Communication for hominins is through sound and sight. Sounds that were expressed emotionally formed patterns that became music. Visual expressions of what was seen diverged into symbolic representations that were given meanings, either individually or collectively, that became writing and expressing feelings as art. To cooperate, the members had to understand each other, not only through the words but through empathy that the words were being understood and conveyed the intended meaning. Increased empathy yielded increased communication and cooperation, yielding the increased potential for success in hunting or building.

By 100,000 ya, human behavior was changing in the way we expressed ourselves. Symbolic art and adornments were created to add personal identity and express ourselves to others, recognizing individualism beyond the self-awareness of many animal species.

A history of the development of language is difficult to explain due to lack of physical evidence. Using at phonemes, the consonants, vowels, and tones that are the simplest elements of language, lingo-archeologists have found a simple but striking pattern in some 500 languages spoken throughout the world.

Language provided another survival tool. Language allowed for communication between unrelated hunting groups. Not only knowledge of the best methods of hunting but also abstract thoughts that became rules and beliefs.

As language projected thoughts, music projected feelings. The first human-created music is unknown, though all cultures have some form of musical expression. While there is no physical evidence in the development of oral language, there is for visual expression in writing and art. The first visual expressions were in paintings. The oldest were found in caves in Spain, dating to approximately 40,000 ya. They provide a record by the creator of their lives and environment.

Paintings and writing were the first time that records could be passed from one being to another over time and between beings that had no physical contact with each other. Thoughts and experiences were not lost but were human's first steps toward immortality.

Expressions of thoughts and explanations of events evolved into religions that saw the power in animals, the weather, and in beings beyond our comprehension that had controlled their lives.

Pieces of ochre rock decorated with geometric patterns found at Blombos-ocher-plaque in South Africa were dated to at least 25,000 ya. The Lebomo bone, from Swaziland, about 35,000 BCE, indicates marks for records. Maps may also have predated language writing. The oldest map, carved onto a mammoth tusk, found in present-day Ukraine, may date from about 10,000 BCE.

Abstract symbols were understood by the creating group as representing a thing, an idea, or an organization with accompanying values of each entity and what it meant to them.

The Sumerians created the first known cuneiforms in approximately 3,200 BCE. The shape of an animal or its head became a symbol for the animal. Combining symbols gave meaning beyond objects. Continual simplifying and combing led to the alphabet and words we understand today. The contemporary Chinese script is the result of an evolution from depictions of things to stylized symbols, different from the Western use of letters for more complex words or ideas.

The Sumerians "wrote" on clay tablets, while the Chinese used brushes with fluid strokes on skins and later paper. The contemporary alphabet originated in the eastern Mediterranean region about 800 BCE as a proto-Sinatic Semitic system. It was built around simple sounds of vowels and consonants. This was merged with the Greek writing system to create the contemporary alphabet. Written with agreed upon words, it allowed a common set of laws and trade. Ideas like philosophy, theatre, history, and science were written and passed intact to be built upon.

The medias of clay tablets, brush on paper, animal skins, parchment, or chiseled in stone were the primary media for written communicating. The letter and symbol styles were tailored to the media. Even with technologies for mass distribution, as with the printing press, the styles were still familiar fonts.

In the mid 20th century computers created new tools for data transfer between humans and computers and later directly between computers. New fonts were specially designed to also be read by computers. These were still readable to humans as letters. With the text limitations of the smartphone symbols were developed to express ideas, things, and feelings writing in symbols as emojis more quickly than with words. Anticipating computer data transfers Marshall McLuhan wrote in the 1950s that "words…are just too slow to be relevant or effective."

QR and Bar codes can only be read by other computers.

Hominins probably first exchanged one item for another in barter. Different items had to be justified as having an equal value. Exchanges were made, giving both goods a "market value." The symbolic item need not have actual value but was one that had an accepted value to each party. This is a "double coincidence of wants."

Symbolic items of accepted value made trade possible as long as both parties accepted the worth of the item. The first evidence of trade was about 12,000 BCE in the Mediterranean area. The need or desires for goods that are more abundant in one area were exchanged for a different abundant good in another. The Code of Eshnunna, about 1,930 BCE, is the first recorded law that formalized the role of money with the first coins minted about 600 BCE.

Anthropocene of the Mind

Communication plus allowing select people to have time led to a sub set Anthropocene marker, one of the minds, the "Axial Age." It reached its height between 900 and 300 BCE in emerging civilizations around the world. They developed philosophies that set the base for our contemporary morals, religions, and philosophies.

Laws, physical and moral, began to formalize beyond natural observances. Being able to write permanent laws, the Hammurabi Code gave consistent interpretations of actions and consequences. Moses gave a set of laws to the tribes of Abraham. The Buddha, between 563 and 483 BCE, offered an eight-fold path for reaching enlightenment.

In China, Confucius, 551-479 BCE, emphasized a virtuous life of personal morality, justice, and sincerity. Taoism and the teaching of Lao-Tse were roughly contemporary as was the Hundred Schools of Thought (6th century BCE).

Much of distinct Western thought began in the Golden Age of Greece with Plato (4th century BCE), a student of Socrates who thought through problems based on logic. To him there were two realms; the spiritual and the physical. His student Aristotle was the first to bring the concept of the atom along with writings on ethics and political theory.

Medicine

Survival depends on maintaining a healthy body. When the body is injured or limited due to a disease, the probability of survival is reduced.

Primates used many of the same methods and through cooperative pruning, washed in areas that the injured could not self-treat and to pick off ticks, lice, and other parasites. Animals and hominins alike ate soil-like substances such as clay and chalk, a condition called *geophagy*. While of questionable internal use, clays applied on cuts and wounds help to heal.

By trial and observation, hominins used herbs and plants that had healing and therapeutic properties. Without a written language, hominins passed this knowledge orally through stories. New knowledge was added, and the collection of treatments increased. Hominins sought to know why the illness occurred and why a remedy worked. The answers they were able to provide led to the creation of both medicine and religion. Although having no formal "scientific process," efforts were made to explain what happened.

The Neanderthals were the first to show signs of spirituality as they buried their dead. Cro-Magnon cave paintings and stone figures appear to have a religious significance representing ties to both the physical and spiritual world. Early civilizations sought to communicate with the forces that made rain, earthquakes, and disease, trying to influence events that made up their lives. To the Chinese from the Shang dynasty (14th-11th century BCE) Chi, the balance of the forces of yin and yang and the Five Phases were central to their healing. Native-Americans had a similar life force called *ni* by the Lakota and *nilch'I* by the Navajo. From the Greeks to Mayans through sacrifices and prayer, tried to contact the supernatural world and their gods to understand

and hopefully have a degree of control.

They become curious and filled the gap with possible alternatives that are set aside or proven until there is the information for a new understanding. The practice of systematic observation, measurement, and experiment, and the formulation, testing, and modification of hypotheses, proposes a question, creates a hypothesis, creates experiments, and tests the results had been in use since early civilization.

As early as 60,000 BCE, plants, including yarrow, rosemary, and mallow were used to treat injuries. Plants as common as dandelions contain healthful ingredients.

Western medicine is more mechanistic based on the laws of science. Though Western hi-tech medicine offers the best health, 80% of the World's population cannot afford it, and ancient medical myths still persist. The results are still uneven health care and reliance upon remedies that encourage the destruction of certain species (i.e., shark fins, rhinoceros tusks).

The Egyptians were the first civilization to formally write down their medical drugs and procedures about 1,500 BCE with the Ebers Papyrus, though the Sumerians listed medical plants on clay tablets 1,500 years before. Sanskrit writings as early as 1,900 BCE listed herbs also used in India in the Avurveda system. Four thousand years of accumulated medical knowledge is built upon the first recorded observations and curiosity from shamans to brain surgeons. Today we are finding out more of what we don't know and how to address the gaps.

SocioCultural

Culture: *"the customary beliefs, social forms, and material traits of a racial, religious, or social group... the characteristic features of everyday existence shared by people in a place or time"* (Merriam Webster Dictionary)

Humans are the most social species, forming groups beyond their kin through a cultural evolution to cause changes in longevity and scope.

Culture doesn't just happen, it's designed. It's in the design of the town layout that encourages cooperation or segregation. It's the architecture that reflects the inhabitant's values. It's the knowledge from how we process the data and choose to selectively pass it along. It's how we design our foods and portray our art. It's how we relate to other people.

From the first sapiens of about 300,000 ya, to today the body and brain size have changed little, indicating that they were probably as intelligent as contemporary humans so the change that occurred has been in the social development of culture. Early sapiens came together to bring individual strengths to help the tribe. Biologist David Wilson said that between groups, selfish individuals will defeat altruistic ones, but that group of altruistic individuals, who are willing to sacrifice for the greater group, will prevail over selfish individuals. Humans are hardwired to be both selfish and altruistic. They were willing to cooperate, not just for propagation within their tribe, but to unite strengths for the betterment of the tribe, even including helpful non-kin. Naturalist E. O. Wilson (no relation) described the trait in humans as "Eusociality."

Humans took it another step by uniting kin tribes into larger tribes built around a common theme. With the extended tribe, more hominins were interacting, and with language thoughts and ideas, the scope and complexity of culture were transmitted. Interbreeding across tribes improved the gene pool. 'Behavioral modernity" began about 65,000 to 50,000 ya as more advanced technologies started appearing, including complex projectile weapons such as bows and spear-throwers fishhooks plus, ceramics, and sewing needles. They formed cultural inheritances where learned knowledge and tribal mores were passed horizontally across tribes and vertically along generations. The sudden flourishing of technology has been called the "Great Leap Forward,' one of the most important periods in sapiens cultural evolution. One cause of this leap was that there were simply more sapiens to innovate with, create in technology, and share and interact with the arts and ideas.

Innovations allowed the population to increase, which provided more innovators. As technologies became more complex, innovators had to work together highlighting sapien uniqueness in communication and sociability. Population increases with communication, and technology began to outstrip the environment, devastating local megafauna, some to extinction, forcing food control.

Tribes today are built around a national or racial identity, a common economic, political, military, or even intellectual uniformity where people find purpose with one another. Governments are tribes, as are corporations and local sewing bees, where individuals give up some personal identity to be part of a greater tribe.

Sociability is such a part of being human that to be deprived of social contact can have consequences. Isolation is used as punishment or torture.

In each unique manner, all life forms respond to the basic questions for existence and continuation. Questions that are taught to beginning journalism students: *who, where, when, what,* and *how.* A unique question was asked by humans; *Why.* We sought an understanding of our environment, and that has led to our finding an entirely new set of answers to the basic questions.

Human curiosity goes beyond survival needs. We're "Infovores." We've had the need mental for inputs even before artificial intelligence. We have what 17th century philosopher Thomas Hobbes noted as "curiosity is a lust of the mind."

We gained the tools, so how will we use them? How do we design the world to our needs and survival? How will humans use the rules to break the rules we created?

But is the evolutionary path we've taken the best for survival of our species or of the planet we know? Planned agriculture provided food for more people than the hunter-gather system could but it also decreased the diversity of diet including more starches than proteins. Diet dependency upon a limited number of crops leads to vulnerability of crop failure and starvation. Through Roman times body size decreased by an average of six inches.

To grow more food required more workers. Family size increased, especially as non-gatherer women could have a faster rate of pregnancy, but also made them more dependent upon the males. Food storage was centralized requiring communities, protective soldiers, and formal organizations with leaders and a hierarchy of power and wealth. Tightly grouped tribes, especially with close proximity to their animals, were more prone to epidemic disease

When hunter-gathers were in conflict with agricultural societies the former were taller and healthier but the latter were more numerous, math wins.

Natural evolution will continue, especially as a response to climate change, though it will be difficult for humans to physically adapt as quickly as the nature that we are designing.

Nine Billion of Our Closest Relatives
World Population, Problems, and Control

This is written as an analytical view, regardless of moral values other than the value of the continuation and well-being of the human species.

About 70,000 ya *Homo sapiens* almost went extinct just as they got a population foothold. Food became scarce after dust and ash, following the eruption of the Toba mega volcano on Sumatra, blanketed the East African savannah for decades or even centuries. It's estimated that there were less than a couple thousand of our ancestors remaining.

The savannah recovered, and so did the size of that tribal group. In Genesis 1:28, the Judaic god blessed them to *"be fruitful, and multiply, and replenish the earth, and subdue it: and have dominion over the fish of the sea, and over the fowl of the air, and over every living thing that moveth upon the earth."* Divine encouragement or not, they overachieved, and around the year 1804, soon after the start of the Industrial Revolution, the human population had reached 1 billion people. The population topped 2 billion about 1930 with a 3rd billion by 1960. The 4th billion was reached fifteen years later and the 5th twelve years after that. As the millennium concluded, the population topped 6 billion. Eleven years later, it topped 7 billion. At the present growth rate, the human population will exceed the figure of 8 billion within the 2020s.

18th-century economist Thomas Malthus wrote that over-populations would lead to starvation as increases on an exponential scale cannot be met by food production on a linear scale. "The power of population is so superior to the power of the earth to produce subsistence for man that premature death must in some shape or other visit the human race. The vices of mankind are active and able ministers of depopulation." At the time, there were just over 700 million humans worldwide. He couldn't have foreseen advances in health and crop yields.

Many of the problems of the 21st century can be traced to an ever-expanding population. More people, especially with needs for energy, land, and material consuming lifestyles, are straining the limits of the planet. Land is being taken for homes, infrastructure, and food production. When the supply of resources cannot meet the needs of competing groups, conflicts occur. With reduced opportunities, those displaced will react in conflict or migration.

Overpopulation is a difficult issue to address as there are no villains, no polluters, nor mad genetic scientists. Instead, it's caused by the purest of intentions; the act of reproduction, bringing forth new life, cute babies, and honored parenthood. Putting limitations on population growth is perceived as Orwellian and counter to being human.

A few of the major causes of Middle Eastern migration into Europe and Hispanic migration into the United States are a steep rise in local populations, climate disruption, and local political instability. The larger challenge will be to design an equitable economic and environmentally sustainable world as the projected population nears nine billion humans.

Population growth is also undermining efforts to reduce climate change. Even by reducing energy use per person by 10%, while the population increases by 10%, it will still produce, at best, zero pollution reduction as 82 million people are being added to the population yearly. With an average per-person carbon footprint of 4.9 metric tons, 402 million metric tons is automatically added into the global scheme of things.

Basic rule of Economics: ***There is an unlimited demand for a limited supply***. A continually growing population and an anticipated resource driven lifestyle continually enlarge the demand. However, the uncontested truth is that the Earth is limited; therefore, there is a fixed supply of resources and that supply is diminishing from past consumption. Throughout most of history, there was the drive to survive against incredibly challenging odds. The two best ways were to evolve for efficiency in changing conditions and to produce as many offspring as possible.

Attempts to limit population growth face two problems. The first is the forces that are knowingly encouraging population growth. The second is the methods we're using to eliminate traditional means of population control.

Many in the religious community are against birth control by any means, even as medicine finds ways to extend life. "Determination of birth and death should be left to God" with his means to check the population. They were the "Four Horsemen of the Apocalypse:" * **War,** * **Famine,** * **Pestilence,** and * **Death.** In a contemporary view, Pestilence means disease. Death seems redundant as it is the end result of the other three. I use it as meaning a natural death from old age.

War: Despite news reports and personal intuition, percentage fewer people are being killed by war than ever before. A single battle in ancient times ended up destroying entire civilizations. Even Atomic weapons will not kill the percentage of the population equal to a day of slinging broadswords.

Europe was able to go back to war in 1939 with fresh young troops two decades after the blood bath of "The Great War." War also destroys the creations of humans, and the infrastructures, many of which took centuries to build. What the designer created the warrior destroyed, including lives, yet it was all rebuilt. A "war of attrition" focuses on enemies' resources, or access to resources of foodstuffs, trained fighters, and combat equipment.

Famine: This was especially threatening to those in Biblical times. Famine occurs when there are too many people for the local agriculture to feed. One solution is to migrate to an area with a greater supply of food. But we've also taken a different approach. Humans are living tied to lands that change while they won't or can't change in location, food source, or societal rules. All the food and water resources have to be imported, bringing food to those in famine areas, thereby allowing them to live and grow in areas that humans should not occupy for permanent residences. "Feed the World." This is counter to the anti-symbiotic relationship that has allowed for human prosperity.

In 210 AD, Christian scholar Tertullian wrote, "Our teeming population is the strongest evidence our numbers are burdensome to the world, which can hardly support us from its natural elements." Population increases on an exponential scale cannot be met by food production on a linear scale. In 1830 it took 50-300 labor hours to produce 100 bushels of wheat. With the insurgence of new technologies by 1900, only 35-40 labor hours were required to produce the same 100 bushels of corn. Still, in his 1968 book, "The Population Bomb," Paul R. Ehrlich warned again that the worldwide population growth would outstrip food supplies leading to massive starvation.

Pestilence: If ever there is a weapon of God, it's a disease. In my viewpoint, the notion of disease is a killer created by a hand greater than man, for which humankind has limited defenses. Pestilence, include all diseases or natural deaths caused by bacteria, viruses, and unhealthy cell growth, including cancer, heart disease, Covid, dementia, TB, etc.

The Black Plague killed off one-third of the citizens of Medieval Europe, often ending in one area to reappear later in another country: Marseille in 1620, Italy in 1629, and London in 1665. The 1918 H1N1 virus, or Spanish Flu, affected over 500 million people worldwide. 17 to 50 million of humankind died, according to the methodology of fatality reporting.

Covid-19 is thought to have begun in China, then spread worldwide, causing the deaths of millions due in large part to globalization, where an infected person can carry the virus to anywhere on the planet within 72 hours.

Viruses don't recognize national borders or racial differences. Pandemics can only be addressed on a global scale with national leaders and international organizations like the World Health Organization. When the Covid-19 virus spread, world leaders were caught between issues of public health safety and economic stability. Suspicion of the agendas of other governments inhibited the fight against Covid-19.

Viruses are part of the natural world. They are the most diverse form of life on this planet earth. Interestingly, their living status is a debate among scientists. Viruses cannot reproduce and don't have cells. Nobel Laureate Dr. Joshua Lederberg said, "The biggest threat to man's continual domination on the planet is viruses. They are looking for food, and we are meat."

With diseases, entire populations can succumb, but a reservoir colony that is immune or resistive to the disease may survive. From the survivors, new colonies will form that is immune to the disease. This was especially disastrous to indigenous peoples who had no natural immunity when they came in contact with Europeans who were the decedents of the plague survivors.

In contemporary Western medicine, science is continually competing with deadly viruses.

Science is fighting back. Despite occasional local flare-ups and smallpox, polio has been virtually eliminated, and AIDS has become more of an inconvenience than a death sentence. Cultural/political factors have slowed international disease eradication. While the remainder of the world had seen the end of polio, pockets still remained in rural regions of Afghanistan and Pakistan caused by suspicion from the war, and in Nigeria, vaccinations were interpreted as an extension of European colonialism.

Some medical failures are man-made. The drug Thalidomide was created in the 1950s to relieve stress on pregnant women. A dangerous side effect was the malformation of limbs in the developing fetus. About 10,000 babies were affected, with almost half dying at birth.

Death: All humans will eventually expire. The only variable is – when? Science is pushing back the expiration date, and many people today will still be active at one hundred, while a mere century ago, three scores were more than most could expect. In 1840 the average age for women in Sweden was forty-five. By 2010 it was eighty-three. The very definition of old age is being pushed back.

While these forces limit the population, some forces are encouraging the population growth: * **biological**, * **religious**, * **cultural**, * **political**, and * **economic,**

Biological: Humans are mammals, and the fact that we are alive is because our ancestors copulated, resulting in offspring. The primary goal of every biological species is to continue the species. The ability for human female pregnancy can last about thirty-five years for females (12-47). A Total Fertility Rate (TFR) of 2.2 is accepted as a stable population with a replacement child for each parent, plus accounting for unforeseen deaths and inability or disinterest in having children.

Religious: Many religious rules are still preserved in the shape and form of when they were written for a worldwide agrarian population under a million. Members were encouraged to have a large number of off-spring, especially males, as they were strong and agile enough to assist in agriculture. Males are wired by their genes through evolution to fertilize every female, possibly in order to continue their gene lineage. Most religions are still male oriented where decisions on virility are more important than the female's right to control and use her body.

As much as encouraging greater births are the restrictions on preventing population increases. It's a multi-step process;

Restricting knowledge and use of birth control methods,

Restricting sex education,

Restricting the availability of pregnancy termination,

Lack of support of post birth healthcare.

The desire to procreate is a factor in religiously conservative objections to same sex pairings. While same sex interaction is a norm in almost 1,500 species of animals, from bottlenose dolphins and bonobos to dragonflies and western gulls, many religions have made it a taboo.

Cultural: Many cultures still regard the number of offspring as a hallmark of manhood. But cultural influences also affect the female who perceives having a child as a sign of "being a woman." While pregnant, they are the center of attention. The media makes celebrities of famous child mothers.

Another cultural taboo is the self-termination of one's own life. Whether seen as "only God can take a life" or allowing too much potential for abuse and homicide masquerading as self-termination, societies attempt to make suicide illegal. In the moral light, the act of taking one's own life is seen as "a coward's way out" regardless of the conditions of the person's life, while others see it as the final act of self-determination. It's the individual, not the state or an institution that decides when it is time for termination of one's life.

Changes occur with four causes:

Social (civil rights, growing and moving population and cultures)

Technological (chapter15, new inventions to reduce input to results {automation}, access and or create a desire {digital TV} Fire, bronze/steel, concrete, gunpowder, telescope, the compass, printing press, steam engine, vaccines, electrification, the telegraph, the radio/TV, airplane, atom power, computer, rockets, and internet.

Environmental (chapter 11, the cause that humans have only limited control over)

Economic: We live and work in a growth dependent economy. We can only continue growing if more consuming bodies at the bottom layer support the smaller upper levels. In order for the top to remain stable and healthy, there must be a greater number of consumers and taxpayers below.

But what to do when there are fewer new bodies (babies) to grow into future consumers, the economy contracts.

After the Second World War, the economic recovery of Japan was marked by high growths in worker output and a TFR of 2.1. But with heavy workloads and the realization that children require responsible maintenance, little time was left for socializing. At the present rate, with an estimated 17% drop in 12 years, the 2017 population of 124 million may fall to 88 million by 2065. China, meanwhile, will have 25% of its population over 65. To prevent further declines, the government has set up dating services to encourage relational interactions even as the population has declined.

Demographic Political Power: Democracy may have a negative side with regard to population control. Democracy is built on decisions made by the majority or the greatest number of people. One way to assert power is to have more voters of a specific group. It is advantageous for a group to produce more babies, thereby laying the foundation for more voters eighteen years later. Groups with the most extraordinary breeding will eventually become the group with the most political/voting and buying power.

Demographics have become a political weapon. Many industrialized countries in Europe and Asia are experiencing a decline in native pregnancies. For a society to be culturally stable, births have to exceed deaths. If the average woman has a first child at age 20, this is five generations per century. With a rise to the first child's age to twenty five, it will be only four generations per century. In 2019 the worldwide TFR was 2.4, so the total population is still growing. But it's in the national differences where signs of political power are being seen.

As of 2022, France has the highest European TFR at 1.92, Italy at the lowest at 1.34, and Russia is 1.8. Owing largely to the "one-Child" policy of 1979 and keeping male offspring mainly, China's TFR is 1.15. Central and South American rates are between Guatemala at 2.7, Brazil at 1.73, and Cuba at 1.7. The United Arab Emirates is 1.73. While the Muslim TFR in India has fallen from 4.1 to 2.7, the corresponding Hindu rate has fallen from 3.1 to 2.1, closing the population's percentage.

By contrast, the African continent is 4.4, led by the nation of Niger at 7.24, though due to domestic political stability, infant and maternal mortality, education, poverty, and native health is not an indicator of future political or military power. The U.S. has a TFR of 1.8, though immigration will offset the rate to 2.11, allowing the population and economy to grow.

Immigrants have moved into regions for the basic needs of survival, often from oppression or natural calamity. In the late 20th century, Middle Easterners migrated into Europe to escape wars, a move replicated in 2022 by Ukrainians from the Russian invasion and Central Americans as a result of the drug wars at home, each group trying to find safety.

To the receiving country, the influx of non-natives was often seen as an invasion that was changing the demographics of the country. In the United States, resisters saw this as a planned action they called "Replacement Theory" that would change the political power putting "natives" at a disadvantage. In Europe, it was called "genocide by substitution," a theory formalized in 2010 by the French author Renaud Camus.

In Hungary, a leader in fertility encouragement, the TFR has increased from 1.23 in 2011 to a 2020 rate of 1.55, still way below 2.1. In September 2021, the Fourth Demographic Summit was held to discuss how to implement the "Hungarian Model." Regional nations discussed how to increase their native populations as a way to limit what they see as an assault on their national/cultural identity by non-native immigrants, mostly from the Middle East.

To counter a TFR of 1.9 the Russian government, in alliance with the Russian Orthodox Church, severely restricted abortions and circulation of contraceptive pills.

By 2050 the cities of Shanghai, China, Tokyo, Japan, Karachi, and Pakistan, plus the Indian cities of Mumbai, Kolkata, and Mumbai, will all have more than 30 million people living in them. Twenty cities are anticipated to exceed 40 million by 2100, most of them in Africa and South Asia, with Lagos, Nigeria leading at 88 million. Africa will make up 90% of the population growth through the 21st century.

And it's not just the numbers it's the breakdown of the populations. While the rest of the world's population increase is .7% annually, the Muslim population is increasing at a rate of 1.5%.

Migration: Human history is one of migrations. Sixty thousand years ago, a group of Homo *sapiens* left Africa. As the population grew, they migrated to every part of the planet. The forces of economic globalization were preceded by the globalization of human migration, often encountering already-established tribes. The larger or more powerful group in each area dominated the resources and livestock of the area. With additional migrations and births as the group population increased, so did their power to influence. As newcomers, regardless of the fact that they were immigrants or invaders, they settled into a region, and their ethnicity changed.

The histories of the United States and Canada are of migration. From the early 17th through the early 20th centuries, European migrants moved west, often in deadly conflicts with the indigenous peoples, searching for land for farming and grazing. As farming became less labor intensive and with the dustbowl of the 1930s, a second migration began to California or the factory jobs of the industrial north. A third migration traversed into full flow in the late 20th century as factories and individuals moved south to warmer climates.

Two hundred thirty-two million people worldwide migrated to another country in 2013, an increase of 33% over 2000. Europe led with seventy-two million, followed by Asia with seventy-one million and North America with fifty-three million, leaving regions of instability. Migrations can be disruptive as residents of the receiving region may perceive a loss of resource access with the increase of "competitors." These factors will put increased strains on underdeveloped infrastructures, thereby inhibiting growth.

Migration can be used as a planned political tool. Called "migrant instrumentalization" (MI), sufficient citizens are emigrated into another country to become a political factor in the receiving county.

The 21st century is experiencing a new kind of migrant due to climate change. As the sea level rises, many low-lying islands are being abandoned, and coastal cities will either have to be walled or abandoned. Much of South Asia, the Middle East, and Africa will be too hot for human habitation. There are now four times as many climate refugees as war refugees.

The planet's Global Mean Surface Temperature (GMST) in 1900 was 13.9°C. By 1950 it had risen to 14.0°C, and in 2019 it was 14.98°C. Most of the increase has been in the populated northern hemisphere, as land holds more heat than water. Escaping to air-conditioned dwellings only increases the amount of energy consumed which can add to warming. Wealth cannot make countries immune, as Singapore to Kuwait are becoming unlivable. India, by 2050 may have 25% of all climate heat deaths. In Namibia, 20% of the population is at risk of dying due to heat stroke and could be prone to heat-related crop failures.

Modern technology is so far checking God and Thomas Robert Malthus. In the hunter-gather era, there was an estimated population of less than 100 million worldwide. When Malthus issued his warning at the end of the 18th century, there were an estimated less than one billion humans. Yet today, with new technologies for food production, the world's population exceeds seven billion and still increasing.

Why do people want to live longer?

We are living longer, or so it seems. Archeological findings show that until about 30,000 years ago, the life span was only into the early thirties. The potential for infection was high and little chance of surviving even a simple cut or broken bone. Today, with access to the best medical care and enormous luck, a contemporary person might be able to survive even into their nineties, but for what?

Life is a series of learning experiences and memories, a collection of knowledge. Knowledge is something that can be passed on, but with death, all that is lost. All the investments of energy and experiences are gone forever. Immortality is that part of life that remains to be a part of human history and in the memory of others, regardless of size and impact, that all is not lost. A philosophical question is what is the worth of life if it's finite? We build pyramids and space probes to be forever while we, the designers, are not.

The pharaohs of Egypt sought eternal life through mummification, but only after leaving this one. Christians believe in life beyond death beyond the human body. Through reincarnation, one passes from this life, depending on how the life was lived, to return to start the life cycle anew.

The prospect of reincarnation can be explained through the epic story of how Gilgamesh, four and a half millennia ago, sought eternal life. He found an underwater plant that was written to be able to provide immortality, but he lost it to a snake, depriving both himself and mankind of eternal life. The character proclaims that man must accept death."

Not everyone agrees. Scientists find examples of near immortality in nature. The contemporary Gilgamesh Project seeks to understand how disease and death of the organism is caused by the process of differentiation and the growth and division of the cell cycle, especially in advanced age. Through science, can human life continue indefinitely?

In 1967 Dr. James Bedford cryonically froze a human head in an operation called "cryopreservation" to "thaw out" when the disease had been cured.

Popularly known as "suspended animation," freezing people allows storage over extensive time, like a space flight, or to reawake in the future with full faculties.

Google's sub company Calico in 2013 established a mission: "to solve death." Their approach is that death is a failure of technical issues. The body is a biological product made of components that eventually will fail. Replacements for the body can be upgraded.

Effects of longer life? The population is aging. With better health care plus young adults delaying children, the average age, regardless of deaths from wars and accidents, is increasing. In 1800 the Western average lifespan was 35 years. A century later, it was in the mid-50s and 79 by 2020. Projections for 2050 are at 93 years.

With an increase in seniors and lower TFRs, the percentage over 65 has increased. Japan has the oldest population with 22%, just ahead of Germany and Italy at 20%. More people living beyond their productive years will require more productive younger people for economic and health care support, whether assisting in health or as contributors to national retirement funds. Aging causes diminished capabilities in physical and medical issues (dementia, cancer, …) that will require assistance. The medical focus will increase for senior diseases detouring funds and caretakers from general population research. Aging will delay "wealth transfer" to children. Seniors will increase political clout by their numbers, often espousing views learned over half a century earlier.

What are the implications for more humans?

Each person requires so much land and water for sustenance. For each amount of space, something else must lose. More homes, roads, or shops will mean fewer fields for crops or woods for creatures. More buildings require more trees to be cleared, minerals to be mined, and rocks to be leveled. More people will require more energy.

Humans are capable of creating a technology that will allow our present economic growth rate but at what cost? Large scale population relocations are resulting in ongoing political upheaval. The culmination of these trends has resulted in a logarithmic population increase. Have we reached a Full World?

The United Declaration of Human Rights included "… *any choice and decision regarding the size of the family must irrevocably rest with the family itself.*" While being humane in concept, the declaration allowed the individuals to determine how many children they would have without governmental or religious constraints or encouragement. But it also absolved them from the effects of the additional children on the common good.

Then what can we do to reverse the trend? Much of the solution involves paradigm shifts in attitudes and behavior that have been part of human and animal nature since life began on this planet. Somehow the drive for reproduction must be limited. We survived, we prospered as a species, and we no longer need to "be fruitful and multiply."

The United Nations has projected that the world population will peak at 9.22 billion in 2075 and then decline to reach a level of 8.97 by 2300.

Joseph Coughlin of the MIT AgeLab declared, *"Longevity will be one of the greatest drivers of innovation in the next hundred years."*

What is to be done with all the "earthly remains?" The concept of disposal is as animated as uneven as dropping bodies into a mass hole to elaborate ceremonies culminating in placing the body in a lined casket to be sealed from environmental actions and placed in the ground or tomb marked by an engraved stone. Conventional burials in the United States annually use 30 million board feet of hardwoods, 2,700 tons of copper and bronze, 104,272 tons of steel, and 1,636,000 tons of reinforced concrete. The amount of casket wood alone is equivalent to about 4 million acres of forest and could build about 4.5 million homes. Embalming uses three to four gallons of formaldehyde before being laid in the casket. Some of which will leak into the environment decades after the departed.

Cremation has been practiced since ancient times. The body is consumed on a ritual funeral pyre or vaporized at over 1400°F to its basic grey powder. However, in the process, CO_2 and Methane are released, plus any toxins still in the body. For Hindus, the body is burned at Varanasi, and then the ashes are scattered on the holy Ganges River.

As the person no longer has use for the physical body, another method of disposal is to give the gift of the form to a medical study group. Consuming or storing away a body in a sealed box deprives the planet of all the energies and resources used by the person during life. The body is organic, and to treat it as other organic materials and compost it.

By "natural organic reduction" (NOR), the body is placed in a vessel for six months along with wood chips, alfalfa, and microorganisms until it's reduced into the soil and returned as useful compost. Compared to cremation, NOR saves about 500 pounds of CO_2 and 30 gallons of fossil fuels.

"Green Burial" places the unprepared body directly into the ground. It has been long used in Jewish and Islamic burials where the time from death to burial is limited. The process IS the truest expression: "ashes to ashes, dust to dust."

Some logical perspectives on the size and distribution of the human population may seem extreme. Sir James Lovelock stated, "The big threat to the planet is people: there are too many doing too well economically."

Beyond that, the Doomsday Argument claims that we are alive today about 5% through the history of human existence, beginning with the first Homo sapiens. The argument is that there will be 1.2 trillion humans over our existence based on the world population stabilizing at 10 billion.

This Land is Our Land

Control of water is to control the land, life forms, and even our civilizations. Control of water can influence the political and economic value of a country or region, not just for its own welfare but as a gift or as a weapon. Cities are built where vessels have access to rivers, lakes, and oceans for shipping. Communities are built near water that can enable the harvesting of plants or their produce.

The move from a nomadic hunter/gatherer to an agrarian society resulted in the first non-natural alterations to the planet. In order to cultivate crops, trees, and rocks were cleared from the land. They erected water canals to bring water in and dams to keep floods out. The land was opened with holes to get to resources that provided the materials and power for the development of cultures and societies. Along the way, the surface was transformed in accordance with human needs.

While most of the Earth's surface is covered with oceans, it's fresh water that is most usable for our survival. Water is common, but only 2.53% is fresh, and 2/3 of that is in glaciers and permanent snow cover. Another .36% is in aquifers. Only .036% is in freshwater lakes and rivers. Beyond the oceans, the remaining water on the Earth's surface is in clouds above and within the bodies of plants and animals.

Western civilization began with farming communities as early as 8,000 BCE along "The Fertile Crescent" of the Tigris and Euphrates Rivers in Mesopotamia. The earliest Egyptian communities began along the Nile River valley about 3,100 BCE. Both areas are arid except for the lands along the rivers that are periodically flooded or could be irrigated.

The Indian civilization began about 2,500 BCE along the Indus River in the Sindh region and with the first Chinese civilization to similar conditions along the Yellow River about 1,600 BCE.

The rivers and the subsequent flooding were of immense value; therefore, the early Mesopotamian writings include three flood stories; Zeosudra (in which he constructed a vessel that delivered him from great waters), Atrahasis, and the Epoch of Gilgamesh (built a boat in anticipation of a deity-created flood that would destroy the world and to protect his family, his friends, and animals). At a later date, themes were also found in the Biblical story of Noah. Great flood stories are found in the literature of cultures from India and China to Greece and the Mayans, though at different times.

Water availability does not always align with human needs and requirements. Irrigation canals and reservoirs watered the Mesopotamian fields as early as 6,000 BCE in regions that were naturally unsuited for planting. With the intention to bypass the cataract on the Nile, a canal was built around 2,300 BCE using the natural lake of the Faiyum Oasis as a reservoir. The Egyptians constructed levees along 600 miles of the Nile to control flood waters. The oldest known aqueduct in the world, the Jerwan aqueduct, was constructed in Assyria between 703 and 690 BCE.

More recently, Russia irrigated water from The Volga River for farmlands, lowering the Volga River's flow and limiting its ability to regenerate. Water extraction has also reduced the water level of the Caspian Sea. The Aral Sea, once the fourth largest inland sea, is now a toxic desert as the feeding rivers, the Amu Darya and the Syr Darya, were diverted by the USSR to water the arid plains for cotton and crops. The USSR is no longer a gigantic empire, but the conflicts between the states over the remains of the Aral Sea continue to this very day. The sea was divided into the North and South Aral Seas and then disconnected in 2,001 as water levels reduced significantly. What had once been a 26,600 sq miles lake has been reduced to 1/10th of its size.

While irrigation brought river water to fields, levees and dykes were built to restrain rivers and oceans from flooding areas. Dikes have been used to contain sea levels from the Netherlands as early as the 12th century. Levees along the lower Mississippi River made the city of New Orleans possible, and the failure of the levees along Lake Pontchartrain resulting from Hurricanes Katrina and Rita in 2005 caused widespread flooding in certain districts of the city.

The Greeks were the first to use canal locks to regulate water flow as early as the 3rd century BCE. Emperor Charlemagne supervised the first canal in Medieval Europe, the Fossa Carolina, in the late 8th century AD. The capability to economically move resources and finished goods made canals a necessity for the early Industrial Revolution.

The coastal regions have had to build water barriers to offset the effects of global warming that causes more severe storms and rising ocean levels. In 1953 a North Sea storm surge caused over 2,000 deaths in the Netherlands and claimed another 300 innocent lives in England. In response to unprecedented storms, the Netherlands initiated a system of storm surge barriers the following year. Over the next two decades, Delta Works, the world's largest barrier system, was built. Since its creation, it has greatly reduced storm damages while allowing trade along the country's rivers.

Billions of gallons of fresh water flow into the oceans, via rivers, each day. By placing locks at the exit of the rivers with dikes, salt water will be prevented from flowing upstream, keeping the water fresh during tidal exchanges. Freshwater will continue to move, maintaining flow and preventing buildup. A naturally occurring situation is with falls or rapids that are always fresh water upstream but brackish below.

Such a system of locks will interrupt the migratory practices of the fishes like salmon and interfere with regular tidal exchanges. At the same time, ships will move through locks to navigate to river ports. Dams linking the barrier islands to the mainland on America's east coast would be able to retain freshwater even with periodic contamination by ocean waves. Bodies with narrow inlets, like the Persian Gulf, could be dammed at the Straits of Hormuz, providing abundant fresh water for neighboring dry lands.

With the utilization of pipes and pumps, irrigation water can be shifted underground, preventing loss from evaporation. Today, irrigation in warm and dry climates accounts for 70% of all worldwide water usage.

Water was the first use of nature to create power. The Greeks invented the first water wheels to raise water for irrigation. With gearing on the drive shaft, the power of moving water could be transferred and controlled.

Through the Middle Ages, water wheels were the primary source of power for grist mills and foundries into the early Industrial Revolution before a practical steam engine was developed. The latter freed the means of power for production from streams to where input material and coal were most advantageous. The steam engine led to steam trains and boats enlarging distribution beyond the water canals.

In many remote areas, water wheels are still important sources of power. Power from water wheels often serves a dual purpose: grinding flour and pressing oils daily, then turning electric turbines at night. In Uttaranchal, India, water wheels is known as gharats. It provides power for local small-scale industries and then generates 264 megawatts of electricity per hour nightly. The people achieve self-sustainability with no impact on the environment.

The first hydroelectric power source was developed in England in 1878 by William Armstrong. The first US power plant, the Schoelkopf Power Station No. 1 near Niagara Falls, was established in 1881. With the accessibility of mountain river flow and low operating costs, the peak of hydroelectric power sales and utilization was in 1920, when a full 40% of U. S. electricity was generated by hydroelectric facilities.

To meet increased electrical needs and combat the Tennessee Valley Authority (TVA) and the Bonneville Power Administration were built as a series of dams to electrify rural areas. Before the twenty-nine dams of the TVA, the American South, with hot summers and few natural power sources, depended largely on agriculture to create power. The federally owned TVA began in 1933. The dam system provided power for light and air conditioning for homes, offices, and industry, factors that led to the economic growth of the southern states in the 1950s and 60s while displacing more than 15,000 families.

The Colorado River passes through the natural wonders of Arches National Park and the Grand Canyon. Besides the natural beauty, the river has been put to work. Electric power generated from the Hoover and Glen Canyon dams lights up the southwest. Water is diverted from thirteen dams across seven states providing water for almost 36 million people. 15% of America's agriculture is irrigated from the Colorado. And top of that, it is supporting a $26 billion recreation industry, yet very little water reaches the gulf.

In 2012 the Bureau of Reclamation reported that there was not enough water entering Colorado to meet the demands. The problem is exacerbated by an increase in demand from a continually growing population. Since the population is growing, snow supplies are diminishing due to climate change. Since 2000, water storage had decreased by 40 % until the rain bombs of 2023,

Dams are not only responsible for controlling water flows but also the area of economic and political environment. The Mekong River flows over three thousand miles through the nations of Southeast Asia from the headwaters in China to the South China Sea. Sixty million people depend on it for fishing, watering farmland, and hydroelectric power for cities. As of 2020, thirty-nine dams are in China, Thailand, Cambodia, Vietnam, Laos, and over 400 on the Mekong's tributaries.

Hydroelectricity that is produced by Dams is the most widely used form of renewable energy, accounting for 16 % of global electricity generation – and is expected to increase about 3.1% each year for the next 25 years. Hydropower is relatively low in cost, ranging from 3 to 5 US cents per kilowatt-hour. Furthermore, once dam construction is complete, hydropower has no direct waste and emits considerably lower levels of CO_2 compared to fossil fuel plants.

The British built the first modern dam on the Nile River 12 miles downstream of Cairo, opening in 1861 to control flooding in the delta region. After the Egyptian Revolution in 1952, a major dam was proposed to stabilize water flow. The resulting Aswan Dam provides water storage in Lake Nasser for the dry season, with 46 km3 of the 55 km3 of the annually released water used for irrigation. It is fascinating to know that Egypt's wheat production tripled between 1952 and 1991.

The same soil the Nile brought that made Egypt so fertile for the Romans continued after the construction of the Aswan Dam. In the fifty years of dam operation, an estimated 134 million tons of sediment has built up behind the dam annually. This has decreased the depth of the reservoir. Deposited sediment has lowered the water storage capacity, and with greater surface area, more water is lost to evaporation than would have been from a moving river.

The importance of the rivers to India is reflected in the culture. The rivers begin in the high Himalaya Mountains. The terms Hindu and India are derivations of the name for the Indus River. The Ganges River is considered holy, and millions of people make pilgrimages to bathe in its sacred waters. Along with the Brahmaputra River, the three rivers run their courses across the northern part of the subcontinent to empty in the Bay of Bengal.

The water travels to India from the melting glaciers and the seasonal monsoons that bring rain from June to September. 64% of the cultivated land is dependent upon the "wet season" because, in the dry season, the subcontinent receives very little rain.

But with global climate change, the amount of usable water is decreasing across the cryosphere. Glaciers, the source water for Europe (Alps) and central and east Asia (Himalayas) are melting and sending less fresh water down the Rhine and the great rivers of China and India. The Gangotri glacier, the headwaters for the sacred Ganges River, is retreating at a rate of thirty meters per year. Even where the river continues, it is polluted, causing ongoing friction between India and Bangladesh.

According to Indian scientists, Mt Everest's glaciers have lost 2,000 years of ice in the last 30 years. The Hindu Kush Himalayan range could lose 80% of its volume by centuries end. Melting will affect available fresh water for 21 billion people, causing flash floods, avalanches, plus loss of farmland. At the present rate, they forecast the conditions to be "Unprecedented and largely irreversible."

The reservoir behind the Hirakud Dam on the Mahanadi River (India) is the longest in the world, creating Asia's largest artificial lake. It holds water for irrigation in the Chattisgarh Plain while stabilizing river flow to prevent downstream flooding that destroys crops. Everything comes with a cost; therefore, the development of the dam and reservoir caused the displacement of nearly 22,000 families.

While the Colorado is listed as the most endangered river in the United States, it's not unique. Demands for water and silting due to ash from power plants will eventually cause many rivers to disappear.

Lake Faguibine, fed by the Niger River in Africa, has been clogged by sand, shrinking it from 228 sq miles in 1974 to a collection of shallow pools. The Jordan River has been diverted for agriculture and industry, reducing the Dead Sea by three feet annually. Poyand Lake, once China's largest freshwater lake, has evaporated from drought leading it to be at only 5% of its former capacity.

Other lakes are also on the verge of disappearing altogether. Lake Chad provided water for the counties of Chad, Niger, Cameroon, and Nigeria. By 2010 the lake had shrunk by 95% from the 1960s level. Crop failures, livestock deaths, increased soil salinity, and a collapsed fishing industry have resulted.

The adverse effects of dams occur even before it's built. The effects can be described in four ramifications: (1). Removal of native populations, (2) loss of biodiversity, (3) loss of farmland, and (4) loss of cultural heritage.

China's Three Gorges Dam, built on the Yangtze River, crosses 6,418 km with the melting of Himalayan glaciers in Tibet. The resulting reservoir from the dam is over 660 km long and covers 632 square kilometers. River control is intended to lessen the deadly floods that have threatened life, property, and crops annually, including the major cities of Wuhan, Nanjing, and Shanghai, while stabilizing water flow for crop irrigation, especially during the dry season.

The resulting reservoir required the sacrifice of over a million homes and over 1.4 million people, the largest peacetime evacuation in history, all in the official name of the "common good." Flooding covered 13 major cities, 140 towns, and 1,352 villages, as well as over 1,600 factories and abandoned mines. The official catastrophe figure does not include the loss of millions of secondary home loss due to economic displacement. According to a worldwide estimate, 40 to 80 million people have been displaced due to dam construction.

Dams often destroy not only the lands of indigenous people but also their sacred sites and may even threaten the survival of certain groups. Archeologists have found over 1,300 sites, some over 5,000 years old, in the Three Gorges area. They expect that they will only be able to save about 10% of the indigenous population from flooding.

The lake formed behind the Grand Coulee Dam flooded over 21,000 acres of bottomland that had been home to Native American tribes for several thousand years. The inhabitants were forced to relocate, leaving settlements and graveyards behind. Once a prime fishing ground with catches exceeding 6000,000 salmon per year, the Kettle Falls area was inundated and lost. Native tribal life centered on the salmon, but without a fish ladder, the salmon migration was blocked, removing the salmon's spawning grounds.

Governments have an obligation under Principle 9 of the Guiding Principles on Internal Displacement to protect groups with special ties to the land, but it is up to the individual country to designate sites for protection. Not all cultural issues are recognized for governmental protection.

Dam failures are rare, but the results are catastrophic when they occur. They store a great deal of kinetic energy in the form of water, and when released in an unplanned and uncontrolled fashion, downstream towns and fields are severely affected. Poor construction is one of the main reasons for dam failures. Besides that, the inability to contain large amounts of water from heavy rains may also result in dam failure. The most catastrophic dam failure occurred in China in 1975 with the collapse of the Bangiao Reservoir Dam. An estimated 171,000 lives were compromised, and 11 million people had to relocate due to the failures of all the dams in Henan Province.

No region is immune from dam failures. Other major dam-related shortcomings include the 1889 Johnstown (PA) flood, Ln Eigiau in north Wales of 1925, and the 1928 failure of the St Francis dam in Los Angeles (CA) due to geological instability.

Not all failures are natural or due to construction inadequacies. In World War Two, the destruction of three dams situated on the Ruhr and Eder rivers by the famed "Dam Busters" disrupted the supply of electric power to war industries in the area. Early in the war, the Germans destroyed sections of the Dutch dike system flooding large areas of civilian farmland and villages. Today, since dams are considered so crucial to the area's environment, life, and property, intentional destruction of a fully functioning dam is considered a violation of Article 56 of the 1997 International Humanitarian Law and Protocol 1 to the Geneva Convention.

Threats to biodiversity from dams are worldwide. The World Commission on Dams reports that the Emenek Dam threatens the wildlife of the delta of the Goksu River in Turkey. The Chalillo dam in Belize has flooded 1,000 hectares of pristine rainforest. Despite reports made after guidelines for construction, environmental damage has continued with the Burnett Dam in Australia.

Loss of water access is every bit as much a threat to local populations. To exemplify this threat, the conflict in Honduras élites can be viewed. A group of Honduras élites diverted water from the Gualcarque River in western Honduras via a 3-kilometer-long channel to the Agua Zarca Dam. Resistance came from the loss of sacred farmland and fishing rights of the indigenous Lenca people.

Submerging vast areas of productive land for dam reservoirs decreases the amount of arable land available for future food production. In areas like China and India, where farming has been active for millenniums, the best land is already being utilized. Without new lands, vast populations that are only skilled in farming are left to landless poverty. The indigenous people are often more impoverished and less self-sustaining than before the dam.

The government of Guatemala borrowed from the World Bank in the 1970s to build the Chixoy hydro-electric dam with a life expectancy of 135 years. Yet from increased erosion silt, buildup will result in projected life of fewer than 30 years, leaving the country with loans and industries dependent upon "Cheap, clean energy."

The westward expansion of the United States was farmers, miners, and ranchers supported by the infrastructure of roads and rails protected by the military. The tribes that had collectively held land were forced back to lands determined by "legally defined" boundaries lacking historic sustainability.

Irrigation canals and reservoirs were built in the Indus River valley as early as 2,600 BCE. The oldest water diversion dam, which is still in use, is located on the Kallanai River in Tamil Nadu, southern India. The diversion dam was built in the 2nd century AD, and the diverted waters and canals irrigate the fertile delta region.

With the Chavin culture, simple irrigation canals were used in the Zana Valley in Peru as early as the fourth millennium BCE. The Inca Empire enlarged the system to over 700,000 hectares on the coastal zone, but when the Spanish focused on mining rather than agriculture, the systems were reduced, and so was the agricultural production.

The Romans created large-scale water movement with a carefully planned use of gravity water which was brought through a system of aqueducts as elaborate and impressive as their roads. The first aqueducts were built as early as the third century BCE with some still in use in the 21st century.

The man-made waterways do not carry the water solely but also serve as artificial rivers for boats and the movement of goods and people. As far back as the warring states of the 4th century BCE the Chinese connected provinces through the Hong Gou Canal. During the Sui Dynasty, the canal was enlarged, becoming the Grand Canal. The longest canal in the world, at over 1,115 miles, connected the two major rivers in China – the Yangtze and the Yellow, allowing easy trade between the two commercial regions.

Canals are also beneficial when there is too much water. In 1991, over 100 square kilometers of low-lying land in the northern suburbs of Tokyo were flooded, resulting in 52 casualties. The flood water was unable to be emptied into Tokyo Bay fast enough. So to prevent a recurrence, a $2 billion project was undertaken, which involved the construction of a 6.4 km long channel leading to five 65m tall silos. These silos were built within a massive structure resembling an "underground temple" tank.

The scenic city of Venice, Italy, is in danger of being lost to rising sea levels. Saltwater flooding has inundated over 60% of the city, eroding building foundations. If precautions are not taken promptly, the city will be underwater as the wood and stone supporting the building's frame will rot and decay. The best hope is the MOSE (Modula Sperimentale Elettromec-calico), a series of retracting floodgates that are submerged at the inlets but can rise to hold back high tides or surges.

In Austin, Texas, the Waller Creek Flood Tunnel, a 26ft diameter shaft, conveys 14,000 cubic meters of floodwater protecting homes and 12 roads.

Through the employment of competent engineers and efficient planning, canals can be linked to waterways. The Erie Canal opened in 1825, connecting the Hudson River system with Lake Erie through 82 locks, effectively linking the Great Lakes and Middle America with the Atlantic Ocean and world commerce.

Canals were not just to provide waterways where nature had been missing. Many rivers were unnavigable, so canals bypass rough sections, like the C&O canal around the rocks of the Potomac River near Washington D. C. The Welland Canal bypasses Niagara Falls, providing ocean ships access to the four upper Great Lakes.

Since the 1830s, the Russians have actively proposed canals that allow waters from the Pechora, Northern Dvina, Tobol, Ishim, Irtysh, and Ob rivers that naturally flow north into the Arctic Ocean to be diverted south. Supporters point to the amount of freshwater lost into the Arctic Ocean that could be used thousands of miles to the south.

Large-scale canals allow ocean ships to bypass entire continents. With the Suez Canal inaugurated in the year 1869, European and Asian ships could now transverse without sailing around Africa, realizing the goals of Marco Polo and Columbus' quick route to the East. The Panama Canal was opened as a trading route in 1914. The canal eased transit between the Atlantic and Pacific Oceans, eliminating the time and dangers of circumnavigating South America and the Straits of Magellan. The two canals, namely the Suez and Panama, are critical for globalized commerce.

95% of freshwater in the U. S. is underground in aquifers, the largest of which is the Ogallala that stretches from South Dakota to Texas, containing an estimated 1/3 of the country's underground water. When western farmers drilled for water, it was to the Ogallala aquifer. While it has taken millions of years to form, depletion occurs at three to five feet yearly. Without the water's support, soils give way, resulting in sinkholes that have swallowed entire homes.

Withdraw of ground waters shows a change in the planets' tilt by as much as 31.5" between 1993 and 2010. In that period, 2,150 gigatons of water have been pumped out of the interior reserves.

Not all human-induced holes in the ground are intentionally designed. A sinkhole is a portion of the ground that opens up, producing a sizeable hole in the massive ground. Soon the number of sinkholes increases, resulting in the expansion of the already opened up hole. Sinkholes can occur naturally with underground rivers dissolving rock.

The growth of sinkholes is often due to human actions. In urban areas, underground storm drains, sewers, and water pipes wash away the surrounding dirt, leading to collapses. Where land surfaces are artificially contoured with dirt or rocks, there is an unnatural balance between the added and native material. The deeper the pipes the greater the sinkhole.

While most are small and resemble a pothole, some can be dramatically large. In 2007 a 330-foot-deep hole opened in Guatemala City. Leaking sewer pipes were blamed for the occurrence. In 2013, a hole almost the width of the street, resulting from heavy rainfall, carried through old pipes opened in Chicago, consuming three cars. Even the Corvette Museum in Kentucky was not immune as in February 2014, a twenty-foot-deep hole opened, swallowing eight of the iconic sports cars.

Mexico City is sinking, not from aquifer extraction, but compaction. It's sinking from pumping out its own foundation. The Aztec city was built around a series of lakes that were drained and filled in by the Spanish, creating the present Mexican capital. But with 80% of the cities' water withdrawn from the aquifers, the city has dropped an estimated nine meters in the last century.

Surface mining produces 85% of non-petroleum minerals in the United States. "Open-pit mining" as the name implies, is done by creating a giant hole in the ground. The world's largest open pit mining is present in the Bingham Canyon Mine near St Lake City, Utah. It is 0.6 miles (0.97 km) deep, 2.5 miles (4 km) wide, and covers 1,900 acres today. The pit has yielded more than 17 million tons (15.4 Mt) of copper, twenty-three million ounces (715 t) of gold, 190 million ounces (5,900 t) of silver, and 850 million pounds (386 kt) of molybdenum. Some mines are just big holes in the ground. The abandoned Mirny diamond mine in Russia is 1,722 feet deep with a diameter of 3,937 feet.

Beneath the surface of the Earth are resources that have been instrumental to societal growth when mined. Such resources were found in Neanderthal flint sites in Hungary, dating back to about 43,000 years old. The contemporary "Lion Cave" is in Swaziland. The Egyptians mined gold from Nubia from the earliest dynasties. Early technologies were dependent upon the mining of copper, tin, lead, coal, and silver.

The ironically named New River, as it is believed by scientists to be the oldest river in North America, begins its cross of the Appalachian Mountains in western North Carolina, passes through western Virginia, then winds through the canyons of southern West Virginia forming the Kanawha River that flows into the Ohio River.

Along the way, the New River provides the setting of some of the best natural activities in the United States, with internationally recognized white water rafting sites. The 1400 single pitch sport climb sites along the rock sides are challenging but exciting adventures for even advanced climbers. The New River Gorge Bridge, the world's third-largest arch bridge, is open annually for base jumping. The combination of natural beauty and traditional mountain craft lifestyles has made the region a popular tourist destination. In 2010, tourists spent $988 million and were responsible for 44,000 jobs, providing $582 million in revenue to West Virginia.

Through erosion, the river has exposed an extensive stretch of shale, sandstone, and four veins of the finest bituminous coal worldwide. This, however, brings about a conflict arising from human actions.

Insert two West Virginia images, Gauley River and MTR,

West Virginia takes the lead in underground coal production within the United States. Surface mining, commonly known as Mountain Top Removal (MTR), accounts for a significant portion of the annual extraction, amounting to forty-three million tons out of the total of 144 million tons. MTR involves the use of explosives to remove the upper 500-700 feet of the mountain. Distressingly, approximately 1.4 million acres of forested hills have been demolished as a result. The excessive debris from these activities enters over 2,000 miles of seasonal streams, carrying toxic substances, causing significant ecological damage in West Virginia alone. In addition, more than 400 mines have been established throughout Appalachia, where excess rock and soil are deposited into adjacent valleys. This process leads to the entry of acidic pollutants into the underground water source, which ultimately flows into the streams and local drinking water reservoirs. Environmental studies conducted by the EPA reveal that streams near valley fill from MTR mines have exhibited higher mineral levels in the water, resulting in decreased aquatic biodiversity. The same studies estimated that between 1985 and 2001, 724 miles (1,165 km) of Appalachian streams were covered by valley fills. While the land is reclaimed once MTR operations are concluded, the efforts have mainly focused on erosion control and rock stabilization, making it difficult for native animal and plant species to be reintroduced.

Furthermore, not all disused mines are reclaimed. A common practice involves declaring the mine as still operational, thereby circumventing reclamation requirements, even if no active mining is taking place. These mines are often referred to as "zombie mines," as they neither function nor undergo restoration.

To minimize costs, one convenient method employed is the use of rock and soil debris to construct dams for water containment. However, due to the absence of an internal core, these dams tend to be unstable, resulting in catastrophic failures. In 1972, the failure of one such dam, despite prior warnings that were disregarded by the Pittston Coal Company, occurred during heavy rainfall. This failure unleashed 132 million gallons of black water, which is rendered unusable for any human needs due to chemical contamination, human waste, and diseases. The torrent surged through the valley, devastating the nearby mining community of Buffalo Creek. Tragically, 125 people lost their lives, and 4,000 individuals were left homeless. The damage caused by this disaster was estimated to exceed $50 million dollars.

As a consequence of the extensive clearing of approximately 300,000 acres of timber for MTR, roughly 75% of West Virginia streams are now polluted, primarily due to increased erosion. Compounding this issue, the Appalachia region experiences some of the highest poverty rates in the country, with 17% of the population living below the poverty line, compared to the national average of 13%.

The case of West Virginia serves as a poignant example of the delicate equilibrium between the economic advantages derived from energy production and the imperative of preserving both quality of life and the environment. Unregulated Mountain Top Removal (MTR) may yield cheaper coal, yet without adequate environmental safeguards and the diligent restoration of cleared hilltops into vibrant grasslands and, eventually, thriving forests, along with the revitalization of clean streams, the repercussions of MTR will inevitably wreak havoc on the tourism industry, which heavily relies on these invaluable natural resources.

Furthermore, as easily accessible mineral deposits are exhausted and the demand for rare Earth elements increases, particularly for electric vehicles (EVs) and data processing, alternative sources must be explored. These reserves may lie within the oceans and even in the cosmos.

Back in 1873, a research vessel discovered black oval modules comprised of manganese, cobalt, and other minerals on the ocean floor. Initially overlooked due to the lack of specific applications, these black polymetallic modules were eventually recognized as a valuable source of rare Earth minerals with the rise of computer circuitry. The Clarion Clipperton Zone, where these modules are found, requires trawling across the ocean floor, an activity that not only involves collecting modules but also disrupts the delicate ecosystem of corals and sponges. Astonishingly, the seabed holds three times the amount of carbon as what human beings have emitted throughout modern history.

While 167 nations, excluding the United States, have developed regulations under the International Seabed Authority, their implementation has been hindered by economic infeasibility at the time. However, with the surging demand for batteries and smartphones, nations are now beginning to engage in seabed mining, with China alone trawling more than the rest of the world combined. These elements are crucial for cleaner technologies, but the extraction process releases seabed "blue" carbon that escapes into the atmosphere, further exacerbating CO2 emissions.

Mining asteroids and extinct comets, especially those classified as Easily Recoverable Objects (ERO), offer access to the fundamental minerals (such as nickel and gold) and water that constituted the early Earth. Although the concept of astro-mining was initially confined to the realm of science fiction, the realization of its potential became plausible with the Apollo 8 mission, marking humanity's first step beyond Earth's gravity. The Outer Space Treaty of 1967/68, signed by 98 nations, asserted that space belonged to all of humanity and that all nations were free to utilize and explore it.

The asteroid belt predominantly lies between the orbits of Mars and Jupiter. With the advent of reusable SpaceX launchers, both manned and robotic probes can establish commercial processing facilities in zero gravity or on celestial bodies with weaker gravity, such as the Moon and Mars. Astro-mining endeavors have the advantage of being free from pollution and ecological disruption. The extracted minerals can be utilized for space construction, orbital solar collectors, permanent commercial habitats, or transported back to Earth. Estimates suggest that even small asteroids could possess a value in the billions of dollars. Due to the inhospitable nature of these environments, much of the work will need to be carried out by autonomous robots.

The aspiration to alter the contours of the land has been a goal since ancient times, as evidenced by references in the Old Testament, such as Isaiah 49:9-11: *"I will cut a road through all my mountains, and make my highways level."* Over 2,700 years ago, Hezekiah's Tunnel was constructed beneath Jerusalem for the purpose of water transportation, marking the earliest recorded example of such an achievement. The Semmering railway tunnel, which opened in 1848, became the first tunnel to traverse the Alps, spanning a length of 1,431 meters. Over a hundred rail and road tunnels have since been carved into the Alps, facilitating seamless connectivity between Italy, France, Germany, and Austria, with Switzerland alone boasting over fifty tunnels. These tunnels have played a significant role in fostering economic unity within Europe, rivaling the impact of treaties themselves.

Tunnels held such immense significance in the growth of nations that they became the stuff of legends. Among the most renowned tales is that of the "steel drivin' man" John Henry, who faced off against the steam drill in the construction of the Big Bend Tunnel near Talcott, West Virginia, from 1869 to 1871. Although the steam drill emerged victorious John Henry's story transcended into mythology.

While the Channel Tunnel, also known as the Chunnel, connecting France and England beneath the English Channel, may not be the longest tunnel, its economic importance cannot be overstated as it physically links England to the continent.

As early as 800 bce, there was the fully functional multi-level underground city of Deringuyu. Tunneled from the soft tufa of Turkey it could hold as many as 20,000 people as protection from the invading Romans, Mongols, and later Byzantines. The city was as much as 280 feet deep and extended for over five miles to smaller caves and was used into the 20th century.

And tunnels are changing the nature of urban warfare by adding a third dimension. In addition to fighting on the surface and from the air. war is being fought underground.

Tunnels had been used to overcome an opponent's defenses by undermining the walls of medieval castles to the Petersburg crater of the Civil War. The Japanese in the Pacific theatre and the Viet Cong dug an extensive series of tunnels for mobility and to fight below America's superior surface weapons. Hamas expanded the concept with over 150 miles under the surface of Gaza, some as deep as over 150 feet, in the terror attack on Israel in 2023. The tunnels included food, weapons, and fuel storage plus hospital and command centers. They built all the infrastructures for modern urban warfare, but below the field of combat.

Similar to water, land doesn't always align with our desires or needs, prompting the creation of new territories. As the population and businesses on Manhattan Island continue to surge, the demand for additional land persists. In the early 18th century, landfill operations shifted the Hudson River shoreline from Greenwich Street to West Street, while Belmont Island was constructed using rocks removed during the subway system's development.

However, filling in wetlands alone falls short of meeting the housing requirements of the 21st century. By 2030, estimates project a global population of over 9 billion people, with 70% residing in urban areas and a projected population exceeding 11 billion by 2100. These additional inhabitants will necessitate housing. Since the establishment of the People's Republic of China, over 600 new cities have been built. Hundreds of new cities, distinct from urban expansions, have emerged across Asia and Africa to accommodate the growing populations.

In Bahrain, the exorbitant cost of real estate has rendered land reclamation financially viable. Islands are formed, creating lagoons with geotubes hydraulically filled with sand to enclose them. Dubai, for instance, is constructing three palm-tree-shaped islands and an oval-shaped island called "the World" by dredging sand from the seafloor, covering it with erosion-resistant cloth, and topping it with rocks. However, the underlying ground proved inadequate, resulting in the sinking of the islands.

Hong Kong's International Airport exemplifies a trend seen in several new airports across Asia, where land near coastal cities is deemed too valuable for expansive airport facilities. The airport is situated on the reclaimed land of Chek Lap Kok Island, spanning across Hong Kong Harbor and detached from the city, with 9.38 cubic km of harbor bottom used in its construction. Japan's Kansai International Airport, on the other hand, was built on dredged and silted soil from Osaka Bay.

Island construction can also carry political implications. According to the United Nations' Law of the Sea Convention, a nation's territorial rights extend for twelve miles into the ocean, granting control over an additional two hundred miles for mineral and fishing rights, as well as air and ship navigation. In the South China Sea, numerous islands have been claimed by multiple Southeast Asian countries. With the discovery of underwater oil reserves, along with fishing rights and control over a critical trade route, the stakes of these claims have escalated. China, despite being over 500 miles from the mainland, has undertaken extensive dredging operations, transforming sandbars and coral reefs into larger islands equipped with airstrips, ports, and structures to exert political, military, and economic influence over the disputed region.

During the 18th and 19th centuries, settlers followed the patterns of human migration throughout history. Hunters ventured into new lands to exploit wildlife for sustenance or trade, while farmers succeeded them, replacing native vegetation with crops to suit commercial needs. However, a shift in perspective emerged in the mid-19th century. The untamed wilderness of the American West surpassed any previous experiences, prompting some to recognize the loss of its unique qualities.

Traditionally, land had been reserved by royalty for personal use, with little consideration given to public usage or the preservation of non-human-centric environments. As the Industrial Revolution progressed, people became increasingly detached from nature and open spaces, feeling disconnected from their own land.

The first Western explorers and later mountain men recounted tales of extraordinary geological wonders.

However, it wasn't until the mid-18th century that the scientific community began to grasp the significance of these areas and their connection to human-induced transformations of the planet's design.

In his 1971 book "The Lorax," Dr. Seuss wrote, *"I am the Lorax. I speak for the trees, for the trees have no tongues."* This story served as a condemnation of environmental destruction perpetrated by corporations driven by the incessant pursuit of "bigger," leading to the destruction of natural infrastructure.

So, who truly speaks for the trees? Who advocates for the birds, the lakes, the seemingly insignificant insects, and the wetlands?

Throughout history, non-human entities such as the church and the crown have been recognized as having legal rights to protect their own survival. As other groups, clubs, organizations, and civic bodies gained influence, they, too, acquired a legal voice. In the 2012 US Supreme Court decision "Citizens United," corporations were granted freedom of speech under the First Amendment.

However, does a species have the right to survive? Does it deserve maintenance of the conditions necessary for its survival? Does its value extend beyond what can be quantified on a financial balance sheet? The relative worth of a natural object within the planetary design is determined by humans.

To counterbalance the rapid exploitation and commercialization of the wonders of the American West, governments began setting aside land to be preserved or restored to its natural state. In 1864, the government designated Yosemite as a grant to be managed by the state of California, later becoming a National Park in 1890. Yellowstone, the world's first National Park, was established in 1872, marking the first time any nation reserved such a vast expanse of land for non-commercial use. Through the establishment of national parks, the government assumed the role of spokesperson for the natural world.

Following America's lead, other nations have embraced the concept, resulting in over six thousand parks across more than one hundred countries by 2015. Sagarmatha National Park in Nepal is known in the Western world as Mount Everest. In India, the Ganges and Yamuna rivers have been granted the legal status of "living human entities."

Today, the planet bears little resemblance to its state fifty thousand years ago. We have transformed deserts into arable lands by providing water and creating islands and land where water and marshes once prevailed. We harness the power of moving water to generate energy. New materials and designs are being developed to combat challenges such as desertification, particularly in North Central Africa.

If an alien race were to visit a post-human Earth, it would find evidence of our presence in the altered landscape. Flat expanses would exist where mountains should have stood, and cuts would traverse solid rock, accompanied by surrounding hills and earthworks. Egyptian and Mayan pyramids would endure, albeit potentially covered by sand and forests. Non-natural, linear ditches would lead from former water bodies, and colossal pits would remain, even if they were filled with water or soil, their contours betraying their non-natural origin.

In a 2020 report, the full extent of human-induced changes to the planet was unveiled. For the first time, the mass of man-made structures, encompassing dams, buildings, canals, roads and bridges, airports and ports, islands, and homes, surpassed the total global biomass of all living organisms on Earth. This "anthropogenic mass" has doubled since 2000. Co-author Ron Milo remarked on our impact, stating, "We are already a major player, and I think with that comes a shared responsibility." However, given that a significant portion of the economy revolves around construction, it is unlikely that this trend will decelerate.

While nature may eventually reclaim even the grandest of our structures without human intervention, the alterations we have made to the planet will endure as permanent monuments to our time here.

The Culture of Agronomy

Humans are unique in an animal kingdom of specialized symbiotic relationships between eater and eaten, humans are unique. We are omnivores, and our physiology has changed. We are not tied to specific foods; we have one versatile design. With canines, we can eat meat like carnivores. With a sliding jaw and molars, we can eat plants and fungi like herbivores. We eat parts of plants across the spectrum: roots and tubers (potatoes), stalks (celery), leaves (lettuce), seeds (nuts and beans), skin (watermelon rind preserves), flower (cauliflower), bark (noodles from white pine bark), fungus (mushrooms), sap (maple syrup), and fruit flesh (apples).

If the food isn't edible in its natural state, we boil it until the fibers break down, crush it until it's a manageable texture, and bake it until the chemical composition is altered or combined with other plants. Cereal grains have to be dried and ground to make flour or boiled to softness. The hunter-gatherer's diet was varied but inconsistent, limiting tribal size and foraging locations to the changing seasons and herd movement. However, it was with the seeds of the grasses that sapiens changed our evolution.

On the great plains of central North America and the Asian steppes, seed grasses were present in great quantity. Hominins picked the seeds and have been eating grain seed in some form for over seventy thousand years. Grain seeds have a distinct advantage over other parts of plants that humans use for consumption. Grains can be used immediately, stored, or transported for future consumption, expanding beyond localized sources for themselves and their animals.

For easy consumption, some were boiled, while others were crushed to make flour. To maximize production, farmers focused on the large seed producers, though they needed to be planted annually, tying the farmers to their fields.

The agricultural revolution began about 12,000 years ago, permanently altering human society, turning from hunter-gatherer nomads to village builders. By planting specific seeds, humans decided the type and quantity of plants grown, even changing the environment to fit the plant. They took control of what and how much was available to maximize the plants.

The oldest records that are still preserved for research indicate that the Agrarian Revolution first occurred in the Fertile Crescent, though it occurred independently in multiple cultures around the world at different times. Gathering and processing native plants provided a more secure food source with a selection of easy-to-grow edible plants.

Collective farms were limited in size. As farms became larger power became centralized and private ownership. This created a hierarchy that led to kings and rulers.

Different parts of the world were more favorable to different grains. Grains are divided into "warm-season" varieties, including millet, rice, maize, and sorghum, and "cold-season" cereals like barley, oats, rye, wheat, and wild rice.

Wheat was first domestically grown in the Middle East about nine thousand years ago, and lentils about eight thousand years ago. Barley, a highly adaptable crop, is grown from north of the Arctic Circle to Ethiopia. In the current day as well as in history, Rye is grown across northern Europe and Russia and was also widely grown in colonial America. Rice has been harvested in warm, humid climates for over nine thousand years and is the premier grain for half the world.

To the indigenous farming peoples of pre-Columbian America, the primary cultivated grain was maize. North Americans refer to maize as corn. It was the centerpiece of what they called the "Three Sisters." Maize provided a pole for beans, while squash spread out from the base restraining weeds. Through selective breeding, the size of a corn ear was raised from about 4 cm to the present size. Corn is the most widely cultivated grain worldwide, at 717 million metric tons annually, with the United States leading production, followed by China and Brazil. While popular as a food, its primary use is as foodstuffs for livestock and processing into fructose as an additive and sweetener.

Pseudocereals, such as buckwheat, chia, quinoa, and pitseed goosefoot, are non-grasses that can be ground into flour.

The use of grains is divided into whole grains and refined grains, with the latter being milled to remove the bran and germ, then enriched with vitamins. The process increases the active life between production and usage but often lacks the fiber of the original grains.

Non-cereal grains (pulses) include peas, beans, legumes, soybeans, and peanuts. While higher in proteins than the cereal grains, they are incomplete, lacking amino acids.

Cultivation required changes in the environment for grains to be stable food sources with a stable water source. Trees and rocks had to be cleared, and fences built to separate the crops from native herbivores.

Agriculture, though, presented its own set of problems. Replacing a varied foraging diet with a cultivated crop reduced diversity, making the plants more vulnerable to insect invasion or disease. Agriculture also put a strain on human physiology. Humans evolved upright for reaching and running, not stooping over as needed in planting and collecting.

The farming economy and diet remained little changed until 1492 when the Ottoman Empire closed off the Silk Road and access to Asian goods. In 1453, Europeans were forced to the seas to obtain spices, some of which were so valuable as to have more worth than gold. With stronger ships and improved navigation led by the Portuguese, Europeans circumnavigated Africa to spice-rich India, China, and present-day Indonesia.

Christopher Columbus convinced the new monarchs of Spain to bypass Portuguese dominance of the "spice islands" by crossing the western ocean. While missing his target, he landed in North America. Numerous Europeans had reached North America before, but none had an incentive for trade routes and colonization.

Renaissance Europe did and began an age of exploration and colonization that lasted for over three hundred years. So began the "Columbian Exchange" as the two hemispheres were linked together again, this time by trade.

From the New World came corn/maize, vanilla, squash, peanuts, quinine, potatoes, pumpkins, avocados, peppers, strawberries, nuts, onions, quinoa, yams, papaya, tomatoes, and cocoa, along with resources of gold and silver. Over two-thirds of all types of food crops grown worldwide are originally native to the Americas, including the potato, which became so ingrained in the Irish diet that the famine of the mid-1800s led to a migration of thousands to America. The tuberous root Cassava, also called Yuca, was first cultivated in Brazil. Today, it's the third-largest source of food carbohydrates in West Africa.

The Europeans brought coffee, apples, onions, citrus, grapes, peaches, blackberries, pears, and bananas to the Americas, along with wheat, rice, barley, oats, and sugar, a crop that the New World proved to be ideal for cultivation. Sugar cane was first domesticated in New Guinea about 10,000 years ago, reaching mainland Asia around 1000 BCE and brought to Europe by the Crusaders. Columbus planted the first sugar cane in Hispaniola. Rainforest and native populations were cleared and replaced by large plantations. High prices resulting from the European demand for sugar led the English to call it "White Gold." Sugar has become a major internationally traded commodity, with over 170 million tons produced annually. The average person consumes fifty-three pounds annually, with people in the developed West averaging over seventy pounds.

Ethanol is made by fermenting sugars with yeast and has been used for beverages and as an antiseptic. In recent years, ethanol has gained importance as a renewable fuel source.

While cotton was native and used for producing clothing in the New World from Mexico to Peru since about 5,000 BCE, Europeans found the southern region of the future United States to be ideal for growing the plant. But before the invention of the cotton gin by Eli Whitney in 1794, the task of separating the cotton was too labor-intensive for mass profitability. The machine made it so practical that a second wave of slave trafficking, even larger than the first used for harvesting sugar cane and tobacco, commenced.

To the victors belong the spoils, including the resources. Armies took gold and food from the losers, including the resource of other humans. Human trafficking had been ongoing for centuries, with local chiefs selling captives to Muslim Arab merchants. The Europeans were just the latest customers for the same old product. Until the trade, known as the "triangular trade," was finally made illegal in the early 19th century, over eleven million people were taken from Africa in the largest forced human migration in history. In addition to the agricultural south of North America, the major recipients were Brazil and the Caribbean islands, taking over half of the stolen humans. The loss of large numbers of young males disrupted West African societies for centuries.

Much of the economic growth of 18th and 19th-century England was from the acquisition and use of African slaves. Planting and harvesting crops on the plantations, shipping slaves to the Americas, and marketing commodities back home created a need for manufacturing machines such as the steam engine, cotton gin, better reapers, and looms. The owners made fortunes by providing, at low cost, what were once luxury items to large portions of the population.

Coffee began its world domination from East Africa. Arab traders, along with European explorers, introduced the drink to Europe, from where it was carried around the world. Today, it's grown in tropical countries worldwide and is one of the most traded products globally.

Globalized industrial farming has focused on four plants: soy, palm oil, canola, and maize.

Palm oil, originally cultivated in Egypt, has been used for cooking for over five thousand years. The growth of palm tree plantations in Indonesia has resulted in the loss of natural habitats for the endangered orangutan, Sun Bear, Pygmy Elephant, and Sumatran Tiger, partly due to the loss of small self-sufficient local farmers' habitat and partly due to poaching for unique pets. In response, the Malaysian government has publicly committed to preserving 50% of its land area as forest.

One change humans can make is to eliminate diseases. DDT was created in the 1940s as a replacement for contact insecticides that were harmful to humans. However, as exposed in Rachel Carson's Silent Spring, it caused unintended harmful effects. A worldwide ban on DDT and similar organochlorine pesticides has allowed most bird populations to recover.

Carson's focus was on the damage to birds, but another kingdom is more threatened: bees, especially honey bees, which are the primary pollinators of the plants on which humans and all herbivores depend. Due to parasites and disease, insecticide and herbicide use, habitat loss, and global warming, bee colonies are collapsing. Populations of butterflies, bumblebees, and other solitary pollinating insects have also steeply declined in many places. Bees are responsible for pollinating 80% of flowering plants. In the US, honey bees pollinate $15 billion worth of agricultural products each year, including more than 130 types of fruit, nuts, and vegetables. Proper control of insecticides and moving whole colonies to better-controlled environments has stabilized bee populations.

The Supreme Court of the United States, in Chakrabarty v. Diamond, ruled in 1980 that "the fact that microorganisms are alive is without legal significance for purposes of the patent law." The ruling gave General Electric Corp. the legal rights to a bacterium of GE's creation for gobbling crude oil. Life can be owned by a corporation.

Genetically Modified Organisms (GMOs) are the controversial result of new plant creation. They are hailed as either the answer to the perfect plant for an unlimited supply of safe foods or the introduction of Frankenstein foods by bullying monopolistic corporations. Despite the ongoing pronouncements of food scientists on the safety of GMO foods, public skepticism and resistance have continued to hamper widespread usage.

Those who oppose GMOs have two concerns. One is that GMO plants are not "natural," and people are wary of how they will affect consumers. The other concern is the potential domination of the food supply by a few corporations. GMOs are patented products, and the patent holder has exclusive rights to the use and sale of the product for the patent's effective life. Farmers need to annually buy new seed from the corporate supplier.

Traditional farming involved setting aside seeds from one crop to be seeded at the next planting. This ensures the survival of the best seed for ongoing plant strength. However, with nearby GMO fields, pollen crosses between fields, adding GMO DNA to the native plant. For a farmer, using these seeds for planting is legally held as an unapproved use of a patented product. Monsanto has filed lawsuits against hundreds of farmers for possession of seeds with the Monsanto gene. Farmers have requested legal protection from inadvertent pollination from GMO plants onto their traditional plants.

In 1996, Monsanto's Roundup seeds were used for 2% of the American soybean crop. By 2015, 91% of soy, plus 85% of US corn, 88% of cotton, 90% of canola, and 90% of sugar beets were GMO, produced by three chemical companies: Monsanto, Dupont, and Syngenta. 165 million acres in the US and 420 million acres worldwide are planted with GMO plants. Using GMO seed, the yields of corn and soybean have doubled in the past decade.

Despite increased yields, international resistance to GMO foods has not abated. Sixty countries have banned GMOs, including Haiti, the poorest country in the Americas. Local farmers protested against Monsanto seeds, fearing a lack of local control in buying seeds.

The next step is the use of CRISPR-Cas9. It uses the natural defenses of bacteria with a Cas9 enzyme that tracks the patterns of attackers. Researchers employ a plant's RNA to spot the harmful genome and replace or remove it. The process has been used in both animals and plants to repair genetic diseases. As it is not a GMO but rather involves adding or moving a gene from another plant or animal, it potentially will not face the resistance that GMOs have encountered.

In the 19th century, new technologies were applied to farming. Stronger metals for bridges and steam engines were used to build bigger and stronger plowing and harvesting machines. First steam, then gasoline-powered tractors pulled implements, followed by specialized combines, planters, irrigators, balers, and backhoes. To increase food production during the First World War, Henry Ford created a tractor called the Fordson. Like his Model-T, it was low-cost, making mechanized farming available even to the smallest of farmers.

Stalin, in an effort to prove the superiority of his communistic system in the USSR, which was lagging behind western agricultural countries, embraced the pseudoscience of Trofim Denisovich Lysenko. Through collectivization of agriculture, Stalin created state-run farms called kolkhozes that replaced small independent farms. Modern machines like tractors were introduced to be managed by the party. The most prosperous farmers, the Kulaks, revolted and destroyed machines, slaughtered between 20% and 35% of the livestock, and burned crops. From 1932 to 1934, about 7 to 20 million Kulaks were killed per Lysenko's orders, while approximately 5 million Ukrainians died of starvation. Stalin ordered the production of cash crops grown for foreign sales, often leaving farmers without access to the food they grew. Peasant farmers were tied to the kolkhozes in a form referred to as "neo-serfdom." In 1938, private farms were allowed 3.9% of total sown land, but those plots produced 21.5% of gross agricultural output.

The big increases in post-war food production in the West came in what has been called the "Green Revolution." American scientist Dr. Norman E. Borlaug experimented with wheat in Mexico in the 1940s. By the 1960s, Mexico was able to supply its own people and even export wheat.

In 1963, Dr. Borlaug went to India to attempt duplication and prevent a massive famine on the subcontinent. The prevailing opinion was that the human population was outgrowing potential food production, and mass starvation was inevitable. After overcoming delays, his team was able to produce a wheat strain that yielded higher than ever recorded in Asia.

The techniques were applied to Latin American countries and to other grains. In the 1930s, farmers planted 30,000 corn plants per hectare. Today, the yield is in excess of 80,000. Dr. Borlaug received the 1971 Nobel Peace Prize.

The Green Revolution has critics. Worldwide production of corn, wheat, and rice products makes up 75% of the world's diet, thereby reducing biodiversity. The efficiency of monocultural crops uses large amounts of water and pesticides, herbicides, and fertilizers, large specialized machines, and standardized techniques. Mass food production is dependent upon annual seed purchases and the use of large-scale farm implements. These are costly prohibitions for small farmers who have to borrow, putting them in debt, or else production is taken over by large-scale international companies.

The romance of the individual farmer will become an artifact, sidelined to boutique farmers producing low-volume unique vegetables and fruits. Industrial corporate farming, like its manufacturing counterpart, will dominate in production and distribution.

The Brown Revolution addresses local food production. Specialized plants encourage stronger specialized weeds and insects. Biodiverse ecologies can better withstand environmental changes using local knowledge of plants that have been successful for centuries. Biodiverse ecology techniques maintain the soil with a minimum of outside inputs. Within the soil are thousands of fungi, bacteria, and microbes necessary for soil quality. To ensure that soil remains rich, farmers and agriculturists often seek the help of herbicides. While Herbicides and pesticides can kill destructive weeds and insects they can leave the soil sterile.

But are there better methods of farming? Can techniques as old as civilization be incorporated into modern agriculture for sustainable, healthy yields best suited for localized areas?

Alternative planting methods have their origin in primitive and natural farming. Pasture Dropping involves planting annual crops among living perennial plant pastures. Intercropping, a practice used by Mesoamericans, mixes grasslands and animals with trees for sustainable yields by removing a minimum of carbon and nutrients from the ground.

Silvopasturing seems counter to modern monocrop plantation farming. Domestic animals are grazed in natural landscapes of local trees and plants. The trees provide food for some species, plus shading the land reduces water loss and offers protection to the animals from wind and snow. Worldwide, 1.1 billion acres are being silvopastured, creating as much as three times the carbon capture as with industrial farming.

"Black Earth" is an ancient method where waste food and vegetation are burned in the ground without air. The resulting biochar holds nutrients and increases organic mass in the soil. Healthy soil is rich in carbon, necessary for the structure of all plants and animals, as microbes feed on the sugars in plant roots, reducing the need for induced fertilizers.

Food is most often separated from the consumer by time and distance; therefore, it is essential that food is persevered for longer periods. Keeping food preserved over long distances required new methods of food storage. Through the 18th century, storage was basically unchanged since the Neolithic times, with hides and baskets. Napoleon recognized that food supplies were necessary for an effective army. In response, Frenchman Nicholas Appert developed a method whereby food is sealed into a container while hot, forming a vacuum seal. In 1810, Englishman Peter Durand applied the process using tin cans.

Freezing or keeping food cold in storage units has been employed for over three thousand years, but cold storage ties the users to the cold units. "Ice boxes" were the preferred method of home cooling storage.

Clarence Birdseye researched how to quickly freeze vegetables, culminating in 1927 with a patentable process. By 1930, he was commercially selling frozen vegetables that could be kept indefinitely yet were crisp when thawed.

To feed soldiers in World War Two, complete meals were frozen on aluminum plates to be heated in convection ovens for consumption. After the war, these "meals" were sold commercially, creating the "TV Dinner."

Waste

Even with a growing world population, there is sufficient food to supply the needs of the entire population. Yet hunger still exists.

"In theory, we have plenty of land to grow stuff," says FAO director Kostas Stamoulis, *"But the world may move in on land that they shouldn't move in on."* About 75% of newly farmed land is in environmentally sensitive ecosystems such as forests and wetlands in Africa and Latin America.

The needed 60% growth can be partially accomplished by reducing food waste. It is estimated that nearly one-third of all food produced is wasted, never completing the journey from field to stomach. That is approximately 1.4 billion tons of food annually, with the US alone wasting 35 million tons of food. $165 billion worth of food is discarded monthly. Only 72% of US grains are consumed, while fruits and vegetables are at about 56%, and roots and tubers at 53%. Dairy has the greatest consumption rate at 84%.

While the "sell-by" date implies that the food is no longer edible, many foods and packaging methods are still safe. Better information references are "best if used by" or "best before," which indicate when the food is at its premium, though the food of lesser taste quality is still consumable for days longer.

A misshapen fruit or vegetable has not lost nutritional value

Photo credit: James Martin

The "Food Date Labeling Act of 2021" by the FDA and USDA encourages manufacturers on a national basis to standardize labeling to indicate when their product is at its best, usable, or should be discarded.

Food is also lost as so-called "ugly food." Consumers will pass over bruised or misshapen fruit, leaving it to go unsold past the magic date. In the US, over six billion pounds of ugly food are discarded annually. Still, the food, whether past the date or blemished, is still full of the same nutrition as the prettier items.

The Christian New Testament speaks about food waste: John 6:12 *"gather pieces that are left over, let nothing be wasted."*

The concern of charities is the risk of liability. The issue was addressed with the Emerson Good Samaritan Food Donation Act of 1996, absolving the donor if given "in good faith."

In underdeveloped countries, providing an adequate food supply has additional issues. Where electrical service is limited, so is consistent refrigeration. They often lack good roads to transport grown foods to markets, or processing centers lack water sanitation, making even the most basic consumption a source of disease. In areas of conflict, warring factions forcibly take food. Reducing food waste reduces the need for new resources. With agriculture utilizing 70% of fresh water and causing 80% of deforestation, any reduction in food production, while increasing food supplies, will help reduce harmful emissions, such as 30-35% of human-generated greenhouse gases.

The UN's Kostas Stamoulis says, "technology exists to fulfill 80% of the increased need for food by 2050 by simply increasing productivity with methods like 'double cropping' and 'triple cropping,' or growing more than one crop in rotation in a single field. The problem will be getting the technology and education to make some of these changes into the hands of everyone who needs it."

Forests

Forests are natural filters for pollution and CO_2. The largest forest is the Amazon River basin. It has been called "the lungs of the world" for the amount of weather it creates, carrying water from the mountains to the ocean, so vast that it creates its own rainfall and provides 20% of the world's oxygen, as well as 20% of the freshwater. It is so diverse that it includes one-third of all life forms, including over one hundred species of monkeys.

The Amazon is a "biotic pump." The trees transpire lots of water vapor. In theory, they could transpire more water than can evaporate from the oceans. The air around the trees becomes lighter and rises, sucking in more air from outside the area. The rising air gets colder as it rises until the dew point is reached and it falls as rain.

However, the trees are being cut down to create new farmland for both crops and cattle ranching. This will result in the winds no longer blowing from the ocean, which won't bring rain. Moreover, despite the apparent lushness of the jungle, the soil is poor, depending on decaying trees for nourishment.

Organized deforestation of the Amazon basin began in 1940 as part of what the Brazilian government called "rational exploitation." Clearing, mostly through burning, increased in the 1960s with a worldwide increase in demand for beef. Brazil is the world's largest beef exporter. Since 1970, the rainforest has been deforested by almost 800 thousand square km, and by 2017, 17% of the rainforest had been cleared.

With the 2019 election of Jair Bolsonaro, who saw the environmental laws for the forest as a detriment to the economic growth of mining, logging, and large cattle ranches, deforestation increased by 300% in his first year..In that year, 88,816 fires broke out in the rainforest, with most attributed to agricultural interests of farmers and ranchers. They proclaimed "a day of fire" on August 10.

Deforesting the Amazon basin is becoming a significant contributor to warming, as about 75% of Brazil's emissions come from rainforest clearing, as vegetation burns and felled trees rot. Removing the protective trees leaves the land open to the sun and drying. Most of the ground is made up of peat that, when unprotected, dries out and becomes more susceptible to fire, releasing the carbon within as CO_2.

Second to the Amazon is its African counterpart, the Congo River. The river basin in west-central Africa covers 1.4 million sq. miles. The basin contains 8% of the world's forest-based carbon, which affects rainfall across the eastern Atlantic.

For years, southern Spain was an arid region, but with a major investment in 26,000 hectares of greenhouses that kept interior temperatures at 45°C, the Almeria province has become a major exporter of vegetables across Europe. The controlled environment negated exterior temperature rises, and while temperatures in the rest of Spain have climbed at rates above the world average, the local temperature has dropped an average of 0.3°C every 10 years since 1983.

Food production encompasses large acres of land and is usually separated from processing centers and consumers. Vertical Farming with food towers provides fresh local vegetables on a year-round basis by building controlled units near urban centers or immediate consumers using hydroponics. Separate floors can focus on different plants for maximum productivity, and as shown with people-centered skyscrapers, height is not a limitation. Vertical farms can be independent of external weather extremes, able to supply fresh vegetables locally or transport them year-round. "Farm to Fork" is almost immediate, as the store can be in the same building as the farm. Rural vertical farms can provide a wide variety of vegetables without the need for extensive transportation from centralized warehouses.

The plants can be grown without pesticides or herbicides under controlled LED lighting. Being inside and using a much smaller footprint, vertical farming reduces the need for deforestation. Water loss due to evaporation is almost eliminated.

The concept of the "farmer" is changing as there is no connection to the land. Other facilities are being constructed around the world. The vertical farming market reached about $5.5 billion in 2020, with expectations to reach about $20 billion by 2026.

One under-utilized resource is not under our feet but under water. Kelp is an ideal supplemental food source. Naturally growing in the ocean at up to five inches per day, it doesn't need fresh water, so it doesn't compete with human needs, nor does it need fertilizers and pesticides or take up arable land. As a side benefit, it's a natural ocean filter and a safe area for growing fish.

Kelp provides an ocean forest for a diverse variety of free-range fish and crustaceans, from the base to the upper branches. Kelp is a biological pump that draws carbon upwards along with nutrients that feed the plankton, the base of the food chain. When dried, kelp is also used for biofuels. The DOE (Department of Energy) estimates that kelp biofuel produces 30 times more energy per acre than field grasses.

Livestock fed on dried kelp, as kelp is easier to digest than land-based leaves, produce less methane while producing more milk, as methane is a waste product created by inefficient digestion.

Food is indispensable for life, and plants are the most efficient way to produce food for animals and humans alike. To continue to grow, humans will have to depend more on plants and develop ways to grow more on less land acquisition while reducing the impact on other life and still providing a flavor choice that humans will happily utilize.

Man's Best Friend, and Dinner

"Man's Best Friend," that is, of course, the dog. Fortunately, we have many other friends and many more animals that are of service to us and how have interacted, exploited, and even changed them.

Early hominins, as omnivores, were on both sides of the food chain. They were often the prey. From their tree homes, they ate fruits, nuts, and berries, but upon moving to the savannah, they needed animal protein, usually obtained by scavenging. Using early tools, they broke open bones to obtain the protein-rich marrow and developed canines for tearing into the meat. In groups and with crude, sharpened rocks, they became hunters of larger prey.

The first recognized herding was with sheep and goats and later with cattle, probably following the herds as much as leading them. The herders did provide protection from the carnivores as being near humans was safe.

Early teachings of Judaism proclaimed that animals were part of God's creation and they were to be treated with compassion. The teachings suggested that no pain should be caused to the animals. Killing animals for food was allowed, but hunting and killing animals for sport was disallowed. The Qur'an 40:79-80 states, "*It is God who provided you with all manner of livestock, that you may ride on some of them and from some you may derive your food. And other uses in them for you to satisfy your heart's desires.*"

In primitive Hebrew and then later in Muslim cultures, sacrifices were necessary as recognition to God as an awareness of heavenly gifts. The most important sacrifices had to be made from the most important lives, those of the best animals. Ritual slaughter was a religious event done with a *chalaf,* which directed the slaughterers to let the animal bleed out.

The Hindu doctrine of Ahimsa preaches against doing harm to all living beings, and the Buddhist doctrine of Right Livelihood preaches against inflicting harm to animals.

For most of the *sapien* existence, the relationship with animals as well as the combined nature was referred to as "animism," the belief that all things have a soul. Animals, plants, and the rocks have a spirit and a connection to everything. There is no distinction between humans and the food they eat or the animals they hunt.

The relationship changed with the Agricultural Revolution. Crops and animals became property as humans started to control their lives. Early in the Judeo/Christian Bible, mankind is given a different relationship from pantheism to other life on Earth. As stated in Genesis 1:26, "*and let them have dominion over the fish of the seas and over the fowl of the air and over the cattle, and over all the earth and over every creeping thing that creepeth upon the earth.*" Humans saw nature as separate, something for which they were to make decisions over, a resource.

Domestication

When humans take on an animal as a pet or a domesticated farm animal, they assume the responsibility of feeding and caring for the animal till the day it dies. Often that responsibility is longer than the intended period for care. A pet may be cute for a few years, but the life of the animal may be much longer, and it is the human who has to make sure that the animal remains healthy.

Responsibility for the life of a "pet" is necessary. Before domestication, humans controlled 2% of the animal mass. Today humans control 98%.

Dogs, a subspecies of the gray wolf, were the first animal tool to be companions and tools for Neolithic *sapiens.* Fossil remains of wolves have been found in close proximity of the humans as early as 400,000 BCE in England and 300,000 BCE in northern China. Offspring of the wolves with the lowest "flight distance" (how close an animal will allow humans to get) and were less fearful were bred. As a result of that breeding, those wolves eventually became domesticated.

More than any other animal, dogs have had a partnership with humans as hunting companions. Their superior sense of smell, hearing, stamina, and speed is a great compliment to the human vertical sight and superior communication. Humans and dogs find interaction with each other easy because both humans and dogs are pack oriented with a leader and social position.

By specialized breeding, humans developed the various breeds of dogs, from the pocket size Chihuahua to the small horse size Great Dane for specific work tasks. With greater wealth, individuals are able to create personalized hybrid "vanity" breeds;

Cats were unique in domestication as they served a use but weren't classified as tools. They're not as much domesticated as they were opportunistic for the human created environment. Originally from Egypt, cats hunted rodents that fed on the stocks of grain.

Worldwide there are an estimated 300 million domesticated and feral dogs, with 77.5 million in the United States. Counting cats (93.6 Million) and other domestic animals (171.7 million freshwater fish, 11.2 million saltwater fish, 15 million birds, 15.9 million small mammals, 13.6 million reptiles, and 13.3 million horses), Americans spent $45.4 billion in 2009 on pet supplies and medical care.

Horses were hunted animals as they are shown with other prey in Paleolithic cave paintings of over thirty thousand years old. There was no certainty when horses were first domesticated, but some studies suggest that they were domesticated as early as 4,500 BCE.

For much of history, horses carried warriors into battle. The first depiction of horse drawn chariots was in Mesopotamia around 3,000 BCE. The chariot was a major weapon system as the horse would clear away foot soldiers, and the rider could accurately unleash spears or arrows, especially on flat open ground.

By the Middle Ages, to protect the horse, armor plating was added to the horse's frame. The heavier armory obviously necessitated a bigger, heavier horse. Bigger horses were also more efficient for plowing. Other human induced evolutions led to faster horses for racing, survival in the cold, and maneuverability for herding. All in all, there are now over 3,000 breeds of horses.

The Spanish conquistador's military reintroduction of the horse into North America was originally deadly to the natives. But on the Great Plains, the horse gave native tribes mobility to hunt the buffalo at an equal speed and move across the vast grass oceans, thereby changing their societies.

The first sheep and goats to be domesticated as a food source occurred in Mesopotamia, about 9,000 BCE. Nomadic herding societies that moved from hunter/gather were less dependent upon the seasons. They took their food source with them. The small mammals known as pigs were first domesticated in China and were part of a settled community. With domestication, humans took on the responsibility for the welfare of the animals providing food and safety with a stable supply of grasses and enclosures.

Camels were domesticated in Mesopotamia around 1,500 BCE. Being able to go for long periods without water, they were hugely important as the beast that could be burdened for transportation across the arid regions of North Africa and Central Asia.

Bovines have been an important group since about 4,000 BCE. Size and brute strength have been used to great advantage to pull plows, increasing the yields of early agriculture. The same qualities were put to use for pulling carts and wagons, as well as being important food sources for both meat and milk. About 10,000 ya bovines, called Aurochs, were domesticated in the Turkey to Pakistan region. Free range cattle have traditionally been raised on land unsuitable for growing crops due to terrain requiring minimum protection. Their dropped manure was naturally recycled into the grasses.

The other major animal food source is the chicken. Chicken descended from the red jungle fowl of the Indian and Southeast Asian jungles. It was first domesticated about 2,000 BCE, spreading into the Middle East and Europe by 1,500 BCE. Today chickens are the most prevalent food source.

Some animals are helpful without our domestication, even when we find them undesirable. Bats may be scary as the creatures of the night and the most endangered species of mammal, but to farmers, they are invaluable because they feast on insects. Where bats have been removed, the corn earworm larvae that gnaw on corn ears have increased by roughly 60%, as has the corn loss due to a fungus.

As hominins became hunters, predators, from bears and lions to wolves, were competitors. With the domestication of sheep and chickens, the predators went after livestock, and farmers went after the predators, in the case of wolves, leading to near extinction. This created an imbalance in the biosphere. For the purpose of safeguarding the herds, predatory animals were often hunted to near extinction.

At the end of the last ice age, the planet began to warm, became wetter, and CO_2 levels increased. This was good for grasses opening new areas. About 5,700 BCE, with the domesticated sheep, goats, and docile cattle, numerous tribes changed from hunter/gathers to herders. In cattle and sheep milk, they had a consistent source of proteins. Milk has five times the calories of meat, providing greater energy for growth Herders were able to move into otherwise uninhabitable areas and transit to other tribes increasing trade. As the herders moved onto the steppes and grasslands, horses were able to feed themselves on the prairie grasses and travel over greater distances.

Herders had no permanent "home" and as their range and needs increased, so did the size of the herds. This led to conflict with the early farmers who were committed to specific areas. It's a conflict that has repeated from the prehistoric era to the cowboy-rancher conflicts, a main theme of the musical *Oklahoma*.

To hunter-gathers and farmers, the EuroAsian steppes had been a barrier for transiting, lacking fruits and plants other than inedible grasses and rivers. However, for herders, the plains grasses were feed for the herds. Horses were the major "beast of burden" for herders carrying people and goods. Horses are a necessary component of human endeavors in opening the steppes and great plains to *sapien* expansion. Horse based Mongols easily moved from their grassy steppes to conquer fixed civilizations.

After hunting large herbivores, we replaced many with favored herbivores of cattle and sheep. To predators (wolves and lions), the contained flocks and herds were the same. They became predators to ranchers. To protect the favored herbivores, they hunted the predators, not for meat or sport but for perceived damage control, often eradicating entire packs of wolves, coyotes, foxes, pride of lions as well as the lone cougars and tigers.

By the early 1900s, the grey wolf in the western states was nearly extinct. This upended the natural balance, and populations of the former prey (deer, elk) increased. The federal government reclassified the gray wolf in 1978 as an endangered population throughout the US.

In an attempt to restore the balance, wolves were reintroduced from Canada to Yellowstone Park in 1993.

The greatest impact was controlling the deer and elk population and eventually rebalancing the entire biosphere

Reducing the number of deer and elk allowed native grasses, small trees, and berry bushes to prosper, bringing back birds. More trees gave food to beavers, who built dams creating ponds where fish flourished, attracting muskrats and otters. Wolves reduced the number of coyotes bringing an increase in the mice and rabbit population. They did this by attracting foxes, hawks, and eagles. The increased vegetation controlled river bank erosion.

Domesticated Food

At the dawn of the Agricultural Revolution, the idea of animal domestication replaced hunting in providing a steady supply of meat. This marked the beginning of the human-animal relationship (HAR).

These animals provided milk, and with that, the human became the first species to seek milk from another species. Success provided a mobile source of fat and proteins, and the prosperity of the herds depended upon finding a constant supply of grasses and water. Food and water had to be provided for the herds, so farmers began to grow crops exclusively for animal feed.

CAFO cattle
Photo credit: James Martin

While the image of the cow grazing in the field of grass is idyllic or a part of the American legend of the cowboy bravely trailing longhorns from Texas to the rail heads of Dodge City, most farming is done via CAFO (Concentrated Animal Feeding Operations) or factory farms where animals are kept and raised in confined areas. A cluster of animals including dairy cows, feedlots, and poultry farms are controlled by the space the animal lives in, the grains it's fed, how manure is removed, the introduction of antibiotics and growth hormones, and how the animal is removed. Free ranging requires ten acres for every one and a half cows. A CAFO raised cow takes only fifteen months to maturity, a saving of eight months of food and water, grassland usage, and manure /methane production. Fed on corn and mill instead of grass, CAFO cattle produce less methane. There are approximately 450,000 CAFOs in the United States.

Well into the 21st century, production of all meats has become a major industry. Worldwide, 300 million tons are consumed annually, with a projection of 450 million tons by 2050. Though the high beef consumption per capita in the 1970 consumption has been reduced by 40%. This reduction has caused chicken to rise up the ranks as the most popular meat in the United States. Pork is the most consumed meat worldwide.

Intensive farming requires less land per output, produces larger animals, so fewer are needed for the same protein output, and has fewer losses due to predators and diseases. However, when a disease enters the group, it is easily transferred to the entire flock or herd. The concentration of animals produces a concentration of manure on the ground that, when rained upon, can run off into streams causing excess nitrogen and "dead zones."

Production of all meats is a major producer of greenhouse gasses and environmental problems. The United Nations estimates that livestock production causes 55% of erosion in the United States. Without grass, soil to hold water is blown away or into streams polluting at least one-third of the United States and reducing the productive worth of the land. One trillion pounds of manure produced annually releases ammonia and hydrogen sulfide. On the other hand, Methane can cause air pollution for as much as five miles downwind.

Methane is one-fifth as common as CO2 but eighty-six times as destructive to the atmosphere. Much of the output in the US originates from cattle. Grazing cattle eat grass and produce four times the methane than their grain fed CAFO. Together an estimated 10-12% of methane production is from cattle. Of all domestic animal types, beef and dairy cattle were by far the largest emitters of CH4. Excess nutrients run off to waters, where they encourage phytoplankton growth. As they die, the decay further acidifies the water.

United States livestock produces 116,000 pounds of manure per second, 130 times as much waste as humans, and may contain pathogens, pharmaceuticals, hormones, and antibiotics. Yet while human waste is treated for contaminants, animal waste is not. 90% is realistically recycled for organic fertilizer; the remainder is washed into streams and onto the ecosystem

Manure has traditionally been beneficial to agriculture. Neolithic farmers worked animal manure into the soil, returning nutrients and as fuel. CAFOs not only separate cows from the fields but also their manure from the process of decomposing. The manure has to be physically removed, often after the cow has walked through it, to a disposal site.

Animal waste is destructive to the environment when not contained. In 1995 twenty-five million gallons of hog manure were spilled into the New River in North Carolina. Over five hundred square miles of wetland were harmed, killing an estimated ten million fish. In 2010 Brazil cleared 1.6 million acres at a rate of about two to three acres per minute for cattle production. In the following decade, from political actions, the rate has increased. 91% of the rainforest loss is for livestock and feed for livestock.

Production of livestock is not an efficient method of protein production for humans. Plants produce fifteen times more protein per acre than meat, and livestock need water, lots of water. Animal protein requires one hundred times more water than grain protein. Water usage worldwide for all of agriculture, including crops and animals, is about thirty-four trillion gallons. Four hundred gallons of water are needed to produce one egg, still less than the 660 gallons of water for a pound of hamburger, and poultry requires only 20% of the land for equal amounts of protein as beef and releases 10% of methane. Two thousand five hundred gallons of water are needed for one pound of beef. Nine hundred gallons of water are needed for a pound of cheese and one thousand gallons for one gallon of milk. 51% of US water is used for agriculture and 30% of the world's needs. Only 5% is for home use. 47% of land is for food production, 70% of that is for livestock or feed for livestock. Beef requires fifty times the land for the same amount of protein as vegetables. Only 1% is used for growing fruits, nuts, and vegetables. Worldwide, clearing land for livestock is the foremost reason for deforestation.

The United States is leading the race to consume the most meat. The worldwide average is 41.90 kg, whereas the American figures show 120 kg or 260 lbs. American males consume 40% more meat, eggs, and fish than the FDA recommends, with females consuming about 15% more. Overall, Americans eat three times the amount of red meat as any other country.

The United States is the largest producer of protein from meat. It's also the largest consumer, at two hundred pounds annually, twice as much as any other national group. By contrast, the European Union collectively produces about 13%, and China, at 11%, produces almost exclusively for the growing internal market.

Animals are an inefficient source of protein. Compared to plants, beef requires one hundred times the water, eleven times the fossil fuels, and five times the land for the same end amount of grain protein. The figures come from the amount of resources over the life of the animal and the energy to process and transport. Presently, one half of the land is dedicated to animal agriculture. Texas alone uses forty trillion tons of water to produce fourteen million beef cattle. One pound of beef requires twenty-five hundred pounds of water. Worldwide, raising animals for food uses 30% of the total fresh water. Humans use only 5%.

With CAFO, per-hen-egg production has doubled while broiler weight has tripled. Growth enhancements for "broilers" make their bodies grow faster than their legs and organs, causing weak knees with joint and heart problems.

A free-range bird will yield about 20 eggs annually; a CAFO chicken produces an average of 269. While free range birds can live about twenty years, an industrial chicken, raised in a "laying" cage with about 100,000 hens per building, has less than two years. To efficiently grow CAFO animals, twenty–eight million pounds of antibiotics are introduced annually, four times human poundage.

The average time from hatching to slaughter for cows has been reduced from 70 days in 1950 to 48 days in 2008, limiting full growth in all components. A CAFO cow takes 15 months to maturity. A pastured cow takes 23 months plus additional water and feed while producing another eight months of manure and methane. Beef production per cow has increased from less than 250 pounds per cow in 1950 to over 660 pounds per cow and 60 % more milk from 30% fewer cows, as each cow produces over 2.5 times as much milk.

Legally companies are required to make a profit, meaning to maximize output and profits while minimizing costs, what Thomas Jefferson called "the selfish spirit of commerce." The two major expenses are the cost of animal production and factory conditions (meaning employee salaries and factory upkeep).

Turn-of-the-century factory conditions were publicized in Upton Sinclair's 1906 book *The Jungle*, with political fiction highlighting conditions in meat packing plants at the beginning of the 20th century. In response, President Theodore Roosevelt directed actions against the conditions leading to the 1906 Meat Inspection Act and the Pure Food and Drug Act of 1906, leading to the Food & Drug Administration (FDA).

Aquatic

If there was any resource that seemed limitless, it was the oceans. Fish, mollusks, crustaceans, and sea mammals were abundant and familiar. The oceans went forever, and so did the sea life with a biodiversity that was unparalleled, containing over 80% of life on the planet, and humans found ways to harvest and use every type.

Simple boats allowed early humans to venture beyond the shoreline, giving access to almost all aquatic life.

As with land resources, through mass acquisition and processing, humans have overdone, and the oceans are in peril. According to the UN Food and Agriculture Organization's twice-yearly report, 52% of fish stocks are fully exploited, 20% are moderately exploited, 17% are overexploited, 7% are depleted, and 1% are recovering from depletion. Nations continue to subsidize their fishing industry which could not survive without these subsidies. Japanese subsidies are estimated at $4.6 billion, with China subsidizing to the tune of $4.1 and the United States at $2.3 billion.

There are about twenty-three thousand industrial fishing factory ships worldwide of various sizes and capabilities employing various methods to collect masses of fish. Longlining nets, miles long, scoop up everything in the ocean, though only a limited percent are the intended catch. Benthic trawling, involving dragging trawl nets along the sea floor, is highly non-selective and comes with a large amount of by-catch and destruction in the trawled path. The UN Food and Agriculture Organization published that 52% of the fish stocks are fully exploited, with an additional 20% moderately exploited. Almost 3/4 of the world's fish stocks are in a state of collapse.

Trawling not only indiscriminately scoops marine life off the ocean floor, but the disruption of the surface is releasing CO_2 that has been trapped in the seabed, releasing it into the ocean. The ocean absorbs about a third of CO_2 emissions, and the additional seabed carbon sink release, greater than emitted by all airlines, may overwhelm the natural system.

70% of the planet's oxygen comes from the photosynthesis of plants near the sun light rich surface, as the ocean supplies about two-thirds of the oxygen.

Rather than relying on exploiting natural aquatic life, efforts are being made to make seafood another domesticated crop in the form of Aquaculture. About 4,000 years ago, ponds were built specifically for raising sea life. The Chinese developed a polyculture system. Animal manure fertilized pond algae that were eaten by carp that also ate parasitic insects and weeds. The carp were, in turn, used as fertilizer for crops.

The most common contemporary farmed fish are salmon, carp, tilapia, and catfish, with farming shrimp beginning in the 1970s.

Integrated Multi-Trophic Aquaculture (IMTA) is composed of interdependent species, so it has an inherent function of self-cleaning. This can allow parasites to pass between bred fish and wild fish. One pound of farmed fish requires two pounds of feed fish. Salmon and Tuna require even more with a five-to-one ratio.

Aquafarmed salmon is different than free ocean salmon. Farmed salmon are higher in fat and about 46% higher in calories. Though both natural and farmed salmon are high in Omega-3s, natural salmon are higher in minerals, including potassium, zinc, and iron.

Even the average farmed fish requires two pounds of feed fish for every resulting pound. The alternative is to feed corn or grains, but such fed fish have low levels of Omega-3, one of the benefits of consuming fish.

Fish farming is more efficient for proteins than for land animals. In cooler environments, they require fewer calories and mass to counter gravity. Compared to 6.8 pounds of feed for one pound of beef, 2.9 pounds for pigs, and 1.7 pounds for poultry, the fish only requires 1.1 pounds for one pound of fish.

Whales

Whether hunted in an Eskimo kayak or on a whaling ship/ocean going factory, the size and abundant supply of meat and blubber could not be ignored.

Humans have been hunting whales for over five thousand years, But In 1986, faced with reduced demand and public pressure, the International Whaling Commission (IWC) put a limited ban on commercial hunting whales. Native cultures, where whale hunting is part of their culture, were excused by the IWC as Aboriginal Subsistence Whaling.

With the oceans covering 71%of the Earth's surface yet providing only 2% of the world's food, there is vast potential for intelligently designed sustainable use of the oceans in the new "Blue Revolution."

But increased consumption of sea life has consequences on the climate. Sea animals also take in carbon from the consumption of other sea life and the atmosphere, but with death, the carbon stored body sinks to the bottom of the ocean, sequestering the carbon often for thousands of years known as "blue carbon." When caught, the fish and the sequestered carbon are prevented from being naturally recycled.

Columbian Exchange

The "Columbian Exchange" was different in a way since it brought the European Settlers with Old World animals. Horses, pigs, cattle, sheep, chickens, dogs, cats, bees, and even earthworms, useful in Europe, became useful to settlers in the Americas. Some cows and horses became adrift and evolved into animals that could thrive in the Great Plains as mustangs and long horn cattle, the former adopted by the native tribes.

Sparrows were introduced as a familiar sight and sound from the old country.

Other introduced species include the bullfrog, green iguana, large-mouth bass, big head carp, blue tilapia, and amur catfish, many of which have become so ingrained as to seem to be native while competing with native species.

The introduction of sheep into Patagonia led to the loss of grazing lands of the native Guanaco, a llama-like herbivore.

The age of exploration also brought non-invited species along with the settlers. Rats, a constant stowaway, found the new lands to be rich with opportunities, especially in areas that had no similar rodents and, therefore, no natural predators.

Introductions went both ways. New World species brought to Europe included the turkey and guinea pig. The American grey squirrel thrived in England, partially due to its larger size and aggressive manner, as was the raccoon, muskrat, and rainbow trout.

Globalization has caused an increase in invasive species. Most cargo ships take on water for stability and then purge the tanks at the final terminal. This action takes an organism in one port and deposits it in another. One method to reduce contamination is for ships to purge their bilge tanks while still in the open ocean rather than wait until moored in port.

The North Sea and Bering Straits are open shipping areas, but there has been little invasive species interaction due to the cold arctic water, inhospitable to warm water invaders. As the waters warm from climate change, especially if the Arctic Ocean becomes navigable and as the ice shelf melts, these areas might become more susceptible to ecological invaders.

Niagara Falls provided a natural barrier for non-native fish or mollusks from reaching the four Great Lakes beyond. But the opening of the St Lawrence Seaway in 1959 allowed full access to the entire Great Lakes estuary. Since then, over 180 invasive species have entered.

Without natural predators, the invaders can grow unrestricted. The quagga mussel has become so dominant in Lake Michigan that they form a bottom density of 35,000 per square meter. A new invasive species has been located an average of once every six months.

The example of the Great Lakes is repeated in the Black and Caspian Seas, the Gulf of Arabia, the harbors of Tokyo and Singapore, river ports of Amsterdam, London, and Shanghai, and such where localized ecologies have been transformed by species brought in from other ecological areas. Especially for freshwater species, the oceans provided a barrier limiting each to a specific area. But human traffic has removed those barriers by lifting the species over the salt water to other freshwater environments.

Imported animals do not always stay where place. Burmese pythons, brought in as exotic pests, escaped into the Everglades in 2000. The favorable environment, including no natural predators, allowed the giant snakes to prosper, to where in instances, they preyed on young Florida panthers, themselves an endangered species.

The Nutria, a large rodent, was first discovered in South America as a fur source. The wetlands of the Chesapeake Bay proved ideal for their diet of aquatic plant roots destroying over fifty thousand acres of the environmentally sensitive region.

Post-war America was a move from the cities to the suburbs with trees, shrubs, and real grass. What was created was an ideal nature, a pseudo-nature with plants added for aesthetic enhancement, even plants unnatural to the region.

Deer also live in the transition zone between open fields and deep forests. Despite centuries of being hunted for meat, furs, and sport, in this environment, free of predators, they thrived in an ideal dietary environment of leafy plants, shrubs, and flowers. Today the number is about the same as in 1492, but the distribution is different. "No hunting zones" have given deer a safe haven alongside humans, putting them in conflict for eating decorative plants. Unchecked deer populations overeat the environment creating starvation for the younger and weaker members of the herd.

Few views are as naturally awe inspiring as a V formation of migrating Canadian Geese. But they all don't migrate. An estimated four million of the eight-ten million geese stay put. With many natural areas remaining unfrozen in the winter as well as man-made food sources, there is no reason for migration. With their size, a bird can disrupt an aircraft. The famous "Miracle on the Hudson" began with two geese hitting the engines of an Airbus A-320.

The beaver is one of the species that was trapped to near extinction. Before it could go extinct, natural predators were removed, and it prospered when protected. They flourished, spreading into the suburbs.

The most dangerous feral hunter is the common house cat, whose natural instinct is to hunt small animals. They are silent and adept in trees, either day or night. While this was helpful in killing mice and rats, it also included small birds as prey. An annual wild bird loss of $17 billion is attributed to feral and outside house cats. They have been responsible for the extinction of at least thirty-three species of birds.

Hunting

Hunting animals was necessary for survival. The meat was a concentrated supply of protein, and the increase of meat, especially once softened by cooking, allowed for an increase in brain size. As humans migrated into new regions finding a readably available supply of meat was essential. With cooperative hunting practices and killing tools, they were often too effective as soon after humans entered new regions. The megafauna populations decreased, and some were even subjected to extinction.

Hunting has continued for several reasons. There is the tradition of hunting as a link to a more self-sufficient-individualistic lifestyle. By hunting, the individual or group reenacts entry into the natural world, where humans are the interloper. To reduce some of the advantages hunters use bow and arrow, black power guns, and restrictions on hunting locations. Wildlife is perceived as a renewable resource to be controlled and exploited. By estimate, $38.3 billion was spent in 2011 related to hunting through firearm and support equipment sales, state hunting fees, transportation and lodging, and butchery. Taxes and fees revenues are used through the Wildlife Restoration Act of 1937 to maintain open areas and monitor herds.

Feelings and protection

Charles Darwin wrote that *"there is no fundamental difference between man and the higher mammals in their mental facilities."*

From ancient religious writings, humans have questioned if animals feel emotions such as pain. So to address these concerns, laws have been enacted to protect animals from abuse, recognizing that they are living beings with a nervous system and brain not that dissimilar from the human brain. DNA testing shows that chimpanzees live in social groups, laugh and grieve. They are 96% identical to humans, closer than to gorillas.

Even the "humane" religious slaughters cause pain. The animal has to be alive when the ceremonial slit is made, and being hung up by the hind legs causes fear.

There is a difference in how animals are legally protected. *Animal Rights* laws and the organizations that oversee these laws are based on the premise that animals are sentient beings and humans have no right to use them for food, clothing, labor, or entertainment. *Animal Welfare,* though accepts that humans have the right to use animals but to treat them humanely. Animals can be used but not mistreated or to cause pain, whether in growth methods leading to slaughtering for the meat, pulling wagons, or cock fights.

Humans have not always lived up to their part of the relationship.

Animal Rights were gained on July 7, 2012, when an international group of cognitive neuroscientists released the Cambridge Declaration of Consciousness. They stated that non-humans have the substrate of consciousness and the capacity to exhibit internal behavior. *"Humans are not unique in possessing the neurological substrates that generate consciousness."*

Three years later, New Zealand passed the Animal Welfare Act recognizing that animals are sentient beings.

Major cultural activities based around the destructive use of animals have changed. In 2005 fox hunting was banned in the United Kingdom, cock fights were banned in Louisiana in 2008, and bullfighting was outlawed in Catalonia, Spain, in the year 2010. Companion animals and farm animals have shown the same level of intelligence, and it is administered by the scientist that they feel pain. There are more animal protection laws for the former. PETA (People for the Ethical Treatment of Animals) was founded in 1982 with the purpose of peacefully working in public for animal welfare.

Through the 1990s, investigative reporters presented stories about unfavorable conditions in CAFOs and slaughterhouses. In reaction to the news, laws were passed in the United States to protect animal research, livestock, and processing centers. After the 9/11 attacks, the 1992 Animal Enterprise Protection Act (AEPA) was amended in 2006 with the Animal Enterprise Terrorism Act (AETA) under the blanket of the importance of food to a nation's security. It's illegal in thirteen states to disparage the meat industry.

One theory on the origin of the Covid-19 pandemic goes back to a human consuming bat meat at Chinese wet markets of wild animals. Pandemics like Ebola, Sars, and HIV have previously been found to have come from the consumption of wild animals.

Alternatives sources of meat proteins

"This is neither a condemnation of an animal-based diet nor espousing a vegan diet but a comparison of economic use of resources. Meats are tasty and an efficient source of proteins."

We need animal products, but do we need animals as a source of protein? With the inefficiency of creating animal products via an animal, there are quests for alternatives.

A Vegetarian diet requires one-sixth of an acre to produce the necessary amount of proteins. With the addition of eggs and dairy products, the land required rises to half an acre. And when meat is added, the necessary land requirements rise to three acres. Compared to an omnivore diet, a vegan diet saves 1,000 gallons of water, forty five pounds of grain, thirty five square" feet of forest, ten pounds of CO_2, and the life of one animal. 50% of all grains and legumes are eaten by livestock. Three hundred seventy-five pounds of meat require the same amount of water as 37,000 pounds of vegetables.

The World Health Organization (WHO) stated that proteins from soy, farina, peanut butter, and refined wheat are easier for the human body to process than meat or fish. And Americans have twice the obesity and diabetics and three times the reports of cancer than the world average and are fiftieth in longevity. Meats produce what is described as "diseases of indulgence." Treatment of these diseases from meat consumption is estimated at $314 billion annually. An approximate of almost thirty four thousand deaths worldwide annually are attributed to the highly processed meat diets, with another fifty thousand to red meats.

Non-meat proteins are not the thing of the unknown. Tofu has been a staple of Asian diets since the Han Dynasty.

"Flexitarianism" is a dietary transition that allows some meat consumption while maintaining a mostly vegan diet. Chicken and other fowl, fish, and vegetables have been shown to lower levels of cholesterol and saturated fats.

Recent non-vegetarians have sought to simulate meat products with vegetable based foods. The advantages of non-animal meats have enormous implications. Minced meats made from vegetables emit one-eighth of the greenhouse gasses and use 95% less land and a quarter less water.

Using bovine cells, the Modern Meadows Company has lab grown sheets of collagen duplicating leather, but without the hair and fats from animal skins or the toxic chemicals of tanning.

There may be a way to have meat without the disadvantages of needing a living animal. Built on tissue engineering, in vitro meat offers the potential to have all the advantages of meat without the accompanying conditions of livestock yards or processing facilities. It would not be contaminated with feces, chemicals, or pesticides. Called "shmeat," it is made of sheet meat, which consists of layers of cell cultures from animal tissues.

Hampton Foods was founded in 2011 to develop plant-based foods that could replace animal-based foods. Their initial work involved using yellow peas to replace eggs in both direct consumption and as ingredients for other foods, starting with non-egg mayonnaise and cookie dough. While an artificial egg requires only two units of food input for a single unit of output, a natural egg requires thirty-eight units.

Cultivated or "cultured" meats are grown directly from real animal cells. This concept is an outgrowth of decades of stem cell, cell culture, and tissue engineering research. The first commercial companies began operations in the mid-2010s. The Singapore Food Agency approved chicken products in 2020, and American UPSIDE Foods completed consultation with the FDA in 2022. Other meat alternatives include with mycoproteins. A high-fibre, high-protein food with a lean chicken like texture is produced by fermenting Filamentous fungi in a lab. Other funji-based foods are replacements for bacon and fish.

Nature's Fund uses *Fusarium strain flavolapis*, to make meatless patties and a cream-cheese alternative

Red-algae supplements, found in seaweed, reduce methane burps, especially in cattle, by 80%

The cells used for cultivated meats are taken from the source animal, such as chicken, beef, pig, or fish, without the need for harvesting or slaughtering the animal. These cells are grown in bioreactors/cultivators using controlled antibiotic and disease-free nutrients. The process takes a few weeks, after which the cells can be harvested and molded into consumable products. The cell line can be stored, reducing the need for additional sources.

The resulting meat has the attributes of the source animal without the need for resource-consuming large herds or flocks, and the source animal remains unharmed. The creation of cultured "meats" requires 7-45% less energy, uses 99% less land, and emits 78-96% fewer greenhouse gases. Additionally, the production can be located near consumers, reducing travel, packaging, and cooling costs.

The traditional meat industry has raised resistance to non-animal-grown "meats." Several states have passed regulations restricting the use of meat-like labels for plant-based foods. In Europe, a proposal was put forward to prevent non-meat products from using meat-associated titles in their labeling. For the meat industry, this is seen as an issue of false advertising since "meat" traditionally refers to raised and slaughtered animal tissue. On the other hand, the alternative meat industry sees it as a free speech issue, allowing them to market products that serve the same demands while encouraging innovation. Turkey and chicken burgers and sausages have been on the market for years without notable dissent.

This issue is already playing out with nut and plant-based "milks." It is not just about consumer clarity on options, as plant-based meats are projected to account for $85 billion in sales by 2030. Ultimately, consumer taste, rather than labeling, will lead to acceptance.

Entomophagy: *the consumption of insects by humans*. While insects have a negative connotation in developed Western nations, they serve as an important source of protein for about a quarter of the human population. Crickets are twelve times more efficient as a source of protein than cattle. A pig requires 269 pounds of feed to produce a single pound of protein, while a mealworm requires only 88 pounds.

There are more than two thousand edible insects, with 31% of them being beetles and 18% caterpillars. Other edible insects include crickets, grasshoppers, ants, various larvae, and even bees,

With the continually growing human population, reduction of farmland, and the effects of climate change, there is a growing awareness of the viability of insects as a human food source. At the 2013 International Conference on Forests for Food Security and Nutrition, the Food and Agriculture Organization of the United Nations released "Edible insects - Future prospects for food and feed security."

Other meat alternatives include with mycoproteins. A high-fibre, high-protein food with a lean chicken like texture is produced by fermenting Filamentous fungi in a lab. Other funji-based foods are replacements for bacon and fish.

Nature's Fynd uses *Fusarium strain flavolapis*, to make meatless patties and a cream-cheese alternative

Red-algae supplements, found in seaweed, reduce methane burps, especially in cattle, by 80%

In western countries, flour made from pulverized insects is already being used as a baking ingredient for items like cookies and pancakes. Cricket farming has also experienced significant growth. In Mexico, "pest" insects are being trapped as they provide more protein than the crops they were previously "destroying."

Viewing insects as a food source rather than a flying plague may lead to the cultivation of crops specifically for insect food, subsequently reducing the need for numerous pesticides. Increased use of food insects will reverse the historic relationship, shifting from protecting plants from insects to raising crops specifically for insect feed.

One universally accepted insect food is honey. The first honeybees were brought to the Virginia colony in 1621. Today, China produces almost 28% of the world's honey, followed by Turkey (5.9%), Iran (4.5%), and the US (4.1%). The USDA reported that the average American consumes more than 1.75 pounds of honey.

Microalgae, an even more primitive food source for energy and fats, can be grown in the dark with only a minimal amount of land and water. In the ocean, it converts water and carbon dioxide to biomass and oxygen, which is beneficial in light of increased atmospheric CO_2. Microalgae can be up to 70% protein and produce 15 tons of protein per hectare. The major challenge will not be technical but social, as Western diets need to accept what they once considered disgusting pests as a major source of protein due to the "ick" factor.

Testing

Due to biological similarities, faster reproduction cycles, and ethical considerations regarding human usage, animals are used as test subjects for cosmetics and medical research, a practice that has been ongoing for at least five hundred years. An estimated twenty-six million animals are used for testing and research in the United States alone, despite the controversy surrounding its continued use.

DNA research has demonstrated our biological similarities. Chimpanzees share 99% of their DNA with humans, and rats are 98% genetically similar, meaning that chemical and bacterial reactions in these animals will be similar to those in humans.

In the US, animal testing is regulated by the Animal Welfare Act (AWA) of 1966 and approved by the Institutional Animal Care and Use Committee (IACUC), which limits the conditions in which animals can be housed and tested.

Poaching and Smuggling

Non-food hunting has been a part of human endeavors for at least 5,000 years, with animal parts like bear claws or lion heads having spiritual symbolism. Ivory has been obtained from the tusks and bones of hippos, narwhals, and even frozen mammoths by the Russians. However, the primary source has been elephants. Before plastics, ivory was used to make billiard balls.

In the global economy, animals are often worth more for their parts than for their meat. The Chinese use of ivory has been found to be over three thousand years old, primarily among the nobility and the wealthy. With the growing middle class, seventy percent of illegal ivory is headed to China, where it sells for over $1,000 per pound. In Japan, due to low manufacturing costs and an increasingly affluent society, the traditional Hankos was changed from traditional wood to ivory.

African elephants are killed for their tusks, and rhinoceroses are killed for their horn. Due to poverty and corruption, African natives kill their natural wildlife, often using military weapons or cyanide poisons. This not only eliminates the prized animals but also affects non-tusked young animals and other creatures that rely on the same water sources or feeding grounds, such as vultures and hyenas.

Between 2000 and 2016, 140 rangers were killed in the Congo, with over a thousand killed throughout Africa. Many rangers are unarmed or under-armed compared to poachers, who often possess military weapon systems left over from civil wars. The International Ranger Federation reports an average of two ranger deaths per week. Dian Fossey, known for her work with mountain gorillas in Rwanda, was murdered in 1985 after living with them for almost twenty years.

Despite the presence of national parks and "safe zones," poaching continues. In one African country, 62 elephants were poisoned by poachers in October 2015, while 22 elephants were killed with cyanide in Zimbabwe's Hwange National Park.

Some elephants have evolved being born without tusks making them worthless to poachers

photo credit: Marco Freire

In 2014, China imposed a one-year ban on ivory imports amid criticism that its citizens' huge appetite for ivory has fueled poaching, which threatens the existence of African elephants. Equally worrisome is the killing of rhinoceros for their horns. The trade in horns can fetch prices ranging from $3,000 per pound in Africa to over $30,000 in China or Vietnam, and even more when ground and sold by the ounce. Poachers remove the horn by killing the animal and then hacking it off with a machete, leaving the carcass behind. Profits from killing rhinos contribute to governmental corruption, instability, and international crime.

To reduce poaching in South Africa, rhinos are kept in private farms. Periodically, farmers sedate the animals and saw off their horns for sale. Revenue generated from rhino horn sales is then used for rhino protection.

In the Democratic Republic of Congo (DRC), a self-funded sanctuary is taking in seized chimpanzee babies. Chimpanzees are poached in the wild for food and sale. Although the DRC, home to 40% of the world's population, has ratified regulations for primate protection, little action has been taken, leaving our closest relatives in danger of going extinct in the wild.

The pangolin, a toothless anteater, is the most trafficked animal on Earth, accounting for 20% of the world black market in wildlife. Fifty thousand pangolins are killed annually in Vietnam alone. Despite a ban on pangolin trade in Asia since 2002, the meat and scales are still being sold for hundreds of dollars per kilogram to the Chinese, who believe they have various curative properties for ailments.

The origins of traditional Chinese medicines, according to legend, can be traced back to Shennong (The Divine Farmer) with the compilation of a catalog of 365 species of medicinal plants. There are approximately 1,000 endangered plants and 36 animal species included in the *Neijing*, the basic medical authority still used in Asia today.

Poaching is not limited to skins and ivories. Live exotic animals are profitable items for smuggling. Although the importation of primates has been illegal in the U. S. since 1975, the value of over $3,000 for a monkey to $30,000 for an ape has made smuggling financially attractive.

There are already an estimated 15,000 kept as exotic pets in the U. S. The World Wildlife Federation (WWF) estimates the global illegal wildlife trade is estimated to yield at least $19 billion per year, comprising the fourth-largest illegal global trade after narcotics products, currency counterfeiting, and human trafficking.

An elephant would cost $120,000 in sport hunting, while a tourist pays only $10 to view the same elephant. Money from sport hunting plays a crucial role in conservation efforts. In January 2014, a permit was sold for $350,000 to hunt an endangered black rhinoceros. In 2000, Namibia alone generated $11 million for its economy from nearly 16,000 trophy hunts. These hunts often involve the "big five" popular African game: lion, elephant, Cape buffalo, leopard, and rhinoceros.

Wealthy "hunters" are willing to spend on obtaining a trophy of a large animal they have "killed" in a controlled and staged environment.

Traditional big game hunting has been replaced by private game ranches, where trophy hunters pay thousands for permits to shoot one of the big five. The animals are raised on the ranches and eventually released for hunting in what is referred to as "bred for the bullet." To the farmers, there is no difference from raising a chicken for slaughter.

Ecotourism
photo credit: Marco Freire

The goal of the African Wildlife Foundation (AWF) is to protect unique African wildlife through tourism in official parks. Ecotourism is the second-largest source of foreign exchange income in Madagascar and generates $2.4 billion for South Africa's economy.

Ecotourism has been increasing by 10-15% annually. Wildlife safaris can provide relief, as keeping animals alive for tourists is a more stable and less dangerous alternative to poaching. Kenya alone receives over a million safari tourists annually. As ecotourism grows and more locals get involved, deforestation and poaching decrease.

However, tourist safaris alone cannot guarantee the survival of endangered species as human activities encroach further into their habitats. Only 3% of revenue from trophy hunting ever reaches the local communities.

Animal destruction is always an unintended consequence of war. The Vietnam War, in particular, had a devastating impact on wildlife. The United States dropped thirteen million tons of bombs, creating craters and deforesting "landing zones" across the landscape. To clear the forests of vegetation, twenty-two million liters of defoliant, including Agent Orange, were sprayed. The chemicals not only defoliated the trees but also poisoned the fruit that tree-dwelling animals relied on for food. While wildlife was not the intended enemy, it became caught in ecological warfare—a war against nature.

In Vietnam alone, there are one hundred fifty species of birds, accounting for about 10% of the world's total variety. There are also twenty-four primate species, of which twenty-one are listed as threatened, including the Red-Shanked Douc Langur. 70% of all Asian primates are classified as either threatened or critically endangered.

Where the military has designated "no go zones," native populations have been able to rebuild.

Equatorial Africa, another region with a large number of vulnerable species, has been the site of numerous localized wars for decades. The ongoing wars have also resulted in millions of people being forced to leave, often moving into regions that are home to species that would otherwise not be in contact with human encroachment.

Image credit: World WildLife Fund

In an update to the Red List, four out of six of Earth's great apes are now critically endangered, "only one step away from going extinct." These include the Eastern Gorilla, Western Gorilla, Bornean Orangutan, and Sumatran Orangutan. As humans are primates, and chimpanzees, bonobos, and gorillas are our closest DNA relatives, killing these animals is akin to cannibalism.

Extinction and restoration

In the late 18th century, the French biologist Jean-Baptiste Lamarck first proposed that humans might be able to cause the extinction of animal species. At that time, such human impact may have seemed inconceivable.

Biodiversity relies on differences in breeds and species due to the functionality of the animal or plant. Animals coexist as each variation has a different food source or different method of acquiring food. When a species is eliminated, the function it provided within the ecosystem disappears, disrupting the natural balance. In pre-human nature, herbivore populations were kept in check by carnivores, maintaining this balance.

DDT (Dichlorodiphenyltrichloroethane) was effective for its intended purpose of controlling unwanted animals but proved to have major unintended consequences. As a tasteless and odorless insecticide, it was beneficial in controlling malaria during World War II. After the war, it gained commercial acceptance for insect damage control. By the late 1950s, the World Health Organization was using DDT to control malaria, leading to its elimination in Europe and North America, and significant reduction in the Caribbean and major parts of the South Pacific.

In her 1962 book, Silent Spring, Rachel Carson sounded the initial alarm against DDT. The reaction to her book eventually led to the ban of DDT in the US and Sweden in the early 1970s.

The recent loss of species is called the Holocene Extinction or, more recently, "the Sixth Extinction," as large numbers of species of plants and animals have gone extinct, many due to natural actions but many now to the actions of humans as the Anthropocene extinction. Extinctions are occurring now 100-1000 times higher than the historical rate of extinction.

By the species-area relationship (SAR) theory, up to 140,000 species are going extinct per year. First correlated in 1921 by the Swedish ecologist Olaf Arrhenius SAR it states that as the amount of usable land is decreased, so is the diversity and number of native species. The 703 species and sub-species

According to naturalist and author E. O. Wilson, at the current rate, half of the higher life forms will be extinct by 2100. Even over half of our closest primate relatives, due to large scale destruction of their habitats through burning and clearing of forests and the illegal wildlife trade, are on the verge of extinction.

Human activity has caused the extinction of whole species. The last of the great Auks, at three feet tall, the last flightless bird in the Northern Hemisphere, was killed in Iceland in 1844. Passenger Pigeons once dominated North American skies, but the tasty bird was a nuisance to farmers as well as an easy food source. The last bird died in the Cincinnati Zoo in 1914. Logging and predation by foxes and domestic pets threatened the Quokka, a marsupia that lives on islands off Australia's west coast.

Other animals faced other threats. The Kakapo, a very large flightless parrot of New Zealand, has suffered from extensive hunting and the introduction of predatory animals like cats and ferrets. Continuous civil violence and deforestation make conservation measures almost impossible to enforce for the Okapi. While it may look like a zebra, it's closely related to the giraffe.

Extinction, through eradication, may not always be a negative, especially when the survival of the animal is detrimental to human health. Mosquitoes carry infectious pathogens, including malaria, West Nile virus, yellow fever, and Zika. Annually, over 700,000 humans die from mosquito carried diseases. Rather than attack the pathogen, eliminate the carrier, the mosquito. The ethical question is that even if we can, should we? Mosquito larva is symbiotic with several species of amphibians and fish, while adults are food sources for birds and bats. There are over 3,500 mosquito species, but only about a hundred spread diseases to humans. That would still leave a large supply for natural predators.

The May 2019, the United Nation's Intergovernmental Science-Policy Platform on Biodiversity and Ecosystem Services issued a report that concluded that human activity might well cause the extinction of a million species. The international conference of 145 scientists from 50 nations reported that extinctions of all forms of life; reptiles, amphibians, plants, corals, insects, birds, fish, and other marine life, and mammals (where humans fit in) are going extinct at a rate up to 100 times natural species turnover.

The report concluded that the loss was due to human activities:

* Changes in land and sea use.
* Development in marsh areas, damming rivers, and deforestation.
* Climate change causing loss or change of habitat environmental conditions
* Pollution of chemicals and plastics into the soil, air, and oceans
* Invasive species that destroy the native ecosystem for which many native species have no defense, nor the time to evolve a counter.

Species Preservation

While having the capability to destroy species, humans also have the capability to save them.

Conservationist John Muir founded the Sierra Club in 1892 to protect the environment resulting in early public awareness of how pollutants and loss of habitats were affecting the natural environment.

Protection by the Endangered Species Act of 1966 led to the preservation of the American Bald Eagle and Grizzly Bear in the lower 48 states. This was followed up by the 1969 Endangered Species Conservation Act acknowledging that protection was needed worldwide and prohibited the importation and sale of endangered species, regardless of regional origin.

President Richard Nixon signed the Endangered Species Act in 1973 to protect imperiled species and those on the brink of extinction. The United States Fish and Wildlife Service and the National Oceanic and Atmospheric Administration were charged with the implementation of the act that divided protected species into Endangered Species, Threatened Species, or Critical Habitat.

Species protection and biodiversity is a worldwide issue. With recognition, the World Wildlife Foundation (WWF) was created in April 1961 to save species and the environment.

For eons, a natural balance of predator, prey, and habitat had prevailed in the American west. Native indigenous tribes hadn't affected the balance

Humans set up a conflict with domesticated cattle herds. Not recognizing human created boundaries and the difference between bison and cattle, predators became competitors. They were labeled as varmints to be hunted. Beginning in 1914, the U. S. Biological Survey implemented a plan to kill off all the wolves in Yellowstone National Park. The final two were killed in 1927 herds.

With wolf removal, not only were domestic herds now "safe" from predators, but so were the herds of large herbivores (elk, bison, and deer) free to grow unrestrained. Overgrazing and plant life destruction led to habitat destruction, soil erosion, and starvation from over-eating available food sources. It is safe to say that human actions have changed the balance of nature.

Bob Paine first noted the importance of "Keystone species" impact on the natural balance with starfish. He found that keystone species top down stabilized local ecosystems. Among the kelp beds it's the sea otter as is the large mouth bass in mountain streams and alligators in the Everglades. When humans, through hunting or destruction of the environment, remove the keystone species the diversity of the entire ecosystem was disrupted.

Recognizing the keystone value of wolves a Yellowstone recovery plan was instituted. By 2014 there were an estimated 400-450 wolves in the Yellowstone ecosystem and the balance was improved. The controversy though has continued between ranchers, environmentalists, and game hunters.

And even extinct might not be forever. Advances in cloning are taking DNA from the retrieved cells of an extinct animal and then recreating a copy with the use of a similar animal (e.g., mammoths and elephants). Since we can't go back in time to prevent extinction, cloning allows a way to bring past animals into our present.

While it may be possible to clone a human being, there will be ethical questions. President Bill Clinton made research for human cloning illegal.

Zoos have reversed the safari experience by bringing exotic species to viewers. Animals that aren't native and even local animals that urban viewers are not in contact with are brought for viewing and animals that might be known as only in pictures are viewed up close.

Zoos range in size from roadside petting zoos to sanctuary farms that take in injured wild animals to large scale attractions like Disney's Animal Kingdom. Disney World in Florida contains 1,700 animals of 240 species in a recreated natural environment void of metal fences.

For several species, the only livable environment is in zoos. Recognizing that the numbers were declining in the natural environment and that their environment was being changed by human induced invasive species, chemicals, and development, animals were collected for protection and sent to zoos.

Thirty-one species, listed as extinct in the wild, are being held in zoo captivity. Among the animals "saved" are the New Guinea Singing Dog, the Guam Rail, and the black footed ferret.

But there are practical reasons for species reintroduction. The northern Siberian tundra is warming faster than the world average. One local factor is that heat holding trees have replaced grasses. There are fewer large animals to pack down the heat reflecting snow. Mastodons had kept the trees in check, allowing for grasses. Their reintroduction might return the tundra to a balanced ancient ecosystem slowing the warming and release of methane.

While none of these will cause worldwide celebration in their salvation, any more than there would be worldwide regret in their loss, each pull-back from forever is a testament that humans can be a part of the solution.

In many primitive and Native American societies, as late as the 19th century, there was a pantheism that revered animals and plants as equal in rights to humans, hunted only for food. The hunter asked permission of the animal's spirit first. We have a *"kinship with all creatures of the earth, sky and water,"* stated Lakota Chief Luther Standing Bear.

Sticks & Stones and Nanos

"In the beginning God made the heavens and Earth." But the world was without bronze, concrete, or styrene so humans created these and many other then formed them to design the world.

Humans design and build tools, shelters, clothing, and even electric hair curlers. To construct these things, materials are needed. Nature provides many of the materials, but when nature is lacking, humans create new materials and find ways to shape and combine them in manners impossible through natural processes.

Nature provides 92 elements. Oxygen, being unstable, combines with hydrogen to produce water and with carbon to produce carbon dioxide. Carbon and hydrogen combine to form hydrocarbons, which we consume as oil and coal. Sodium and chloride are individually poisonous to humans, but as the molecule salt, they are necessary for life on Earth.

Beyond the 74% of the Earth's surface covered in water, the rest of the surface is composed of soil, sand, rocks, and minerals. Igneous rocks (formed from cooled magma within the planet's surface) and metamorphic rocks make up 90-95% of the Earth's crust. An accumulation of rock particles under pressure becomes sedimentary rock. Fine rock particles mixed with organic materials form soil.

During pre-civilization, often referred to as the "Stone Age," the development of tools and shelters was a significant step. Sticks and hides were also important, but they lacked the permanence of stone. Stones were used by hominins to create shelters or were broken to form cutting tools. Flint was especially useful, as it could be chipped to produce a sharp edge and struck to create sparks, useful for producing fire.

However, natural shapes were not always the best fit. By altering materials with sharpened stones, humans improved the efficiency of joining pieces together to create a unified whole. The easiest and most available material for this purpose was wood. Although temporary, wooden structures defined an area and provided protection.

When heated, clay chemically changes into ceramics, becoming more durable and permanent. Ceramic containers can hold liquids and withstand high heat for boiling water and cooking soups and stews. Clay bricks were the first synthetic materials created by humans, not found in nature.

Mesopotamian and Egyptian builders used metal tools to cut pieces of sandstone and create magnificent temples, shelters, and statues. In Mesoamerica, Mayan craftsmen shaped limestone blocks using only wooden tools for their structures.

Iron and copper, the first metals used in construction, are not found naturally in large quantities but rather as oxidized ores or small deposits. Smelting of metals began around 7,000 years ago by heating the oxides to remove oxygen and impurities, leaving behind pure metal.

Copper was initially found as simple nuggets and then hammered into amulets and other personal items. Copper and tin compounds were smelted to create bronze, and with the addition of zinc, brass was produced.

Compounds were used to enhance the strength of the base elements.

Bronze was the first of many materials created by humans. It is harder than copper, making it better suited for weapons and cutting tools. The dominance of bronze began around 3,000 BCE, giving that era its name: the Bronze Age.

The first use of iron smelted from ore is estimated to have occurred around 1,200 BCE. Iron was more readily available than bronze, allowing for a wider range of applications. The smelting and compounding of copper and iron occurred at different times in different cultures. Bronze was created earlier in the Middle East, while the Chinese developed superior iron smelting techniques.

Stronger metals revolutionized the arts, enabling the cutting of harder rocks. While Egyptian statues and buildings were created using bronze tools on sandstone, Greek artists and builders were able to shape harder marble with steel tools, allowing for greater detail.

Until the Renaissance, the prevailing thought in the West was that the world consisted of four elements: fire, water, air, and earth. In China, the world was believed to consist of five elements: wood, earth, water, fire, and metal. Both systems were more philosophical than scientific, dealing with various aspects of life from medicine to astrology and relationships, rather than providing an understanding of the elements that compose the world. It was Aristotle who first proposed that everything was composed of "atoms."

Through observation and isolation in the ancient world, copper, tin, lead, zinc, mercury, antimony, sulfur, and carbon were identified as basic materials or elements. The first element to be chemically identified was phosphorus in 1669 by Henning Brand. Oxygen was discovered in 1773 as an individual element that combines with other elements to form the four ancient elements (hydrogen in water, iron in earth, nitrogen in air, and carbon in fire). Science had replaced philosophy in understanding the physical world.

From the mid-18th century until 1940, scientists identified and published the characteristics of the natural 92 elements. Dmitry Mendeleyev created order with the periodic table, even though he had only sixty known elements to work with. The discovery of additional elements later fit precisely into his table.

Within a year, the next step in the study of elements took place with the creation of Neptunium, the first transuranium element not naturally found in nature, by bombarding uranium atoms with protons. Twenty-two new elements, up to Copernicium (Cn), have been created by bombarding existing elements with other elements or protons. In our world, these elements are unstable and exist only momentarily. In 2016, four more were created: Nihonium (Nh), Moscovium (Mc), Tennessine (Ts), and Oganesson (Og). There may be other elements beyond those, but they currently exist only in theory.

Glass modules are created by subjecting naturally occurring silica (sand) to intense heat. In Neolithic times, glass was used for trade and as sharp cutting tools. The first human-created glass was made in the third millennium BCE in the Middle East, primarily for decorative purposes.

Natural materials and human-created materials have significant differences. Natural organic materials are hydrophilic, meaning they form bonds with proteins and water at ambient temperatures, making them easy to break apart for recycling by natural and living organisms. On the other hand, human-created materials are formed through heat and pressure and are cooled for use. They can be simple molecules, composites of two or more blended molecules, or multiple parts combined into a larger whole. Recycling requires additional heating and cooling.

The alteration of materials into useful products is accomplished through various methods:

1. Subtractive: Removing material, as seen in classical sculpture.
2. Additive: Putting pieces together to create a larger item through mechanical screws, chemical bonding, painting, and welding.

3. Reshaping: Pounding or forming flexible materials to change their shape or thickness.
4. 3-D printing: An additive process where molten material is applied layer-by-layer, guided by a CAD (computer-aided design) program to achieve the desired shape. 3-D printing can be used with metals, concrete, foods, and plastics. There is minimal material waste, as dimensional subtractive fine-tuning may be necessary. Concrete-type materials have been used for cementing stones in structures over eight thousand years old. With the development of concrete, stones could be held together, allowing for strong and intricately designed shapes. The Romans were the first to exploit the advantages of concrete as a large-scale building material. Roman concrete was a mixture of quicklime, pozzolana (from volcanic ash), and an aggregate of pumice. When mixed with water and dried, it hardened into a durable bonding material. Roman architects used concrete to create structures, buildings, bridges, aqueducts, and baths that are still structurally stable two millennia later. After the fall of the Roman Empire, the use of concrete was limited to medieval forts and cathedrals.

In the 19th century, the addition of reinforcing metals to concrete increased its strength for bridge supports, road surfaces, and structural building walls. The use of concrete as a liquid during forming allows for more flexibility in creating curved structures. In the 20th century, poured reinforced concrete was first utilized to construct large integrated dams.

In 2019, global concrete production reached 4.4 billion tons, with China leading at 2.2 billion tons. The largest increases in production have been observed in India and Vietnam.

However, the growing impact of concrete is affecting the environment. To produce clinker, the primary component of most contemporary concrete, limestone must be heated to over 1400°C. Cement carbon concentrations range from 5% to 8%. During the manufacturing of concrete, CO_2 is released through the chemical process and the burning of fuel, contributing to approximately 5% of global man-made emissions.

Due to its fluid nature during creation, concrete has a promising 3-D material future. In 2016, a concrete building in Dubai was 3-D printed, and this method may prove to be the most practical way to construct structures on Mars.

CAD files for 3-D printing will need to be patented as intellectual property, similar to songs or other copyrighted materials.

Wood has been an important building material since the earliest structures, but it has limitations due to its linear fibers. Wood can withstand compression but is easily split along the grain. In the late 18th century, plywood was developed by gluing multiple pieces of veneer together with alternating grain directions, creating a material that is resistant to splitting. Cross-laminated timbers (CLT) are boards bonded with alternating grain directions. Besides being a renewable material, even infected woods can be recycled. Projections suggest that CLT can be used as a structural material for buildings up to forty stories high, serving as an alternative to steel and concrete. CLT can absorb side loads, making it a more flexible material in earthquake-prone areas.

Plastics have become the wonder material of the latter 20th century and into the 21st, representing a family of human-created materials. Plastics can be molded to serve a multitude of purposes and can replace various natural materials. For example, Plexiglas is as transparent as glass but won't shatter, nylon can replace silk, and polypropylene can substitute for rope. Through compounding, plastics can be flexible and soft or hard enough to form the basis for bulletproof vests. Plastics are inexpensive and commonly used for disposable items and as wrapping for shipping.

Plastics are derived from hydrocarbons like oil and coal. While fossil fuels are consumed and produce CO_2 when united with oxygen in combustion, the hydrocarbons in plastics form their permanent structures.

The first plastics were created by chemists in the 19th century. In 1839, Eduard Simon discovered polystyrene, a material with a chemical composition similar to rubber. However, it took another hundred years for practical production of styrene. The first commercial plastics were based on cellulose, organic materials derived from cotton fibers. The first synthetic polymer was invented in 1869 by John Wesley Hyatt as a substitute for ivory. Bakelite, invented in 1907 by Leo Baekeland, was the first fully synthetic plastic that contained no molecules found in nature.

Plastics account for over 50% of the mass of cars and planes. More clothing is made from polyester and nylon than from cotton or wool.

Almost all plastic products are essentially single-use. Some items, such as medical supplies (gloves, needles, etc.), need to be rigorously discarded to prevent contamination. Other plastic containers, like those used for weed killer and bleach, retain toxicity. Para-aramid synthetic fibers like Kevlar and Nomex have high tensile strength-to-weight ratios, making them ideal for flexible protective applications and serving as the foundation for fiber-resin combinations that surpass most natural fibers.

Plastics were not initially created with disposability in mind. It's because of the universal use of plastic that alternatives must be developed. Eventually, all plastics will degrade and break apart into microplastics. The characteristic of relative permanence has proven to be a disadvantage, as plastic debris is found in oceans, waterways, and landfills worldwide. Unlike products made of wood, steel, and paper that can be recycled by nature, plastic replacements can remain intact for centuries. Plastic bags, which float like jellyfish, are ingested by fish, leading to choking. Bottle ring carriers entrap seabirds. Visually attuned animals cannot detect chemical additives. Plastic pellets are found across the world's surface and in the deepest ocean trenches. The "Great Pacific Garbage Patch," the largest of several immense floating trash heaps, is approximately the size of the state of Texas and consists predominantly of plastics. Plastics account for over 10% of the material in the world's landfills. Almost every bit of plastic ever produced still exists in some form.

Plastics contain various additives, such as dyes, fillers, or flame retardants. Very few plastics can be recycled without a loss in performance or aesthetics. Polybrominated diphenyl ethers (PBDEs), added as flame retardants for seats and carpets, pose additional challenges for recycling. Even the most recyclable plastic, polyethylene terephthalate (PET), used to make plastic bottles, is recycled at a rate of only 20-30%. Typically, it is shredded for recycling, and there is no method to recycle PVCs. The variety and characteristics of plastics hamper plastic recycling, as each type of plastic has its own production history, and few are compatible with other types for reformulation. Symbols indicating plastic types are often misunderstood by non-professionals, and the presence of a symbol does not necessarily mean that the plastic can be recycled economically

One reason why so little plastic is recycled is because it's difficult to break down. The processes typically used to remold old plastic weaken its chemical structure. As a result, recycled plastic is normally only used to make low-value products.

The promising plastic PBTL maintains its original qualities when recycled and has excellent strength, toughness, and stability. It's created by joining together chemical building blocks called bicyclic thiolactones. The plastic can be cleanly broken down into its original building blocks through heating at 100°C for chemical reassembling. However, it can only be recycled infinitely if it's separated from mixed plastic materials.

The most commonly used plastics for single-use are polyethylene and polypropylene. Although they have high temperature resistance, they are difficult to break down at about 100°C. Efforts are being made to break the chemical bonds down at 70°C using an alkylation catalyst for less than three hours. The resulting material can be used as fuel.

Plastics require energy in the form of heat to be molded into usable shapes that retain their form when cooled. Thermosetting plastics are formed once, while thermoplastics can be reheated and remolded, making them recyclable but not disposable.

Various approaches are being designed to create alternative materials.

Biological composites are divided into three groups: sugars, proteins, and minerals. These natural materials form at ambient temperatures and take on shapes determined by DNA. The advantages of natural-based materials are that they are temporary in water and can easily be recycled to be formed again or allowed to return to the soil.

Biodegradable polymers (bioplastics) are often made with polylactic acid, polyhydroxyalkanoates, cellulose and lignin, and starch from renewable sources such as corn, potatoes, and soy. However, even some plant-based bioplastics are not fully biodegradable, which creates uncertainty in recycling.

New generations of plastics are made of PDK (poly diketoenamine), with bonds that can be reversed by an acid bath, creating a material that can be re-manufactured along with water. PDK polymers can be reformed multiple times without any loss in performance.

Corn starch-based bioplastic polylactic acid (PLA) can withstand high temperatures and will break down within 12 weeks. The wax moth, Galleria mellonella, can digest polyethylene.

Another bioplastic is made from marine algae, an abundant and renewable natural resource that captures carbon from the atmosphere throughout its life.

Keratin is a natural protein found in various fibrous structural components, such as hair, scales, skin, feathers, claws, beaks, silk, and nails. Keratins can hold liquids and dissolve over time.

Chitin, a derivative of glucose in the sugar group, is a natural protective cover found in the exoskeletons of crustaceans and insects. When deacetylated with sodium hydroxide, it becomes chitosan. Both materials can be ground into a powder and extruded to create structures through 3-D printing or extrusion.

Calcium carbonate, a material found in eggshells, is another natural material that can hold liquid and is biodegradable. Collagen, the most abundant protein in the body, is used to give structure to bones, skin, and muscles. Elastin forms the main constituent of elastic connective tissues.

MarinaTex is made from waste fish scales and skin, with a red algae binder. Processed with low energy at ambient temperatures, it biodegrades in four to six weeks. Its creator, Hughes, declared: "It makes no sense to me that we're using plastic, an incredibly durable material, for products that have a life cycle of less than a day." Approximately 40% of plastics are used only once.

Spider silk is recognized for its flexibility and strength, ten times that of steel. An approach is to assemble sustainable plant materials like soy to mimic spider silk without using an actual spider, creating "vegan spider silk." Mycelium, a strong fungal-based material, can be combined with natural substrates to form a strong yet open-cell material that can be used as a filler.

Alternatives to plastic also address other materials. Mettlewood is a natural wood compressed under mild heat, creating tight hydrogen bonds. It is up to ten times as strong as the original wood and one-sixth the weight of steel while providing superior puncture resistance.

By bleaching thin slices of wood to remove lignin and adding epoxy for clarity and strength, wood can be made almost as transparent as glass, yet stronger. A layer of sodium over a sliver of wood can store electricity as a nano-scale battery.

Strengthened wood from fast-growing trees can replace slower-growing, denser but stronger woods in traditional wood applications, and wood is a renewable resource. Even after wood is cut, it can capture CO_2. Without lignin, the wood, when boiled and immersed with metal-organic framework (MOF), forms strong CO_2 bonds, making it an alternative to plastics and steel in construction.

Anaerobic digesters (AD) utilize microorganisms to break down biodegradable materials in the absence of oxygen, producing a renewable energy source.

Other materials, while not renewable bioplastics, use natural structures to increase strength while decreasing weight. Metallic Microlattice is made of hollow tubes 1/1000 the size of a human hair and is one hundred times lighter than Styrofoam. With a 99.99 open-volume structure, it exhibits greater energy absorption and compression recovery than any natural material discovered.

Graphene, made of carbon atoms, is only one atom thick but two hundred times stronger than steel. It can be applied to another material, which can then carry an electrical current as it offers little resistance. Translucent Silica Aerogel, composed of 99.9% air, can be used for insulation.

Aerogels are gel derived synthetic ultralight materials that are of low density and low thermal conductivity. They are solid to the touch and applications.

Nanotechnology refers to technology on the micro level, with dimensions of less than 100 nanometers, too small to be seen by a common microscope. At this size, nanos can act as binding agents for fabrics or carry electrical currents. They can be custom programmed for specific characteristics. Nanotechnology introduces a new set of parameters to various synthetic materials. Nanos and graphene can be found in everything from food and medicines to building materials.

Existing atoms don't always possess the desired attributes, even when combined into ordinary molecules. However, clusters of atoms known as "superatoms" behave like single units with designed attributes. The properties of "designer molecules" are tailored to fit specific functions. Electrons form an orderly nucleus center arrangement called an Aufbau.

K. Eric Drexler, a founding father of nanotechnology, proposes that with existing manufacturing techniques, our industrial civilization is approaching the limits of Earth. New techniques are needed at the molecular level. The manufacturing processes in nanomachines promise to use less carbon, even extracting materials from the atmosphere.

To perform more sophisticated operations in the macroscopic world, behaviors will need to be integrated. Molecular nanotechnology (MNT) is a technology based on the ability to build complex structures with atomic specifications through mechanosynthesis. Mechanosynthesis refers to hypothetical chemical syntheses in which reaction outcomes are determined by using mechanical constraints to direct reactive molecules to specific molecular sites. This enables obtaining the correct atomic specifications. Drexler stated that mechanosynthesis will be fundamental to molecular manufacturing based on nanofactories capable of building macroscopic objects with atomic precision.

Bridging the gap between the current generations of synthetic molecular machines are natural biomolecular machines. They operate similarly to biology, where inertia and momentum are irrelevant, providing integrated moving parts. While scientists have been working with simple molecular machines since the 1990s, showing great promise, they are still experimental.

From bronze to nanos, humans have designed materials that nature couldn't. The unique manufacturing methods of 3-D printing and nanomachines will present opportunities for materials and methods that will push the boundaries of our current imagination. As Aristotle, with rare insight for his time, argued, technology supports nature by supplementing and completing what nature herself leaves imperfect. Now, technology is going beyond the imitation of nature to create naturally impossible materials.

We Have the Power

Everything requires energy. Energy is responsible for creating movement and restraining movement. Society, as well as life itself, depends on the acquisition and application of energy. Fortunately, energy is abundant on planet Earth.

The creation and utilization of energy is one of the most distinguishing factors of humans. Early hominins recognized the potential of fire to provide heat for cooking food and to transform materials like clay or steel. Fire became a mobile and controllable source of energy. Every design and unique achievement by humans has been a result of the creation, application, and transmission of energy. As the world's population continues to grow in both size and prosperity, the demand for energy will only increase.

The Industrial Revolution unfolded in two phases. The first phase involved the invention of the steam engine. Prior to this, wood was the primary source of energy for most human needs. However, the steam engine, powered by wood or coal, exponentially increased power directly to machines used in industry and transportation, providing energy at the required location and time.

The second phase occurred in the late 19th century when energy production was first used to generate electricity. Electricity could be stored and transmitted to remote locations, providing heat, light, and power for various purposes. It could also be stored in batteries. The usage of electricity quickly became the primary application of energy. Energy consumption was no longer restricted to the time and place of production. The means of energy production (steam, fossil fuels, wind, water) became a means to an end, with electricity being the ultimate goal. The focus shifted to finding the most efficient and least damaging methods of electrical production.

In terms of physical strength, humans are not as strong as animals of a similar size. We lack their strength, dexterity, and speed. To succeed, humans had to design ways to amplify available energy through the use of six basic mechanical machines (lever, wheel and axle, pulley, inclined plane, wedge, and screw). These machines provided a "mechanical advantage," allowing a small force to generate a greater reaction. For example, an inclined plane enabled the movement of large rocks and logs uphill, while wedged-shaped tools could tear apart materials that would be resistant even to the natural claws of a raptor or a bear. Animal power applied to these tools increased the ability to perform increasingly complex tasks, such as pulling wagons (wheel and axles) and plowing (wedges). The wheel, a human creation, does not exist in the geological or biological world. Nature has no device for rotary motion around an axle. Rotary motion is applied in various applications, from water wheels to electric motor shafts. A propeller is a rotary inclined plane.

The term "renewable" can be misleading, as we cannot renew the sun, tides, or wind themselves. Instead, these forms of energy are means to generate usable electricity. While the term "renewable" is universally accepted to refer to non-fossil fuel energy sources, more accurate terms will be used here.

Energy creation can be achieved through three means:

1. **Fossil Fuels as Consumable Energy:** Fossil fuels involve the use of long-stored energy sources that are consumed within a short span of time. This includes carbon-based fossil fuels such as oil, gas, and coal. Burning wood is also a form of consumable energy, but the time frame for replacing wood is relatively short and can be planned. The use of fire for heating and later smelting played a significant role in hominin progress over several million years. However, it was with the beginning of the Industrial Revolution in the 17th century that the widespread utilization of coal and later oil began to impact societal development and the environment.

2. **Biomass as a Renewable Energy Source:** Biomass includes biological materials such as trees, crops, and animal fat. These materials, which are carbon-based, can be interacted with oxygen to produce heat and CO_2. The intention is for the CO_2 to be absorbed back into other plants, making biomass a circular source of energy. Depending on the timeframe of this circular process, biomass can be considered a renewable energy source.

3. **Harvestable Energy as Renewables:** Harvestable energy refers to energy collected naturally without human intervention, which is then transferred into forms that are useful for human endeavors. This includes energy derived from sources such as the sun, wind, water movement, and geothermal heat, which can be converted into usable heat, power, or electricity. The energy is present whether humans harness it or not. Renewable energy is a zero-sum game.

Consumable Energies

Fossil Fuels, Coal, Natural gas

Carbon is the basic solid mass of all plants and animals. It constitutes 18% of the human body, second only to oxygen, and 65% of plants.

While wood served as the primary heating source for most of human development, "King Coal" took over in the last two centuries as the dominant energy source for factories and transportation during the Industrial Revolution. Even in the twenty-first century, 40% of the world's electrical production still comes from burning coal. Coal is easily accessible worldwide and requires minimal technology for utilization. According to the International Energy Agency (IEA) global coal demand is projected to grow by 33% through 2040, with the greatest increase expected in Southeast Asia.

Coal production is estimated to increase by 0.7% per year through 2035, while natural gas and oil are expected to increase by 1.6% and 1.1% through 2020, respectively, followed by 0.7% through 2035. In 2017, China was the largest consumer (51%) and producer (46%) of coal, followed by India (11% and 9%) and the United States (9% and 9%).

Coal-fired plants also consume large amounts of water. The US Geological Survey estimates that coal production uses enough water to meet the needs of a billion people.

Coal usage has declined in recent years due to several factors, including the use of mountain top removal (MTR), which requires fewer workers for coal extraction, the transition to cleaner natural gas, increased deployment of renewable energy sources, and changing public perceptions of coal. Despite marketing claims of "clean coal," it remains the most polluting source of energy.

The romantic image of "Foggy London Town" during the Victorian Age was not solely due to fog off the Thames; it was also the result of the man-made cloud of dust created by the inefficiencies of the Industrial

Revolution. Additionally, coal mining posed a threat to miners due to the risk of cave-ins, and breathing in coal dust was especially harmful, contributing to "black lung." A 2011 World Health Organization study revealed that approximately 1.34 million people die each year due to coal dust particles smaller than 10 microns (μm).

For many developing nations, coal may still be seen as a means to escape poverty, regardless of the associated environmental issues. Coal plants can be located anywhere, and their construction and operation costs are relatively low compared to the high electrical output they provide. Particularly for poorer countries in Africa and South Asia, which experience the greatest population growth, there are few accessible energy sources. These countries are striving to rapidly and economically transition to an electrified society, making coal a quick solution. They need to import fuels and construct low-cost coal plants to power their development. Coal plants are also used as backup sources when there are gaps in the production of solar and wind energy. Since it is inefficient to stop and restart a coal plant to match irregular harvestable outputs, the coal plant needs to be in operation full time.

Oil, Drilling, and Fracking

The Chinese began drilling for oil in the early 4th century, while the Persians were the first to refine oil into a kerosene-like fluid in the 9th century. The discovery of easily accessible oil fields in Texas and the Persian Gulf between 1920 and 1925 marked the beginning of the era of cheap energy.

With much of the on-land oil fields already utilized, exploration expanded to include offshore drilling. There is always a degree of leakage, which is not a major problem on land but can be catastrophic offshore. Platforms have capsized, sunk, exploded, and caught fire in disasters from Brazil to India, and from the Gulf of Mexico to the North Sea. However, as long as there is a continuous demand for power in transportation and heating, new offshore locations will continue to be sought.

Oil is trapped between layers of shale deep within the Earth. Traditional drilling can only recover a small amount of this oil. In the late 1940s, experiments found that shale could release a greater amount of oil through induced pressure. Hydraulic fracturing, or "fracking," combined with horizontal drilling, has allowed for the extraction of up to five times the amount of recoverable oil.

The extraction of oil through fracking leads to the production of as much as fifty times more chemically contaminated water. For every gallon of oil, ten gallons of toxic water are brought to the surface, and this water must be disposed of properly. Improper disposal can result in contamination of local water supplies.

The injected water used in fracking reduces the friction between rock layers, causing them to slip over each other and often leading to the creation of earthquakes. A U.S. Geological Survey indicated that these earthquakes may have been caused by increased fracking activities in a region stretching from New Mexico to Arkansas. Oklahoma, an oil-rich and geologically vulnerable area, has been particularly affected by these earthquakes. Most of the recorded quakes have been in the magnitude range of 1.7 to 3.5, although a 5.6-magnitude quake was recorded in 2011.

Oil can also be obtained not through drilling, but by mining a tar mixture of sand, clay, water, and bitumen, in a process known as "unconventional" extraction. This method, long overlooked in favor of drilling for liquid petroleum, became commercially viable due to increased oil prices and improved recovery technologies. The oil is separated from the mixture in separation cells using hot water, resulting in a slurry. It takes about two tons of tar sands to produce a single barrel of oil. The use of a citrus-based solvent may reduce the environmental impact. However, the water used in the process is toxic. The extraction of Canadian tar sands has required the elimination of native forests for access roads and processing facilities, polluting nearby streams and harming wildlife.

Natural Gas and Methane

Natural gas consists of four parts hydrogen to a single carbon atom. It is abundant, reliable, and cleaner than coal. Coal produces over 200 pounds of CO_2 per British thermal unit (BTU) when burned, while natural gas produces 117 pounds. When used as a mobile fuel, natural gas is 15-20% cleaner and less polluting than gasoline. This makes it a potential "bridge fuel" between fossil fuels and clean, renewable, and harvestable energy sources. To facilitate transport, the gas is cooled and liquefied, becoming liquefied natural gas (LNG).

Accompanying natural gas, methane often leaks into the air during the extraction process. Methane occurs naturally in the ground, trapped for millennia within frozen soil in cold climates such as the Arctic, Antarctic, higher altitudes, and deposits below the ocean floor. As the planet warms, observations in Alaska and Russia have shown that permafrost temperatures have increased. The melting of permafrost will release trapped methane into the atmosphere, where it acts as a greenhouse gas, intensifying the effects of global warming. Although methane remains in the atmosphere for a shorter period than CO_2, it has a greater impact in terms of trapping more of the sun's heat.

Renewable Energy

Wood & Biofuels

Plants absorb carbon from CO_2 in the air, and it can make up to 50% of the dry mass structure of a plant. When wood is burned, carbon unites with oxygen to form CO_2, and the process starts anew, making it net CO_2 neutral. The time it takes for plants to become usable as fuel can range from months to centuries, which falls within human time frames. Today, 7% of the world's energy still comes from burning wood, primarily in developing countries where 77% of the population resides.

Biofuels, derived from living plants, are considered a renewable energy source. Biomass can range from a personal compost pile of scrap food to the industrial-scale clearing of century-old trees to be ground into wood chips for combustion. The most common commercial biofuels are ethanol, made from the sugars of maize (corn) and sugarcane, and biodiesel, made from palm oil. Plant sugars are broken down to create combustible alcohol. However, the cultivation of crops for biofuels requires equipment for planting, harvesting, and delivery, as well as the use of pesticides and water.

A biofuel variation derived from algae was first proposed as a source for food or fuel by Edward Harder and Hans Van Witsch in 1942, though there was little interest until the food and energy crises of the early 70s. Algae removes atmospheric carbon through photosynthesis and has gained increased interest as it can be grown on waste, saline waters, and on land unsuitable for other forms of agriculture. While still experimental and more costly than other biofuels, algae yields between 10 and 100 times more fuel per unit area. It also causes minimal harm if spilled and is biodegradable.

Biogas is produced through the process of "anaerobic digestion." Over forty million home units are already in use in China, with another four million in India, processed from local agricultural waste. A side benefit is that the remaining solid waste can be used as fertilizer, turning "waste" into something useful.

Wind

Wind, the earliest known renewable energy source, was utilized to power primitive sails on boats approximately 5,500 years ago. It was later harnessed for power on land. Greco-Egyptian scientist Heron of Alexandria built a wind-powered machine, and practical horizontal windmills, known as "Panemone Windmills," were employed in the Near East by the 9th century. Today's giant wind turbines are direct descendants of those early windmills. Additionally, wind towers can reduce the impact of hurricanes.

James Blyth of Scotland pioneered the use of wind power to produce electricity for his home in 1887. However, it was not until the mid-20th century that large-scale wind farms were constructed to supply electricity to the power grid. The United States, Germany, and China have been at the forefront of wind-generated power. The London Array, which opened in 2013 and spans 100 square kilometers, is the world's largest wind project, with 175 turbines in the English Channel off the outer Thames estuary. The Array provides electricity for over half a million homes, eliminating the need for 900,000 tons of carbon that could be released into the atmosphere.

In a vertical-axis wind turbine (VAWT), the wind rotates internal rotating blades, resembling the reverse of a vortex vacuum cleaner. Some vertical shaft generators appear more like kinetic sculptures than machines. They can harvest wind regardless of its direction, and some models can enclose the blades. A solid-state wind energy transformer utilizes electrohydrodynamics.

The construction of any form of wind generator still requires fossil fuel furnaces for steel production, transportation to the construction site, and the installation of transmission lines to deliver the energy to its destination. To manufacture a single wind turbine, 800 yards of concrete (the third leading source of CO_2 emissions), a concrete base, 140 tons of steel, and fiberglass for the blades are required. Wind turbines have a useful life of 15-20 years and then need to be refurbished or replaced.

Hydropower

Greco-Roman engineers were the first to create water wheels, which converted the flow of streams or waterfalls into rotary power through gears for pumping water. They also used water power to operate bellows for fires used in metalworking. English improvements to the vertical water wheel in the 18th century led to its application during the Industrial Revolution.

In 1882, the first hydroelectric plant, located in Appleton, Wisconsin, connected a turbine to an electric generator. Hydroelectric power usage proliferated in the United States, accounting for over 25% of electric power generation by 1920. In 1933, the Tennessee Valley Authority (TVA) was established to build a series of dams to provide electricity to the southeastern United States. This electrification powered the economic growth of the region, including the establishment of manufacturing plants and the widespread adoption of air conditioning in offices. By 1940, hydropower generation accounted for 40% of the American grid, but its growth is now limited.

Older dams are being dismantled to allow for the natural movement of rivers, enabling fish to return to their natural spawning grounds. China is the global leader in hydroelectric generation, followed by Canada and Brazil, with the United States in fourth place. Hydroelectric generation dams face challenges, as they are initially expensive projects, often requiring loans from international banks for poorer nations. Lakes formed behind dams can cover plant life, which then decays and releases CO_2 and methane. Additionally, hydroelectric power output is dependent on seasonal and weather irregularities. The development of power in one area can negatively impact native fishermen by disrupting the natural flow of rivers that migrating fish depend on for survival.

The biggest threat to hydroelectric power generation comes from the effects of global warming. Record-low water levels in rivers and reservoirs behind dams are being observed. Reduced snowpacks, drought conditions, and increased agricultural demand are putting hydroelectric power output at risk. In 2021, the two major hydroelectric power generators from the Colorado River, Lake Powell behind the Glen Canyon Dam and Lake Mead behind the Hoover Dam, were at 36% capacity, but their capacity increased due to the heavy rainfall of 2023.

Tidal, Waves, and Open Sea

Utilizing tides to generate electricity offers two significant advantages. Many major cities worldwide are situated near oceans or seas, making tidal forces readily available, and tides are a predictable energy source.

Since at least the 8th century, tides have been used to generate power. In high tides, water was trapped in ponds and then released as the tide went out, powering water wheels. In the late 19th century, this output was first used for electrical generation. The French Rance Tidal Power Station, built in 1966, was the first large-scale electrical generation facility of its kind.

Tidal stream generators (TSGs) are turbines placed in areas with high tidal flows. Power can be generated in either tidal direction or in response to water movement.

Parallel to tidal power, generators in the open sea also utilize the movement of currents. While tidal generation is most effective in areas of concentrated water movement along coastal inlets, the potential for open sea current movement as an energy source is recognized worldwide. In 2020, tidal energy generation made up only 3% of the United Kingdom's electrical input, but it is projected to increase to over 11% by 2050.

Geothermal

Each year, thousands of tourists marvel at Old Faithful, the geyser in Yellowstone Park, which is a visible surface feature of the underlying geothermal energy. Iceland, sitting on a volcanic base, produces 78% of its energy from geothermal sources.

Passive applications use steam directly for heating, such as in ground-sourced residential radiators. The only external energy input is a pump to circulate the water beyond convection. An active system uses the rising water to turn electricity-producing turbo generators. Approximately 55% of operating geothermal plants are located in Europe and North America.

The geothermal system is environmentally neutral as the water, having not been contaminated by chemicals or radiation, makes no negative impact on the surrounding area. While geothermal plants are expensive to set up, they are inexpensive to operate and require minimal land use.

Solar Radiation

The most basic energy source, the sun, which sends 3,766,800 exajoules (EJ) equal to 10^{18} (one quintillion) joules to Earth annually, has been the last to be realistically utilized. Presently, all human activity uses only 500 exajoules. According to the 2000 World Energy Assessment by the United Nations Development Program, the annual potential of solar energy is estimated to be between 1,575 and 49,837 EJ, several times larger than the total world energy consumption in 2012, which was 559.8 EJ.

There are three methods of converting solar radiation to energy: 1. Direct conversion to collectors, 2. Solar thermal heating a medium that drives generating turbines, and 3. Growing plants to biomass that can be burned.

Experiments for using the sun for direct energy go back to the late 19th century, concentrating light onto liquid-filled tubes to raise the temperature and drive a steam engine. The same principle of concentrated solar power (CSP) is used in the Crescent Dunes Solar Plant in Nevada, which utilizes over 10,000 mirrors to concentrate sunlight on a single post. Liquid salt is heated for storage to drive generators during the night or when covered by clouds. The CSP Noor 1 plant in the Moroccan Sahara uses 500,000 mirrors. Solar-generated electricity has been known since the experiments of Charles Fritts in 1880, but the first direct use of solar-generated electricity through photovoltaics (PV) was with satellites beginning in the late 1950s. Solar panels on the International Space Station and space probes directly convert light into electricity. The largest commercial CSP plant is the Solar Energy Generation Site (SEGS) installation in the Mojave Desert of eastern California, with a capacity of 354 MW.

In 1972, a solar panel with a capacity of 1 watt cost $75. By 2015, the cost had decreased to less than one dollar per watt, making it cheaper than coal. With the declining price, the International Energy Agency estimates that solar power can generate as much as 27% of the world's electricity by 2050. Existing panels convert about 25%, but maximum efficiency is projected to reach 33% optimistically.

Solar panels are made of mined quartz and rare earth elements mixed with coal and heated to 1,500°F, often by coal consumption.

Large solar panels require a significant amount of land. However, their impact can be reduced by placing them atop land already disturbed by buildings, within traffic islands, or on degraded land such as old mines. Placing solar panels over parking lots provides shade, keeping the road surfaces cooler. Home panels can be designed to replace traditional roofing shingles, making them less disruptive within the overall home design.

In 2020, multiple research groups developed "transparent photovoltaic" (TPV) devices made of metal-oxide conductors that conduct solar inputs to the electrodes, producing electricity. Unlike conventional opaque solar cells, TPVs only capture light in the longer-wavelength ultraviolet range, outside our range of vision, making the receptive cells invisible. Visible light passes through TPV cells, allowing them to be placed anywhere, such as on windows, electronic devices, clothing, cars, and in offices, without affecting the aesthetic appearance of the product.

The World Solar Challenge, conducted in Australia with abundant solar light, began in 1987. The first winner averaged 42 mph. By 2007, the speed had increased to 56 mph, limited only by Australia's speed limit.

The Astroflight Sunrise, the first solar-powered plane solely driven by electrical motors, made its initial flight in 1974. Energy came from batteries and solar panels. The Gossamer Penguin made the first solely solar-powered manned flight in 1980. In 2016, the Solar Impulse 2 completed a journey around the world in segments, relying on solar power and supplemental battery storage. Solar power, with its ability to store energy through battery storage, is an ideal source of electricity. While solar energy is not geographically equally available, it can be found across the globe. However, the production of solar power panels involves mining and refining rare earth elements.

Depletable Energy, Fission

Electric power from nuclear reactions is neither a consumable nor strictly a renewable source. Like fossil fuels, nuclear reactions consume a material and produce heat that turns a dynamo. However, no carbon is consumed, so no CO_2 or any toxic gases are produced. Instead, the large amount of energy produced in nuclear reactions also generates radioactive waste that must be contained.

One of the most famous equations in science is $E=MC2$, Albert Einstein's 1905 statement of the equivalency between matter and energy. The release of atomic energy creates a significant amount of heat that can be controlled to drive steam-driven electrical generators or, if uncontrolled, can be used as a nuclear bomb. The NSS Savannah, built in 1955, served as a showcase for nuclear power in cargo and passenger ships as part of the "Atoms for Peace" program. However, concerns about nuclear discharges forced the closure of the program, and the NSS Savannah is now a monument to what could have been.

The first nuclear reactor to produce electricity was started in Idaho in 1951. By the mid-1980s, nuclear power accounted for 16-17% of total electricity generation worldwide. A total of 218 reactors, an average of one every seventeen days, were built worldwide, with forty-seven in the United States, forty-two in France, and eighteen in Japan.

Fission reactions have some problems. The reaction splits the heavy atom of uranium, U-235, into smaller atoms, giving off heat that turns electricity-producing generators, as well as radiation. To contain the radiation, the reactor requires enormous shielding and large amounts of cooling water, which can become radiation-contaminated. Toxic waste from water and spent rods can remain radioactive for centuries. Additionally, fresh water is needed for cooling. Failures of reactors at Three Mile Island (USA), Chernobyl (Ukraine), and Fukushima (Japan) contaminated the local areas and caused fear and distrust among the public.

Although only a small mass of uranium is needed, it is scarce, and access to supplies is prone to disruption due to political interactions. Currently, nuclear power accounts for 20% of American output, which falls far short of France's dependence on nuclear power, at 70%. Nuclear power sites are the most efficient in terms of land use and construction material per output, and they are carbon-free and provide reliable power 24/7. With renewed interest, several new designs are in the prototype stage.

The Natrium-style reactor functions as both a generator and a storage unit. The generators are remote from the reactor. Developed by TerraPower, the "Traveling Wave Reactor," a Thorium-232 molten salts reactor, is relatively safe and inexpensive, producing a lower amount of radioactive waste than uranium plants. Additionally, thorium is more abundant than uranium. Studies, including those published in the English journal Landsat, have shown that nuclear power is the safest form of energy production, particularly when compared to the pollution caused by fossil fuel consumption. Forty companies in the U.S. and China are working on reactors that run on waste and are cheaper than coal, making them economically exportable. The operational life of a reactor is 40-60 years, with an additional 20 years required for decommissioning.

However, demand for nuclear power has declined by 7% between 2000 and 2014. Nuclear power output peaked in 2006 at 368 GW and has been declining since then. The U.S. has taken plants offline, and Japan has eliminated all its nuclear plants. Most of the decline has been replaced by renewables, which can only produce energy 10-20% of the time due to weather fluctuations and low natural gas prices. Renewable sources have only made up half of the loss resulting from the reduction of nuclear power.

As a proven backup for the variability of wind and solar power, nuclear energy offers a reliable and cost-effective source of electricity. Nuclear power is especially important in regions with limited natural or renewable resources.

Fusion

No energy source holds as much promise, or frustration, as fusion. Unlike fission, which involves splitting atoms to create energy, fusion involves forcing atoms to fuse together. This process is the basic energy force of the universe, as elements are combined within stars to form heavier elements. At the core of fusion is hydrogen, the most common element in the universe. Through fusion, hydrogen is converted to helium, with the interaction creating energy. The byproduct of this process is a harmless gas, and no radiation is produced. In theory, electricity generated through fusion will be abundant and inexpensive.

Fusion produces at least three times the energy of fission, and the source material, hydrogen, is readily available in the form of deuterium and tritium, two isotopes of hydrogen that fuse at a lower temperature of 100 million Celsius, hotter than the core of the sun. To be useful, the fuel has to be in the plasma state, which is an unstable fourth form of matter that is neither solid, liquid, nor gas.

Other attempts, such as the Tri Alpha reactor, involve firing two plasma clouds at each other, thereby heating the plasma to over ten million Celsius. In June 2015, the reactor held the plasma stable for five milliseconds, a significant achievement in the development of the process.

The record for a tokamak was set by the French "Tore Supra" at six minutes, but it consumed more energy than it generated.

The goal is to reach the break-even point, where more electricity is produced than is needed to initiate the reaction. For fusion to be viable, it must be able to produce electricity at a lower cost than current fossil fuel methods. If accomplished, it could be the most significant advancement in energy since the development of the steam engine. In December 2022, scientists at the Lawrence Livermore National Laboratory announced that they had achieved fusion for the first time by producing more energy than was inputted. Although the output was short-lived, it marked a significant milestone. The full-scale application of fusion may not occur until around 2050.

Applying Energy, Steam

When water is heated beyond its boiling point from any heat source, it expands and becomes steam. The pressure from expansion can be used to move objects, such as a piston or turbine wheels, for various forms of energy production.

In the first century AD, Heron created the first turbine, called the "aeolipile," by boiling water contained in an axle-mounted sphere. Two bent vents directed the steam out offset from the axle, causing the sphere to rotate and creating the first steam-powered movement. The movement was continuous and had no limit in revolutions. However, it was initially regarded as no more than a toy

Thomas Savery patented the first practical steam engine in 1698, an External Combustion Engine (ECE). It did not use pistons but worked on the principle of a thermal siphon. Fourteen years later, Thomas Newcomen created the first piston steam engine. James Watt's steam pressure-driven engine, developed in 1781 and powered by steam pushing a piston, proved to be practical for commercial usage.

The potential high rotary speeds of the turbine, the descendant of Heron's "toy," were too fast for manufacturing but ideal for turning an electrical generator or dynamo. The first electrical generator was built in Paris in 1870. Today, steam generation from coal to nuclear is different only in the means used to create heat to force steam through the blades of the dynamo.

Electricity, Motors, Generation, and Transmission

While the development of the steam engine grew more efficient with the invention of the steam turbine in the early 19th century, even the smallest size was prohibitive for portable use. It was the development of gas and electric motors in the 19th century that led to mobile power applications, from ocean-going boats to nano motors.

Power is not always conveniently located near the point of need. Windmills and water wheels need to be near water sources. The steam engine could be located at a convenient application point, but fuel had to be sourced elsewhere and transported to the power facility. Factories were fixed in place due to the size of the engine, and workers and raw materials had to come to the site. These factors limited mobility. Until the 19th century, energy applications were limited by the size of the energy source.

In the early 19th century, scientists began working on applying the theories of electricity to practical applications. English scientist Michael Faraday established the principles of the electromagnetic field using a magnet and a moving loop of copper wires, demonstrating the relationship between magnetism and electricity and how one could cause the other. His applications generated electricity using a motor to move objects, and he also discovered that moving an object through a magnetic field created electricity. Hungarian physicist Anyos Jedlik invented the continuous rotation of the commutator using electromagnetic coils. In May 1834, Moritz von Jacobi created the first true rotating electric motor. When electrified, the coil movement created a motor. James Clerk Maxwell's equation laid the foundation for electrical generation and utilization by explaining that electricity and magnetism were both manifestations of a single phenomenon: electromagnetism.

An electric motor is quiet, non-polluting, and can be scaled down to be used in miniature products. Since there are no flames involved, electrical devices can be used in environments prone to gas-related hazards. Electric motors are applied in various sizes, from watches to trains, and account for more than half of electric energy consumption in the U.S.

The first commercial electricity-producing dynamos were developed by a team within Thomas Alva Edison's Edison Illuminating Company in 1882. Edison favored Direct Current (DC), which worked best at 110 volts for distributing electricity over short distances, such as city blocks, with generating stations located about every mile.

In Europe, Alternating Current (AC) was preferred because it could be stepped up in voltage for transmission over long distances. This allowed energy usage to be separated from the source of energy creation. Nikola Tesla, who had worked for Edison, unsuccessfully tried to convince him of the advantages of AC. Tesla left to develop AC and sold his patents to George Westinghouse, who commercialized AC and challenged Edison's DC system in what became known as "The Battle of the Currents." Eventually, AC prevailed, and it is AC that connects countries and the world through a wired electrical grid.

Electricity is the linchpin of contemporary human applied energy. It can be transmitted with minimal loss across great distances, used to create heat and light, and power machines that produce movement.

The initial creation, distribution, and access to electricity mark the beginning of the second phase of the Industrial Revolution, which is as important as the development of the steam engine two centuries earlier. Power was now decentralized, and it could be brought to the point of need. Electrification brought power to users and led to significant changes in society. There was light for reading, schooling, and street safety, as well as refrigeration and the preservation of food and medicine. Air conditioning and elevators became possible, enabling space-efficient buildings. Access to electricity will become even more critical in transportation with the increased use of electric vehicles.

The continual growth of sustainable economies worldwide depends on increased access to electricity. The methods of transmission are important, as they account for a third of electrical costs. However, transmission can be influenced more by political issues than technical ones. Electricity transmission lines may need to cross several international borders to reach customers in more northern regions. International transmissions, like international oil or gas pipelines, require connection agreements that can be disrupted by nations with political issues along the route. One party, whether it's a producer or consumer, may see the dependence on another country as a violation of their national sovereignty and self-interest. In the United States, there are over sixty microgrids, some of which have no connections to nearby grids.

Liquid-Fueled Motor

In an internal combustion engine (ICE) heat is created internally to expand a medium, pushing a piston or turbine blade. The movement turns on a central axis to perform a task. The gas motor's range is only limited by the capacity of liquid fuel storage. A Diesel engine is also an ICE that uses compression-ignition. It was invented by Rudolf Diesel in 1897. The third type of ICE is the rotary engine, developed by Dr. Felix Wankel, for whom it is named.

The first examples of liquid-fueled motors were developed in the mid-19th century, starting with the experiments by Belgian engineer Etienne Lenoir, and later improved by German engineer Nikolaus August Otto with the four-cycle motor. The terrors of World War One were amplified by the capabilities of gasoline-fueled weapon delivery systems such as airplanes and tanks. For over a century, the gasoline motor has been the preferred power source for a wide range of products, from string trimmers to cruise ships.

Individually or in combination, electric and gas-fueled motors have provided portable power, allowing humans to expand into the air, space, and the depths of the oceans, making all of Earth open to human exploration and exploitation.

Batteries and Energy Storage

The development of increasingly efficient batteries has made smaller personal computers/phones, portable power tools, and effective cars practical. There is archaeological evidence near Baghdad of a simple battery that has been dated to around two thousand years ago, although there is no evidence of what it was used for. The first lead-acid battery was created by Raymond Gaston Planté in 1859, while Thomas Alva Edison created an alkaline battery. Other battery materials include carbon-zinc, nickel-cadmium, and alkaline-manganese. However, 20-40% of electrical energy is lost when it is contained and then released from a battery source.

The first electric-powered car (EV) dates back to the beginning of the automobile in the late 19th century. By pre-World War 1, electric cars made up 1/3 of the cars sold. However, their lack of range and the growth of the gasoline infrastructure led to their decline. However, with the increase in air pollution, mainly from gas-powered cars and trucks, and the gas shortage of the 1970s, electric-powered cars were given new consideration. The California Air Resource Board (CARB), under Governor Reagan, set limits on exhaust emissions. In response, General Motors developed the all-electric EV-1, but within two years, all the cars were recalled. Silicon Valley startup company Tesla built a sporty, high-performance roadster, showing the potential of EVs with cash and support from Elon Musk.

Electric cars are quiet and have excellent torque. Without the complex fuel ignition-exhaust systems, electric cars are less prone to mechanical failure, but their range is dependent upon battery capacity and recharging time. However, even though they are electric, they still depend on the means of electricity creation, which could still involve the use of fossil fuels. Electric power also has potential in light local personal aircraft, helicopter-drone taxis, and short-range commuter aircraft. Motorsports is at the forefront of applied electronics for transportation, with Audi, Toyota, Ferrari, and Porsche winning the 24 hours of Le Mans with hybrid fuel-electric cars.

Fuel cell devices convert chemical energy from a fuel via a chemical reaction to create electricity. The by-products are heat and water. Unlike a battery that stores electricity and discharges it until it is "dead," a fuel cell continues to produce electricity as long as fuel is supplied. The concept of the fuel cell was discovered in 1838, but it was the needs of NASA for energy for space probes and satellites that led to its development and potential. The Alstom-developed Coradia iLint hydrogen fuel cell train began operations in Europe in 2018. Unlike conventional electric trains that depend on external power lines, the Cordia is a multiple-unit system, with each car being self-powered and having a range of almost five hundred miles.

Looking Ahead

Human development on Earth has been possible because it has two elements that, when combined, create energy: oxygen and carbon. Nowhere else do we know of a readily available source with both elements, neither on Mars nor Titan. The six habitable continents are crossed and connected through a series of electrical and virtual grids. There are over 150,000 miles of high-voltage lines efficiently transmitting electricity from 5,400 power plants in the United States alone.

Whether it's coal mining, vast oil sand fields, wind turbines, hydropower dams, nuclear storage, or solar panels, an estimated 20% of the world's remaining land will be used for energy creation and transmission by 2030. As electricity is produced, it has to be transmitted along power grids, and even the most efficient power transmission stations and lines lose power over distances. These grids are vulnerable to disruption by natural forces or by physical or cyber-attacks. With societies dependent on a steady, reliable source of electrical power, disruptions will have almost immediate consequences for security and health.

While fossil fuels are the most abundant source for power plants, different areas will be able to provide energy in different ways. Wind power is readily available in the American "tornado alley," and the southwest has abundant sunlight. The coasts can generate power from tides, while mountainous regions will continue to supply hydroelectricity. Regardless of the source, electricity can be sent to any part of the country or beyond through transmission lines, putting power where it is needed in a balanced manner. The United States has a more balanced internal energy production available. Solar energy collectors in Phoenix, AZ, can cool homes in Malibu, while wind turbines in Texas can warm homes in Chicago. A surge in demand or drop in supply in one area can be easily supplemented from another. Appalachia and Wyoming have an abundance of coal. Kansas has wind, while Arizona has sun. Oil is pumped from old fields in Oklahoma, new sources in Alaska, and offshore rigs in the Gulf of Mexico. Internationally, solar grids in Egypt can warm ovens in Stockholm. In contrast, Africa has abundant sunlight but lacks great mountain ranges for hydropower, and its realized oil deposits are limited.

As of 2020, China had eighty times as many interregional high-voltage transmission lines as the United States, and Europe had fifteen times as many, enabling seamless connections between providers and consumers across borders in milliseconds. Power can shift as needed due to weather or emergency needs, allowing distribution in either direction. An international, intercontinental grid of high-voltage direct current (HVDC) cables that lose less energy than conventional AC could connect the world on a global scale.

Yet, despite all the energy production in 2020, an estimated 1.3 billion people worldwide still lack access to electricity. Access to electricity is necessary for development, and the lack of energy availability is a limiting factor in local health and economies, which can be causes of political instability. In 2011, the International Energy Association defined the basis of energy access as 250 kWh per capita per year of electricity for rural areas and 500 kWh for urban residents. "Universal Energy Access" is based on access to an efficient refrigerator, a mobile phone per household, and a small computer or television. Additional urban energy is needed for businesses, industries, and public service facilities. Lighting provides safety and enables reading, while refrigeration makes buildings hospitable and preserves food and medicine.

The increasing independent need for electricity is leading people and companies to explore new methods of energy creation and storage. Google, through Makani Power, is developing turbine generators mounted on kites with cables connected to ground-based storage units. Elon Musk developed The Powerwall, a home or factory electricity storage unit. When connected to solar panels, the "gigafactory" can potentially make homes, offices, or factories energy independent. He has estimated that 10,000 units can supply the necessary power for a city of over 100,000, and 160 million units could provide ongoing electricity for the entire United States and the world. The BEET (Building Energy Efficiency Through Innovative Thermo devices) project is using microorganisms to create liquid transportation fuels in a new and more energy-efficient way than current biofuel production methods. The GENSETS (Generators for Small Electrical and Thermal Systems) program aims to develop transformative generator technologies to enable widespread deployment of residential combined heat and small natural gas-fueled power systems. HEATS (High Energy Advanced Thermal Storage) is seeking to develop revolutionary, cost-effective ways to store thermal energy.

The *Energiewende* or Energy Revolution has pushed Germany to generate over a quarter of the country's

We Are The Intelligent Designer

energy needs from renewables, while the U.S. still only produces 13%. Germany has also moved away from a centralized energy distribution grid, and local communities are becoming energy self-sufficient.

A long-term process for solar energy collection is to place a series of solar sails in space, where they can continuously collect energy from the sun. Using microwaves, the electricity will be transmitted to Earth-bound stations.

Buckminster Fuller viewed fossil fuels as a stopgap energy source while renewable energies were being developed. In 1969, he wrote: *"the fossil fuel deposits of our Starship Earth... must be conserved... for the exclusive function of getting the new machinery built with which to support life and humanity at ever more effective standards of physical energy. We cannot afford to expend our fossil fuels faster than... the rate at which the fossil fuels are being deposited within the Earth's spherical crust."*

However, consumables became too easy to use, too cheap, and too deeply ingrained in the economy. The economic wealth of fossil fuel producers is supported by an infrastructure of workers and support companies, including miners, distributors, HVAC technicians, and transportation industries that depend on consumables for their livelihoods.

It is impossible to compare time scales for replacements, so society will continue to depend on unreplaced fossil fuels to maintain stable economies for decades to come while renewables are gradually integrated into mainstream usage. For the foreseeable future, there will be an additional cost on renewable energy sources, known as the "Green Premium," which is the cost difference to achieve zero additional emissions.

Human activities have caused atmospheric heat beyond natural methods of dispersion. Burning consumable fossil fuels produces heat beyond natural temperatures and alters the pH and acidity levels of the planet's oceans. Burnt gases mix into the atmosphere, creating a blanket effect on a global scale. Additionally, the release of CO_2 from fossil fuels contributes to further warming. Since 1880, when the fossil fuel-powered Industrial Revolution was in full swing, the average global temperature has increased by over 2°F, with two-thirds of that increase occurring since 1975 at a rate of about 0.3°F per decade.

Expanding electrical outputs will increase the amount of available electrical energy. However, due to human nature, rather than replacing fossil fuel producers, the additions will contribute to the overall output mix, creating a greater supply that will be followed by increases in demand.

The need for increased energy creation to sustain economic growth has led to oil production and distribution becoming a geopolitical weapon. The 1973 OPEC (Organization of the Petroleum Exporting Countries) oil production reduction, partly in response to the war between Israel and several Arab nations, resulted in inflation and recessions across much of the developed world. Subsequently, several OPEC countries experienced a significant increase in national worth, transforming them from former colonies into major economic power centers. The periodic disruptions of global oil and natural gas supplies caused by cartel boycotts, pipeline protests, and political upheavals continue to reshape the worldwide economic landscape. Only through local energy independence, supporting the global energy grid, can local economies remain stable and sustainable.

The choices for energy production are vast and varied, and each has advantages and limitations. Providing long-term access to affordable power will require a mixed repertoire of suppliers. There will be an ongoing conflict regarding the makeup of the energy mix, as fossil fuels have become too cheap, too easy to use, and deeply entrenched in infrastructures, employment, and businesses. Full replacement may take a long time, if ever. Mature suppliers will resist new technologies as they fight for what they perceive as their economic survival. With the current pace of population growth and the increasing number of electronic devices, energy needs will continue to rise, potentially reaching over ten times the current demand by 2050 without a foreseeable leveling off. Developing countries will strive to emulate the prosperity of the developed West, and this will require access to reliable electricity without disrupting the world's economy. Energy must be universally available. Since renewable technologies are still in development and full implementation is decades away, a hybrid energy portfolio will need to include consumables, nuclear power, and renewables. Otherwise, developing countries may resort to using the cheapest and most readily available energy sources, fossil fuels, and the planetary climate situation will continue to deteriorate.

Energy creation is the major cause of climate change. To reduce climate change, there must be a reduced demand for energy, not just a replacement of means, but a shift toward more satisfying means that do not involve unchecked consumption. Energy is necessary for building societal necessities, such as products, construction, transportation, and food. Until consumption can be maintained at a sustainable level worldwide, the "crisis" will persist.

Regardless of the commitment to renewables and nuclear power, the results will not be instantaneous. New infrastructures will need to be constructed and connected, and accommodations will need to be made to interact with existing power suppliers while facing resistance from the status quo providers. Consumable energy sources will have to remain as bridges for the foreseeable future.

The Market for Self-Destruction

"Earth provides enough to satisfy every man's need, but not every man's greed." Mohandas Gandhi

But humans have and accumulate 'things' that often go beyond those necessary items for survival. Tools and clothing were our first possessions. These tools helped in survival by taking down game animals, or they protected us from the elements. Baskets and jars were used for food storage, allowing nutrition on a need-to-consume basis rather than an acquired basis. When more food was obtained than needed at that time from hunting or gathering, it was stored, providing humans with means for survival into the future.

Trade of surplus is a foundation of civilization as it requires cooperation and communication in production. There must be trust in trading partners and a peaceful environment where creation is more important than destruction. Innovation is needed to create greater value in goods offered. A tribal system of order and laws is necessary. Trade was made possible by human attributes of communication, cooperation, and acceptance of an agreed worth of symbolic items.

While demand remained constant, supply did not come evenly. There were too many variables, such as weather, conflicts, or distance.

Bartering was workable on a small local scale but inefficient for larger transactions and those that required extensive travel. To simplify trade, items were given worth by the group.

Faith, whether in money, government, science, and truth, has been a necessary foundation in the growth of civilization. Without faith in the transfer of wealth, transfer of goods would have been limited, and the economy would have stagnated.

With the greater scope of trade, some items became the recognition of wealth. Local economies remained stable as sufficient goods were produced to satisfy the immediate needs of the group. Advances were made only as knowledge from one tribe was acquired by the trading partner. Innovations were made for immediate situations but with little regard for finding other applications. As a hierarchical society did not recognize or encourage innovation, there was little reason to question why things happened. The past, not the physical future, was revered.

With the Renaissance, the Enlightenment, and the Scientific Revolution came the admission that even the greatest thinkers of the time, like Leonardo da Vinci, didn't know everything. Rather than filling in the blanks with supernatural answers, they logically sought the unknown, even if there was no immediate gain from their research. They went to make the future, a new concept, greater than the past or present. The Enlightenment exalted individual rights of identity and ownership, a change from medieval God-given ownership.

Trade between Europe and the East brought not only goods but also new knowledge of medicine, innovations, and materials. Europe made practical use of eastern inventions like the compass, gunpowder, moveable type, and other items. The compass gave direction for exploring, then colonizing the entire world in ships. Gunpowder, used for fireworks in China, formed the portable energy for guns and cannons, giving greater destructive power. And moveable type, when combined with the grape press, was used to print documents and books.

Competition took on two forms. In the ideal, each group competes for the attention of the buyer with a superior product. This drives innovation and benefits everyone. The other is a zero-sum fight where one party attempts the destruction of the other, leaving the market exclusive to the winner.

The growth of the merchant class resulted in a change in how wealth was collected. The nobles had enacted taxes that were to be paid, collection by force if necessary, to support the army to be called upon at the noble's discretion. Wealth given to the merchant was voluntary for a good or service. The more the merchant had to offer, the greater his wealth. His wealth was only limited by supply availability and consumer demand.

But is the accumulation of goods a positive? As early as the fifth century, Saint Augustine, in 'City of God,' wrote against the lust for things, which he equated to the lust of flesh.

Banking came with the first money, though 'money lenders' were not highly regarded as in the New Testament's Matthew 21:12 account of Jesus throwing them out of the temple. In the Quran and Old Testament, loaning to receive interest was not allowed. Originally, banks were another type of storage where units of wealth (shells, gold, gems, or currency) were protected. Lenders offered support to farmers in return for a portion of the following season's crop, and to governments to wage war with anticipation of receipt of a share of the spoils. When legal responsibilities for safeguarding were made on the bank, depositors felt their wealth was secure. The banks began to lend out the money to others on the promise of repayment with interest. Money began to move, and borrowers were able to build beyond their present capabilities with aspirations of future wealth.

The world changed in 1492 when Columbus 'discovered' the New World, followed by DeGama into Asia, beginning the period of exploration, exploitation, and cultural genocides. The world began to be a single inter-related Euro-centered market economically and culturally. With globalization, the financial excesses, profits of these ventures were invested into better means of production that became the Industrial Revolution.

But while the intellectuals of the Enlightenment were writing of equality and scientific reason, slaves were being used, without personal compensation, to create wealth. Larger, more powerful machines, and standardized production were possible with centralized industrial cities and agricultural plantations requiring masses of workers. Profits for wealth and investment were maximized by minimizing expenses (wages, working conditions).

Trade created new nobilities, the merchant classes. They controlled the exchange of goods.

By the 15th century, ships were safer for ocean-going trade, making the discoveries and opportunities possible. To grow and keep up with the increasing demand, farmers and plantation owners needed to buy more equipment, more ships, and especially more laborers (slaves). Slavery, the worst of human institutions, was at the center of the economic growth of western civilization.

Goods, previously only available to the nobility, were accessible to the greater populations of Europe. They saw and could buy the goods without seeing how the sugar and cotton were grown, didn't see the conditions for those who grew the commodities that local industries turned into goods. But there are other forms of slavery besides physical shackles. With availability and low cost, the mass population could buy things previously unreachable, increasing the demand for more. Expectations increased. To acquire, they needed money that was available with urban factory work. To buy goods and pay rent, they needed a steady income, a job. They became serfs to the factory.

Even the merchants were captive to the slave triad. Due to the time for growing and ocean transit, it may well be a year before income is received for the investment while bills are still accumulating. Only through bank credit could the merchant survive until payment is received.

Adam Smith, the acknowledged father of capitalism, published The Wealth of Nations in 1776, describing how wealth can be increased. His basis was that profits beyond needs were to be reinvested to acquiring additional labor and machinery that increased production, resulting in greater profits. The collective wealth is increased as it's shared among a greater number of people. Wealth was moral as it gained prosperity for all. Profits were to be invested in infrastructure, education, and research for means of production improvement. He saw profits set aside for self-glorification as egoism as they did not enhance the greater wealth. For Smith, 'consumption is the sole end and purpose of all production.'

Smith wrote in 'The Theory of Moral Sentiments' of self-interest as the lifeblood of the human economy, as social creatures with a natural sympathy. Individuals look out for what is best for themselves but in doing so find cooperation and assistance to others that will ultimately return in personal reward. Self-interest is not the same as selfish, where the needs of others are not taken into regard, often alienating those who could be of personal use, even to seek approval as others see us.

Adam Smith lived and wrote in a world without limits. With the discovery of the New World's exploration/exploitation and ongoing increases in industrial capacity, they seemed to be able to go on forever.

The resulting profits from the endeavor are to be reinvested into the endeavor, giving the opportunity for further growth. Profits removed from the endeavor for personal consumption are decreases to the resources of the endeavor and serve only the ego of the owner.

Consumption of produced goods didn't require effective consumption by the user, only a payment to the producer. Some products like food have utility when immediately consumed (eaten). Storage delays consumption. Food is a temporary product. Clothing has a longer life but will wear out to be replaced. Some items, though, like stone buildings, guns, or art works do not effectively wear out. While there is consumption by the user from the producer, there is no complete consumption by the user. Artificial needs are necessary for the user to purchase another, either by destroying useful items or accumulating/collecting additional units.

With global trade, countries specialized in specific products or means of production. Each region or country is more effective in one area: manufacturing, growing food, or extracting minerals, allowing other regions and countries to produce to their relative best advantage. In 1817, David Ricardo identified this as the Principle of Comparative Advantage.

Large-scale industrial machines were cost-prohibitive to individual producers. That required financial resources from a bank or wealthy supplier. That took capital and the rise of capitalism. The owner of the machine controlled the means of production. Cross-production skills, necessary in cottage industries, were made unnecessary. Machine operation required lower skill levels. Controlling capital controlled the machines and the operating labor.

The introduction of the more efficient machines in the 18th century moved production out of the cottage into a centralized plant. Poverty, on the farm, was replaced with poverty of mill towns and dangerous factories.

Workers became biological cogs of the machine, losing identity and self-worth of creating personalized goods. Rewards were not directly in response to their actions. The production line, while a maximization of performance, is counter to human nature. The assembly line requires specialization. Humans have succeeded as generalists.

Two philosophies of economics came out of the surpluses of the 18th and 19th-century American and European economies. Progressive Social Democrats saw industries that encouraged people to buy things they didn't want or need, with money they didn't have, as wasteful. They decried the artificial wants that replaced authentic needs. To them, consumerism was the new totalitarianism.

By contrast, Classical Liberalism desired maximum freedom of choice as a prerequisite for democracy (vote) and prosperity (ownership). Markets were to be unhampered by governmental regulations. Each person became an island looking out for self rather than a collective good.

Classical Liberalism had alienated the worker from the financial and cultural fruits of his labor. The sense of self in the creation of a finished good was removed. The factory shifted work from task-oriented to time-oriented as no one individual created the end product. Efficiency was measured by how quickly the good was produced.

The owner/laborer relationship had replaced the king/serf, but it was still based on a few powerful rich individuals and the poor working masses. From 1811 to 1816, a group of English skilled textile workers, collectively called the Luddites, rioted against the new weaving machines operated by unskilled workers. The machines were causing a decline in their livelihood to support their families. To understand the workers, John Ruskin wrote in 1853: "Men were never intended to work with the accuracy of tools, to be precise and perfect in all their actions. If you have that precision, you must dehumanize them. Let him but begin to imagine, to think, to try to do anything worth doing and the engine-turned precision is lost… and out comes the whole majesty of him also…"

A 19th-century alternative perspective was that everything was a social product and that everyone who contributed to production is entitled to a share of it. Society should own or control property for the benefit of all. However, the courts and government favored the stability of the owner.

With the Industrial Revolution, machines were able to produce goods at an unprecedented rate. When production output exceeded demand, the question became what to do with the surplus goods? Decreasing production was not a viable option. There had to be an increase in demand. The supply of basic goods, and later luxury goods, increased to where people had multiples of goods so that by the early twentieth century, the economy depended on not being able to produce goods but how to sell the goods made. Society turned from a producer-economy to a consumer-economy. It was the social responsibility of the user to consume in order to maintain a healthy growing economy.

Production can be directed as Supply Side or Demand Side. In the former, the emphasis is to continue to produce goods in hopes that competition will force the lowest price, and the consumer will benefit by purchasing those goods.

With demand-side production, production awaits the need for the good. For the economy to continue, consumers must purchase goods beyond necessities, as "Conspicuous Consumption," to satisfy an emotional need. Thorstein Veblen coined the term egoism of the purchaser in his 1899 book, "The Theory of the Leisure Class," referring to consumers who buy expensive items to display wealth and income rather than to cover the real needs of the consumer. Excess wealth is spent for the individual without plans for investing in the economy as a symbol of financial success, even if it's beyond actual success.

From the exuberant spending of the 1920s, the middle and upper classes seemed to have everything they needed. Through standardization and the assembly line, manufacturing had reached a maximum level of efficiency. So by the late 20s, they stopped spending, beginning the 'Great Depression." Production had over-reached consumption. With no spending, there was no need to manufacture and no need for workers.

Ernest Elmo Elkins' concept of "artificial obsolescence" was to create new products that would make existing products undesirable, leading to purchasing new products that are produced, keeping the economy moving. Elkins saw Consumer Engineering as the scientific business way to encourage consumers to purchase new products as fast as they could be made. He wrote, "Prosperity lies in spending, not saving."

He saw products as either goods we use, like cars, or goods we use-up like toothpaste. The goal is to make the car seem to be a use-up good that needs to constantly be replaced. "Consumer engineering doesn't end until we can consume all we can make."

He was proposing a way out of the depression through advertising and design. GM's head of research, Charles Kettering, equated perpetual change with progress. In a 1929 article called "Keep the Consumer Dissatisfied," he stated that: "It is a question of change, change all the time – and it is always going to be that way because the world only goes along one road, the road of progress."

Planned Obsolescence has to produce new products that offer a new look or function that made the previous product out-of-date in the mind of the consumer. New or luxury items are intended to gain recognition to the consumer. One-car families become two or three car families as larger homes are "needed," even when the number of occupants remains the same.

The clean streamlining and futuristic streamlining styles of the 1930s were visual counterparts to the popular song "Happy days are here again," things would get better. Design created newness and freshness. It created optimism.

Pencil Sharpner,   *The "Mercury,"*
Raymond Loewy   *Henry Dryfusss*

Streamlining

The cultural shift towards a world of consumer products was highlighted in the 1939 New York World's Fair. In 1955, Victor Lebow wrote that "our enormously productive economy... demands that we make consumption our way of life, that we convert the buying and use of goods into rituals, that we seek our spiritual satisfaction, our ego satisfaction, in consumption... we need things consumed, burned up, replaced, and discarded at an ever-accelerating rate."

Barbara Kruger paraphrased Rene Descartes for the consumer society, "I shop, therefore I am."

Peter Drucker was on the demand side as *"it is to supply the customer that society entrusts wealth-producing resources to the business enterprise."* The customer is the foundation of a business and keeps it in existence.

The average American home has 300,000 items. $1,700 is annually spent on clothing, while discarding an average of 65 pounds. American children, at 3.1% of the world, own 40% of the toys. The Wall Street Journal estimates that Americans spend $1.7 trillion on unnecessary unneeded stuff.

What is to be done with the additional items? They can be stored in the home, taking up living space, or relocated to a shed. Americans spend almost $38 billion annually to store excessive stuff in storage units. This old, still usable stuff is just moved around to a new location.

Wealth has been destroyed, not physically but in the imagination of the consumer. These are problems of a society with too much "stuff," an overabundance of material items. Recognition of wealth or status has historically been through the display of items. Acquisition of things can create the illusion of status, implying wealth or power.

With the Industrial Revolution, the symbols of wealth were available to a greater portion of society and the growth of the middle class. Status was recognized in the amount or worth of things. Success could be measured and displayed. Shopping became a leisure activity, an end unto itself. It was a world of desire; stores became what Emile Zola described as Cathedrals of Commerce. Extravagance became a virtue.

Repair and reuse are counterproductive to a consumptive society. Aldous Huxley wrote in Brave New World, *"Ending is better than mending."*

In the 1920s, following the sacrifices of World War One, the public was urged to buy, even things they didn't need, to cause the economy to grow. Every economic indicator rose at an unparalleled rate in "the Great Acceleration," the third marker of the Anthropocene. The chairman of President Eisenhower's Council of Economic Advisors stated that "the American economy's ultimate purpose is to produce more consumer goods."

In the 1980s, President Ronald Reagan planned to defeat the USSR by outspending them on weapons, even ones of questionable need, till they couldn't afford to respond and failed. In response to the 2001 September 11 attack, President George W Bush encouraged people to show how strong our economy was by shopping, "patriotic consumption."

Happiness through consumption is not universal. The 2019 World Happiness Report listed Finland, followed by Denmark, Norway, and Iceland, as the happiest countries based on responses by inhabitants on the quality of their lives. The United States was rated 18th. China, the second-largest economy, came at 86th.

Middle-class affluence began with European merchants and spread to America, then to Japan. Stable governments, first in South Korea, Singapore, Hong Kong, and Taiwan, called the "Four Asian Tigers," then to other Southeast Asian countries, led to growing economic strength and the desire to move beyond an existence lifestyle to "the good life." Globalization made all the world's countries interdependent. Resources moved to any place in the world provided access previously unavailable, adding to global wealth. What happened in one country affected everywhere.

The downside of globalization was shown in 2020 when the Covid-19 virus began to spread. Through international travel, it quickly spread worldwide. People began dying worldwide from the disease. Goods didn't move, and economies suffered as container ships couldn't unload and trucks lacked drivers.

Nationalism, a counter to globalization, is putting the nation-state first regardless of the effect upon others.

Henry David Thoreau promoted personal sufficiency by reducing his needs of consumption to the basics through Voluntary Simplicity, a philosophy earlier promoted by Leonardo da Vinci, "Simplicity is the ultimate sophistication," and Chinese philosopher Lao-Tzu, "He who knows he's had enough is rich."

Thoreau reduced his lifestyle to the necessaries of clothing, shelter, and food. He built his own house on Walden Pond, raised his own food, and had only clothing necessary for body warmth and protection, repairing housing and clothing as needed in a life of frugal abundance. His perspective was that the cost of a thing was the amount of life exchanged to obtain it. He was able to supply his needs in less than four months, leaving eight months for personal pursuits.

For Thoreau, it was a decision he made for the life he lived. But for others, it's a reaction to having groups (business, government, etc.) decide. Nineteenth-century art critic John Ruskin stated, "There is no wealth but life." The ultimate economy is one that improves the quality of people's life.

One description of economic growth is the amount of resources consumed.

In his 1960 book The Waste Makers, Vance Packard wrote that the creation of waste and unneeded disposable goods was a moral issue. Both the physical environment and the financial and spiritual character are destroyed through excessive credit buying for unnecessary things.

With increased wealth by "emerging economies" comes the desire to emulate the lifestyle of already affluent nations. In 2009, the developed countries of Europe and the United States accounted for 51% of middle-class spending. William Rees stated at the Ecological Society of America that the world is in a resource overshoot, consuming 30% more of the world's resources than is sustainable.

Population growth, either through births or immigration, is necessary to provide an increase in customers to consume new products. New goods mean new providers as a workforce puts more people to work, even if the goods they produce are unnecessary or even dangerous.

It isn't necessary that a product or service be needed. It's even better if it isn't. New "must-have" products need to be continually produced, not for the need of the consumer, but for the need for growth of the producer, both in profits to the owners and jobs for the workers.

Goods are manufactured for permanence but marketed as expendable. The world's economic system is dependent upon ongoing production of new goods made of new resources taken from the planet. As planetary resources are consumed, the question becomes: Is there a limit?

Thorstein Veblen, in his 1989 Theory of the Leisure Class, first criticized consumerism as a social problem. He stated that the super-rich used things to show their separation. The middle-class displayed that they were no longer part of the underclass.

Victor Lebow wrote that *"Our enormously productive economy demands that we make consumption our way of life that we convert the buying and use of goods into rituals, that we seek our spiritual satisfaction and our ego satisfaction in consumption. We need things consumed, burned up, worn out, replaced, and discarded at an ever-increasing rate."*

Philosopher Bertrand Russell stated, *"It is preoccupation with possessions, more than anything else, that prevents us from living freely and nobly."* Jorge Majfud followed with *"Trying to reduce environmental pollution without reducing consumerism is like combating drug trafficking without reducing drug addiction."*

Compulsive shopping, "Oniomania," is a form of addiction that induces dopamine in the brain. Anticipation of the reward from the purchase, especially if there is the expectation of approval from neighbors or peers.

In the 1972 presentation "Mankind at the Turning Point," The Club of Rome stated: *"A keen and anxious awareness is evolving to suggest that fundamental changes will have to take place in the world order and its power structures in the distribution of wealth and income. Perhaps only a new and enlightened humanism can permit mankind to negotiate the transition."*

There will be resistance, as there has always been to any lifestyle redesign. The design of the present environment is familiar to many. With change, they will feel lost and devoid of worth based upon their proven, but now unnecessary, skills. In a society where worth is based on the ethic of work effort, where is worth without meaningful work?

Historically, wealth inequality has increased with technological innovations. Economists and policy researchers using a Gini coefficient rated this as a 0. Beginning with landowners who collected and passed on wealth, a disparity between members began to grow. By the era of the Egyptian Pharaohs, the value was .68. (The value of total inequality is 1). Localized individually owned self-sustaining communities were replaced by "more efficient" single-owner capitalized farms and factories. Continual reduction of individual ownership of production machinery that reduces or eliminates workers will raise that value. The contemporary United States is at .86.

Production depends upon consumption; someone must buy what is produced. If there are no purchasers, then there will be no market, no need to produce.

Robots can work more efficiently than any human at a lower cost until the price will be dependent upon only the cost of energy and material to produce it (lowered by wage-free robotic acquisition) and desired producer profits.

Science fiction addressed production without consumers, as automated producers brought in resources, manufactured, and continually sent out completed products in a post-human world, although there were no consumers.

Business can continue without workers, but it cannot continue without consumers.

Government programs provide a payment that the recipient will use to purchase goods. The specific type of good is irrelevant as long as it's put back into the economy. Through the multiplying factor, the government's outlay will find its way into multiple layers of the economy.

Traditionally, unemployment and welfare have put funds into non-workers who are still able to be consumers.

In a robot production society, a form of Guaranteed Basic Income (GBI) or Universal Basic Income (UBI), will ensure a continuation of consumers with means to purchase. This will maintain the need for continual production with profits going to provide the economic means for a GBI.

Universal Basic Income is not a recent proposal. Founding father Thomas Paine advocated for a basic income, a capital grant due to "loss of his or her natural inheritance by the introduction of the system of landed property."

A guaranteed basic income based upon the output from robotic and AI production can provide funds for physical needs, but it will take a paradigm shift in attitudes from what has long been considered welfare to be accepted as meaningful. Will the quality of life without toil be better when used for personal fulfillment? Those who are continuing to work, as it is likely that some jobs will not be AI/robotic replaceable in the foreseeable future, will object that their work is propping the needs of the recipients.

Through World War Two, humans lived in an empty world where resources were unlimited, with more than enough for our species. Nature was able to resupply as fast as we could consume.

With the post-war technological innovations, growth in population, and resource demand for a western lifestyle, we have entered a "full world" where consumption exceeds natural replacement. We are in a conflict of growth versus survival, what Dr. Eric Drexler called "a collision between industrial civilization and limits of Earth."

Adam Smith, in laying the concepts of capitalism, recognized that empathy was natural to us as social beings. We feel pleasure when we see people doing things we agree with and pain in the distress of others. Nature has equipped us with socialization and a "conscious" of self-criticism that benefits our species' survival.

Into the 18th century, empathy, expressed from wealth, meant patronage supporting artists and funding charities to give to whom they considered the "worthy poor," those who maintained a moral base.

With the growing wealth disparity of the Industrial Revolution, some of the new super-rich of the "gilded age" found that a simple kindness to widows was insufficient. Philanthropy was created.

In his 1900 book Gospel of Wealth, Andrew Carnegie described what he considered the best use of his surplus wealth in libraries, parks, and hospitals.

By the early 21st century, income disparity had increased to where the 26 richest people equaled the wealth of the poorest half of humanity. Salesforce CEO Marc Benioff acknowledged the inequality and the implications. "Capitalism as it has been practiced in recent decades has also led to horrifying inequality. Business leaders need to embrace a broader vision of their responsibilities by looking beyond shareholder return and also measuring their stakeholder return."

Warren Buffet challenged his wealthy peers to donate half their wealth with his "Giving Pledge." In 2000, fellow billionaires Bill and wife Melinda Gates began their foundation that has donated billions to eradicating malaria and other worldwide health problems. They saw: "Most governments are risk-averse and in poor countries they don't have enough money to invest in R&D, or even to get existing drugs and vaccines to people.

Yvon Chouinard, of the Patagonia outdoor clothing line, transferred ownership of the company in 2022 to the Holdfast Collective environmental nonprofit to help fight the climate crisis. "Earth is now our only shareholder," Chouinard declared.

The acquisition of great wealth is not in itself bad. It shows faith and control of a product or service desired by a large group of people. In adhering to Adam Smith's natural empathy, how the wealth is used is the core of philanthropy.

The Trash Mines of Mumbai

We've become very good at producing and selling things. We've designed and created things of every size, description, and application. We've moved and transferred billions of tons of matter to be products for our use. But we haven't fully addressed what to do with the products post-use. What we can't handle, we dispose of and pretend it never existed. We create trash.

There are no disposal systems for much of human trash, no efficient means to transform the leftovers of a product back into natural materials. We provide trash cans and refuse removal, but that is only intended to collect it and place it out of sight.

We have created a linear consumption system. Minerals and materials are mined or drilled from the ground, produced into products, consumed, then discarded. Measurements of the effectiveness are how the cost of obtaining and producing is minimized. The cost of any recycling or disposal is not factored, thereby encouraging the system of trash production. No one is responsible for trash, so no one bears the costs, though the trash still exists and is indirectly being a cost to everyone.

"Humans are the only species on the planet that actually produces true waste," observed Michael Jessen of Canada's Zero Waste Organization.

Worldwide, humans generate 1.3 billion tons of trash annually, with the projection that, at the present rate and economic growth, it will reach 4 billion tons. The largest economy, the United States, created the most trash, about 292 million tons in 2019. China is the second biggest contributor, followed by Brazil, Japan, and Germany.

Twenty-one million people live in Mumbai, India, with about 62% living in the largest slum in the world, Dharavi. With one million people per square mile, it's the most densely populated area in the world. Mumbai produces 4,000 tons of trash daily into the Deonar dump, a 138-hectare mountain of discarded materials surrounded by slums. The nearby homes are made of sheet metal discarded from shipping containers with no accessible running water.

Mumbai is not alone with too many people surrounded by too much waste. Lagos, Nigeria, with a population of sixteen million, produces over 735,000 tons of plastic waste annually. So much so that there are "Wecyclers," waste brokers who pick through the discarded trash to collect about $300 million annually.

Mexico City, with a population of 24 million, sends about 12,600 tons of waste daily to the Bordo Poniente refuse dump. The government closed the site that covers over six hundred hectares with a concentrated federal effort to recycle the waste. According to the Secretariat of Works and Services of the capital city, "We are tossing valuable materials into the trash, and there is the whole problem of the absence of re-use and recycling. The goal is to recycle at least 60% of our waste. We must establish sanitary landfills that meet health and safety regulations. You can't just improvise a landfill site."

A 2015 plan to collect trash in Jdeideh, Jordan, and send it to Russia failed, leading to a "trash river." The resulting protests were directed toward both the garbage crisis and the political corruption giving rise to a movement called "You Stink."

Trash is not a problem unique to developing or poor countries. Trash is the end result of a "throwaway culture." From single-use paper picnic plates to buildings, immediate usage, at a minimum cost, is the driving economic force.

The United States generated about 254 million tons of unrecyclable trash in 2020, about 1,361 pounds per person, 5.9 pounds daily. Trash consists of everyday items we use and then discard, including batteries, packaging, and laundry containers.

Most of the trash is sent to numerous landfills around the US, but they are rapidly running out of space. In 1988 there were 8,000 active landfills nationwide; in 2006, there were only 1,754.

In 2014, landfills accounted for approximately 25.7% of total U.S. anthropogenic methane (CH_4) emissions, the largest contribution of any CH_4 source in the United States.

One proposal is Extended Producer Responsibility (EPR) that adds the total environmental cost through the lifecycle to the product. The producer and importer are responsible for the take-back, recycling structure and disposal of the product plus packaging.

The strategy was introduced in 1990 by the 37-nation Organisation for Economic Co-operation (OCED), to improve environmental standards in product design. Post-purchase costs would be added that would eventually be added to the cost of the product.

Trash doesn't always stay on land. Much is caught in runoff from streams and eventually ends up in the oceans, ending up in the Eastern Pacific Garbage Patch, a floating pile of trash off the coast of California, and the Western Patch formed east of Japan. Collectively, they are the largest landfill in the world. There are 13,000 pieces of floating plastic per square kilometer. The pieces may break into even smaller pieces called nurdles that can appear as small fish or plankton and be eaten by fish. Plastics are not digestible and can cause the animal to die.

90% of the ocean's five trillion tons of trash is plastics. Each year, a million seabirds and over a hundred thousand sea mammals are killed due to ingestion of human trash.

Ocean action, not recycling centers, tears the material into ever smaller pieces and microbeads.

A 2019 study found an estimated 13.1 quadrillion, 4,000 metric tons, of these microfibers in the environment of California alone. 73% of fish caught mid-ocean contains some microfibers. Most of these fibers, less than 5 mm in length, were from washing synthetic clothing that makes up 60% of what is worn, fibers too small to be caught in washing machine filters.

The U.S. Zero Waste Business Council created certification in 2013 for local facilities that meet zero waste. TRUE (Total Resource Use and Efficiency) is a program that addresses physical facilities and operations through zero waste and cuts in their carbon footprint that can also support public health by diverting solid waste from landfills and incineration.

The problems of trash and demand for resources will only continue to increase as the growing middle classes of China, Brazil, Russia, and India will have an ever-increasing demand for gold, copper, oil, and other finite materials.

The growth of plastics accelerated after World War Two. Even then, there was an awareness of the potential for plastics becoming a major part of the growing trash problem. Modern Plastics editor Lloyd Stouffer stated in 1954 that "the future of plastics is in the trash can." Nine years later, Stouffer proclaimed, "You are filling the trash cans... with literally billions of plastic bottles," and other products. "...nobody any longer considers the plastic package too good to throw away."

Former British Prime Minister Theresa May called plastic trash a scourge and committed the government to a 25-year plan that would phase out disposable packaging by 2042. India claimed it will eliminate six types (plastic bags, cups, plates, small bottles, straws, and certain types of sachets). The Chinese province of Hainan vowed to eliminate single-use plastics by 2025. And the United Nations has declared a war on single-use plastic, though methodology and enforcement are unspecified.

E-waste can't be dropped into a regular landfill. They contain toxic materials, including mercury and bromated flame-retardant materials. Environmental laws by the US and developed countries prohibit uncontrolled disassembly.

China was the world's largest importer of used electronics, disassembling them for the exotic materials within. To address the homegrown trash problem, a result of increased consumption from a growing material society, importation was officially prohibited in 2020.

But other countries, with loose or non-enforced environmental regulations, were willing to accept E-waste. Ghana, Nigeria, Ivory Coast, and Pakistan picked up the business. Short-term income and jobs are more important to them than the long-term environmental effects from burning plastic coatings and releasing toxins into the air and water supply.

Humans have created things that nature was unable to but in doing so created problems of reprocessing the component materials back to a natural condition. Nature doesn't have systems that can deal with our creations, and we haven't designed sufficient systems to supplement nature. Bronze doesn't rust like iron, good for tools, bad for natural recapture. Plywood is natural wood but is held together with unnatural adhesives. And there are few designed processes that can convert petrochemicals, from plastics to toxins, back to a usable natural state in a sustainable manner. We created the problem of trash, we need to design remedies.

Solid waste can be a resource. In Europe, anaerobic digesters (AD) use a natural process to produce renewable energies from food scraps. BDC of Maryland, Generate in California, and Anaergia of Canada are building new plants in the U.S., partnering with waste haulers to create "Waste to Value."

Trash is an underutilized resource. The desired materials are at hand. There needs to be designs that make disassembly easier and processes that separate for new use. To have sufficient resources for future usage, humans must find ways to retrieve resources from trash.

Changing the Environment

eco·cide (merriam-webster dictionary): the destruction of large areas of the natural environment as a consequence of human activity"

What's Causing Climate Change? "It's the Economy, Stupid." For an economy to grow, there must continue to be increases in the sales of goods and services. To make the products, it takes resources of material and energy. Consuming these resources adds CO2, trash, and pollution.

Climate change is not just a scientific problem; it's an economic/political problem. The problem will not be resolved until the economic and cultural causes are confronted and resolved."

In January 2023, the Bulletin of Atomic Scientists moved the symbolic "Doomsday Clock" forward to ninety seconds to midnight. Originally created to highlight the self-made threat to human existence by nuclear weapons, it now also includes the threat of unchecked climate change.

"Efforts at reducing global emissions of heat-trapping gases have so far been entirely insufficient...unless much greater emissions occur very soon, the countries of the world will have emitted enough carbon dioxide and other greenhouse gases by the end of this century to profoundly transform the Earth's climate," stated Richard Sommerville.

The first simple life, called Cyanobacteria, appeared about 3.5 billion years ago through photosynthesis creating food and energy. Sunlight powers carbon dioxide and water to produce glucose and oxygen. Over the next 500 million years, those simple organisms generated oxygen in the process known as the "great oxidation." The first plants appeared on the land about 510 million years ago with the first trees about 360 million years ago. Trees and plants collected CO2 from the atmosphere. As the dead plants and carbon-based algae and plankton bodies decayed, they, along with other minerals like Sulphur and Lead, formed coal and oil trapping trillions of tons of the gas. Through contemporary burning, the gases, held for millions of years, are released back into the atmosphere as CO2.

CO2 occurs naturally in the atmosphere but at trace levels. It's called a "long-lasting" gas. It's naturally released into the atmosphere through animal breathing, flatulence, volcanoes, and naturally occurring fires. With the ascent of humans, the atmosphere consisted of 78% nitrogen, 21% oxygen, 0.93% argon, and 0.038% carbon dioxide.

For the past 12,000 years, since the last great ice age, the planet has been in a stable state referred to as the Holocene era. With a relatively consistent environment of temperature, CO2 atmospheric level, a balance with bacteria and viruses, and sea level, sapiens were able to develop agriculture, build communities, establish consistent safe water supplies, domesticate a stable group of animals, and locate accessible resources.

The climate of the Earth has been ever-changing. From 200 BCE to about 600 AD, there was a warming period, followed by a cooling period through about 900 AD. The medieval warming period (900-1300 AD) was followed by the "little ice age" that lasted until the mid-nineteenth century. These were natural changes that took centuries.

But Earth's climate is changing, and human actions are a major factor. While the date of origination is debatable, we have entered the human-directed epoch, the Anthropocene. Since the late 19th century, Earth has warmed 1.50°F.

In the 3rd century BCE, the Greek naturalist Theophrastus wrote of stones that kindled and burned hotter than wood. It was the introduction of the steam engine and coal-fired furnaces that pushed the Industrial Revolution into the dynamo that created the modern world, and CO2 emissions became a problem. With coal-burning engines, producers became energy independent of rivers or wind.

In the mid-19th century, London, the epicenter of the Industrial Revolution, was so smoke inundated from coal-fired furnaces that it became wrongly called "foggy London town."

The Clean Air Act of 1963 established the National Ambient Air Quality Standards, which regulated air emissions and the creation of the EPA (Environmental Protection Agency) in 1970.

In 2012, estimates showed that the average American consumes goods and services that generated 19.74 tons of CO2 annually. China, with the largest population, leads in total CO2 output, followed by the United States, India, Russia, and Japan.

It's not just the obvious CO2 generation from burning fossil fuels; it's also the emissions produced by the consumption of goods and services by building users and includes emissions from transport, food, clothing, and other goods. The hidden emissions come from the production and distribution of the goods.

In June 2020, the CO2 level was 416.39 ppm (parts per million), the highest in 800,000 years.

The earliest recognized proposal for the human effects on the planet came in the 19th century as "Anthropozoic." Their proposal was dismissed, even by scientists who couldn't believe that humans could have a great effect on the planet, especially when compared to natural forces.

The first recent reference of a greenhouse effect from burning fossil fuels came in 1824 from Joseph Fourier. Whig congressman George P. Marsh, in his 1864 book "Man and Nature: Physical Geography as Modified by Human Action," warned that humans could destroy the Earth if we don't restore and sustain global resources.

The first recognized use of the term "global warming" was stated by Ms. Eunice Foote in 1856 after showing in the lab how the addition of CO2 would raise the atmospheric temperature. Her work was widely ignored as she was an amateur, an American, and a woman.

Swedish scientist Svante Arrhenius stated in 1890 that burning fossil fuels was increasing the world's temperature. He predicted that if you doubled the amount of CO2 in the atmosphere, it would raise the world's temperature by 5 to 6 degrees.

His calculations were correct, but he underestimated the output growth of the coal-burning Industrial Revolution. He anticipated the 50% rise within 3,000 years. By the early 21st century, the rise has been about 30%.

In 1958, Frank Capra produced the movie "The Unchained Goddess." It concluded with a warning that with six billion tons of CO2 annually (1958), almost insignificant compared to 2019's output of 36.8 billion tons, could melt the polar ice caps, raising ocean levels.

Warnings were presented to the top level of the American government. President-elect John Kennedy received a warning that people were transforming the natural environment due to climate change in 1961.

President Nixon's staff noted that air pollution "is caused almost entirely by the combustion of fossil fuels," especially with power plants and cars. The Clean Air Act was enacted in 1963, followed by the Water Quality Act in 1965 and the Air Quality Act in 1967, which were later consolidated with multiple environmental agencies into the EPA. The Clean Water Act was implemented in 1972, followed by the Safe Drinking Water Act in 1974, the Toxic Substance Control Act, the Resource and Recovery Act of 1976, and the Super Fund of 1980.

Twenty million Americans demonstrated at the first Earth Day in April 1970, marking the first in what has become an annual recognition. In 1990, Earth Day was recognized globally, with 200 million demonstrators in 141 countries.

Ever the scientist president, Jimmy Carter understood the impact of the reports on atmospheric changes. He formed the National Energy Plan to address better ways to burn coal and increase the use of nuclear power. In alignment with the national environmentalism of the 1970s, Carter believed in cheap, embargo-proof sources of energy through the use of solar energy. To encourage development, he had solar panels installed on the White House roof and instituted tax credits for wind and solar power installations.

The White House Council on Environmental Quality issued three reports in 1981 on the long-term health threats of CO_2 pollution. The CEQ report suggested trying to limit the global average temperature to 2°C above preindustrial levels, thirty-five years before the same goals of the Paris Climate Agreement.

In the 1980 presidential campaign, Ronald Reagan promised that Americans would not need to sacrifice, and it was back to consumerism. Against Carter's conservation, Reagan easily won.

Reagan cut funding for green energy and removed the solar panels. Donald Regan described them as "just a joke." Candidate Reagan had declared that more than 80% of nitrogen oxide air pollution is "caused by trees and vegetation." He believed that the climate was under control and that the Mount St. Helens volcano spewed more sulfur dioxide into the air than the past 10 years of auto emissions. He cut 90% of the budget for the Department of Energy and eliminated the tax credits.

Still, the planet warmed. In 1988, Time magazine recognized changes by making Earth "Planet of the Year." In the scorching summer of 1988, environmental disasters dominated the news. More than almost two three dozen years have since had hotter summers than 1988.

Bill McKibben's 1989 book "The End of Nature" suggests that humans will have to decide "between our material world...and the natural world. One world will have to change, or the other." The two are tightly bound. While the governments were slow to address global warming, the emitters were aware of the consequences of their product. In 1991, the Shell Oil Company produced the film "Climate of Concern." It began by stating that "our energy-consuming way of life may be causing climate changes, with adverse consequences for us all," and that "changes (are occurring) too fast for life to adapt without serious relocations." They even included a need for CO_2 reduction incentives, including the potential for a "carbon tax."

In a 1977 private report, Exxon Corporation (Exxon Mobil) acknowledged that releasing CO_2 was having an effect on the atmosphere and that in 5-10 years, hard decisions were necessary to combat long-term impacts that might be reversible.

The resulting actions were the creation of the Global Climate Coalition to question other public scientific reports, creating doubt in public awareness. This created a perception that governments were putting barriers for growth rather than a power balance to protect the citizens. Still, governmental agencies, many unaware of these reports and even advised by the very companies, continued to address the issue.

Positive control actions in the 1980s would have been much less disruptive to both the environment and society than any actions taken now. Humanity lost forty years, forty easy years for corporate profits.

The United Nations Framework Convention on Climate Change opened in Rio de Janeiro in June 1992. President George H. W. Bush promised to fight "global warming" and declared at Rio: "The United States fully intends to be the world's preeminent leader in protecting the global environment. We have been that for many years. We will remain so. We believe that the environment and development, the two subjects of this

Conference, can and should go hand in hand. A growing economy creates the resources necessary for environmental protection, and environmental protection makes growth sustainable over the long term."

But he opposed an agreement that would have bound the United States to specific reductions in greenhouse gas emissions to protect economic growth.

In 1995, the United Nations began a series of annual reviews of climate change progress known as the Conferences of the Parties or COP. COP-1 was held in Berlin.

Led by the United States, the delegates of the international community met in 1997 for the Kyoto (Japan) Protocol (COP-3). The protocol stated that climate change was real, and that human activity was the cause. Despite the support of President Clinton, the American Congress refused to sign, declaring that this gave those countries an unfair advantage in the cost of production for trade.

Long an environmental advocate, former vice president Al Gore took his message of warning about climate change in a presentation that became "An Inconvenient Truth." The awareness he created led to international recognition of climate change and the 2007 Nobel Peace Prize that he shared with the United Nation's IPCC.

President George W. Bush promised multiple times to fight global warming. "My administration takes the issue of global climate change very seriously…. I do not believe; however, the government should impose on power plants mandatory emissions reductions for CO2, which is not a "pollutant" under the Clean Air Act." The 2007 report of the IPCC stated that "the phenomenon is real and does pose a significant environmental threat during the next century…" With no further efforts to reduce greenhouse gas emissions, the IPCC baseline is for 1.1 and 6.4°C through the end of the century.

In November-December 2015, COP-21 met to negotiate the Paris Agreement, with 174 nations signing to adapt through their individual legal systems to limit temperature increases to less than 2°C compared to pre-industrial levels.

The major boost to the effectiveness of the Paris Agreement came in November 2014 when President Obama and China's General Secretary Xi Jinping agreed to limit greenhouse gas emissions.

By 2017, every nation, including war-torn Syria and isolated North Korea, had signed the agreement, with the sole exception of the United States. China and India demanded exclusion from the toughest measures due to their status as developing economies.

While President Obama committed the United States to the agreement in 2015, presidential candidate Donald Trump called climate change a hoax perpetrated by China to hurt American business. As president, Trump withdrew the U. S. from the treaty in 2017 as part of his "America Energy First" program, which reduced pollution and safety regulations for the fossil fuel industry, especially coal mining and coal-burning energy plants.

A problem with any environmental agreement is that there is no direct penalty for failure to fulfill a voluntary environmental agreement, and changes in government may result in a change in commitment.

Political action is hindered and undermined by "Climate Deniers." Senator James Inhofe (R-OK) declared that man can't change the weather, *only God can do that.* Political commentator Sean Hannity decried global warming as *a made-up climate change crisis.* In 2011, Florida Governor Rick Scott banned the use of the term "climate change" in state discussions, despite Miami being one of the most vulnerable American cities already allocating $400 million for sea walls, pumps, and raising roads to safeguard the city from the rising ocean. West Virginia governor and coal mine owner *Jim Justice declared:* "If there is such a thing… as climate change, I believe that he [God] will give us time, and the smart people will fix it."

In October 2018, the United Nations' IPCC released its follow-up report, stating that the Earth has until 2030 to reverse the increases in climate change temperature. The report warned that global warming of 2°C will be exceeded during the 21st century, marking a "Code Red for Humanity."

President Trump responded that; *"Something's changing and it will change back again. I don't think it's a hoax…But I don't think its man made…*

The 2021 IPCC, Report highlighted that human influence has warmed the climate at an unprecedented rate.

No American agency is as affected by climate change as the military. The Navy formed the Task Force on Climate Change in 2009 to determine how changes will affect the Navy's ability to accomplish their missions as they are especially vulnerable to rising ocean levels, and ports will be less serviceable. Joint Chief Chairman General Mark Milley commissioned the Army War College and NASA to create "Implications of Climate Change on the US Army." The military focuses on risks rather than absolutes. Bases of all the services were threatened by many of the same violent weather conditions that affected the rest of the country, including constant flooding, drought, wildfires, desertification, and the collapse of an aging electrical and water infrastructure. Flooded runways and lack of local water prevent the service from being able to perform effectively. Secretary of Defense retired Marine general Jim Mattis urged action on climate change, stating, "Climate change is impacting stability in areas of the world where our troops are operating today."

In February 2019, the Navy quietly shut down the task force, and information on the Navy website was scrubbed off. The National Security Strategy (NSS) removed the effects of climate change from the list of national security, focusing instead on traditional threats of terrorism and nuclear weapons.

The political movement for non-renewable energy sources with renewable energies began in the 1970s and gained momentum into the 21st century. "Green" parties were part of the political landscape in most western countries, though always on the electoral fringes. In the United States, they became a faction of the Democratic Party supported by traditional organizations like the Sierra Club, Friends of the Earth, and Greenpeace. The "Green New Deal" became part of President Biden's "Build Back Better" program to meet the 2015 Paris Agreement.

Climate control, however, was dealt a setback when the U. S. Supreme Court ruled in West Virginia vs. EPA that Congress must give the EPA "clear direction" rather than providing a broad delegation of power, reducing the agency's ability to regulate based on their research. Requiring direct congressional direction disallows the flexibility the agency needs to meet the intention of the 1970 Clean Air Act, as the nature of environmental threats is constantly changing.

Poor countries and people are disproportionately affected by climate change. They are more likely to live in areas lacking infrastructure and with less access to capital and full insurance, making them less likely to be able to rebuild after a disaster. Low-income communities are often located in danger-prone, lower, or near industrial sites leading to greater health problems, especially breathing-related diseases.

In 2019, 16-year-old Swedish activist Greta Thunberg, after making a zero-emission Atlantic Ocean crossing and leading a rally in New York, gave a speech at the U.N. Climate Action Summit, concluding, *"This is all wrong. I shouldn't be up here. I should be back in school on the other side of the ocean. Yet you all come to us young people for hope. How dare you! You have stolen my dreams and my childhood with your empty words. And yet I'm one of the lucky ones. People are suffering. People are dying. Entire ecosystems are collapsing. We are in the beginning of a mass extinction, and all."*

Time magazine named Ms. Thunberg "Person of the Year" for 2019.

From September 20-27, 2019, there were 2,500 strikes by students worldwide under the umbrella of the Global Week for the Future, including The Future Coalition and the Sunrise Movement.

Not everyone accepts that increases in CO2 and global warming are bad or man-made. In 2022, 64% of the American public believed that climate change was real, but only 45% believed humans were the cause. It's difficult to address threats that are slow, remote, and impersonal.

For deniers, temperature change is cyclical, touting the mild span between 950-1250 AD known as the Medieval Warm Period, which was followed by a cooling period, the mini-ice age. This viewpoint is Euro-centered, as the tropical Pacific region was cooler during the same period, with the average global mean temperature virtually unchanged until the 20th century. This fits the justification by deniers that the sun goes through periods of a "Grand Solar Minimum," when Earth temperatures will naturally rise and fall without human intervention. However, the temporary natural cooling is in the 0.1-0.2°C range, not nearly enough to offset human activity.

Warming temperatures will mean earlier springs and later falls with milder winters. Melting arctic ice will allow shipping across the northwest passage.

There is a problem of public awareness with "creeping normality," where changes seem to occur slowly, barely observable from day to day. It's difficult to address an unseen threat, especially with a complexity of connections where the causes don't seem immediately relevant to the effect. When it comes to choosing between immediate problems and long-term problems, the present always wins.

For many industries, efforts to reduce fossil fuel consumption are counter to the best economic interest of their business. In order to direct public policy away from climate actions, "astrograss movement" groups give the perception of a (pro-climate) point of view with grassroots support while being supported by special interest energy and related companies.

To nationalists, acknowledging and solving the problems of climate change will require cooperation on a worldwide scale, giving away some power of the individual nation to global institutions being led by those outside the country to create a "united global society." They see international actions on climate change as a Trojan Horse leading to an all-world government. They see "green is the new red."

Bjorn Lomborg of the Copenhagen Consensus Center supports that climate change is real and greatly influenced by human activity, but he argues that the benefits of proposed remedies are far outweighed by the costs and that other problems like hunger and clean water are more addressable. The National Academy of Sciences panel stated: "We have wasted years of response time…the longer you wait, the faster you have to respond and the more expensive it will be."

To counter scientific data, deniers issued disinformation in order to delay climate actions that were commercially problematic. After acceptance that climate change is happening, the actions were to question the reliability of the scientists, claim the actions wouldn't work, and shift blame to individuals (e.g., plastic bags and recycling juice cans). These put the focus on the minor impact of individuals rather than the industries whose profits would be reduced with changes.

Most climate misinformation came from denial vested donors, including the Koch Affiliated Foundation, Exxon Mobil Foundation, and the investment firm Vanguard. Ultimately, the purpose of all climate misinformation was to delay climate action.

Not everyone displayed the anti-climate change view through discussion. Scientists from research labs to local weather reporters have been threatened for public coverage ever since the Weather Channel first introduced the subject in 2006. Meteorologists in Spain, France, Australia, and the UK have also been subjected to complaints and harassment.

In response, a new field, "attribution science," examines how climate change is affecting extreme events.

Scientist believed that if the public was informed about climate change they would change behaviors so that they could survival. Fascinatingly enough, while most people believe the data and see the impacts, they believe that despite switching to EVs and recycling soda cans changes are inevitable. They are referred to as the "climate doomers." Each drought, fire, or hurricane story only reinforces their apocalyptic narrative. Changes are beyond their efforts.

Despite deniers, the world is getting warmer as CO2 levels increase. Each year of the 21st century has been warmer than its predecessor, and the heat is causing changes in both the environment and human activities, leading to widespread hunger from crop failures and medical emergencies from increased allergies and asthma.

A warmer climate has other effects. Shorter winters, or no winter at all, will allow many species of insects, normally held in check by freezing, to survive, increasing diseases to humans, animals, and plants alike.

Relief from the heat through air conditioning will be counter-productive to the net Earth temperature. The energy introduced to run cooling units is greater than the amount of cooled air in the aggregate, regardless of the efficiency of the unit.

The Atlantic Meridional Overturning Circulation (AMOC), of which the Gulf Stream is a part, is often described as a large oceanic conveyor belt that circulates heat through ocean currents, keeping Europe temperate. However, recent studies have suggested that the AMOC is weakening due to melting glacial freshwater replacing colder salty water. The AMOC is driven by the interaction between warmer, lighter freshwater, and colder, heavier saltwater.

Ancient diseases trapped in permafrost in long-dead animals will be released to a population that has not confronted inherited immunity for thousands of years.

The ice sheets on land masses of Antarctica, Greenland, and others are collectively known as the "cryosphere," and they are melting at both poles. At the North Pole, the long-term trend has been around a 3% reduction in ice each decade since measurements began in the 1950s. Greenland has lost up to thirty feet of surface ice with insufficient snow replacements.

Besides the ice, warmer weather will release the CO2 trapped in permafrost across the northern hemisphere, from Russia through Canada. Estimates suggest that there are between 500 billion to 1,000 billion metric tons of carbon trapped in the permafrost soil.

Global warming, causing climate change has scientifically been proven to be real, and the consequences are as lethal and far-reaching as any war in human history. Yet, there is no international protest. In the 2016 US Presidential Election, the issue barely registered, and the denier became the victor.

Changes to the climate are gradual. A hot day is followed by a cool day, and only the weatherman understands that the norm is increasing. There is no Pearl Harbor or 9-11. In those incidents and the Cold War, there was a villain. There is no Hitler, Stalin, or Bin Laden. On the 25th anniversary of the 1992 warning in 2017, 1,700 global scientists from 184 countries issued a "warning to humanity" on the Earth's ecosystem: "Humanity has failed to make sufficient progress in generally solving these foreseen environmental challenges, and alarmingly, most of them are getting worse."

Rising sea levels are threatening human settlements, from idyllic tropical islands to major shipping ports. The Marshall Islands, important in World War Two as bases for the military, are being lost, and other regional islands are already gone. Salt and saline waters are invading fresh water bays and wetlands, making fields unusable for raising crops. One billion people depend upon fish from coral reefs, but since the 1980s, almost half of the reefs have been lost.

To rebuild and help worldwide reefs adapt to the changing environment, groups are using micro-fragmentation and fusion to speed the growth of boulder, brain, and star coral. Pieces of living coral are grown in protected environments and then replanted.

As the glaciers melt, they become rivers that people are dependent upon for crops, navigation, and hydro-electric power. Much of Southeast Asia from Cambodia, Laos, and Vietnam, northern India and Bangladesh, to southern China, is dependent upon the rivers fed by the glaciers of the Himalayas. Equatorial Peru is dependent upon the Quelccaya ice cap in the Andes, and the glaciers of the Andes are melting faster than anywhere else on the planet.

Glaciers are disappearing. When Glacier National Park was created, there were 150 glaciers. In 2015, the number had been reduced to 30, and by estimates, all will be gone by 2030. "The Snows of Kilimanjaro" have been depleted by 80% since 1912. Greenland is losing 270 billion tons of ice annually.

Major cities like Boston, Nagoya, and Hanoi are vulnerable to ocean level rise. Tidal areas like the Chesapeake Bay have always been vulnerable to storms, especially as much of the land is sediment of earlier deposits. Water levels on the bay have been rising at twice the global average increase of 1.7 mm per year.

Rising sea levels and drought will force people to move; they are ocean climate refugees. Estimates suggest that by 2050, between fifty and two hundred million people will be climate-caused displaced.

In areas like Miami and Bangladesh, while the city remains stable, rising oceans will overflow low-lying areas with soil deposits. If left to nature, these areas would be entombed as artifacts for future archaeologists.

Warmer weather will release the CO_2 trapped in permafrost across the northern hemisphere from Russia through Canada, Greenland, and Scandinavia, plus the high plains of the Himalayas. Estimates suggest that there are between 500 billion to 1,000 billion metric tons of carbon trapped in the permafrost soil.

Methane hydrates (MH) are trapped in deep ocean sediments under low temperatures and high pressures. They may become destabilized with higher temperatures and reduced pressure.

Air pollution is the fourth highest global health risk factor, with over 5.5 million dying annually from pollution, and India and China accounting for 55% of the victims. Daily pollution levels in 2013 in Beijing and New Delhi exceeded 300 micrograms per cubic meter, twelve hundred times the World Health Organization guidelines. An estimated 85% of those affected already live in areas that exceed the level for air quality.

CO_2 and acidification are already damaging significant man-made objects. While Renaissance marble statues are moved indoors, buildings cannot escape destruction to the marble and limestone exteriors, including the Great Wall of China, Gothic cathedrals, and the pyramids of Egypt and Yucatan, Mexico.

Carbon Capture and Containment

Carbon is critical to life on Earth, and decarbonizing goes counter to all preceding human development. We, along with every plant and animal, are carbon-based life forms. It is also the mainstay of energy and chemicals for our societies, so there will be no elimination of the need for carbon and carbon-based materials (coal, petroleum, wood, peat) in the immediate future.

The so-called "Blue carbon" refers to the saltwater ecosystems on the shores of kelp, marshes, and mangrove thickets. Countries with extensive and fertile tidal zones, like Indonesia, the U.S., and Australia, capture the most. However, Cuba is the greatest beneficiary with a long coast balanced by a low industrial emission level. Blue carbon collects 81 million metric tons annually.

For direct industry application, "carbon capture" scrubs CO_2 directly from power-plant flue exhaust. CO_2 in the ambient air is 300 times more diluted than exhaust air, making the problem harder.

Direct Air Capture (DAC) removes CO_2, "mining the sky," directly from the air. But DAC towers are expensive.

There are three physical methods of Carbon Capture and Storage (CCS) that trap, transport, and store airborne carbon from burning fossil fuels. **Post-Combustion** (captures at exhaust) is the point at which the CO_2 is very concentrated. **Pre-combustion** capture occurs before burning, and **Oxy-fuel combustion** burns the fuel in pure oxygen.

Other methods being explored are Bio CCS Algal Synthesis, based on earth science photosynthesis using solar membranes for pre-smokestack CO_2 as a source for oil-rich algal biomass used for plastics and animal feed. Scrubbing CO_2 with potassium carbonate can create liquid fuels, though the process requires extensive energy usage. Scrubbing towers have limited range and depend upon natural air circulation but are effective in capturing CO_2 molecules along with other air pollutants.

The bacteria Cupriavidus nectar can ferment carbon sources and produce a biodegradable plastic called polyhydroxybutyrate (PHB).

While carbon dioxide is catastrophically accumulating in the atmosphere, it has positive uses. Companies still mine it commercially for about $100 per ton for various commercial uses, such as carbonating soda, filling fire extinguishers, and making dry ice. Carbon dioxide also promotes plant growth as ground carbon is taken into the body of the plant.

Water Mismanagement

Human water mismanagement can create climate disasters. Following the First World War up through 1931, farmers in the American Midwest, using new mechanized farming equipment, produced record crops by deep plowing under in excess of five million acres of the prairie's virgin drought-resistant grasses. But with overproduction and the financial failures of the Great Depression, many farmers were too in debt to purchase new supplies and equipment, leaving fields bare of new plantings. The once-fertile topsoil was blown away, so when the rains stopped, there were no deep-rooted grasses to hold the soil back. During the Dust Bowl, the Midwestern winds blew the dust, and millions of acres of topsoil were blown away, ruining 35 million acres of farmland.

Droughts and creeping deserts are a natural part of a dynamic planet. Annually, 24 billion tons of fertile soil are irretrievably lost to desertification, leading to 40% of the planet's land surface being considered degraded.

China instituted the Three-North Shelter Forest, referred to as "The Green Wall," in 1978 to slow the desertification by the Gobi Desert.

To address the increasing encroachment southward of the Sahara Desert, the "Great Green Wall initiative" was launched in 2007 by 20 members of the African Union.

While some environmental disasters are natural actions, others are directly human-created without any natural causation and assistance.

In 1986, the nuclear power plant at Chernobyl, in Soviet-controlled Ukraine, suffered a meltdown, releasing four hundred times the radiation of the Hiroshima A-bomb. It is estimated that the accident caused cancer in 100,000 people. Though the plant was buried in concrete, it is estimated that the area will be uninhabitable for two hundred years.

In January 2014, 5,000 gallons of coal-cleaning chemicals leaked from storage tanks into the Elk River in central West Virginia. The chemicals flowed into the Kanawha River, which provides water for more than 200,000 people in what is known as "Chemical Valley" and upwards into the Ohio River.

In a 2023 Supreme Court decision, waters such as wetlands, floodplains, and swamps that didn't share a "continuous surface connection" to a body that is part of "waters of the United States" were not nationally protected by the EPA under the 1972 Clean Water Act. The ruling allowed dredging and filling by farming, mining, and development even when the land is hydrologically connected.

Attitudes

Sustainability solutions are more than changes in physical equipment. Attitudes must change beyond acceptance of what our products are doing to the planet. Our behavior is also a factor. It is the attitude of use rather than the technology that must change.

The Department of Defense is the single biggest user of energy in the US government. The military's

2013 energy bill was $18.9 billion. The Marine Corps Expeditionary Energy Office investigated how to use behavioral science to change habits of energy usage. A 10% energy reduction will save $26 million annually, resulting in an increase in battlefield range by reducing refueling, logistics, and vulnerabilities.

In 2009, Navy Secretary Ray Mabus stated that the focus should be on "not just changing technologies but on changing us." "I think the biggest potential piece is behavior."

Perhaps the greatest change in attitude will be how we perceive and use time and space. We have conquered both, but at a cost.

Time was measured by how long it took to do a task. It was an analog world. Crops grew when they grew, and the next village was a time period away.

With the coming of the train, there was concern in the 19th century if the human body could handle movement over 30 miles per hour.

Moral Issue

Creating a sustainable world climate is not just a scientific or political issue; it's a moral issue. We are more connected than ever before on this planet, and what happens in Vegas or any other part of the world does not stay there. It affects the entire starship Earth and all its inhabitants.

Pope Francis emphasized the quality of life in a sustainable climate as a moral issue in his 2015 Encyclical Letter LAUDATO SI' OF THE HOLY FATHER FRANCIS "ON CARE FOR OUR COMMON HOME." Bishop Marcelo Sanchez Sorondo stated that it was *less about ecology than morality and fairness. It's not God versus science, but followers of God and science together trying to save humanity and the planet. Climate change is a global problem with serious social, environmental, economic, distributional, and political dimensions, and it poses one of the greatest challenges for humanity,"* the bishop said. *"The poor populations are the most severely affected, even though they are the least responsible."*

In 1971, Pope Paul VI referred to the ecological concern as "a tragic consequence" of unchecked human activity: "Due to an ill-considered exploitation of nature, humanity runs the risk of destroying it and becoming, in turn, a victim of this degradation," and, "never have we so hurt and mistreated our common home as we have in the last two hundred years."

Pope John Paul II warned that human beings frequently seem "to see no other meaning in their natural environment than what serves for immediate use and consumption." Pope Benedict stated, "The misuse of creation begins when we no longer recognize any higher instance than ourselves, when we see nothing else but ourselves."

Concerns about the consequences of Climate Change have crossed all religions. The ARC, Alliance of Religions and Conservation, organizes religious groups across the spectrum to address changes from a religious perspective. Prior to the 2016 Paris Agreement, religious leaders issued the Interfaith Climate Change Statement to World Leaders, calling for action by world political leaders.

Seventeen Anglican Bishops *issued "The World Is Our Host: A Call to Urgent Action for Climate Justice"* on March 30, 2015, stating: *"We accept the evidence of science: Human activity, especially in fossil-fuel based economies, is the main cause of the climate crisis. The problem is spiritual as well as economic, scientific, and political. We have been complicit in a theology of domination. While God committed the care of creation to us, we have been careless – but not hopeless."*

The Southern Baptist Climate Change Initiative states: "These issues are among the current era's challenges that require a unified moral voice. Therefore, our motivation for facing failures to exercise proper stewardship is not primarily political, social, or economic—it is primarily biblical."

The Evangelical Climate Initiative (ECI), made up of leading evangelical Christian pastors, expressed the view that global warming will have significant consequences warranting immediate action to greatly reduce the amount of carbon entering the atmosphere. Rev. Rick Warren stated that: "we have a stewardship to take care of the Earth."

The Hindu Declaration on Climate Change, the BHUMI DEVI KI JAI!, states: "A radical change in our relationship with nature is no longer an option. It is a matter of survival. We cannot destroy nature without destroying ourselves. Climate change is a stark symptom of the deeper problem of humanity living out of balance with what Bhūmi Devi, our shared planet, can renewably provide." "Climate change creates pain, suffering, and violence. Unless we change, we will only further this pain, suffering, and violence."

The Islamic Declaration on Global Climate Change states: "Our planet has existed for billions of years, and climate change, in itself, is not new." "Climate change in the past was also instrumental in laying down immense stores of fossil fuels from which we derive benefits today. Ironically, our unwise and short-sighted use of these resources is now resulting in the destruction of the very conditions that have made our life on earth possible." "Moreover, it is human-induced: we have now become a force dominating nature." Our species, though selected to be a caretaker or steward (khalifah) on the earth, has been the cause of such corruption and devastation on it that we are in danger of ending life as we know it on our planet."

"But the same fossil fuels that helped us achieve most of the prosperity we see today are the main cause of climate change. Excessive pollution from fossil fuels threatens to destroy the gifts bestowed on us by God, whom we know as Allah – gifts such as a functioning climate. What will future generations say of us, who leave them a degraded planet as our legacy? How will we face our Lord and Creator?"

The World Jewish Council issued a statement that: "The Bible informs us that the Earth is not subject to man's absolute ownership but is rather given to man 'to use and protect' (Genesis. 2:15). Man's control over the world is restricted. 'For the Earth is Mine' (Leviticus. 25:23): only the Creator may be considered to enjoy absolute ownership of His creation. Man is commanded not to spoil the creation but rather to improve and perfect it."

The Dalai Lama, the Tibetan Buddhist spiritual leader, said: "This is not a question of one nation or two nations. This is a question of humanity affecting the whole world... We have to take serious concern about the protection of the environment... The fate of the Tibetan Plateau, called the "third pole," containing about 40% of the world's fresh water locked in its glaciers, has direct international consequences as the Indus, Ganges, Mekong, Yangtze, and Brahmaputra Rivers provide water to the populations of Pakistan, northern India, Bangladesh, much of China, and all Southeast Asia.

A Buddhist Response to the Climate Emergency, also known as EcoBuddhism, states: *"Today we live in a time of great crisis, confronted by the gravest challenge that humanity has ever faced: the ecological consequences of our own collective karma. The scientific consensus is overwhelming: human activity is triggering environmental breakdown on a planetary scale..."* "Future generations, and the other species that share the biosphere with us, have no voice to ask for our compassion, wisdom, and leadership. We must listen to their silence. We must be their voice, too, and act on their behalf."

Pope Francis' encyclical calling global warming a moral issue moved it beyond theoretical science. U.S. National Academy of Sciences president Marcia McNutt stated, *"You can argue the science until cows come home, but that just appeals to people's intellect. The pope's argument appeals to someone's heart, and whenever you appeal to someone's heart, that's a much more powerful message."*

The Natural World Strikes Back

Nature doesn't compromise. The laws of nature are absolute, and it's up to humans to understand and adhere to those laws. We cannot compromise with 14 billion years of physics to accommodate temporary human wants.

As if nature was making a climate statement in 2019, heavy rains damaged the Noah's Ark reconstruction at Kentucky's Ark Encounter. It was a symbolic prelude to the extremes of the following years.

Since the changes were gradual, the warnings went generally unnoticed. The data seemed unbelievable. Changes to our intuitions and lifestyle to lessen the effects were inconvenient or costly to the status quo, so we let the changes happen. Perhaps it would take a Pearl Harbor or 9-11 type of disaster to awaken humanity to action against these changes.

It seemed in 2020 that nature had had enough and created multiple environmental 9-11s to the point where a new field of science was created, "extreme event attribution," to understand the changes. In 2019, the warmest planetary temperature ever recorded at the time was felt across the entire planet. Los Angeles hit a record 121°F. Siberia experienced daytime temperatures over 100°F, the first such modern recordings north of the Arctic Circle. Wildfires burned over 49 million acres of tundra, a region thought too cold to have forest fires. Some fires were reported as "zombie fires," slow-burning leftovers in the methane-laced bogs from the 2019 fires. Property and wildlife were devastated by heat induced fires, droughts, and hurricanes.

It began in the Australian summer (November through March) of 2019/2020, bringing record fires across New South Wales and Victoria provinces beginning as early as June with what was called "the Black Summer," aggravated by record high temperatures and ongoing drought. The fires burned over 15 million acres, including the deaths of 25 people and an estimated billion animals, including some 100,000 cattle. Many endangered species may have become extinct by the fires. Prime Minister Scott Morrison downplayed any influence from climate change.

Following a severe drought in 2019 in the biome of Brazil's Pantanel wetland region, the soil was dry, and boundary rivers were either lower or non-existent. This set conditions for the fires of 2020 that burned 3.2 million hectares. The dry carbon-heavy soil burned, releasing stored CO_2 while destroying the grasses necessary for large herbivores.

In the summer of 2020, the west coast of North America, after years of drought, began to burn, disregarding national borders. The Canadian province of British Columbia had 5 uncontrolled, 11 held, and 47 controlled fires. In the United States, the National Interagency Fire Center (NIFC) reported 87 active fires across more than 4.6 million acres in ten states.

California had six of the seven deadliest fires in the state's history in 2020, including a gigafire that burned over a million acres. The Pine Gulch fire was Colorado's largest in the state's history, burning 139,000 acres, only to be superseded seven weeks later by the even larger Cameron Peak fire. The Calwood fire produced a rotating flammagenitus pyrocumulus cloud from the intense heat-generated winds.

Europe had its worst year for fires in 2017. More than 800,000 hectares were burnt across Italy, Portugal, and Spain. High temperatures and dry conditions affected even the far north of Finland and Sweden, allowing record fires. Greek Prime Minister Kyriakos Mitsotakis stated that: "If some people still doubt if climate change is real, let them come and see the intensity of phenomena here."

The American Midwest experienced a "derecho," a sudden, hurricane-force windstorm of unparalleled strength with sustained winds over 100 mph.

California Governor Gavin Newsom declared in 2020, *"We are in the midst of a climate crisis. We are experiencing weather conditions the likes of which we've never experienced in our lifetime."* President Trump responded that *"It'll start getting cooler, you just watch...I don't think science knows actually."* Science did know.

While the west coast was burning, the American east coast was battered by two record hurricanes occurring even before the official June 1st start of hurricane season. In August, Laura became the strongest-ever hurricane by wind speed, causing damage of $14.1 billion upon initially hitting Louisiana. Teddy was the fourth-largest wind speed ever to hit Canada. Running out of names, additional storms were given letters of the Greek alphabet, with the first, Alpha, hitting Portugal.

And the extremities hurricanes went beyond the number of events. Storms went from depressions to hurricanes in a matter of hours. The 2020 season concluded in November with a double hit on Central America just before harvest. Eta made the spin-up to a category 4 in only 36 hours, with Iota following only two weeks later. The soil couldn't hold the water, causing massive mudslides. More than five million people were affected, burying dozens of homes and destroying much of the year's crops, forcing natives of Central American countries to migrate northward.

Not locale-limited, 7,000 miles to the south, similar rain bombs deluged Queensland, Australia, dumping 60% of annual rainfall in three days, causing record flooding. In 2021, Belgium and Germany experienced record flooding.

Pakistan is used to monsoon rains, but what hit the central Asian country in the fall of 2022 was unprecedented, with some areas getting six times normal rain. Flooding occurred across a third of the country, causing the loss of crops and animal life. 1,700 people died, with another 33 million affected. This led to starvation and increased political instability.

Triple normal rainfall was exacerbated by extreme surface heat, large and earlier flows from melting glaciers, deforestation, and the warming of the Indian Ocean, the fastest warming in the world. This affected the larger area of India, Bangladesh, and Nepal. The Indian Ocean normally produces two cyclones. In 2022, there were five, with twelve named storms.

The Intertropical Convergence Zone (ITCZ), a belt of equatorial stormy weather, has been staying north of the tropical regions longer. Increased rainfall in parts of northern-western Africa led to flooding, while Tunis, Tunisia, hit a record 48°C.

Eastern Africa had five consecutive years of drought, causing 2,500 deaths in Uganda alone, and the lack of rain in the Horn of Africa resulted in low dam reservoir levels and reduced electrical production.

The full extent of climate change in Africa is difficult to assess due to the lack of historic data and under-reported weather activities in naturally hot and dry areas.

Excess heat in South America led to wildfires in Peru and drought in the Pama-ak Plata basin, and Andean glaciers are melting at an unprecedented rate.

In 2020, there were seven straight years of recorded global high temperatures, over 1.7°F above the standard average, with Death Valley, California, marking the highest temperature ever recorded at 130°F. Beginning on July 4th, 2023, the global average temperature, from a combination of global warming and El Nino, reached a record 62.9°F (17.18°C), continuing for several consecutive days. The World Weather Attribution group showed that "the extreme heat wave would have been 'virtually impossible' without human influence."

With the heat came drought. Snow seasons have been getting shorter, and with less runoff, rivers carried less water to western cities and farms, with much of it lost to heat-induced evaporation. The mega-drought of 2021 was a continuation of ongoing drought conditions that have been growing since the turn of the century, even as the population of the cities of the American southwest and agricultural demand has continued to increase. The demand has increased while the supply decreased. The heat and drought of the summer of 2020 in East Africa allowed the worst infestation of the last 70 years. India will be one of the countries most affected by climate change, as was evident in the 2022 spring when a heat wave brought temperatures as much as 15°F above normal. Due to the "hottest summer ever," wheat yields were reduced by more than 500 kg per hectare in "India's breadbasket."

We needed new terms. A "rain bomb," fed by an "atmospheric river" that can hold as much water equivalent to 25 Mississippi Rivers, flooded the American Pacific Northwest in July 2021, killing 240. In the fall of 2022 and continuing into 2023, over eight atmospheric river-fueled events of up to 7" of rain in a single day hit northern California, causing flash flooding, undermining the parched soil, creating sinkholes, mudslides, and loss of "security of place."

Since 2015, the number of Americans alarmed about climate change has doubled to over 60%. Former Soviet Union Premier and founder of Green Cross International, Mikhail Gorbachev, declared that "We need a new paradigm of development in which the environment will be a priority. World civilization as we know it will soon end. We have very little time, and we must act."

One of the most effective counters to climate change from increased CO2 emissions is with trees. Yet every day, we lose 27 million trees more than we plant. Deforestation is not just a problem of CO2 but also because of the biodiversity in forests as they hold the fertile soil. To deforest the landscape, fertile soil may wash away, and that can't be regrown. It's often an irreversible process. And where there is a forest, there is rain. One tree produces about 5,000 liters of water per day, through clouds. Without trees, the land will become dry in the area.

But the installation of sufficient Harvestable and a parallel reduction of sufficient Consumables will cost money, billions of dollars, Euros, pounds, yen, renminbi, and riyals. So far, governments, for economic and political reasons, have been reluctant to invest in these energy sources while still paying out for damages and investing in "band-aids" of sea walls.

But the design balance is changing. Passivity is no longer possible. For the long-term survival of a human-friendly planet, positive steps must be taken to reduce, halt, and then reverse the effects of our harmful actions.

British scientist David King said, *"Time is no longer on our side. What we do over the next ten years will determine the future of humanity…"*

Geoengineering is defined by the Oxford Geoengineering Program as *"the deliberate large-scale intervention in the Earth's natural systems to counteract climate change."* In the 1960s, a proposal was to float billions of white golf ball-sized objects on the oceans to reflect sunlight. Scientist Mikhail Budyko proposed to release reflecting sulfate particles into the stratosphere. Harvard proposed seeding clouds with sea salt and other aerosols to increase solar reflection. Thousands of flights, at a cost of about $2 billion annually, will be sprayed above 65,000 feet to mimic volcanic clouds that have naturally shown to reduce temperatures worldwide. And who would plan and make the seeding, what would be the political implications to affected states? Could surgical weather control become weaponized?

Upon inauguration, President Joe Biden, by executive order, announced that the United States would officially rejoin the landmark Paris climate agreement. He declared, *"This is the decade we must make decisions that will avoid the worst consequences of the climate crisis. We can't resign ourselves to that future."*

Companies were already responding to the climate threat. Amazon and Global Optimism led a Climate Pledge that called on signatory companies to achieve net-zero carbon by 2040, ten years ahead of the goals of the Paris Accord.

The transition will not be easy. Electric batteries depend on rare Earth minerals that are sourced by polluting methods and energy-extensive mining methods. Demand will cause conflict between industries, countries, and even environmental groups. The minerals are often in countries with questionable worker human rights. Too many agencies will hide behind "greenwashing" to profess positive actions while making few actual changes. There will be political resistance from industries that will be made obsolete or irrelevant. And the costs will be enormous but overcoming the problems is necessary to be zero-carbon by mid-century.

Geopolitical conflicts over oil and natural gas supplies have exacerbated economic climate factors and set climate control actions aside. The 1973 OPEC reduction in oil production had already caused inflation and recessionary forces throughout the developed world, highlighting the world's dependence on oil. However, there was no organized attempt at alternative energy sources. Subsequent actions addressed economic issues rather than climate concerns, even though scientists were already warning about future consequences.

Wars and boycotts come and go, but CO_2 output continues, resulting in a warmer planet, melting glaciers, and more acidic oceans.

Environmental events have even influenced how the problems are identified. In 2021, the magazine Scientific American announced that the term "climate change" will be replaced with "Climate Emergency."

Climate change is affecting the entire planet. Historically, plagues, famines, and wars have been localized, but for the first time, everyone is vulnerable. Environmental internationalism cannot be restrained by laws or border guards.

Al Gore proclaimed, *"We have to fight for the planet."*

But who are we fighting? In 1970, Walt Kelly, carrying a line from an Earth Day poster, wrote in his comic strip Pogo, "We have seen the enemy, and he is us."

Despite worldwide recognition and calls for action by international groups, insufficient actions are being taken. Humans may have reasons for inaction, but nature's actions continue.

Yuri Gagarin, the acknowledged first man in space (1961), first saw the planet from the heavens. He said, *"When I orbited in a spaceship, I saw for the first time how beautiful our planet is. Mankind, let us preserve and increase this beauty, and not destroy it."*

A Sustainable World

(Merriam-Webster dictionary)

Sustain: *To keep up, to maintain prolong and preserve, to conserve*
Exploit: *as: …to make productive use of and to make use of meanly or unfairly for one's own advantage*
Sustain makes with what you have.   Exploit takes more.
Sustaining is symbiotic,   Exploitation is parasitic.

"Mankind is challenged as it has never been challenged before to prove its maturity and its mastery, not of nature but of itself" Rachel Carson 1962

We are finite creations in a finite world (the Earth). Our blue home is only 25,000 miles around, with over 70% of the surface covered with water. Much of the solid surface is sandy desert, frozen ice, mountains, or has already been developed, covered with roads and buildings. Onto what is left, we have to provide for a population that continues to grow, consuming resources, most of which end in some form of trash, useless for reuse. Only 3.2 billion hectares are available for cultivation. The world average is .4 hectares per person for food, with Americans using .9 hectares. And we have to allow for the other life forms that share the planet and to which we are either directly or indirectly dependent.

For most of the hominin era, the world seemed infinite. With the agricultural revolution, there were new forests to clear and always new lands to cultivate. When Europe seemed to have reached limits, a new world (the Americas) and access to an unfamiliar old world (Africa) with infinite resources were discovered. Within three hundred years, almost all the new lands were being exploited. We were living then to the Unlimited Planet Theory that there are no physical limits to growth.

Nature reuses. When a material is no longer useful to one consumer, it's taken by another. A monkey eats a fruit then drops the peel or seeds to the ground. The monkey's trash becomes another's resource. A monkey can ignore its trash as there's already a natural recycle/reuse, and it can go onto consumption of another resource.

But we aren't monkeys. The jungles we have designed are filled with products of our imaginations, and we've shown to have great imaginations on creating but little on disposition.

There are three man-made threats to our existence, ones of which we do have some control.

Since 1945 we have lived under the threat of nuclear war. First with the United States, then with the Soviet Union, the destructive power of the atomic then hydrogen bomb has the potential to destroy entire cities. The American technology was shared with allies England and France but eventually the nations of China, India, Pakistan, and North Korea acquired the technology. Other countries have sought "the bomb" till only the threat of retaliation, Mutual Assured Destruction (MAD) has restrained usage. But the threat is still there.

The second is the global warming caused by the accumulation of CO_2 in the atmosphere and oceans from burning fossil fuels (chapter 11). The gasses released by burning fossil fuels are changing the world in which we have evolved and developed, the Holocene. Our diets, lifestyles, and homes have all been shaped to the Holocene, and all are being changed as we enter the Anthropocene.

It's uncertain if we will be able slow the changes and eventually attain a sustainable world, but it will be different. Alternative sources of energy creation, (chapter 8), can and are providing sustainable power for movement, heating/cooling, and communication.

To grow much of the underdeveloped world there must be access to reliable energy without increasing use of fossil fuels. Clean energy access will be the driving force for upward mobility that will bring them out of poverty.

The third threat is from the accumulation of used stuff including trash, (chapter 10) a result of unchecked consumerism including the increasing use of plastics that threaten to pollute the land and water. Pollution is seeping trash and toxic materials into water systems, and with relatively immortal plastic debris, that are flowing into the oceans and our food supply.

For a sustainable world, there will have to be new ways to create products without further exploiting the resources. There must be a way to lessen the effects through the creation and implementation of new materials and the 5Rs. There must also be a change in attitude toward the accumulation of things.

We cannot continue to use the world as we're doing now. Many of the changes cannot be undone and are creating problems that even our technologies won't be able to reverse. For humans, and any other related life on this planet, means have to be designed that will balance our impact so that future generations will be able to enjoy life on Earth as much as has been offered to existing generations.

Human activities use 50% more than the planet has the bio capacity to renew. We are exhausting natural resources as "ecological debtors" and have been doing so for years.

The Greeks were the first to perceive the Earth as a spherical object. This implied that they knew there were limits to the world. But individual lives were within a limited range with an unlimited world existing beyond their view.

The first time humans saw the planet in its limited entirety was from Apollo 8 in 1968. The 1990 image from Voyager 1 showed how small and limited the Earth is, what Kenneth E. Boulding called "Spaceship Earth." It's all we have.

He described the neoclassical economy as a "cowboy economy" of reckless exploitation of unlimited resources, while a "spacemen economy" is a closed system where limited resources have to be recycled.

Sustainability became important once early agricultural communities were tied to specific land as fields in the agricultural revolution. They had to learn how to keep the land productive, how to make it sustainable. Location stability allowed for cities and the growth of civilization.

The Earth is the great commons. We share it with the rest of humanity and all other life forms, and what affects any one of us affects the common environment. Humans have formally divided the common planet along national borders, sales districts, frequency restriction, and individual property ownership.

The priorities of the present owner are on immediate implications, rather than what the affect is on future owners and the common. What is done within the "owned" property is judged only by the owner. The framework is; if everyone takes responsibility and care of their property, the common good will be safeguarded.

But what is done does not stay within the defined borders. Any form of production emits a form of pollution (smell, noise, runoff, even blocking a view) that influences other properties and rights of the owners.

Great achievements have been made in the last five hundred years. Beginning with the Renaissance and the Age of Exploration, humans have moved to all parts of the planet, and following our imaginations, into the cosmos. We are in awe of the technologies that have enabled us to identify then eradicate diseases, to feed millions even as fewer are involved in farming. Industrial prosperity has increased to be available for a greater part of the population. Each generation has lived better than the one before. With the right technology, there seemed to be no limit to what could be done.

John Stuart Mill, in the early years of the Industrial Revolution, referred to a "stationary state" where the population and production would not need to grow for growth in the quality of life. "The increase in wealth is not boundless; at the end of what they term the progressive state lays the stationary state. A stationary condition of capital and population implies not a stationary state of human improvement."

Mid-19th-century author/philosopher Henry David Thoreau lived a sustainable life of fulfillment with a minimum effect on the environment. His method was not for everyone.

Economics begins with the realization that there is an unlimited demand for a limited supply. As resources are limited, unlimited growth is not possible. In 1969, thirty-three African countries signed a document for future economic development without harming the planet's resources using the title "sustainable development."

In 1987, the World Commission on Environment and Development promoted the term as "a form of development that meets the needs of the present without compromising the ability of future generations to meet their own needs." The Brundtland Report, also known as "Our Common Future," issued "a compelling call for political action on behalf of the environment." Where the Anthropocene describes an epoch of greater human intervention in the world, we should look at how to sustain what we have, to establish an epoch of "Sustainocene."

Neoclassical economics depends on growth in both income and capacity. There has to be new stuff and new consumers to obtain the stuff. Population growth provides an increasing supply of consumers, and with satisfaction of real needs, they consume non-essential or vanity stuff. The worth or necessity of the stuff is irrelevant, only that it was produced and sold. If the stuff was discarded without use, it would still be included in the GDP.

To maintain employment for an increasing population, jobs in both manufacturing and services have to increase, creating demand for additional stuff made of limited resources.

For the producing company, financing for investment in increased capacity and replacement of aged machines came from stocks or bank loans, regardless of the source.

All energy sources, either animal or machine, are replacements for human energy. Each source replaces the efforts of a human with one of greater power, freeing the human from the toil of the effort but also putting the human out of the specific work. As artificial intelligence is given greater control of the means of production, the question is: what will humans do with the non-work time?

In a growth society, the answer is for full employment, which creates new work that will make new products or services, that will take additional drains on resources. Production requires consumption, and consumption requires consumers willing to trade work credits (pay) for the produced stuff. In a stable economy, rather than elimination of a job, individual hours are reduced, sharing the additional non-work time among a greater number of people, time that can be used for personal growth and enjoyment. The solution for the classical Greeks was work by slaves. Our slave work is now being assigned to robots. Philosopher Bertrand Russell referred that non-work time is used for leisure growth rather than product growth.

In post-war America, as real goals were met, the illusion of unfilled goals was created through advertising. Material consumption was kept ongoing by "planned obsolescence," each year producing new stuff, thereby making the existing, though useful, stuff unwanted. Being "out of style" in clothes, cars, appliances, or attitudes was socially fatal.

So, what do we do with the "old stuff?" Discard it, though as quality and durability had a low manufacturing priority, the stuff would quickly be worn out, which caused a demand for new stuff, and the economy rolled on. America went for extravagances in design and resource consumption, fueling an expanding growth economy exploiting resources for economic and lifestyle well-being.

As early as the 1970s, there was an increased awareness that linear growth could not continue, and there was a price for our progress. The environment had deteriorated to where the skies and oceans were at CO2 levels unmatched since pre-human times, causing rising temperatures as ice levels are decreasing.

The population is growing at a rate that the planet may not be able to support.

Until post World War Two, humans were in an essentially "empty world." Whatever we took, nature was able to more than recover. Plants could absorb the additional CO2 from industrial burning. There were always more trees to cut or deer to hunt. Minerals and resources were within easy access.

In a post-war boom with the "Great Acceleration," rapid advances in technology gave humans the means to collect faster than nature could replace. The limitations on fishing were no longer on increasing fish intakes by building more boats but on finding more fish as their numbers dwindled. Fish, trees, fossil fuels could not reproduce as fast as humans captured and consumed. Less fertile land was cleared for planting, and resource hunters had to go to more extremes to locate materials.

For the developed world, all the basic needs were being met. Growth, that had been quantitatively oriented, was sated. Still, the "growth" economy needed increases in consumption, but for most people, more goods did not project to more happiness. Additional work to obtain additional things created no additional satisfaction, often causing the reverse with increased stress and decreased enjoyment time.

Progress is growth, and growth is measured by the Gross Domestic Product (GDP) and Gross National Product (GNP, GDP of net overseas activities), records the total market value of all goods and services produced. The GDP though has no indication of the effects on the environment and measures activities regardless if they are beneficial or harmful. While the GDP has increased since the 1970s, the economic welfare of most citizens has stabilized.

When Simon Kuznet invented the concept of GDP, he noted, "the welfare of a nation can scarcely be inferred from a measure of national income. Distinctions must be kept in mind between quantity and quality of growth."

Jennifer Blanke, chief economist for the World Economic Forum, stated: 'it's easy to forget that it (GDP) was not initially intended for this purpose (measure the health of an economy), it merely provides a measure of the final goods and services... without any attention to what is produced, how it's produced, or who is producing it." She states *the GDP overlooks the questions of is growth fair, is it green, is it improving our lives?*

GDP measures the total of expenditures, but not the increases in value. GNP does not account for the increased value of goods produced. In technological transitions, two items, such as a hand drill and a small power drill, may cost the same, therefore given equal value, though are not equivalent in ability to perform the task. Improvements in the quality of manufacture or performance are not part of the GDP equation. When sales of multiple items of a less efficient technology are replaced by sales of a single superior item, the quantity of money decreases as does the GDP.

Moore's Law, by definition, is a source of deflation. The theory is that every eighteen months, technology will be more powerful and accurate while costing less.

GDP is based on the linear perspective that changes are being made at the same rate as past changes. This fits with a short-time burst, but with the Law of Accelerating Returns, improvements are exponential. Products will be constantly improved in performance, but with a stability of cost, the GDP will show no increase, indicating a stagnant economy.

An alternative measurement of the economy is the Index of Sustainable Economic Welfare (ISEW), developed by Dr. Herman Daly and theologian John Cobb. It includes costs associated with pollution and other unsustainable costs associated with production. The Genuine Progress Indicator (GPI) measures economic, social, and environmental issues in monetary terms. The GPI is a measure of net cost subtracting the costs to the environment (biodiversity, cleanup, and the impact of pollution), crime (loss and prevention), structure of education, and social issues including family from the GDP as the GPI.

GDP is easy to measure and understand, add up all the inputs. But it makes no allowance for negative external costs that resulted from acquisition and transportation, such as a reduced value of a polluted stream from mining and loss of income to the local fishing industry.

While a more accurate GPI will be more controversial, how to measure the costs of rising oceans and loss of property, especially when the loss is elsewhere? Accountants depreciate the value of a property or capital equipment for tax purposes, though the item is still fully functional. But how do they show depreciation and loss of function in an item of civic infrastructure?

To build a sustainable world, there has to be a sustainable economy. There has to be an acknowledgment that we are in a "full world" and that development has to be qualitative.

In an "empty world" perspective, the economy is but a part of the total ecosystem. With a "full world," the economy is pushing against the ecosystem's limits.

Growth was conventionally measured as approaches to the limiting factor in any activity. By the early 21st century, human activity is approaching or pushing against many limits. There is a limit on land. The limits for fossil fuels are forcing developers to go to extremes for additional production, and the planet cannot absorb the additional CO_2 from consumption, hitting the limit. Fresh water is being limited by the supply of water, not on irrigation ditches or pipelines for distribution. Much of what is listed as production is, in effect, transformation, making one thing from another with a net gain of zero when including waste from the transformation.

There are Planetary Boundaries, and humans are reaching, and often exceeding them, at an alarming rate. Some of them may already be at a tipping point for the planet.

Economics, by definition, is amoral.

A limitless economy has to keep pushing into new areas for growth, but as the resources are limited, the growth has to be at the expense of another group. The economies of Europe grew over the last five hundred years by exploiting the resources of the rest of the world, even exploiting the labor resources of their own people. As author/environmentalist Edward Abbey wrote: "growth for the sake of growth is the ideology of the cancer cell."

Humans have prospered in the environment of the Holocene age that has been in effect for the past ten+ millennia. It's been a world that we have exploited and to which we have become dependent.

Humans are not exempt from the laws of nature as we face our limits. We won't go away or go back, and technology cannot be unlearned. For the first time, humans have to look beyond the goals but at the long-range global implications. The challenges of the 21st century are to stabilize growth.

The "Great Acceleration" began in the 1950s, and by the 1960s, scientists around the world realized that humans were pushing many limits and that the problems must be acknowledged. The climate is changing 170 times faster than if by natural forces alone.

Concerned scientists met in Rome, Italy, in 1968 at the Accademia dei Lincei to form the Club of Rome, releasing The Predicament of Mankind as a proposal in 1970. Using the MIT global computer model World3, they identified that current world problems of the economy, population, environment, and manufacturing continued to grow as they became more interdependent into a single value-based situation.

Lead author Dr. Donna Meadows, in the book The Limits of Growth in 1972, analyzed how population and economic growth were pushing the unconstrained consumption of resources over the longterm. It included five variables: * world population, * industrialization, * pollution, * food production, and * resource depletion.

The following year, 1973, German-British economist E. F. (Ernst Friedrich) Schumacher published a series of essays as his influential book Small Is Beautiful: A Study of Economics As If People Mattered. He stated that the existing economic system was unsustainable as it was built upon the exploitation of finite resources and that small appropriately sized technologies were more sustainable. From his observations, he developed the principles he called "Buddhist Economics" (see "moral issues").

However, in the 1980s era of unlimited potential for economic growth highlighted by the presidency of Ronald Reagan ("There are no limits to growth and human progress when men and women are free to follow their dreams."), "Reaganomics" included reductions in corporate and personal income taxes plus environmental regulations. During his term, wealth was increased by $30 trillion worth of goods and services as unemployment fell to under 5%.

Groups like the Club of Rome initiated questions on the basic assumptions of "growth." It's been the basis of western economics. But is it realistic in the long term for a full Earth?

Are humans ready to consider "degrowth"? This is not to create a recession or depression but meant to de-glamorize growth as an economic philosophy, not to be confused with negative economic terms. Degrowth in a sustainable economy replaces one unit, stuff, or people, with another. The replacement can be of equal value, but there is no restriction on the development of improved stuff that has greater value in exchange or use. It's the acknowledgement that there are collective limits, and that we are hitting them.

How society has used its surplus is the nature of the society. To continue the classical economic model, surpluses went to artists, police/military, political, and to idea creators. They, in turn, moved the society to new plans that expanded towards the limits of the physical ecosystem.

Can humans, like the rest of nature, prosper without "more," living happily with the same level as previously done, to sustain in balance, neither over-taking from nature nor from others where the net status is zero, and the economy based on reproduction and replacement rather than expansion?

The 1992 Earth Summit, officially named as the United Nations Conference on Environment and Development (UNCED), or Rio 92, acknowledged worldwide awareness, leading to the Declaration on Environment and Development Agenda 21 and Forest Principles. The Convention on Biological Diversity and the Climate Change Convention led to the Kyoto Protocol in 1999.

A second Earth Summit was held in Johannesburg, South Africa, in 2002.

In 2015 the UN again addressed the problems and potential solutions through seventeen developmental goals.

1. End poverty
2. End hunger and improve nutrition
3. Ensure healthy lives for all
4. Inclusive quality education for all
5. Gender equality, empowerment
6. Sustainable cities and communities,
7. Access to affordable energy
8. Strengthen global partnerships
9. Reduced national inequalities
10. Clean water and sanitation
11. Action on Climate changes
12. Responsible consumption and production
13. Protect terrestrial environment
14. Sustainable seas and marine resources
15. Promote inclusive just societies
16. Build Industry, innovation, and infrastructure
17. Sustainable economic growth and decent work

For the first time in over 800,000 years, CO_2 levels in the atmosphere have passed 400 parts per million (ppm). Our hominin ancestors, plus the familiar plants and animals we rely upon, have come in the last 10,000 years, developing in a world based around a CO_2 of 280 ppm.

The 2014 Sustainable Development Solutions Network at the United Nations released a report created by scientists of fifteen nations on what is necessary to keep the atmosphere from warming more than 2°C/ 3.6°F above the preindustrial average of the late 19th century.

Three transformations are critical to making the world sustainable by 2050:

1. Decarbonize the world economy, eliminating harmful CO2s,
2. Feed the world through sustainable agriculture, the largest single emitter of greenhouse gases and the largest single user of fresh water,
3. Reduce the need for additional mineral exploitation through cyclical material flow.

An international group of 29 environmental scientists and academics met in 2009 through the Stockholm Resilience Centre and set out a framework for planetary boundaries in nine categories:

* climate change,
* biodiversity loss,
* biogeochemical flow,
* ocean acidification,
* phosphorus cycle,
* land use,
* freshwater,
* ozone depletion,
* nitrogen cycle.

The group stated that the sustainable levels of the categories were necessary to "maintain a safe operating space for humanity" before survival is threatened by crossing irreversible thresholds. While the limits are inexact, the loss of the first three has already crossed their boundaries, though they have yet to have passed tipping points.

The concept of planetary boundaries is counterintuitive to our historical perspective of an unlimited planet. There are limits in resources and the planet's ability to absorb what we are doing.

Ecologist Gretchen Daily stated: "it is time to confront the hard truth that traditional approaches to conservation, taken alone, are doomed to fail… The challenge is to make conservation attractive from economic and cultural perspectives."

To attain the Sustainable Development Group, the Transformable Policies are:

•   Rapid renewable energy growth, (halving emissions every decade)
•   Investment in education for all, gender health, family planning (improve well-being with a reduced ecological footprint)
•   Active inequality reduction (insuring 10% richest < 40% income)
•   Accelerated sustainable food chains (1% per year better productivity)
•   New development models in poorer countries (copying successful aspects of South Korea, China, Ethiopia)

British economist Kate Raworth added the social impact of population on health, access to food, jobs, and energy in her 2012 "Donut Economics" theory. The focus is not on the growth of the economy, but on where everyone on earth can be ensured to have access to their basic needs of adequate food and education. This does not limit opportunities for future generations by protecting our ecosystem. She said: "A healthy economy should be designed to thrive, not to grow."

The 1987 UN's World Commission on Environment and Development published in the Brundtland

Report "Our Common Future" with a definition for sustainable development. "Development that meets the needs of the present without compromising the ability of future generations to meet their own needs."

The personification of the planet originated with the ancient Greeks as "Gaia." Like a living organism, the planet reacts to environmental changes. And like a living organism, it will perish when its limits are exceeded.

The 5 Rs

Within the existing manufacturing methods are the traditional R's of material goods for sustainability: Reusing, Recycling, Repair, and Reducing, to which we must add Redesign that affects how the four are possible.

The EPA, addressing the importance of design in 1992, created DfE (Design for the Environment) to minimize environmental-economic costs to consumers. Initially addressing pollution, they expanded to climate issues. Design was a factor in environmental processing, disposal, and energy consumption throughout the product's life. The program was renamed "Safer Choice" in 2015 with labeling to notify consumers of EPA approval for materials and energy consumption.

Reuse is the downcycling of materials into lesser products. In the 1950s, following the sacrifices and make-do of the war years, many companies sold their products (jelly, milk products, pimentos, etc.) in glass containers that were after initial consumption used as drinking glasses and bowls. Designers can improve reusability by making single-use commercial containers to the same aesthetic standards as for permanent-use products. This is where reusable products can or cannot add to sustainability. A product intended for reuse is made of thicker material often requiring longer production times. The product has to be additionally stronger by a magnitude of times used to justify an additional cost.

Recycling and composting, in the natural recycling of organic materials in the U.S., have prevented 100 million tons of material from being sent to landfills and releasing over 170 million metric tons of CO_2. The largest amounts of recycled materials are plastics, including everything from plastic grocery bags and drink bottles to appliance cases and furniture.

Due to the size of the consumption market, the U.S. leads in total material recycled. 21% of the glass, including drink bottles, and 59% of paper packaging, mainly as cardboard and much of that by retail operators, is recycled. In comparison, Germany recycles 81% of glass and 83% of paper, while Japan recycles both at about 98%. Additionally, Sweden and Denmark not only recycle 100% of their own materials but also import material for recycling.

Once separated and cleaned, primary recycled scrap material, rather than virgin, requires lower energy outputs as well as outputs of acquisition, mining, and transportation. For aluminum, the decrease can be as great as 95%, plastics 70%, steel 60%, paper 40%, and glass at 30%. For example, 2,700 kw hours are needed to produce steel, but only 740 kw hours to recycle an equivalent amount of scrap steel.

However, the cost also has to include post-use collection and transportation. Recycling requires inter-industry interdependence. While initial production is a linear process (mine, to mill, to consumer), recycling begins at a variety of sources that move through multiple industries.

Before the 1950s, products were made of recyclable natural materials like wood, glass, and metals. While many products were not built to last, the material could be reused in other forms. During the Great Depression and WWII, material reclamation was a necessity as many materials were expensive and in short supply. Government programs actively encouraged reclamation, even to turn in unused pans. After the war, the instruments of destruction were cut up for aluminum, steel, and glass to become the materials of the 1950s boom.

Plastic usage began to grow as designers were able to create exciting shapes of new products and as the cost of oil, the base material for plastic, was kept low, production of single-use items was economically feasible.

While the life of the useful item is short-term, the life of the plastic material is long-term. Though plastics can be recycled, they don't naturally break down into natural materials. Over time, they break into smaller parts that become plastic chips that find their way into waterways. Due to a visual similarity to jellyfish (plastic bags) and food (plastic chips), they are eaten by fish, many of which are caught for human consumption.

Plastics are the perfect material for almost all applications and, by the 1970s, were replacing metals, glass, wood, and cotton in applications including tools, clothes, windows, and building trim.

Even as they publicly promoted recycling, industry leaders knew that it was doubtful if effective mechanical recycling of plastics on a large scale would ever be economically viable. As early as 1973, six years after the movie "The Graduate" proclaimed that the future was in plastics, industry leaders recognized recycling as "costly," "difficult," and sorting to be "infeasible." Still, they continued to promote recycling as a way to head off proposed governmental curbs or outright bans on plastics, telling the public that recycling was working.

To promote awareness that materials could be recycled, a symbol was designed to be put into the product. Originally created for paper products, variations of the symbols are used for plastics, glass, and metals.

However, there was seldom a structure for collection, material separation, and reprocessing, even for type 1 and 2 materials and plastic. And the addition of the recycling symbol can cause confusion to the public, suggesting that any material containing the symbol can be recycled, when most cannot. Consumers want to feel that they are being responsible. This is "wishcycling."

Not everything can be recycled, though a marketing program called "Greenwash" suggests more can be. While intentions may be sincere, the amount of recycled waste is minuscule. Reduction/recycling can be better done with product/service redesigns that are better oriented for recycling. Corporate efforts may be sincere in trying to recycle, proclaiming their efforts, but sometimes the results are less than the effort. Whether it's due to over-aggressive promotion or failure of an anticipated technological breakthrough, the result is less than advertised. Rather than face adverse reactions to deceptive claims, underperforming companies turn to "green-hushing."

Today, plastics are everywhere and in places that can't be recycled, even if there was a cost-effective way. Designers use the shape freedom to make their designs. Houses have synthetic rugs, vacuum-formed doors, polymer wall paints, and plastic cases for all the myriad appliances that make up the contemporary home. Eventually, cars, houses, and appliances will join the packaging they came in to make up junkyards and trash dumps.

An estimated 400 million metric tons of plastic waste are produced annually, with 51 million tons produced in America. Only 5% is domestically recycled. The remainder is incinerated, sent overseas, or sent to landfills.

What is to be done with the omnipresent tons of plastics? Efforts for recyclable and biodegradable plastics are intended to maintain plastics usage while reducing the environmental impact. Due to the wide range of types of plastics and the pairing of plastics with other materials, separation of plastics that can be recycled is difficult and often labor-intensive.

Recycling and reuse alone can't solve the plastic problem. "We can't recycle our way out of this mess." While economics are built on a balance between production and consumption, there is no consumption with plastics; there is only transformation in time and space. Almost all plastics continue to exist in some form.

Until a method can be created to break plastics back down into their basic elements or create new truly recyclable materials and create new uses for existing materials that can replace plastics in function (chapter 7), piles of plastics will continue to increase, overloading the systems.

The commonly called recycling process of plastics is mechanical. Plastics are physically separated by type, cleaned, chopped into pellets, and then reformulated back into material that can be made into new products. The problems are that only some plastics can be recycled, and even within the same material, recycling is not feasible due to differences in color and food or material contamination.

Alternatives are to break down into base materials by either biological or chemical means. Biodepolymerization is an in-development enzyme-based process that can break down plastics, converting a polymer into a monomer or a mixture of monomers, especially those with ester bonds.

Chemical recycling "unmakes" plastics by converting them into their original raw materials. Their long hydrocarbon chains are broken into shorter fractions or single monomers using chemical, thermal, or catalytic processes. It's not fussy whether the plastic is the wrong color or a composite; it's simply fed into an infinite recycling system.

"Unprocessing" plastics back to their hydrocarbon origin is an opportunity to address two problems. Unprocessed plastics that are presently litter and waste can slow the ocean's plasticification. Plastics are a carbon-hold material as hydrocarbons made into plastics are trapped in a solid form that cannot interact with oxygen to produce CO_2. Unprocessed plastics can be used, reducing the need for newly pumped petroleum. While not reducing usage, it will lessen demand for additional drilling.

The Chinese government, in January 2019, put a ban on importation of materials intended for recycling, announcing that they no longer "wanted to be the world's garbage dump."

China's decision was based on several factors. With increased internal prosperity and trash production, they had less room to take in external trash. While trash intended for recycling was often contaminated, there was still a profit line available. But as the cost of disposing of corrupted "recyclable" material, primarily plastics, rose, and with the cost of oil remaining low, new production is favored.

Material intended to be recycled in China began to mount up. Much of the material was rerouted to Vietnam, Indonesia, Malaysia, and India. But this is merely a temporary solution. Long-term solutions will require a shift in the attitude of throwaway cultures.

A major source of waste material is from single-use products. These are products that go through the entire product cycle but are intended to be used only once and then discarded. But most are items of convenience with no value beyond the moment. Paper plates, stir sticks, and disposable paintbrushes can be made to be cleaned for re-use but are easier to discard, disregarding the downstream cost of disposition and pollution. The convenience of disposability is for the immediate consumer and will continue as long as there are no penalty costs to the producer or consumer for post-use.

True sustainability would involve using the same materials over and over, only adding input of energy for ongoing product transformation and minimum material loss. Things have to be designed to be repaired; otherwise, new things are constantly being made of new resources that only serve the same function, creating no new advances, the antithesis of sustainability, which is not possible without systems for repairing and refurbishing existing products. The best that can be planned is to design products that can easily be repaired with a minimum of energy allotment.

A product is designed, setting its fate of its life cycle even before it's made. The first step is with DFA (Design for Assembly), which puts the emphasis on the most effective method of production.

DIY (Do it yourself) was not just a marketing phrase but a standard for product design.

All products used to be DFR (Design for Repair) as replacement parts were not always convenient. With standardization, repair was as easy as the original assembly.

Being able to repair has always been a part of ownership. From the first primitive tools, there has been a connection between the creator and the user. It means reducing the need for the creation of new items and the resources (material, energy, transportation, labor, and structures), and the accompanying reduction in land use and pollution of trash in that creation.

Without the ability to repair, users are detached with no sense of ownership, even when they legally own the tool. They feel nothing for the tool so have no connection to its place in sustainability. The product/tool is discarded without thought.

Original Equipment Manufacturers (OEM) can require service and repair with their technicians that have access to specialized tools; otherwise, any warranty is voided. But even when the product has gone beyond the warranty, the owner can't perform repairs, as those tools, repair manuals, and settings are often not made generally available. That computer controlling data is often proprietary to the creating companies, limiting access to codes. With the internet, digital controls and data are interconnected. The stated concern by manufacturers is that non-company access to one device will allow access to linked devices and the proprietary codes. Only by using technicians with their proprietary tools can their intellectual property be secured. Control of the data gives them a monopoly on components and the product. Independent repair technicians and third-party services, such as for personal cars and appliances, are denied access to the codes, thereby reducing their ability to provide self-service repair.

Resistance to company control of a product's data began with users wanting to be able to repair property that they own by purchasing repair tools from the producing company. The first Right to Repair legislation came up in Massachusetts in 2012 with the Motor Vehicles Right to Repair Act, intended to allow consumers who own the devices the right to modify and repair them.

The problem for repair will continue to increase as more vehicles, from farm tractors to aircraft, plus home appliances and entertainment systems, are controlled by internal computers and internet connections to the manufacturer's site. Personal repairs by local shops will become increasingly difficult, if not illegal. Personal car upkeep and repair are continuing to be diminished with the market conversion from ICEs to EVs. It's expected to continue with the introduction of self-driving cars, "smart roads," and communication between vehicles, other drivers, and centralized control.

This raises ethical questions of who owns a product when the guiding algorithm is forever controlled by manufacturers. How much modification, if any, can the owner make? Does the manufacturer have a monopoly of costs for replacement parts and service? And can the manufacturer direct how the product is used?

Colorado passed two pieces of legislation in 2023: "Consumer Digital Repair Bill Of Rights, HB21-1199," and "Consumer Right To Repair Agricultural Equipment" HB23-1011, to allow non-manufacturer repairs by equipment owners. Manufacturers are to provide access to parts, tools, and manuals except where access will divulge trade secrets. They were initiated by self-reliant farmers, but as more products became dependent upon proprietary data, the application will affect general users.

The ability to repair, rather than continual replacement, will encourage company quality improvements, increase competition for repair services, reduce duplication of product production, and subsequent unnecessary resource mining. It will increase consumer income by reducing the cost of company-directed repairs and continual purchases of essentially the same product. Being able to repair or customize to the owner's specific need is a liberty of ownership and a direct connection between the owner and user.

Redesign: Designers are the central creators. Ultimately, everything, whether a product (industrial designer), a script (author), or a spreadsheet (accountant), is a design created by someone practicing their version of design. Designers create things that make feelings and passions tangible.

Redesign can increase the ability to repair. Product design can improve sustainability with the selection of materials that can be integrated into efforts to reduce plastic waste.

Redesign can direct the implementation of the original five. 80% of the environmental impact of a product is determined in the design phase: what materials will be used and what is the method of production.

To the contemporary technology-based society, it's difficult to understand that the dominance of technology was not widely considered a thing well into the Middle Ages. One of the first to comprehend the impact of technology was Francis Bacon, who wrote of how the use of our tools extends human power over nature. In an "empty world," the designer had only to consider the factors of creation and use; the function, what materials, and cost.

With contemporary materials and manufacturing processes fueling a seemingly unquenchable consumer society, the design of the artifact has to address issues from creation to the ultimate product death. The entire product ecosystem life span has to be planned out in the initial design. Addressing one moment of product life is of minimal importance if the entire cycle is not addressed.

Product design is at the core of most environmental problems. Some are useful and needed, but many are stuff that will quickly become the new garbage to keep the consumer/producer economy moving, regardless of any actual value. The production line of new products has become both a plaything fulfilling our desires and an insatiable monster we cannot control. The focus is on the production of things rather than the services to humans. It's the responsibility of the designer to establish the relationship between the tool and the user.

"Planned Obsolescence" was an official marketing plan by General Motors President Alfred P. Sloan Jr. in the 1920s. Product sales were reaching market saturation. Ernest Elmo Elkins called it the concept of "artificial obsolescence" (chapter 11), a way to engineer the consumer to change the attitude of "use" items to "use-up" items that have to be routinely replaced, even if still functional. The philosophy became mainstream when, in 1954, designer Brooks Stevens acknowledged it was for "instilling in the buyer the desire to own something a little newer, a little better, a little sooner than is necessary." It was the superficiality that was expressed in the products' visual variety, as humans are more visually oriented to differences. The design gave individuality to the user.

Designers can be planners for a more sustainable and productive society by selecting materials that can be recycled, reducing disposable packaging, planning for the ability to upgrade, considering other functions the object could fulfill, determining the intended product life and appropriate life span materials, focusing on meaningful improvements, and easing repair and component replacement.

Eventually, the lives of all products end. Items that are upgradable and serviced are less likely to be quickly discarded.

John Thackara said, *"we designed our way into situations that face us today... if we can design our way into difficulty, we can design our way out."* Designers have to accept responsibility for the consequences of the designs. Elaine Strijkers wrote about a "designer's paradox" where we're designing products to improve the world, but with consuming resources, we end up contributing to pollution that decreases the world.

International design educator Victor Papanek reinforced that *"In all pollutions, designers are implicated at least partially."*

Designers are not limited by the materials and processes available. The scope of the design is limited by the imagination and willingness to explore beyond what is given to the designer. Looking at the placement of the product within the environment is a function that can reach beyond the accepted concepts.

Design can reorient the world from technology domination to social domination, where humans, not machines, are the focus, as all products are, in effect, services.

It's easy to call ours the Information Age, replacing the Industrial Age, but all the data is not a goal in itself but a means for creating the knowledge to make industry more efficient, to do more and make more with fewer resources, an ever-increasingly efficient Industrial Age.

Design involves a collaborative effort, including specialists from all aspects of manufacturing, social, and environmental that the product touches. The overall design goal is to improve the quality of life, not just of the producer and consumer, but also everyone who touches or is touched by the product life.

Over thirty tons of wastes are created for every ton of a consumer's product, and over 98% of those products are discarded within six months. Yet all attention is on the immediate 2%. The 98% is the dark matter of our stuff. We know it's there but choose not to see it.

It's the responsibility of the designer to address this dark matter and make products that use recyclable materials in energy-efficient facilities that serve a useful life cycle, which do minimum harm, and can be reborn.

Product end-of-life is just as important, though not as exciting, as product creation. But it's only with addressing the former that the true societal cost of a product can be ascertained. The designer and producer have the responsibility to influence the entire product life cycle as smart eco-design through life cycle strategies. A circular economy drives products from creation, to use, to disposal, to creation anew.

A circular economy unites producers and consumers into a wider, total perspective rather than isolating each step responsible for their part. A sustainable society can grow with innovation and minimal ecological impact. Products can be designed to be upgraded and to allow failed or obsolete parts to be removed and replaced, providing an extended product life.

Products will fail. The greater the stress on the product, the higher the likelihood of its failure. Moreover, the more complex the product, the greater the opportunity for a single component to fail. Sustainability of the product can be increased by analyzing the potential for some components to fail more likely than others and putting the potential for failure in a direct relationship with the ease of replacement.

Our things define us as designers, as producers, and as consumers. The question has to be asked: what is the stuff for, and is it really needed? How does it improve our lives? Does it even need to exist? A product exists to satisfy a need. The challenge is to understand the necessary service and design a product to fulfill that service. Our values and human dignity are grounded in these products.

Address the needed service rather than a product that commodifies the service. And the product must be in a form that users understand and desire to use. Too much emphasis is on the Form without a full understanding of the broader Function. More elegantly, Augusto Morello described *"Design is the humanizing of technology."*

Reducing the material used in making common household items can prevent excess materials from being sent to the landfills. Can we have a world without growth and still meet physical and psychological human goals? Growth has always meant progress, obtaining more of the needs for life and lifestyle. As we obtained a "Full Earth," the needs were fulfilled for billions, but the economics that guided development remained unchanged in a world of limited resources while retaining unlimited demands.

Yvon Chouinard, CEO of the Patagonia clothing company, encouraged "Don't Buy This Jacket." Chouinard's purpose was for consumers to think about products they purchase. "It's time for us as a company to address the issue of consumerism and do it head-on. It would be hypocritical for us to work for environmental change without encouraging customers to think before they buy."

By doing this, he was rethinking the notion that only profits drive progress. There must be a reduction in demand. This is counter to growth that depends upon demanding and supplying more. This will require a paradigm shift in advertising/public information.

C2C (Cradle to Cradle) looks at the life cycle of a product, from design creation, material extraction, manufacturing (including excess and processing materials), packaging, shipping and display, usable product life, reparability, and reuse as another product of value, post-use collection, and responsible disposition. There are two certifications for C2C: LEED (Leadership in Energy and Environmental Design) and BREEAM (BRM Environmental Assessment Method) founded in 1990 by the Building Research Establishment for both new and renovated structures.

Most packaging in use today is not designed for post-use and is discarded to the landfill. A third of plastics leaking into our ecosystem are from packaging.

Redesigning how buildings are created offers enormous opportunities for pollution reduction. Buildings, from homes to skyscrapers, produce 39% of CO_2 emissions in the U.S. with almost equal distribution between residences (21%) and factories/offices (18%). Emissions come from direct usage of heating, lighting, cooking, and cooling, and from the indirect production of power creation.

A building is one product that still consumes energy, even when not in immediate use. Building design can reduce emissions by making the structure energy self-sufficient with electricity and hot water generation from solar panels and photoelectric windows. Rooftop gardens absorb both CO_2 and solar heat, while natural lighting reduces the need for electrically generated light (12% in residential, 25% in commercial). However, the greatest energy consumer is the HVAC system (39% in residential, 32% in commercial).

The South London city of BedZED (Beddington Zero Energy Development) is both a goal and a location. It was created as a carbon-neutral sustainable eco-village, using design and architectural features to prove that a community could work at 1 Earth (a design that, if adapted universally, could be sustained with a single Earth). It includes the use of photoelectric panels, passive heating from sunspaces that heat materials during the day to release heat in the cooler night, green spaces, and recycling waste water. Despite having the best intentions, the United Kingdom, with an average footprint of 3 Earths, could only achieve 1.7 Earths with BedZED.

The goal of the Living Building Challenge, by the International Living Future Institute, is to eventually design buildings that create more energy than they consume.

President Clinton's Council on Sustainable Development suggested EPR (Extended Producer Responsibility) to target different participants in the product life cycle. EPR was introduced to add all environmental costs associated with a product throughout its life cycle to the market price of that product. EPR uses financial incentives to encourage manufacturers to design environmentally friendly products and hold them responsible for the costs of managing their products at the end of their life.

Nine states have introduced EPR legislation. To comply with a circular economy, companies would need to redesign products through material change of either degradable plastics or alternative materials or institute a "Take Back" system at the end of the product's life. The manufacturer could recycle the material to be reprocessed into new products.

China's rapid industrial acceleration from the late 1980s has been paralleled with an output of pollution in Chinese skies and rivers, second only to the United States. By 2015, the world's largest coal consumer burned three billion tons, more than India, Europe, and the United States combined.

China publicly committed to a "Green Wall" by 2050. Three thousand miles of grasses and trees will be planted to hold back encroachment by the Gobi Desert. China is already the world's leading creator of electricity from wind and solar generation and investing $100 billion in policies of "ecocompensation" that reward conservation and restoration.

Is there too much prosperity? Has too much emphasis been placed on the production of things? Progress has been measured by new products intended to satisfy human needs and improve the quality of life for an increasing number of people.

Each product is the result, not only of human creativity and labor, but also of the resources utilized to produce it. More products mean more resources utilized. There are limits to the amount of land that can be used for planting and for cities and residences, the amount of forests that can be cleared, the species that are displaced for human economic growth, and the amount of trash that can be discarded on the land and in the oceans.

But what is all the stuff for? How do the additional things improve our lives? Are the products being designed and manufactured to improve a people-centered world, or are they filling output in the economic engine, designed to keep the factories running regardless of the real need or fate of the product?

Freedom is being without limits, no boundaries, or restrictions. But it's the unfreedom of those boundaries that defines the function of the effort that gives form. The function now has to be sustainability. The question is if a sustainable economy can exist within a democratic-capitalistic society? Can we change from a quantity of living based on stuff to a quality of living? Cultural values have changed before; they can change again as the need is recognized.

But while the aim should be for sustainability, we may have to settle for resilience.

Evil

$$P \times I \times 1/A = E$$

Predator times **Imagination,** times inverse of **Accountability** equals Evil

Evil is a uniquely human-created condition. No other species has shown the capacity to exhibit evil. Only humans seem capable of imagination and creations of the mind, such as philosophy, religion, love/hate, prejudice, and future predictions, to justify evil acts. Primate expert Dr. Jane Goodall stated: "I believe only we are capable of true calculated evil."

Nature itself is not evil. The act of conflict is not inherently evil; it is in the execution that humans demonstrate the potential for evil.

But what do we mean when we describe something as evil?

Noun: profound immorality and wickedness, especially when regarded as a supernatural force.

What do we consider as EVIL?

Genocide

Terror

Destruction Maiming and mutilation

Serial murder

Sadism

To disrespect the consciousness of others, violating the anti-Golden Rule

To deliberately go against the human created moral code

Supremacy, actions by one person or group that believes itself to be inherently superior to all others

In Dante's "Inferno" (John Ciardi translation), it is stated that "Malice is the sin most hated by God."

To be considered evil, it must be intentional.

Early humans perceived natural evils as events like earthquakes that caused destruction and loss of life, which seemed to be outlets of evil. Disaster victims often suffered maiming and mutilation. These acts, such as a volcano eruption or tsunami, were attributed to supernatural beings (gods) in response to human acts that displeased them. In an attempt to understand the causes of calamities, they sought to establish a connection with human control through prayer or sacrifices, often involving blood. It was a primitive effort to comprehend the relationships between effects and their causes in their human-centered worldview.

From childhood, we learn about the "Big Bad Wolf," the "evil" animal that preys on gentle lambs and misbehaving children. However, the wolf itself is not inherently bad or evil. Like any other carnivore, wolves must kill for sustenance to survive. Every organism takes a life to ensure its own survival. If survival is considered good, then what is often deemed evil is, in essence, a means of securing life.

Humans possess the capacity to control their actions beyond instinct and survival needs. Empathy can be extended to other humans and even to other species. Acts of evil arise when a human goes against empathy, disregards the rights of another human, or intentionally inflicts pain on animals.

In Western religions, evil was often attributed to a destructive force guided by a supernatural anti-god, referred to as the Devil, Lucifer, Beelzebub, Mephistopheles, Satan, or Ahriman in Zoroastrianism. Regardless of the name, it represented an inexplicable evil that purportedly influenced humans to engage in destructive behaviors. When something adverse occurred, it was attributed to the devil's work, allowing humans to absolve themselves of responsibility, as humorously portrayed by Flip Wilson's character Geraldine: "The devil made me do it."

A predator is an individual, whether human or animal, that hunts a smaller, weaker person or animal. The predator, through deliberate behavior, plans to stalk someone and harbors harmful intentions towards them.

Humans are indeed predators and highly proficient ones. Through communication and tools, our hominin ancestors thrived despite encountering stronger and faster prey. Human success often required the suppression of empathy for the animals we hunted. Even in cultures that honor the hunted animal, the ultimate goal is to take a life for the sake of human success and continuation.

Being a predator does not inherently constitute an evil act; it is a part of our ancestral evolution, stemming from our roots as instinctive predators who survived and thrived. While animal tribes may engage in fighting to annihilate another group, only humans knowingly exterminate entire other groups.

Evil acts encompass actions that go beyond survival and deliberately inflict harm upon others. This harm can be directed towards both animals and other humans, with the intent to cause pain, suffering, or loss.

Humans, whether acting individually or as part of groups, can engage in predatory behavior for various "evil" reasons.

Tribal unity can lead to collective efforts in building or, conversely, the destruction of one tribe by another to prevent the victorious tribe from becoming victims of future retaliation or revenge. Genocide, a practice dating back to pre-recorded history, has been perpetuated through the ages.

Too often, humans have acted as predators towards their own kind. What drives otherwise morally upright individuals to commit evil deeds under altered circumstances?

It wasn't inherent instinct that drove humans to commit harm against their own species. Despite the residents of Jericho being fellow humans, descendants of Adam and Noah, the Bible states in Joshua 6:21 that God ordered the city's complete destruction: "put to the sword every living thing." This biblical narrative continues with the Israelites enacting similar orders throughout their campaign in Canaan. Was Joshua acting in an evil manner? Homer's epic, the Iliad, recounts the total destruction of Troy by the victorious Greeks. Numerous instances of such destruction are documented throughout history, spanning various civilizations.

Fast forward three millennia, and tribal genocide endures. Between 1491 and 1691, the indigenous population of Mesoamericans experienced a staggering 90% decline due to European diseases and military actions.

In 1493 Pope Alexander VI issued "Inter Caetera" or The Doctrine of Discovery that all peoples of newly discovered lands of the New World must be made Christian. For the indigenous peoples it was either convert or die.

In 1519, when Hernan Cortes arrived in the Aztec capital city of Tenochtitlan, it stood as one of the largest and most magnificent cities in the world, with a population ranging between 200,000 and 300,000. It boasted a twin-channel aqueduct system that surpassed any seen in plague-ravaged Europe of the time. Through a combination of disease, indigenous alliances, superior weaponry, and tactical advantages, the Spanish succeeded in eradicating the Aztec people and culture, reducing Tenochtitlan to ruins.

Under the banner of "Manifest Destiny," systematic genocide of native peoples was endorsed and embraced by both governments and invading colonists in pursuit of resources such as gold, land, and later, oil. Indigenous tribes were forcibly relocated from their ancestral lands, treaties were violated, forced sterilizations were carried out, bounties were placed on native scalps, and forced assimilation was enforced. Buffalo hunting grounds and fields were devastated, and tribal identity was suppressed. In the eyes of European law, Indians had no legal recourse.

The 1830 Indian Removal Act, known as the Trail of Tears, uprooted entire tribes from their fertile ancestral homes to desolate lands, a pattern repeated with the 1893 Oklahoma Land Rush and the 1920s oil rush that reclaimed the land.

Was "Manifest Destiny" inherently evil? To immigrants, it represented an opportunity for a better life, often oblivious to the impending consequences. However, policy-makers were aware, yet instead of fostering coexistence or cultural fusion, they endorsed actions rooted in ancient evil.

Since 2009, China has designated the Uyghurs in Xinjiang province as an Islamic separatist terrorist group. This classification has been used to justify long-term detentions, language and "education" erasure, forced relocation, and sterilization in an attempt to culturally annihilate the Uyghur people.

Indigenous genocide has persisted in the Brazilian forests under President Jair Bolsonaro.

The Holocaust witnessed the extermination of six million Jews and non-desirables at the hands of the Nazis. In Bosnia and Rwanda, millions of individuals from one ethnic group were slaughtered, with shifting fortunes of war leading to the subsequent killing of millions from the opposing group. ISIS executed "non-believers" and later extended their brutality to anyone even remotely suspected of affiliation, resulting in the revengeful killing of both innocent individuals and guilty parties.

Even Japan, a nation known for valuing self-control and harmony, saw its soldiers engage in unprecedented rampages of destruction during World War II. These atrocities, committed by ordinary Japanese soldiers, often appeared rooted in pure evil. The Japanese army carried out an infamous "Three All" extermination policy, "loot all, kill all, burn all." The Japanese Unit 731 experimented on prisoners with plague weapons.

The Holocaust was a planned orderly mass extermination of Jews, Romas, dissenters, gays, and anyone less than of the pure Aryan race. The term "Genocide" was coined when the German doctors used "undesirables" for medical disease and sterilization experiments on Jews. After the war, they justified their atrocious behavior with "*Befehlsnotstand,*" they were exempt as they were simply following orders.

Sociologist Martin Shaw described the Cambodian genocide by the xenophobic Khmer Rouge in Cambodia as "the purest genocide of the Cold War era." Over two million people; a quarter of the countries' population, were killed, including most of the educated in "the Killing Fields."

Humans have evolved to build tribes based on other issues. There are religious tribes, economic ideology tribes, professional tribes as well as the locality tribes. These are tribes of our imagination because they actualize in our minds. The tribes don't always have a physical feel and the reason they fight or have conflict are generally not pragmatic. Unlike a watering hole, there is no physical worth to the idea of a political party.

Similar to biological connection, these connections that we form with our tribes encourages us to protect our tribe and allow reduction of empathy towards another tribe. The evidence of this intangible phenomenon is the religious wars and the wars the happen between peoples of the same race and culture.

Memory of past transgressions by another can cause "empathy erosion." An act can cause a need for revenge, even against a friend or member of one's tribe when a difference in opinion is observed or when a crack in the structure of the tribe is revealed. It can be as mundane as a sister "stealing" a boyfriend or multiple groups seeking a limited resource undermining previous co-operation. Blood feuds and vendettas have continued for centuries.

In time of war, a conscious effort is made to distance our tribe from the enemy. This effort is often made with the use of terms to dehumanize the enemy so the evil actions can be justified and acceptable. Germans became "krauts," Japanese became "nips," and Viet Namese became "gooks." To white racists "Negros" became "coons." Besides that, the indigenous peoples became "godless savages," definition of which suggests a lowly animal whose life is sub-human with no value and whose killing is easily acceptable.

Racial epitaphs push the perception of the other tribe as being non-human and undeserving of any empathy. The Nazis claimed the Jews were "a life not worth living." It is important to remember that the gangs of even a few members create "evil" actions, attacking other groups or individuals following the same excuses of revenge. To justify their "evil actions," the perpetrators see themselves as the true victims. The Ku Klux Klan played the victim following destruction of their "genteel southern culture" by union carpetbaggers during Reconstruction. Al Qaida justified the attack on Twin Towers as retaliation for years of European colonialization on Arab soil. In wars, both sides may justify their actions regardless of the heinous nature of their actions. In the view of themselves, they believe that they are as righteous as they are the true victim. "We are getting justice against their evil."

Unfortunately, the truth is ordinary people will do almost anything if it seems normalized by peers, whether it's burning trash, driving too fast, or taking part in a lynching. An individual may be criticized for unethical behavior, but if a group does the same thing, the unethical behavior is acceptable. Group norms provide "psychological camouflage."

But some acts are intentional by a single person. A sadist has no one to hide behind, though they may still see themselves as victims since they commit acts that intentionally cause harm to larger audience. They feel personal elation in the pain of others.

The extreme of lack of empathy is the condition of anti-social behavior. Anti-social Personality Disorder (ASPD) is described by the American Psychiatric Association's Diagnostic and Statistical Manual, as an Axis II personality disorder characterized by: "a pervasive pattern of disregard for, and violation of, the rights of others."

Each human develops internal filters which work as self-imposed limits on actions. The best example of this is when we stop ourselves from cussing or using profanity in our speech. The brain may think of a hurtful word or destructive action, but the filter can stop implementation.

By nature, and nurture filters develop that holdback thoughts, and limits thoughts from becoming actions. In disorders the filters do not always work removing empathy for potential victims.

Imagination, a uniquely human trait, surpasses the capabilities of animals. Our aptitude for planning extends across vast spans of time. Humans possess the ability to envision solutions to problems and mitigate perceived threats, even if these threats exist only in our imagination.

As a species, we harbor an innate curiosity. We observe the world around us and endeavor to decipher its mysteries. Why did the boulder tumble? What caused the sun to vanish? Why did illness befall me?

Certain answers are readily comprehensible, or at the very least, easily accepted. However, the principle that every effect stems from a cause remains ingrained in our minds. When a cause is not immediately apparent, we conjure explanations. We weave narratives that link known elements of our environment. Even today, our imaginative faculties are employed to fathom the reasons behind unfortunate occurrences that befall virtuous individuals.

In the realm of potent actions, there demands a forceful actor. Thus, we fashioned myths that magnified such actions. Deities emerged, orchestrating events and influencing human behavior. Rainfall, for instance, was attributed to the gods; if the heavens remained dry, the gods were displeased and only appeasement through blood sacrifices could soothe their anger. These mythical beings provided explanations for occurrences and served as scapegoats for personal misconduct. It was easier to attribute one's actions to Buluc Chabtan, Apollo, or Thor.

Animals, lacking our level of imagination, perceive situations pragmatically. Imagination, when channeled for evil, can be cultivated or, more aptly, "nurtured." Members of a group often fuel each other's inclinations, driving them to surpass one another in their malevolent pursuits.

Ego is inherently self-centered, prioritizing self-wants and desires as the foremost and sole concerns, devoid of any filters. Ego propels us forward, compelling us to strive for more, amass more, and become more.

Paleoanthropologist Daniel Lieberman astutely remarked, *"We are not only evolved to cooperate, innovate, and communicate but also to steal, lie, cheat, and murder."*

Accountability serves as the final component of the equation, tethered to one's participation within the tribe. In animal tribes, codes of conduct exist and failing to adhere to these norms incurs disciplinary actions from the group. Humans, however, have instituted laws and learned morals to establish consequences for misconduct.

When an action is sanctioned or endorsed by the tribe, individual accountability diminishes. Deeds that might be perceived as malevolent, yet align with the values of the tribe, are deemed virtuous rather than sinister—sometimes even hailed as heroic. Such acts are deemed empathetic to the group's principles, revealing the collective's lack of empathy for the victim. Soldiers, for instance, are absolved of personal accountability for their actions, regardless of the cruelty displayed, when these actions occur within the larger context of warfare and align with the overarching goal of safeguarding the tribe.

Society has endeavored to institute accountability for evil through individual actions, ranging from internments to executions. In the aftermath of the Second World War, the International Military Tribunal was established to hold those responsible for their malevolent deeds accountable. German leaders who orchestrated the Holocaust faced trials for their crimes against humanity.

Subsequent trials have addressed crimes against humanity as well, such as the 1993 International Criminal Tribunal for the former Yugoslavia (ICTY), which was created by the UN Security Council to investigate and prosecute international crimes committed within the region.

The subsequent year witnessed the establishment of a criminal tribunal in response to the genocide in Rwanda, addressing systematic assaults against civilian populations rooted in ethnic, racial, or religious motives.

Accountability manifests in various forms; actions that transgress the law are met with punishment within a legal framework or condemnation from one's peers. Alternatively, accountability can reside within the realm of imagination, whether intrinsic—a result of one's conscious—or extrinsic, perceived as actions being judged by an unseen entity akin to Santa Claus ("he sees you when you're sleeping") or a higher power like God.

The truly malevolent lack any internal sense of accountability, devoid of remorse for their deeds. Irrespective of the nature of their actions, whether trivial like shoplifting or grave like serial killings, a sadist harbors no empathy for their victim, deriving satisfaction solely from their internal gratification.

Evil is a creation of humans. Can we transcend it to become a superior species? Can we attribute it to a vestige of the reptilian aspect of our brain's evolution, or is that merely another justification for the subjugation of reason?

While the three components of the equation persist, the Predator, originating from survival instincts, can be tempered by the logic stemming from our conscious awareness of our impact on others and on ourselves. Imagination will continue to serve as a tool for creation, comprehension, and exploration, facilitating the expansion of our knowledge, particularly of our own beings. Enhanced communication, especially through direct exchanges between parties involved, will heighten awareness of accountability and the far-reaching consequences of one's actions. Humans have demonstrated a greater capacity for empathy toward others and even other species than observed anywhere else in nature.

Empathy serves as the most potent counterforce to Evil, recognizing the other as a fellow human harboring similar needs and a shared desire for life. Adam Smith, an 18th-century economist, acknowledged that while we are fundamentally self-centered, our greatest achievements arise from the identification of common interests that promote mutual growth.

With our evolutionary trajectory encompassing both intellectual prowess and emotional empathy, being human will eternally entail an internal struggle between these two forces. The question then becomes: How will we manage our instinctual self-interest against the impulse to sacrifice for the well-being of others?

How to Not Make War

Only humans engage in fights and killings driven by abstract concepts not rooted in the physical world. We wage conflicts over intangibles such as borders, economies, religions, sales territories, and even philosophies.

Humans occupy the position of apex predators, perched atop the food chain. While we hunt for sustenance, we've escalated our predation to include our own kind. As sapiens encountered other hominins, they encountered established rivals. Armed with superior tools and a penchant for cooperation, sapiens emerged victorious, leaving other hominins extinct.

Dante famously stated in *the Inferno*, *"Fraud is the vice of which man alone is capable."* We possess the ability to betray the trust of others, a vital pillar supporting society. We can manipulate the truth to suit our personal desires.

Throughout history, war has been an ever-present fixture, often deemed necessary and inevitable. Even the Bible alludes to wars: *"And you will hear of wars and rumors of wars. See that you are not alarmed, for this must take place, but the end is not yet."* (Mark 13:7, English Standard Version). Alexander Hamilton echoed this sentiment, viewing war as an inescapable facet of human existence: *"the fiery and destructive passions of war reign in human breast with much more powerful sway than the mild and beneficent sentiments of peace."*

Around seven million years ago, hominins branched off as a separate species of the primate family tree.

Chimpanzees and bonobos encompass the Pan genus. The separate paths of evolution occurred approximately 1.5 to 2 million years ago as a result of the formation of the Congo River physically separating them.

Idyllic depictions of "the lion lying down with the lamb" remain in the realm of fairy tales, incompatible with the laws of survival. The lion, a carnivore, is naturally inclined to prey on the herbivorous lamb for sustenance. Coexisting peacefully would deprive the lion of its food source, leading to its eventual starvation causing the extinction of other hominin species.

Around seven million years ago, hominins branched off from the primate family tree. The Pan branch encompasses chimpanzees and bonobos. This split, occurring approximately 1.5 to 2 million years ago, coincided with the formation of the Congo River. While visually similar, these primate species embody two contrasting aspects of hominin nature. Chimpanzees often exhibit violence and suspicion toward outsiders. With muscles situated for greater strength, chimpanzees possess roughly four times the strength of equivalently sized humans, potentially providing an evolutionary advantage in physical conflicts.

In contrast, bonobo society is characterized by a female-dominated structure that's more welcoming to strangers. Bonobos showcase cooperation, compassion, empathy, and sensitivity. Their smaller canines and larger emotional brain regions set them apart. They exhibit enhanced cooperation and an aptitude for learning.

These differences mirror the dual facets of human personality—reacting to fear (akin to chimpanzees) or pursuing pleasure (similar to bonobos). Hominins needed aggression to defend scavenged resources, yet the development of agriculture and sophisticated tools necessitated cooperation.

However, conflict resolution is not limited to fighting. Gorillas, for instance, employ chest-beating as a means of intimidation to avoid physical confrontations. Such evolved communication techniques demonstrate that conflict isn't always advantageous.

Human beings are unique in their ability to make choices in conflicts that go beyond natural instincts, impulse, or logic. Our decision-making extends to choosing between alternatives like turning left or right, eating or abstaining, and moving forward or stopping, based on our volition.

Aristotle asserted that *"the ability to reason is the one capacity or function which separates humans from other animals; being rational is our defining quality, our 'final cause,' our 'telos.'"* True excellence lies in those individuals who genuinely reason well and base their actions on rational thought.

A philosophical query arises: "What defines our humanity?" Answers span from our tool usage, communication skills, and capacity for empathy to our ability to create and appreciate art.

However, we are also the sole species known to fight and kill over imaginary constructs and myths (such as borders, religions, philosophies, wealth, tribal identity, and ownership). Conflicts often stem from one group's refusal to acknowledge the myths held by another. These myths may be intangible, but the suffering inflicted by wars is all too real.

Beyond mere resource depletion, empathy has played a critical role in tempering human conflicts. The ability to recognize our shared species and feel the pain of loss can foster restraint. Evolutionary theories posit that maternal care contributed to the development of empathy, with human females generally exhibiting higher levels of empathy than males. Humans are capable of both empathy and competition, a duality present in advanced primates. Depending on the context, we can manifest either trait, and our intellect can override our innate competitive instincts.

Humans possess a unique form of restraint: an understanding of the consequences of our actions. Whether termed consciousness or guilt this inner sense prompts a feeling that we're being watched—by God, Santa, or the law. Our behavior, aligning with moral values, promises reward, while deviating from morality invites punishment. Morality stems from empathy—a recognition of justice and equality among members of the tribe.

Conflicts, whether personal or global, emerge from the fear of loss—fear that something will be taken from us. Philosopher Bertrand Russell stated, *"Fear is the main source of superstition, and one of the main sources of cruelty. To conquer fear is the beginning of wisdom."*

Religious values, initially conceived to promote higher human standards, have paradoxically ignited wars. These religious conflicts persist to this day, exemplified by the enduring struggles between Catholics and Protestants in Europe, as well as Shias and Sunnis within Islam. Tribalism fuels these conflicts, as evidenced by the 2022 Russian invasion of Ukraine—a forceful assertion of disparate tribal identities over the same physical territory.

President and five-star general Dwight Eisenhower, having witnessed war firsthand as a career military officer, recognized the growth of the military-industrial complex. Throughout the Cold War era and his presidential term, he grew increasingly wary of the potential hazards posed by a permanent weapons industry. In his 1961 farewell address, he warned, "In the councils of government, we must guard against the acquisition of unwarranted influence, whether sought or unsought, by the military-industrial complex." Eisenhower underscored that every fired bullet, launched warship, and propelled rocket extracted a toll from those who yearned for sustenance, warmth, and basic necessities. The collective labor, scientific ingenuity, and aspirations of humankind were being diverted toward weaponry.

It's a disconcerting paradox that nations often lack the means to feed their citizens but boast multimillion-dollar tanks. The world remains flooded with AK-47 assault rifles, legally manufactured in various countries. These instruments of destruction, whether domestic or international, stem from a fear of fellow humans.

The concept of revenge stems from the desire to restore equilibrium and rectify wrongs. Interactions driven by revenge typically involve participants who are unlikely to cross paths again. The motivations often pivot on personal gratification, deriving pleasure from the "sweet taste of revenge" that triggers pleasurable responses in the brain's reward centers.

Alternatives to revenge do exist. Some may consider the offense too trivial to warrant retaliation, prioritize preserving an ongoing relationship over immediate retaliation, or execute a defensive maneuver to thwart further harm. The decision to strike back hinges on evaluating whether it's worth the cost, or if restraint will instead empower the aggressor.

Forgiveness, on the other hand, aims to mend strained relationships. Religious teachings offer guidance in this realm—Christian doctrine suggests "turning the other cheek," Aristotle's "Golden Mean" advocates a balanced approach, and Ludwig von Bertalanffy's concept of "Flow Equilibrium" posits that living organisms strive to maintain order and organization by avoiding entropy's increase.

Human beings transcend natural forces and instinctual responses. We possess the unique capacity to choose. This capacity isn't exclusive to individuals; entire nations can also opt for peaceful coexistence. As 16th-century observer Father Matteo Ricci noted of China, "*in a kingdom of almost limitless expanse and innumerable population and abounding in copious supplies of every description, though they have a well-equipped army and navy that could easily conquer the neighboring nations, neither the King nor his people ever think of waging a war of aggression They are quite content with what they have and are not ambitious of conquest. In this respect they are much different from the people of Europe, who are frequently discontent with their own governments and covetous of what others enjoy. While the nations of the West seem to be entirely consumed with the idea of supreme domination, they cannot even preserve what their ancestors have bequeathed them, as the Chinese have done through a period of some thousands of years....*"

Forgiveness, as opposed to revenge, is more plausible within close relationships. However, a sense of balance must be maintained to prevent perceived vulnerability, which could inadvertently invite further harm.

Human empathy possesses the potential to extend beyond immediate tribes to encompass even those tribes embroiled in conflicts. Understanding the underlying causes of conflicts can pave the way for mutually beneficial resolutions. Viewing adversaries as fellow humans with needs enhances comprehension of how those needs can be addressed without inflicting harm. Through logical reasoning, empathy, and understanding, the probability and impact of war can be diminished.

Numerous conditions that once fanned the flames of war have been reduced. Formerly, conflicts often centered on resource scarcity. Today, increased food production and international aid have dramatically curbed starvation. Neutral mediators and dialogues have emerged as effective tools to settle disputes between neighboring nations, defusing tensions without resorting to armed aggression. Global media ensures that local conflicts gain international exposure.

While oppressive news making regimes persist, the number of individuals enjoying varying degrees of free speech is on the rise. Such individuals are less inclined to embrace hostilities as a means to voice their grievances. A 2011 study underscored the success rate of non-violent resistance movements, exceeding that of violent counterparts by a wide margin.

The quest for nonviolent resolutions to conflicts has gained heightened significance due to technological advancements. Through most of history, conflicts mirrored animalistic struggles—predominantly one-on-one or group clashes.

In 1948, the United Nations General Assembly introduced the Universal Declaration of Human Rights—a monumental initiative outlining the basic rights to which every person across all nations is entitled. While its realization isn't always absolute, the Declaration presents a universal ideal that illuminates the potential of humanity. Since its inception, progress has been evident—slavery has receded, free markets, education, access to electricity, and women's rights have flourished.

In contrast to earlier centuries when war claimed 15% of lives, the 20th century, despite two world wars and numerous regional conflicts, witnessed a reduced death rate of 5%. This trend has endured well into the 21st century, underscoring a promising trajectory toward greater global peace.

The numbers may appear counterintuitive given the daily reports of localized and systematic killings. However, what often goes unnoticed is that historical wars and casualties far exceeded recent conflicts in terms of scale, particularly in relation to population size. Yet, these significant conflicts occurred in different corners of the world. The Mayas of the 14th century, for instance, were oblivious to Europe's "Hundred Years War," just as 17th century Europeans were unaware of China's "Ming–Qing Transition." In today's interconnected world, local conflicts are swiftly disseminated globally through international communication channels.

Global conditions have consistently improved. Following the horrors of the world wars, a period of "The Long Peace" settled over Europe, characterized by the absence of major wars between European states—until the Ukrainian invasion. Despite extensive emigration the actual loss of life, though devastating, remained relatively small compared to previous national conflicts. While major conflicts have arisen as proxies for major powers, participants in each conflict have shown restraint, refraining from total warfare.

Since 1945, nuclear-armed nations engaged in an arms race that had the potential to obliterate humanity. However, the realization of mutual destruction led to a state of equilibrium known as MAD (Mutual Assured Destruction). Even after Israel, India, and Pakistan acquired nuclear capabilities, each exercised restraint, understanding the catastrophic consequences of a retaliatory strike.

Millions perished under the Nazis, with additional millions falling victim to Stalin's and Mao's purges, as well as failed forced agricultural policies. The "Year of Living Dangerously" in 1965 Indonesia saw over 700,000 casualties, while Cambodia's "Killing Fields" claimed the lives of 2.5 million in the late 1970s. The 1994 Rwandan genocide, orchestrated by the Hutu government against the Tutsis, resulted in an estimated death toll between 500,000 and 1 million.

Nevertheless, fatalities stemming from genocidal conflicts have decreased worldwide.

Ongoing fighting in the middle-east, from Gaza to Iran, continued into 2024 due to ancient ethnic, religious, and tribal grudges pitting tribes against each other and governments materially backed by outside countries. Thousands of combatants and collateral damage civilians have been killed by fighting.

The 2023 terror attack by Hamas upon Israel resulted in thousands of civilian deaths on both sides. Wholesale killings targeted upon civilians, for revenge or planned opportunity, disrupted an uneasy peace and reduced the potential for future peace through understanding.

Advancements in weaponry, from catapults and mangonels to cannons, have continually heightened the distance between attacker and victim, as well as the lethality of the weapons employed. Warriors are no longer required to face their adversaries or even recognize their victims. Torture and slavery have been formally eradicated in developed nations. The interdependence of the global economy renders conflicts with trading partners financially irrational.

In the wake of colossal human and material losses incurred during the two world wars, the allure of war has markedly diminished. While individuals may still perform heroic acts, the concept of war as heroic has largely waned. Commencing a war is increasingly regarded as an act driven by madness.

While conflicts persist and are likely to continue, casualty numbers are decreasing even as the global population continues to grow.

Peace treaties, however, cannot halt climate change and its far-reaching impacts on lands and populations. With rising seas and arid lands, those affected have little choice but to migrate, becoming climate migrants.

Yet, where can they go? The answer lies in seeking countries with habitable land, leading to migration and subsequent conflicts with existing residents. This situation often pits migrants from struggling states against their more developed neighbors.

Once the root causes of migration are comprehended, stable nations could collaborate with migrants to address or alleviate these factors, enabling them to remain in their homelands. Migrants with low local total fertility rates (TFRs), equipped with training, could help sustain the population, serving as workers, consumers, and taxpayers. Alternatively, residents might resist this course of action.

Opting for conflict may seem straightforward, while the rational choice involves exercising restraint through negotiations that maximize mutual benefits. This calls upon uniquely human capabilities, setting us apart from other animals – we can quietly listen, share perspectives, and pursue shared objectives. We possess the capacity to choose between our inner chimpanzee and inner bonobo; war need not be an inherent curse but rather a cultural invention.

Human progress has been built upon communication and inter-group cooperation, neither of which war embodies. Trust, shame, mercy, sympathy, and gratitude have been instrumental in our successes, enhancing our chances of survival.

Humanism, associated with altruism, mutual compassion, and fundamental ethical principles, experienced A resurgence during the Renaissance, elaborating on Aristotle's concept of human dignity. In contemporary times, it forms the bedrock of "human rights." A foundation of the Enlightenment was that all men had equal natural rights to individual life and liberty.

We have acknowledged the peacemakers – those who find alternatives to warfare. Annually, the Nobel Peace Prize is bestowed upon individuals actively working to mitigate the threat of war for the betterment of humankind. As scripture suggests, "Blessed are the peacemakers, for they shall be called the children of Heaven."

In earlier times, when early sapiens inhabited a seemingly boundless world with ample tribal abundance, expansion, and migration possibilities, the need for conflict was largely constrained by the vision of those involved.

However, as the human population has burgeoned, resources have not kept pace. Despite advancements in food and energy production efficiency, humanity faces what appears to be a "Full world." Survival hinges on our ability to communicate and collaborate in pursuit of the common good of humanity.

Throughout history, much conflict has arisen from the pursuit of material acquisition, such as iron, oil, and agricultural land. Since the "Great Expansion" of the 1950s, western nations have amassed substantial wealth.

For those living in abundance, questions emerge about how much is truly sufficient and what constitutes life's essentials. Gandhi's words resonate: "Live simply so others may live." Can comprehending genuine needs diminish the clamor for excessive material possessions and mitigate the conflicts that arise from unbridled acquisition?

We have the capability to look beyond physical differences of race, sexual orientation, intelligence, physical size and differences of the mind: nationalism, religion, or economics to find our mutual human betterment.

The Unnatural Species, Genes, AI, the Synthocene, and Transhuman

After designing the planet, the subsequent vital endeavor revolves around us. Could our next evolutionary step be driven by human design, increasingly involving the integration of synthetic creations of our own making?

In 1964, author Arthur C. Clarke pondered: "I suspect that organic or biological evolution has nearly reached its end, and we stand at the inception of inorganic or mechanical evolution, which will progress thousands of times more swiftly. To contend with the information explosion, we might develop a mechanism to directly record information onto the brain."

Thus, we find ourselves as the architects of our own existence. Design theorist Tony Fry asserts: "We don't just extend ourselves through technology; technology now extends itself through us." Technology has permeated so deeply and been so embraced that it has become an intrinsic part of our lives. The configuration of technology parallels the design of our culture.

The origins of designed technology trace back to the Enlightenment, marked by a faith in technology born from the Scientific Revolution. This faith ushered in remarkable advancements in steam power and electrical communication spanning the 17th through the 19th centuries.

Yet, the true extent of technology's power manifested during the First World War. Motorized tanks, airplanes, poisonous gases, and electric battery submarines elevated warfare to unprecedented levels of space and devastation. The application of physics further amplified its potential during the Second World War with radar, communication, computers, and ultimately the atomic bomb. These events raised questions about technology's impact on us and the forces we had unwittingly unleashed.

The apprehensions regarding technology's potential were evident in the political climate of the Red Scare and McCarthyism. Popular media mirrored these fears, portraying biological threats like "*Invasion of the Body Snatchers*" or physical dangers like "*War of the Worlds.*" Had we begun to alter the very laws of nature? Did enigmatic phenomena like UFOs, which emerged in 1947, suggest an external presence trying to halt our self-destruction, as depicted in "*The Day the Earth Stood Still*"? Such inquiries compelled us to scrutinize our technological utilization, particularly as we harnessed new tools in biology and physics to shape our future.

Biologist Julian Huxley reflected in 1957: "*Up till now human life has generally been...nasty, brutish, and short.' The human species can, if it wishes, transcend itself—not just sporadically, with an individual here and there embodying certain characteristics, but in its entirety, as humanity.*"

Hominins have already engineered modifications to enhance bodily performance. Surgical interventions in the Bronze Age Middle East addressed injuries or diseases, repairing damaged bodies.

Art and writing, external mediums, amplify human capabilities, complementing the brain's functions. Hominins were the pioneers of communicating symbolic thoughts across time and distance through visual and auditory means. From painting and sculpture to the advent of photography, thoughts gained permanence and transferability. The phonograph immortalized sounds and spoken words. Today, simple computers store more data than all previous media combined.

As we gain greater control over our evolution, the next strides could be truly revolutionary, possibly transcending conventional evolutionary pathways. Synthetic adaptations could be meticulously tailored to provide optimal solutions for specific needs, unencumbered by historical solutions.

In this context, "synthetic" encompasses any human-created design or feature, spanning metals, ceramics, plastics, biological elements, or silicone-computer components.

Biological

Mary Shelley's "*Frankenstein*" encapsulates the notion of humanity assuming mastery over its evolution. Written during the early stages of the Industrial Revolution, a period characterized by the belief in human capacity to achieve through science, Shelley employed biological components, including a reanimated brain, to fashion her "creature." This being, constructed from lifeless parts but reanimated through the then-emerging technology of electricity, epitomized humanity's newfound dominion over nature.

Organ transplantation found initial success in the period immediately following the donor's death. Living donors facilitate compatible kidney and skin grafts, ensuring donor survival and enabling recipient regeneration. The challenge of incompatibility and rejection has been mitigated through immunosuppressant medications.

Medical procedures expanded beyond internal organ and bone repairs to encompass alterations in physical appearance. Facial implants can enhance attributes like chin and cheek structure, correct misshapen heads, and address cleft palates.

The discovery of DNA (Deoxyribonucleic Acid), the molecular repository of all life's genetic information, including that of humans, dates back to 1869. However, comprehension of DNA's structure and function, enabling compatibility assessments, was achieved in 1953.

The first successful organ transplant, involving kidneys from identical twin brothers with matching DNA, occurred in 1954. Subsequent years witnessed pancreas, heart, and liver transplants, followed by advancements in addressing various organ failures.

Sadly, the supply of organs falls short of demand. An estimated 20-35% of patients awaiting transplants succumb before finding a suitable match. Up to four out of five individuals seeking kidney replacements perish during the wait, which can extend up to four and a half years.

Leveraging 3-D printing and biological materials, customized organs like livers and kidneys can be produced to precisely fit recipients. Natural splints are implanted, and as patients grow, the cells proliferate. By 2030, a bright outlook envisions widespread availability of 3-D printed livers, intervertebral disks, heart valves, skin, sphincters, bones, jaws, cranial plates (composed of heated titanium fused by a potent laser and coated in biocompatible ceramics), and lungs.

One alternative lies in xenotransplants, where organs or living material are sourced from non-human mammals. In 2001, the first patents for "knock-out pigs" were granted through genetic engineering work, demonstrating the concept of creating genetically modified pigs by "knocking out" specific trait-controlled genes.

An initial endeavor involved transplanting a baboon organ into a young human female. Though the girl did not survive, subsequent attempts were made using baboons. However, these organs deteriorated more rapidly than human organs, and the recipients experienced hyperacute rejection of the foreign tissue.

Pigs have emerged as a focal point due to their controlled growth and organ similarities with humans. Through CRISPR (**C**lustered **R**egularly **I**nterspaced **S**hort **P**alindromic **R**epeats), ten pig genes were modified, and six human genes were inserted, making pigs potential sources of lungs, pancreas, kidneys, and livers. Notably, on January 7, 2022, a pig's heart was successfully transplanted into a human at the University of Maryland Medical Center. While the patient's life was brief, this achievement validated the viability of the procedure. A second transplant was performed in July 2023.

CRISPR, introduced for practical use in 2012, enables the precise alteration of DNA by adding or removing specific sequences.

As early as 1975, concerns emerged regarding the ethical implications of "recombinant DNA," described as a "God-like power" capable of gene correction and life-saving, yet potentially spiraling out of control.

The DNA's double helix carries the four code letters that define the unique attributes of each life form. DNA manipulation can activate or deactivate genes to achieve desired outcomes. Individuals capable of affording gene alteration could tailor perfection to their preferences, while others might remain "flawed." The dilemma transitions from technological feasibility to ethical desirability, raising the prospect of DNA with desirable traits becoming a commodity to engineer "perfect" offspring.

Another avenue of hope revolves around developmentally native stem cells, which have the potential to differentiate into various tissues. Stem cells, be they embryonic or adult, possess the ability to stimulate growth. They can serve as an artificial scaffold to cultivate new organs, though progress has been gradual. The term "stem cell" was first coined in 1908, with definitive evidence of ongoing stem cell activity in the brain emerging during the 1960s.

By injecting human cells into meticulously prepared animal embryos, like pigs, the integration bypasses the animal's capacity to assimilate human DNA into its own genetic code. Consequently, the host remains essentially untainted except for the desired human DNA-specific organ. By using cells from the recipient, the transplanted organ is genetically aligned, reducing the likelihood of rejection. Skin or gut cells from adults can be reprogrammed into *induced pluripotent stem cells* (iPSCs), offering a more ethically palatable solution and ensuring genetic compatibility with the recipient.

The ethical quandary accompanying these advances revolves around the incorporation of animal DNA into humans. Could animals become *chimeras*, embodying traits of multiple species? These legal and ethical inquiries extend beyond biological research. To address these concerns, presidents have sought counsel from experts, with policy direction shifting along with administrative changes. In 1996, President Clinton established the National Bioethics Advisory Commission, which was replaced by President George W. Bush's conservative President's Council on Bioethics (PCBE) in 2001, resulting in limitations on stem cell research and abortion. The PCBE was then succeeded by the Presidential Commission for the Study of Bioethical Issues during the Obama administration. This evolution of leadership elicited both criticism and praise along philosophical and religious lines.

Detractors of bioethical opposition have been dubbed "bioluddites," drawing parallels to the 19th-century resistance to mechanical progress. They oppose invitro fertilization, cloning, genetic enhancements, reproductive self-determination, and GMOs, favoring what they perceive as "natural law." Their standpoint maintains that humanity should remain unaltered, preserving human dignity. The question arises: would enhanced humans render normal humans unequal?

Bioluddites were integral to the "deep ecology" movement of the 1970s, advocating for reduced interference with nature. They challenge the necessity of these transformations, questioning whether we are inherently sufficient. Their stance hinges on the belief that no individual should exceed the bounds of humanity.

Evolution is a complex process. Mutations occur randomly and can prove advantageous, neutral, or harmful. These mutations form the bedrock of evolution, driving species to permanent improvement. However, mutations can also lead to harm. Physical or cognitive mutations may diminish an individual's ability to survive.

To date, random DNA mutations show no preference for their impact on a species. Whether advantageous, irrelevant, or detrimental, these effects are equally likely, and the process exhibits no favoritism. Furthermore, multiple mutations can occur during the replication of a single DNA strand.

Could biological nature be enhanced beyond its fundamental DNA structure? Early thinkers like Aldous Huxley, in "*Brave New World*" (1931), believed so. Visions of perfecting the human body by eliminating imperfections such as allergies, dwarfism, ADHD, Autism, and vulnerability to diseases have been depicted. Huxley envisioned perfection through controlled fertilization, aiming for a harmonious society of nearly identical individuals—a response to the turmoil of the "Great War" and the societal upheavals of the 1920s. He anticipated a standardized biological counterpart to Henry Ford's assembly line, envisioning maximized efficiency. Huxley hailed from an era of boundless population growth. In his fictional society, the drug "soma" optimized production by inducing happiness and tranquility in workers. He foreshadowed concepts like test-tube babies and gene manipulation's potential impact on human development.

Formal eugenics emerged in the early 20th century in the United Kingdom, intended to enhance population quality by promoting "desirable" traits and discouraging those deemed inferior, including through forced sterilization.

Unfortunately, the philosophy was co-opted by the Nazis in their quest for a "master race," perpetuating claims of German superiority and inferiority of other groups. The Lebensborn program exemplified this ideology, selecting officers and Aryan women to produce the "purest" offspring.

China has been actively developing an eugenics program since the 1980s, marking the post-Mao Zedong-Cultural Revolution era. BGI-Shenzhen, with over four thousand researchers, is at the forefront, sequencing over fifty thousand genomes annually—a remarkable undertaking that stands as the world's most ambitious program for optimizing DNA.

Genetic modification opens the door to "designer babies," offspring meticulously crafted for perfection. Imagine a child possessing the athletic prowess of Michael Phelps, the tennis prowess of Althea Gibson, the charisma of Charlize Theron and George Clooney, the compassion of Fred Rogers and Mother Teresa, the intellect of Ruth Bader Ginsburg and Elon Musk, and the artistic talents of Lin-Manuel Miranda and Meryl Streep. The child's DNA could be engineered, akin to ordering a custom-made car.

However, this engenders potentially unreasonable expectations for the child. While Michael Phelps boasts an exceptional athletic physique, his unparalleled work ethic played an instrumental role in his achievements. Althea Gibson's journey was marked by overcoming racial barriers, showcasing that even enhancements can't replace the determination required for success. Thus, while manipulation provides an edge, achievement hinges on multifaceted factors, raising questions about the implications for parent-child relationships.

Genetics constitutes a technology that, like others, advances each year. A child designed using one level of technology could lag behind a later-sibling designed with more advanced tools. How will interactions unfold between Daughter 0.1 and the succeeding generation of Daughter 0.2?

As with any technological revolution, concerns abound about potential misuse. There's the unsettling prospect of creating super soldiers armed with bio-weapons, crafting designer babies, shaping compliant workers through specialized castes, engineering crop-killing diseases, or unleashing invasive mutants.

Interestingly, superior offspring might not necessitate a eugenics lab. Over the past two centuries, improved diets, medical breakthroughs, and sanitation have boosted the average American male's height by nearly five inches—a rapid transformation far exceeding the pace of conventional evolution. In essence, humans, rather than the environment, are now architects of the species. The human lifespan has nearly doubled within a century, leading economist Robert Fogel to describe these changes as "techno-physio evolution."

Numerous perspectives on designing our descendants deliberately, as discussed in "*Homo designus*" (Chapter 17), revolve around potential technological advances. Ray Kurzweil's "Human 2.0" presents a theoretical exploration of a human body built with cutting-edge technology. Nanobots, minuscule robots measuring 0.1–10 micrometers, are introduced into the body for controlled distribution of nutrients and cellular repair—one cell and one molecule at a time, ensuring precise nutriment delivery. They even hold the potential to eliminate organs like the liver and kidneys by maintaining internal system cleanliness and insulin administration. Bloodstream-based Bio-MEMS (biomedical microelectromechanical systems) actively combat pathogens, administer medications, and promote blood clotting.

Rob Freitas introduced Respirocytes, robotic red blood cells capable of storing and delivering ten times the oxygen carried by regular cells, thereby diminishing the lungs' role. Nanorobots, mere virus-sized entities, could construct materials within the body, editing out aging genes while introducing bacterial and fungal counterparts to break down cholesterol and brain proteins.

The concept of cloning has permeated science fiction since primitive experiments emerged in the early 20th century. Notably, in 1958, John Gurdon made the first successful attempts at cloning using adult somatic cells, focusing on African clawed frogs. Dolly, a female sheep, became the pioneer mammal cloned using nuclear transfer in 1996. Subsequently, more than twenty species were successfully cloned, solidifying the practical viability of the process.

Media portrayals of cloning underscore its ambiguities and ignite debates about permissible human applications. While scientific challenges can be surmounted, ethical concerns are likely to steer or hinder the progress of human cloning.

The pivotal question arises: What is the overarching purpose? Are scientific endeavors driven by the aspiration to create superhumans, or do they aim to rectify natural imperfections? Achieving these objectives necessitates equitable access to biotechnologies.

Are we approaching the era of "*Homo evolutus*"? Could we be just a few generations away from DNA modifications substantial enough to usher in "a new kind of hominin"?

Synthetic

Robot, (Britannica dictionary): *any machine operated automatically, even if it doesn't resemble humans or function in a humanlike manner.*

Artificial intelligence (**AI**): (Britannica dictionary) *"the ability of a digital computer or computer-controlled robot to perform tasks commonly associated with intelligent beings."*

The lineage of robots traces back to the Automaton—a mechanical entity boasting some form of internal control. This concept dates back to ancient China and Egypt, where engineers crafted devices mimicking human actions. The Greeks introduced the term "Ex Machina," signifying "god from the machine." Czechoslovakian writer Karel Capek first coined the term "robot" in his 1921 play "R.U.R.," referring to a mechanical humanoid. The term "robot" now encompasses a diverse array of machines, from assembly line robots to knowledge-dispensing phones.

However, the term "Artificial Intelligence" (AI) proves somewhat misleading, as original intelligence isn't involved—only programmed instructions generating actions or decisions. AI operates as a data processing machine, executing calculations through selected algorithms to achieve desired outcomes. The accuracy of the outputted result hinges on the quantity of input data.

Similarly, the term "intelligence" doesn't accurately encapsulate human understanding. It's a swifter processor of "data" > "information" > "understanding." While AI might outperform humans in the first two stages, it falters when it comes to acquiring true understanding. AI can mimic and analyze, but its capabilities are confined to executing pre-programmed responses. AI is adept at processing data, leveraging its unlimited access and expansive reach, unaffected by emotional biases or preconceived notions. However, the domain of understanding remains firmly within the realm of humans for the foreseeable future.

Two categories of robots exist: Specific Task Robots (STRs) and General Purpose Robots (GPRs). STRs are programmed to perform a single designated task, such as repetitive drilling, delivering payloads, or vacuuming floors.

A GTR, a General Task Robot. This is the robot of science fiction that like a human is designed to perform multiple types of tasks. These are the most human like robots.

Robots of all forms are still tools to do a directed action without input into the action. Even the computers that led to the Turing Test (is the dialogue with a human or computer?) were from a series of programmed responses.

Ethical questions arise as with any new technology, where is the potential for things to go poorly? How will humans deal with robots?

With the popularity of robots in 1930s science fiction literature led author/scientist Isaac Asimov to create the three laws of robotics:

1. A robot may not injure a human being or, through inaction, allow a human being to come to harm.
2. A robot must obey the orders given it by human beings except where such orders would conflict with the First Law.
3. A robot must protect its own existence as long as such protection does not conflict with the First or Second Laws.

To ascribe to Asimov's laws a robot would have to have AI in order to recognize that its actions might harm humans, an ability not available to an STR. Safety programs have to be initiated by human programmers.

Other authors have added additional laws:

* A robot must establish its identity as a robot in all cases.
  (Lyuben Dilov)
* A robot must know it is a robot.
  (Nikola Kesarovski)
* A robot must reproduce. As long as such reproduction does not interfere with the First, Second, or Third Law.
  (Harry Harrison)
* All robots endowed with comparable human reason and conscience should act towards one another in a spirit of brotherhood, the AIonAI law.
  (Hutan Ashrafian)

GTRs or Mechanical "people" have been a recurring theme in movies since the 1927 German film "Metropolis," featuring a mechanical human-like figure that mimics an actual person's form. The portrayal of mechanical individuals in media gained traction during the 1950s, exemplified by characters like I TOBOR from TV's "Captain Video" and Robbie from the movie "Forbidden Planet." Despite their interactivity and humanoid appearance, these entities remained programmed tools. Artists rendered them in human form as it was the most recognizable model available. However, one might question the wisdom of replicating human fallacies in design. The presence of GTR characters in movies and TV offers enhanced relatability and simplifies costuming. Yet, the creation of these characters primarily aimed to delve into the essence of human existence rather than predict future AI advancements.

The 2011 DARPA Robotics Challenge (DRC) was initiated to "*develop human-supervised ground robots capable of executing complex tasks in dangerous, degraded, human-engineered environments, promoting innovation in human-supervised robotic technology for disaster-response operations.*" The objective was to stimulate innovation in human-supervised robotic technology for disaster response. The goal was to create self-acting robots proficient in handling a diverse range of perilous tasks typically performed by humans. After a span of several years marked by robot mishaps, the KAIST team from South Korea emerged victorious with DRC-HUBO in 2015. Within five years, numerous robots were autonomously running without assistance.

In 2017, Boston Dynamics, eschewing anthropomorphic design, conceived Handle. By synthesizing the optimal mobility attributes of legs and wheels, they engineered a self-contained robot surpassing human physical capabilities.

As robots undertake more intricate tasks, they must evolve towards greater autonomy, resembling GTRs, and relying less on human programmers. Beyond merely executing assigned tasks, robots should be capable of downloading and adjusting their programs to suit the task at hand. This autonomy necessitates three fundamental characteristics: Perception, Decision, and Actuation. The ability to execute actions devoid of human intervention is paramount, especially for robots on extraterrestrial expeditions where communication delays could prove detrimental.

However, a crucial question arises: How will robots navigate unanticipated scenarios? Similar to early life forms on Earth, a robot's AI algorithm must undergo changes or evolution to best address unforeseen challenges and ensure survival. Termed "artificial evolution," this process can occur within hours or minutes within the robot, whereas biological evolution spanned billions of years. Equipped with an onboard 3-D printer and suitable materials, a robot could design, produce, test, and employ necessary components, thus transforming into a craft distinct from its original design. In essence, this innovation could herald Deep Space 2.0.

Nonetheless, it is imperative to remember that humans remain the responsible agents, not robots.

AI, or Artificial Intelligence, represents the integration of computer inputs and controls, extending its influence from toasters to autonomous self-driving vehicles, wheelchairs, delivery carts, boats, golf carts, and even integrating seamlessly within buildings. Entire buildings can adopt self-regulation, adapting internal environments to occupants' needs and external weather conditions. Moreover, buildings can self-repair and update, relying on self-sustained energy sources. Drawing parallels to the computer in the Star Trek series, the AI in the form of the cloud serves as a repository of data accessible to all. This AI won't merely respond to commands; it will function as a collaborative partner akin to the fictional KITT in "*Knight Rider*" or Hal from "2001: *A Space Odyssey*"—a synthetic co-pilot interacting with the human crew while managing ship operations.

The capabilities of AI encompass data processing, converting raw data into valuable information. While the artificial nature of AI is undeniable, the question of true intelligence remains. Are even the most advanced AI models nothing more than highly sophisticated calculating devices, devoid of emotions, morals, or ethical considerations? Historical devices initially used the term "thinking intelligence," acknowledging their limitations. While a computer is essentially a calculating machine, the term "Artificial Intelligence" is widely recognized and understood, referring to machines that process data through synthetic interactions, yielding informational outcomes.

Humanoid robots, imbued with affective computing, could find utility as companions or in contexts seeking interpersonal connections, such as therapy. For instance, "social robot" Sophia, designed by Hanson Robotics, serves as a companion and can engage in simple verbal interactions. Sophia can process language input and incorporate facial tracking for emotional responses, generating relevant and appropriate conversations. Although Sophia initially possessed limited facial expressions conveying understanding, subsequent iterations have made significant strides in recognition and physical expression. The miniature counterpart, Little Sophia, playfully interacts with children, offering a glimpse into a future where AI robots become lifelong companions.

The creation of artificial intelligence can be categorized as Mechanical Intelligence or Electronic Intelligence, dependent on the decision-making process. All computers hinge on the binary principle, translating input into either an off/on or open/closed signal, denoted by one or zero, to trigger actions. Irrespective of data origin or the programs and processing algorithms involved, the inputs are ultimately crafted by humans. Hence, the term "artificial" loses some relevance, as everything is essentially conceived by humans.

As far back as 1637, René Descartes contemplated the prospect of a thinking *automaton—a mechanical creation comprising gears and cams capable of interacting with humans.* Samuel Butler speculated in 1863 that, with continual progress, machines would eventually surpass humans. By the 18th century, English naval vessels were voyaging worldwide, and in 1821, spurred by the Astronomical Society's encouragement, Charles Babbage designed his mechanical "Difference Machine," employing gears for calculations. While Babbage's theories underpin modern computer design, his unfinished "Analytical Engine" and his 1832 work "On the Economy of Machinery and Manufactures" outlining the "Babbage Principle" demonstrated how profit-generating goods could be produced using unskilled labor and machines.

In a testament to Babbage's ideas, a "Babbage Engine" was constructed based on his designs in 2002 and successfully tested. Weighing over five tons and comprising 8,000 mechanical components, this feat underscored the value of Babbage's contributions.

Charles Babbage's "Analytical Engine"

In the 19th century, looped punched cards were used to set patterns for weaving machines. The foundation of digital computer logic was laid out by George Boole in his 1847 work, "*The Mathematical Analysis of Logic*." The three possible interactions, namely "this and this," "this or this," and "this but not this," are now known as Boolean Logic. While Boole's ideas were brilliant, they lacked practical applications at the time. Nevertheless, in the 1930s, Boolean Logic found use with electromechanical relays, which mechanically opened and closed circuits for communication switching. Vacuum tubes were eventually succeeded by electrical flow relays. The invention of solid-state transistors in 1947 introduced smaller, faster components that produced less heat than vacuum tubes. By the mid-1950s, these transistors were integrated into large-scale computers and portable radios.

During the Apollo program's moon mission, vehicle control systems needed augmentation through an onboard computer due to communication challenges during extended periods on the far side of the moon. This necessity gave rise to Integrated Circuits (IC) as onboard calculations and decisions became crucial. While early ICs were expensive, they now form the foundation for all electronic devices in 21st-century technology, including AI.

Machines have subtly replaced humans in numerous ways that often go unnoticed. When a vehicle is assigned a task and navigates to a destination, it effectively functions as a robot, even if the cargo being transported is a human. Tasks that once required human intervention can now be executed mechanically. By the 2030s, it's estimated that around 47% of existing jobs will be either replaced or enhanced by AI devices, signifying a shift in the machine-human dynamic. The focus may evolve from questioning "what tasks can machines perform better than humans?" to "what can humans do that machines cannot?"

Leveraging post-Second World War advancements in computing power, Alan Turing's 1950 report "Computing Machinery and Intelligence" introduced the eponymous Turing Test, which aimed to discern interactions between humans and machines. Turing posed the question, "Can machines think?" Six years later, John McCarthy coined the term "Artificial Intelligence" as it became evident that machines were proficient in solving problems previously exclusive to humans, and often at a faster pace. As awareness grew regarding the diminishing gap in data processing capabilities between humans and AIs, AI expanded beyond rudimentary tasks to encompass games of thought and logic.

In 1996, IBM's Big Blue defeated chess champion Garry Kasparov, while IBM's Watson triumphed in the TV quiz show Jeopardy. Additionally, Google's AlphaGo bested multiple Go champions in 2017 while "learning" the game during the process. Kasparov's emotional response upon losing highlighted the crucial distinction between biological humans and AI. Big Blue remained unemotional, lacking the capacity to comprehend the significance of the victory. AI devices adhere to programmed instructions without true understanding, whether it's Big Blue or an algorithm-guided drill press. AI is amoral.

While AI demonstrates problem-solving capabilities, it has yet to replicate the intricate emotional dimensions of human behavior. For instance, Watson's victory on Jeopardy didn't evoke an internal "thrill of victory" within the supercomputer, despite its vast interconnectedness. Questions emerged about the nature of AI and its relationship with humans. The aforementioned AI triumphs represent Narrow AI, designed for specific tasks. However, can AI process information across a wide range like humans? This broader capability, termed Broad AI, is projected to be attainable by the late 2030s.

As AI's processing power increases, its capacity for calculations expands, enabling rapid computations within shorter timeframes. Advanced intelligence is attained when a machine can outperform even the most brilliant humans, processing information across a diverse array of scenarios.

AI's vitality lies in data. Increased data input and processing contribute to a wider reference range. Just as the human brain's development relies on processing numerous examples to comprehend norms and exceptions, algorithms analyze billions of data inputs statistically to establish mean values or intended outcomes. AI employs pattern recognition algorithms to tackle specific tasks, including facial recognition.

AI "learns" analogously to a baby's development. Through accumulating inputs, AI recognizes discrepancies and similarities, building a framework of identity. Initially, distinctions are drawn between basic shapes like circles and squares or differentiating letters like O and H. Progressively, more complex recognition emerges, distinguishing between entities like whales and giraffes or individuals like Jennifer Lawrence and Tom Brady. These distinctions pave the way for reading and personal recognition. The acquired information is stored and categorized in memory units, ensuring accurate output actions. Unlike human learning, digital devices are interconnected, enabling instant access to knowledge.

AI can employ the same data sets to detect disparities or anomalies in health conditions or landscapes. This ability aids in recognizing early signs of disease, seismic activity, or changes in enemy troop deployments, long before human observers might identify such changes.

The United States and China are at the forefront of AI development, given their substantial access to relevant data and robust engineering capabilities. The United States emphasizes quality data and analysis, employing groups of highly trained scientists and engineers centralized in technology hubs. Notably, President Obama increased funding for governmental AI research, recognizing its advantages. However, President Trump reduced funding for the National Science Foundation upon assuming office, disregarding the AI's worth. Nonetheless, AI research has persisted within private companies.

The American concern revolves around failure and potential criticism from both the government and stockholders, leading managers and entrepreneurs to be sensitive to risk. Additionally, Americans prioritize privacy, harboring concerns about government or corporate intrusion into their personal lives. In contrast, the Chinese approach emphasizes minimal government involvement and the acquisition of vast amounts of data from various sources.

Starting in July 2017, China initiated a national AI mobilization, capitalizing on the increasing tech-saviness of its population. This has been facilitated by the widespread use of smartphones equipped with apps like WeChat, which process a diverse array of transactions, providing valuable buying and movement pattern data. The Chinese government offers funding and support, encouraging local centers and individual initiatives. This approach is often likened to a gladiatorial contest of entrepreneurship between groups, with the government accepting individual failures for the sake of overall growth. The United States and China, possessing superior data access, trained engineers, and robust applications, are projected to dominate AI for decades. American giants such as Amazon, Apple, Facebook, Google, and Microsoft compete with Chinese counterparts like Baidu, Alibaba, and Tencent.

As with any emerging technology, AI presents both positive and negative facets. A deeper understanding of customer preferences can curtail costs and waste. Access to extensive legal precedents could mitigate racial, cultural, and economic biases, fostering a more equitable legal system. Legal professionals might focus on advocacy rather than administrative tasks, thereby improving efficiency. AI's global database of medical cases could lead to more responsive treatments surpassing human accuracy.

In 2022, global data centers consumed approximately 416 terawatts of electricity, equivalent to nearly 40% more than the entire United Kingdom's consumption. U.S. data centers alone utilize over 90 billion kilowatt-hours per year, requiring approximately 34 coal-powered plants each with a 500-megawatt capacity. The growing complexity and speed of computations necessitate increased electrical power. While some power is derived from renewable sources, others rely on non-renewable generators. Heat generated by processors must also be electronically cooled. Around 43% of power requirements cater to provisions and cooling, mirroring the demand for servers. Consumption is expected to double every four years. However, greater reliance on renewable energy sources and enhanced server efficiency could mitigate resulting CO2 emissions.

AI possesses the capacity to create false realities surpassing traditional Photoshop capabilities. Images can be manipulated for ulterior motives, stretching beyond the boundaries of truth. AI programs can process data to present another's visual and vocal attributes, effectively fabricating a deceptive image that's indistinguishable from the original.

Deepfake technology that uses AI-based deep neural networks called "encoders" that find patterns and correlations from large data sets began appearing in 2018 by hobbyist has evolved to create false realities against individuals putting them in compromising situations that question the truth of the image. For the subject, Deepfake is an invasion of privacy and loss of control of their image and identity. For women it has often been used for "involuntary pornography."

Images can be created with 2D pictorial scans to produce 3D models and even full body images that can be recreated with 3D printing. The scans can be attached even with voices to actual pictures or objects.

Hollywood's 2023 strike by writers and actors underscored concerns about compensation, ownership, and AI-driven deepfake technology, which can simulate individuals indefinitely.

Development of ChatGTP and other AI applications are driven by profit. The more used, the more profit regardless of the impact on the cultures, environment and resources. AI is already moving faster than human understanding, legislation, and social cultural changes.

The Center for Humane Technology promotes an ethics panel to address harmful uses of AI. While open AI allows access for anyone and any content regulation of data centers and chip makers can provide a degree of control to what is acceptable.

The US lags behind the EU in the regulation of AI. In 2020 the Digital Services Act was enacted by the EU to "govern the content moderation practices of social media platforms" and address illegal content for 19 online platforms and search engines.

Founded in 2010 and later acquired by Google in 2014, the English company DeepMind operates as an AI research center. It utilizes neural networks to learn how to play video games like a human. The non-profit organization OpenAI, established in 2015, focuses on developing safer AI. Their approach ensures universal access to AI algorithms, thereby promoting equal opportunity for innovation.

In 2018, OpenAI introduced the language model GPT (Global pre-trained Transformer) to capture global knowledge. Subsequent iterations, such as GPT-2 with 1.5 billion parameters and GPT-3 with 175 billion ML parameters, have advanced capabilities, outstripping Microsoft's Turing 10 billion parameter NLG model. GPT-3 utilizes only a small fraction of its training data to span an extensive range of articles from the English Wikipedia.

The core function of ChatGPT, commonly referred to as "ChatBot," was unveiled in 2022. It mimics human conversation, generating music, teleplays, fairy tales, student essays, and answers to questions. While it facilitates expedient research, it lacks the nuanced understanding inherent in human interaction. Co-founder Musk expressed concerns over potential issues such as cheating, job displacement, discrimination, misinformation, and uncontrollable military applications.

Other nations like China (with Baidu's "Wenxin Yiyan"), Korea (with Search GPT), and Russia (with YaLM 2.0) are also developing similar AI programs. Leading tech companies, including DeepMind, Amazon, Google, Facebook, IBM, and Microsoft, are members of the Partnership on AI, an organization dedicated to the intersection of society and AI.

Initially acclaimed for producing papers and visuals, ChatGPT inputs data from existing materials to generate "original" content in a similar style. It can draw from massive datasets, raising the question of human originality, as everything is essentially a synthesis of past experiences, presented in a unique manner. Similar to Kasparov's Big Blue, AI exhibits a lack of emotion in its creative processes, distinct from human creation.

However, ChatBot has created a challenge in distinguishing between reality and manipulated content. Political opponents or celebrities could be portrayed making statements they never uttered, placing the responsibility on viewers to discern truth. Issues of legal and ethical ownership surrounding source material have also arisen. The use of immortal AI avatars, such as Tom Hanks or Beyonce, raises questions about rights, citations, and the role of human manipulators. Hollywood's 2023 strike by writers and actors underscores concerns about compensation, ownership, and AI-driven deepfake technology, which can simulate individuals indefinitely.

The United States Supreme Court ruled that the contents authors must be human beings, highlighting the importance of human creative control. However, this distinction becomes more complex as AI generates new content with minimal human input. By spring 2023, some creators questioned whether AI development should be halted. Notably, 1,000 experts called for a six-month moratorium on "out-of-control" machine learning systems that defy human understanding and prediction. Geoffrey Hinton, a pioneer in the early development of image analysis neural networks, warned that future versions of such technology could pose substantial threats. Although most initially deemed these concerns distant, attitudes have evolved over time. He estimates indicate that around 80% of the workforce will be impacted by AI's advancement.

Can the evolution of AI be contained? Is AI just another in a list of inventions for creating, and moving forward? New things have always been a part of being human. We move forward for more.

But when do we say no? Have we over designed beyond a sustainable level (chapter 12) where unregulated AI can create more harm than good? The techno luddites are not about destroying AI, rather how to use positive applications.

AI in smartphones can provide a myriad of applications but it also inputs the applications of the user. Behind the screen it takes the users looks then provides output that amplifies those interests. With continual use the output pushes to the extreme of interest whether in purchases, opinions, or interactions hijacking to verification amplifying disgust and prejudice of those extremes. And it can also cause a breakdown of social interactions. Looking for "likes" can create an Artificial Intimacy (AI) and isolation.

AI is undergoing evolution. Basic AI, referred to as "weak AI" or ANI (Artificial Narrow Intelligence), pertains to devices capable of storing data and performing a singular task. Watson and Big Blue exemplify ANI as they are programmed for specific tasks, even potentially surpassing human intelligence within those parameters. Algorithms, employing human-defined parameters, facilitate the recognition of visual and behavioral features, a category in which we currently reside.

The concept of the "technological singularity," a term introduced by Stan Ulam in the early 1950s, signifies the theoretical point where AI equals human processing and intelligence. Beyond this juncture, technology may embark on an autonomous self-improvement trajectory, triggering an explosion of "intelligence" that exceeds human capabilities.

The notion was initially envisioned by British cryptologist I. J. Good in 1965. Good postulated that an "ultra-intelligent machine," surpassing human intellectual activities including machine design, could usher in an "intelligence explosion." The resulting intelligence could leave human intelligence far behind. Good's prophecy was one of promise, not menace.

"Strong AI," also known as AGI (Artificial General Intelligence), demonstrates the ability to perform any task within the human purview, encompassing reasoning, abstract thinking, problem identification, and experiential learning. These are capabilities that humans currently possess, which AGI computers are on the brink of excelling at. This is often referred to as Human Level Machine Intelligence (HLMI).

The third tier embodies the true essence of the Super Computer, **ASI** (Artificial Super Intelligence). ASI can autonomously enhance its intelligence in accordance with Ray Kurzweil's Law of Accelerating Returns (LOAR), with limitless potential for expansion.

Two acknowledged pathways lead to ASI achievement. The ANI route entails enhancing processing hardware efficiency and developing learning algorithms. Alternatively, reverse engineering the human brain, unraveling nature's blueprint for the epitome of intelligence, offers an alternative. "Whole Brain Emulation" seeks to simulate the brain's architecture, refining the design and introducing additional circuits.

Regardless of the chosen path, or a combination thereof, ASI will inevitably materialize. However, questions abound. While even conservative experts foresee ASI by the 21st century's end, its ultimate form remains enigmatic. ASI's processing power will enable machines to design increasingly intelligent computers, with no apparent ceiling to the capabilities of an ultimate thinking entity. The entirety of human-generated data will be accessible within moments. Within a few generations, ASI could transcend human comprehension.

Prominent individuals, including scientists, Silicon Valley CEOs, and visionaries like Stephen Hawking, Elon Musk, Bill Gates, and Steve Wozniak, jointly voiced concerns. They presented a cautionary letter at the 2015 International Joint Conference on Artificial Intelligence in Buenos Aires, Argentina, suggesting that AI might pose a greater threat than nuclear weapons. Hawking postulated that AI's success could mark both the most significant event in human history and potentially its last, unless safeguards are established.

The Machine Intelligence Research Institute (MIRI), initially the Singularity Institute for Artificial Intelligence (SIAI), emerged in 2000 with the objective of preparing for the day when machine intelligence surpasses human cognition. While they foresee initial challenges related to AI control, they question whether control will ultimately be attainable. Other institutions, such as the James Martin 21st Century School at the University of Oxford, and the Future of Life Institute, are also addressing the potential risks of AGI and ASI.

The behavior of ASI towards humans remains uncertain. Perspectives vary, with some envisioning a future where humans serve as tools to ASI, while others foresee ASI enhancing human capabilities, similar to how submarines enable underwater movement. An alternate scenario postulates that ASIs, significantly more intelligent than humans, could disregard human interests, akin to how humans perceive fish. Disregard, however, is an emotion, suggesting that humans may be irrelevant in the ASI algorithm. This perspective potentially addresses the Fermi paradox, speculating that an advanced spacefaring species might regard humanity as an inconsequential curiosity, akin to moss on Mars.

Elon Musk, while cautious, also envisions potential partnership with ASI. He proposes that humanity faces the choice of either lagging behind as AI surpasses human processing or establishing a symbiotic relationship with AI. Musk acknowledges the inevitability of AI surpassing human intelligence beyond human control.

ASI holds the promise of propelling the world towards a near-Utopian state. Capable of analyzing limitless sources, ASI could propose and implement optimal solutions while addressing profound human questions. ASI may offer answers, albeit human guidance will remain essential for effective implementation.

Irrespective of the eventual outcome, the nation or group that achieves ASI or AGI first will gain significant advantages in commerce and cyber warfare. This potential dominance, unattainable by others, could destabilize the global equilibrium.

As processing power continues to increase, the question arises: can AI communicate with humans on an equal footing? Existing data programs can recognize word patterns and compose stories, legal briefs, term papers, and poetry in specific styles. Autoregressive language models employ deep learning to generate text and responses reminiscent of human communication.

Alan Turing's initial query aimed to differentiate between a human and AI in both queries and conversations. AI companions have amplified the complexity of this issue.

AI companions presently offer solace to the lonely and alleviate personal losses. They serve as conversational partners and, coupled with AI-generated CGI, can take on the full appearance of a person, complete with expressive visage. Such companionship's precision has therapeutic applications, enabling individuals to confide or form relationships, even while cognizant of the AI nature. Integrating AI with a robotic body yields an autonomous entity capable of physical interaction. On a smaller scale, robots can anticipate needs, perform actions, or engage in games within personal or interpersonal contexts.

As AI assimilates into daily life, it will become "wearable," seamlessly enhancing commonplace scenarios. It will integrate invisibly, much like clothing, housing, or vehicles.

Despite our perspectives on AI, it remains a program, conceived by human minds and imbued with human values. It lacks aspects of reason, intuition, and creativity, although it can learn and adapt with new data. Consciousness, however, remains unattainable—can synthetic consciousness emerge? If so, how would we ascertain it? We comprehend neither how electrical impulses in biological cells underlie consciousness in our brains nor whether analogous actions within non-biological connections can evoke consciousness.

Current synthetics make decisions based on provided alternatives, devoid of moral judgments (e.g., targeting a school bus with a smart bomb). Can synthetics independently discern right from wrong? Could they employ an internal moral processor, dissociated from external programming, to make decisions and feel emotions? Is it possible to program or internally cultivate morals and emotions? Might a conscious synthetic experience the elation of defeating Garry Kasparov?

Should a synthetic demonstrate moral decision-making, should it be granted equivalent rights to humans, including self-preservation? How will bio-humans respond to this sharing? This will be the entry to the Synthocene.

Humanistic Intelligence (HI) systems, exemplified by Apple's Tom Gruber, are designed to meet human needs through collaboration and augmentation. HI and AI values will mirror human values. For AI to be wearable, programmers must possess competencies beyond the technical realm, encompassing philosophy, history, literature, sociology, comparative religion, and the humanities. Additionally, they must grasp human qualities such as ambition, self-confidence, empathy, artistic discernment, judgment, and congeniality.

Staying within Moore's law and the Law of Accelerating Returns, the Singularity's advent is projected before 2040. The subsequent generation, akin to Einstein's level, emerges eighteen months later, propelling AI into an intelligence realm beyond human reach. At that juncture, AI will design its own enhancements, akin to human achievements in prior stages. Human involvement will be imperative for remaining part of this design process.

Anticipating the end of the 21st century entails modifying the basic human design to accommodate AI integration. ANI specializes in specific tasks (winning Jeopardy, fastening screws) and optimizes task performance. Its value is intrinsic to task requirements. The transition to AGI broadens the spectrum of achievable tasks.

Whether AI can attain sentience remains uncertain. Ethical quandaries arise should AI attain self-awareness, independently making decisions beyond presets. Will humans embrace self-aware AI as equals? Might the fully bionic *Homo sapien* render the traditional human body obsolete? Could striving for physical "perfection" lead to extreme narcissism? Will human consciousness reside within a silicon-based entity, virtually eternal? Will the barrier between person and machine blur to insignificance? How will society reconcile moral implications, or will a revolt arise against AI-enhanced entities perceived as aberrations? Might uneven access to technological enhancements breed a digital caste system, more inescapable than historical slavery or serfdom? How long before a connected synthetic human brain becomes a component within a larger brain, equivalent to cells within our own? When will these changes factor into human evolution?

Central to this discourse is the human-synthetic relationship. Will computers assume the role of companions like R2-D2, performing programmed actions, data retrieval, and exceeding human capabilities? Synthetic devices are increasingly mobile, mirroring our own movements. They will be seamlessly integrated into clothing, watches, glasses, and our built environment. These devices, even though machines, will become an unobtrusive extension of ourselves, much like we are to them.

Transhumanism (Oxford Dictionary): *"The belief or theory that the human race can evolve beyond its current physical and mental limitations, especially by means of science and technology."* Transhumanism is seen as a transition between biological humans and post humans, for whatever that may be.

Extropy: the prediction that human intelligence and technology will enable life to expand in an orderly way throughout the entire universe is the opposite of entropy where matter is moving towards disorder and predictability. The goals of extropy are towards a destiny marked by an increased order of intelligence, energy, and functionality.

The concept of technologically enhanced humans has its roots in the 1923 publication "Daedalus: or, Science and the Future," a series of lectures by British geneticist J. B. S. Haldane addressing the future control of human evolution. Haldane was notably intrigued by eugenics, aimed at improving the human race by discouraging inferior traits and promoting superior ones, as well as ectogenesis, the creation and sustenance of life in an artificial environment.

Pierre Teilhard de Chardin introduced the term "transhuman" in his 1949 book "The Future of Mankind." Transhumanism is both a philosophy and a collection of technological advancements. By the mid-20th century, scientists recognized that biomechatronics could surmount the limitations of the evolved human body.

For religious, ethical, or traditional reasons, some may resist science's intrusion into the natural course of life. Since the Renaissance, a conflict has persisted within the Catholic Church regarding the primacy of logic versus faith, with official stance tilting toward faith. This conflict has resonated across various religions and sects, spanning debates from the Earth's age and shape to evolution. Bioconservatives are concerned about potential compromises to human dignity.

Pope John Paul II established the Pontifical Academy for Life to address ethical issues stemming from biomedicine advancements. Initial concerns centered on cloning and cell modification, later encompassing the domain of roboethics. In 2018, at the World Economic Forum, Pope Francis called for technology's service to humanity and our shared environment, stressing that technological progress should be accompanied by enhanced human responsibility, values, and conscience.

To prevent AI from superseding the human species, humans can merge with AI to create a new Human-AI hybrid, blending biological and synthetic elements. Here, humans provide a comprehensive overview, drawing upon contextual knowledge, while AI robots offer specialized skills for data processing. The AI can be fine-tuned and upgraded, though humans must retain ownership of the algorithms and data.

Interactions with synthetic devices will evolve into both a moral and ethical issue, as well as an engineering concern. As AI advances, it will increasingly make decisions synthetically. These thinking machines will wield greater influence over the planet and environment, potentially supplanting human influence. The era of Anthropocene might eventually give way to the Synthocene.

A **"Cyborg" (cybernetic organism)** (Merriam-Webster) *as "a person whose body contains mechanical or electrical devices, granting them abilities surpassing those of ordinary humans."* Despite its menacing connotations, this encompasses individuals with pacemakers or artificial hips. With scientific progress, the number of mechanical and electrical devices integrated into human bodies has surged.

To enhance understanding of human-robot interactions, lifelike robots have been developed. These entities, resembling and behaving like humans, facilitate more natural and effective communication in real-world interactions.

Assistive technologies, aimed at enhancing human capabilities or mitigating disabilities, have been integrated into the human body for decades. Historical examples include the insertion of a dog bone into a human in 1682, albeit removed due to religious objections, and J. A. McWilliam's 1889 use of electrical impulses to stabilize an irregular heart. Innovations like the first kidney dialysis machine in 1943 and the Jarvik-7 artificial heart in 1982 have continued this trajectory.

Early instances of electrical brain stimulation date back to the Roman Emperor Claudius, whose physician employed electric eels on the royal head to treat stuttering. The link between electricity and nerve activation was recognized almost three centuries ago by Luigi Galvani, who discovered nerves and muscles' electrical excitability. Subsequent researchers like Giovanni Aldini in 1802 and Luigi Rolando and Pierre Flourens in the early 19th century utilized electrical brain stimulation to study brain functional localization in animals.

Heart pacemakers in various forms have been in use since the late 19th century, operating via electrical impulses to stimulate the heart. Adjustments to impulse rates enable rhythm control.

The electroencephalograph (EEG), created by German physicist Hans Berger in 1924, measures brain electrical activity, or brainwaves, when attached to the skull. However, the signals are weaker and may be distorted due to the head's composition, placing the receptors between the skull and brain.

Electrical brain stimulation (EBS) was first used to elicit aversive or pleasurable responses in test animals as a behavior reward. Employing brain stimulation reward (BSR), researchers found that direct brain region stimulation could control behavior and task performance. Deep brain stimulation (DBS) targets specific brain regions using a neurostimulator to send therapeutic electrical signals, benefiting conditions like chronic pain and addiction. EBS, a tool enhancing and modifying the brain like any other, merges human and hardware for improved performance. Professor Kevin Warwick's 1998 installation marked the first instance, where DBS controlled temperature and house lighting, leading him to remark that *"Being human was okay...but being a cyborg has much more to offer."*

Incorporating direct two-way links between prosthetics and users' nerve endings and muscles, new control systems enable rudimentary actions, providing sensory feedback. These prosthetics "learn" user actions for more natural movement, integrating biomechatronics to meld mechanical, electrical, and biological systems. Users feel greater control over prosthetics, viewing them as integral to their bodies, not just external tools. Such feedback can discern pressure and texture.

The Human Brain Project, Brain Research through Advancing Innovative Neurotechnologies (B R A I N), initiated by President Obama, collaborated with the National Institute of Health, DARPA (Defense Advanced Research Projects Agency), the National Science Foundation, and the Food and Drug Administration, along with private companies, with a focus on comprehending the brain's functioning and its information transmission.

DARPA's Biological Technologies Office is engaged in utilizing neural signaling from cortex-based electrodes to activate movement in arm or leg prosthetics.

The exoskeleton stands out as an immediate device. Comprising metal beams, servo motors, and electronic connections, it's fitted onto the wearer. A non-invasive skull cap enables thought control of the motors, maneuvering both the unit and the wearer. To expand human capabilities, brain augmentation is essential, as human augmentation thus far has centered on the physical body, the operative shell.

The ultimate connection between humans and machines will occur in the brain. Human synapses will interface with computer circuitry through a brain-computer interface (BCI), alternatively known as a mind-machine interface (MMI), direct neural interface (DNI), synthetic telepathy interface (STI), or brain–machine interface (BMI). Transcranial Direct-Current Stimulation (TDCS) is employed for brain disorder management, such as headaches and depression.

Is it conceivable to directly record, transmit, and potentially store thoughts from one brain into a synthetic device or another brain? How much of this is still conjecture in terms of physical feasibility?

Thoughts are brain impulses. Memories are temporarily stored in the hippocampus before being transferred to the prefrontal cortex.

BCI's initial development dates back to the 1970s, aiming to create a neuroprosthetic for damaged brain areas associated with sight, hearing, and basic movements. The brain's cortical plasticity allows natural sensors to process signals from prostheses. Brain impulses were transmitted as signals to activate an artificial hand. By the mid-1990s, human implanted devices became practicable. Synthetic telepathy, based on reading alpha brain waves on EEGs, was first utilized in the 1960s.

Duke University's efforts in 2011 resulted in a feedback system involving rhesus monkeys, wherein brain activity governed actions. In 2013, two rats' brains were interconnected, marking the first direct brain-to-brain interface. The next step involves direct human brain-to-brain connections.

In 2015, French and Indian scientists employed Transcranial Magnetic Stimulation (TMS) to transmit thoughts. Using BCI, the Indian sender communicated the thoughts of "hola" and "ciao" to three recipients in France. Although the reception entailed rudimentary lights, the message was successfully conveyed.

How will the computer interface with the brain? A range of methods, both non-invasive and invasive, are presently in development. Virginia Commonwealth University created an electronic array akin to a tattoo on the skin. External TMS generates electrical impulses within the brain. Minimally invasive approaches involve injecting through veins and arteries, like D. J. Seo's "neural dust" – tiny silicone sensors distributed throughout the cortex, connected via ultrasound. The University of Chicago's interface employs rolled-up silk inserted into the brain, which subsequently extends across the brain. In an alternate method, a neural mesh can be injected using a syringe, or bundled carbon nanotubes can be sent to the brain via the bloodstream. Ontogenetics employs a light-stimulated virus that attaches to the brain. Full invasive implantation is costly and requires intricate surgery by specialized surgeons, rendering it impractical for widespread use.

In 2017, Elon Musk led a team of scientists to establish Neuralink, initially to treat brain ailments and restore communication and mobility via direct interaction with external computers. Initial human trials were hindered by regulations and animal test subject mortality rates. However, in 2022, the Australian company Synchron commenced approved trials on six paralyzed patients.

The ultimate objective is human enhancement, termed "transhumanism." The Neuralink team approximated that a functional BCI would necessitate the recording of one million neurons simultaneously. With an increase of five hundred neurons every eighteen months, this milestone is projected to be reached by 2040. Existing electrodes are still too sizable to record individual neurons; a probe with 48 ultra-thin threads was used.

Initially, brain impulses will be transferred from a brain to a computer and subsequently to another interconnected brain. The development of algorithms for a universal decoder recognizing brain idiosyncrasies, crucial given the diversity among brains, will facilitate mutual understanding between computers and other brains. The connection supplements damaged brain regions, and additional computer programs can enhance not just specific areas, but overall functions.

While the idea of copying the mind and personality has been confined to science fiction, many now view it as plausible. If thoughts can be transmitted to another individual, can those thoughts and memories be stored post-death?

The next phase might involve the transfer of thoughts. Memories could be backed up to an external hard drive, with additional information being downloaded externally. Specific programs could be loaded into memory for particular needs. As ASI advances, BCI-linked humans will also see an increase in capabilities.

Thoughts may control external actions. The ultimate aim of AI-focused transhumanism is to utilize technology for enhancing human life, potentially leading to a state akin to "living forever" in a god-like form. Humans won't merely use AI, they might become AI.

Supplemental external synthetic memory storage boasts several advantages over a biological brain, which has to retain every memory, regardless of its relevance to the task, thereby limiting specific task memory capacity. Synthetic memory doesn't degrade over time, even if not actively recalled. Access to an unlimited knowledge base, with hyper calculations and rapid downloading speed, will equip users with complete memory and nearly instantaneous access. Individuals might be able to store their thoughts, knowledge, and skills in a brain storage unit, as a contingency in the event of future brain function loss.

The "mind" could be transferred into multiple bodies across various locations. Linked minds would form a community sharing information universally and instantaneously. Thoughts would evolve into group thoughts, shaping collective decisions. Each mind contributes to the group thought, forming what's termed the "hive mind."

The line between individual and group minds could become inconsequential, as every mind would have access to the knowledge of all others. Different problems would require different skills and perspectives, a process at which hominins have historically excelled.

Future hominin design will still need to revolve around the brain, the core of our humanity. It serves as our conscious mind and subconscious processor, extending beyond a mere biological CPU. It's the source of our creativity. Other body parts function as support systems for the brain.

Imagine if a brain could receive an oxygen/nutrient solution via the carotid artery and return it through the jugular vein. External machines could supply oxygen and nutrients while cleansing the returning solution. In the absence of a body, many regulatory organs and sensory inputs like taste and touch would become unnecessary. Visual, smell, and auditory inputs would remain crucial.

With ongoing advancements in BCI, an isolated brain could connect to a computer or other brains for communication or to operate mechanical devices. Replacing a 200-pound person with fifteen pounds of thought and support equipment would be advantageous in situations where weight and size matter. A supported brain would require fewer resources.

The HEad Anastomosis VENture (HEAVEN) is a collaborative medical project between teams in Italy and China, aiming to perform a Body-Head Transplant (BHT) by transferring a healthy brain from a damaged body into the body of a brain-dead donor.

The subsequent step would be transplanting a healthy brain into a different, healthy body. This procedure has faced resistance on bioethical and legal grounds. Questions arise: Should it even be attempted, and if so, is the identity of the final entity determined by the body or the brain?

Many of these proposed changes will likely meet resistance. Unlike previous alterations to the hominin design that occurred over millennia, these changes could unfold within a single lifetime or even a generation. The conflict between "normal" and enhanced humans might resemble the dynamics of the fictional X-Men, with one group advocating cooperation with "normal" humans while another, acknowledging their differences, seeks separation but with a desire for more than just equality.

Companies may find the concept of BCI and AI, enhanced humans, or cyborgs unsettling, as these changes challenge established norms. The question of equitable work and compensation arises.

Historically, the replacement of human efforts by machines has rarely been seamless. Each labor-saving device displaced human labor. Though the Luddite revolt has faded, the term still designates those who resist technological changes.

An essential query of the Information Revolution is: What occurs when everyone gains access to everything?

With AI devices performing tasks once deemed exclusive to humans, the trend is clear: "If your job can be done by a machine, it will be." By 2035, an estimated 47% of current jobs could be susceptible to algorithms.

Elon Musk envisions a future where robots handle monotonous, perilous, and repetitive tasks, liberating humans. "Essentially, in the future, physical work will be a choice."

Gerd Leonhard describes the best-case scenario as "Exponential Humanism," a forward equilibrium embracing technology while retaining human essence. Ray Kurzweil envisions a Bio-AI future as our next evolutionary phase, both within our world and extending outward. He notes, *"Waking up the universe and then intelligently deciding its fate by infusing it with our human intelligence in its non-biological form is our destiny."*

The pursuit of perfection might counteract our humanness. Humans are unique and flawed, and within imperfections lays our identity. John Ruskin, amid the Industrial Revolution's proliferation of perfect products, expressed that *"Imperfection is in some sort essential to all that we know of life."* Imperfection signifies vitality within a mortal body, representing a state of growth and transformation. To eliminate imperfection is to stifle expression.

Predicting *Homo sapiens'* trajectory into the 22nd century remains speculative. Will we attain mental and physical perfection, free from disease and affliction? Will we merge with technology, becoming cyborgs or partnering with AI? Will the concept of privacy become obsolete as everyone's information becomes transparent, yet the true essence remains elusive? And how will we define "human" amidst these changes?

Homo astro and Homo cosmos

We are extending the Anthropocene beyond our planetary confines. Probes have already been dispatched to the major bodies within our solar system, and one-way probes have ventured beyond the solar system's planetary boundaries. Our presence is being broadcast to the universe, and how we navigate this path is a subject of speculation. The journey will necessitate technologies yet to be conceived, but human determination will pave the way for cosmic colonization.

In the words of Carl Sagan, *"We're made of star stuff. We are a way for the cosmos to know itself."* Our essence is intertwined with the stars, and venturing into space aligns with the ongoing evolution of hominins.

At the turn of the 20th century, humans became the first Earth species with the capability to chart a course beyond our home planet. Merely eight years after Kitty Hawk, Russian scientist Konstantin E. Tsiokovsky stated, *"Earth is the cradle of humanity, but one cannot live in a cradle forever."*

Both astronauts and cosmonauts have shared an experience known as the overview effect. Gazing upon Earth from space, they saw no man-made borders, only a fragile blue orb representing all that we possess.

The human spirit is driven by curiosity to explore the unknown. As Stephen Hawking remarked, "I don't think the human race will survive the next thousand years, unless we spread into space. There are too many accidents that can befall life on a single planet. But I'm an optimist. We will reach out to the stars." Adaptation is key, as space won't conform to us.

Surviving in space will demand new accommodations to simulate Earth-like conditions. As far back as 1964, Arthur C. Clarke envisioned "planetary engineering," enabling humans to live on other planets without the need for space suits or airtight cities.

FACTS

Due to the vast expanses of space, travel to habitable exoplanets will take centuries, if not millennia. Space is incredibly immense. Even the New Horizons Pluto probe, the fastest man-made object, reached speeds of 36,373 mph or just 0.000005422% of the speed of light (670 million miles per hour), requiring over nine years for its journey. At this rate, reaching our nearest neighbor, the triple star Alpha Centauri, would take 793,664 years. New worlds will differ from Earth, with unique conditions and potentially different forms of life. Some environments may closely resemble Earth, necessitating minimal adaptations.

A compelling incentive is required to justify the expenditure of resources for space travel to new worlds. How far can we venture beyond space tourism without a favorable return on investment? Will our quest for knowledge suffice until we find another habitable world?

While many may be unfamiliar with space's conditions on Earth, commercialization is on the horizon. Zero gravity and the vacuum of space in Low Earth Orbit (LEO) will facilitate the production of pharmaceuticals and semiconductors of significantly higher quality. Unprecedented research opportunities and space tourism will also arise.

However, realizing these prospects entails extensive periods of zero gravity for human workers. To optimize operations, individuals tailored for zero gravity work will be necessary—humans whose bodies can adapt to the absence of a fundamental condition that shaped our evolution.

As humans embark on deep space migration, our bodies will need to adapt to the novel environments. Extended stays aboard the International Space Station have already revealed the inadequacy of our bodies for space. In the absence of gravity, designed for our 1g (gravity) environment, our bodies behave differently. Astronauts returning to Earth exhibit reduced bone density. The effects of Space Adaptation Syndrome (SAS) manifest in the zero gravity of space.

Long-term challenges stemming from gravity deprivation encompass heart and blood circulation, as well as muscle tone. In microgravity, blood and fluids accumulate in the upper body. The brain's sensory centers react by releasing hormones to decrease fluid levels, depriving the lower body of essential blood supply. Within the initial three days of weightlessness, this loss can be as much as 22%.

To establish permanent human residency in space, the current conditions are untenable, necessitating a transformation in humans themselves since space cannot be altered.

To counteract SAD (seasonal affective disorder), which results from changes in lighting, especially due to insufficient natural light, artificial lighting will be devised. Additionally, sunlight prompts serotonin production, boosting concentration and mood.

Minerals and water from asteroids and extinct comets will be mined and processed for use as we initiate colonization on low-gravity bodies like the Moon and Mars (38%). Exoplanets may possess larger size and greater gravity, placing extra strain on the human body. Unfamiliar physiological conditions may arise, including variations in atmospheric composition such as oxygen, nitrogen, humidity, and CO_2 levels. The star around which these planets orbit could be red rather than yellow. Humans must be tailored to match specific environments.

Space is fraught with hazards. Prolonged exposure will entail dealing with radiation. In the absence of protective shielding, radiation can be lethal to live cells, impacting humans, food supplies, and seeds required for future colonization. Traditional lead shielding methods are cumbersome. Research by the ESA aboard the International Space Station suggests that lichen, algae, and bacterial seeds can survive unshielded in space. Gaining insights into how these Earth-based life forms endure can lead to techniques that enable plants, animals, and Homo species to survive radiation without cellular destruction.

To thrive, humans will harness their adaptability, as they have throughout history. This could entail creating environments conducive to human physiology or adapting physiologically to space or new worlds.

SPECULATION

Humanity will venture beyond the stars, driven by our innate inclination to explore beyond our boundaries. Like traversing hills and valleys, navigating an ever-expanding cosmos will be another stride. Speculations include the potential for new resources in asteroids or space tourism, but our journey is inevitable.

As of now, speculation remains just that. Liquid-fueled rockets that propelled interstellar probes, exemplified by the New Horizons mission to Pluto, require years, not including the return trip.

Voyages beyond our solar system are relegated to the realm of science fiction. Star Trek introduced Warp

Drive, enabling speeds exponentially greater than light. Jumping was vital in the *Battlestar Galactica* reboot and *Star Wars*. The Heiliners of the Dune series employed the Holtzman effect to fold space.

Hibernation or suspended animation through torpor will maintain the body's temperature at 89°F in a safeguarded metabolic state, offering protection to the organs and diminishing the requirement for blood oxygen. Metabolic suppression involves specialized diets designed to initiate and regulate metabolic rates. This approach reduces muscle atrophy, prevents bone loss, and curbs biochemical processes along with excessive oxidative stress, mitigating damage caused by radiation exposure. In order to preserve limb and joint flexibility during extended periods of inactivity, robotic arms will intermittently move the limbs while monitoring bodily functions. Decreased brain function will also minimize the allocation of resources until revival at the destination becomes necessary.

Another conceivable approach, based on current scientific understanding, involves "cities" of intergenerational travelers within enclosed environments that cater to their needs, including rotational gravity. These voyages could span centuries without plans for a return to Earth. Eventually, these travelers could become the pioneers of a new hominin settlement.

We can draw lessons from plants. A seed can remain untouched for thousands of years, yet when introduced to the appropriate conditions, including water and nutrients, it will sprout, grow, and eventually produce more seeds. Though it may not align with our traditional definition of "living," a seed can transition into a living organism, exhibiting all the attributes of a plant. The seed isn't inert or merely dormant like hibernating organisms. Speculatively, could there be a hominin seed capable of remaining inactive for centuries, only to grow into a human upon activation?

Human embryos could be pre-fertilized or paired at the intended location, growing with the guidance of AI assistance. If the prospect of uploading a mind becomes feasible, a file could be transmitted, downloaded, and integrated with an avatar tailored for the environment, allowing the mind or data to traverse vast distances intact.

Alternatively, new hominin species could emerge. To adapt fully to perpetual zero gravity, ***Homo cosmos*** might exhibit primate ancestry traits, such as limbs of equal length with four opposing thumbs. This transformation would necessitate significant circulatory changes without the influence of gravity. Absent an overhead sun or extreme temperatures, the need for hair might diminish. Within a contained environment, light could be regulated, reducing the requirement for melanin.

Nevertheless, each world reached would present distinct conditions. While initial colonists might be cyborgs, long-term evolution could lead to the emergence of a specialized hominin, ***Homo astro***. Through natural evolution or expedient DNA manipulation, they would be tailored to fit the gravity, atmospheric composition, and light of their world. Despite potential communication with other *Homo cosmos* variants, physical interaction might be hindered by the differences originating from their respective home worlds.

Perhaps a *Homo cosmos* entity could control the vessel, subsequently activating and training *Homo astros* for survival on the designated world, even if they never descend to it.

Equally vital to the survival of our descendants is the sustenance of food supplies. Can Earth seeds adapt to alien environments, and if so, will they offer adequate nutrition? Traditional Earth agriculture might prove unfeasible, necessitating alternative approaches to securing long-term dietary needs.

Even with yet-to-be-imagined propulsion methods, it may take hundreds or thousands of years before humanity ventures beyond our solar system. Nonetheless, the human presence will expand. Our design and approach on Earth will determine our trajectory into the cosmos.

The presence of intelligent life beyond Earth could become irrelevant, as some form of hominin may carry Earth's life to the stars. At the dawn of the space age, Pope Pius XII stated, *"God has no intention of setting a limit to the efforts of man to conquer space."*

Over the past 3.5 billion years, Earth has fostered millions, if not billions, of species and life forms. While they've left their mark on the planet, their existence has been confined to the atmospheric envelope. Through *Homo sapiens* life may extend into the interstellar realm. The colonization and exploration of space might act as catalysts for new strides in hominin evolution. Humanity could play a role in endowing the universe with intelligence and empathy.

The Intelligently Designed Human, *Homo designus*

The term Intelligent Design implies the existence of an intelligent designer, someone who creates a design that is as close to perfect as possible given the conditions and available materials. From a religious standpoint, it is often used interchangeably with an omnipotent God who "created the heavens and the Earth." Critics of the concept of an intelligent designer employ the "argument of poor design" or the dysteleological (purposeless-ness) argument, which asserts that the design of the human body, created by a supreme being, is suboptimal.

I'm not the first to make these observations. As early as the 19th century, biologist Ernst Haeckel raised questions about the presence of useless organs. In 2005, Donald Wise popularized the term "incompetent design" to describe aspects of nature perceived as flawed in design. The "dysteleological argument," or the "argument from poor design," posits that an all-powerful, all-knowing intelligent designer would not have crafted an imperfect being containing numerous errors and vestigial organs. Despite its imperfections, this is the design we have to work with.

I don't challenge the belief in a supreme being. That, with humility, is beyond my understanding. However, I do question the resulting design of humans. Our existence does not show significant indications of having been influenced by an intelligent being (IB). There are numerous issues in the design of the human body, problems that a superior designer should have foreseen, particularly an omnipotent one.

Homo designus is only concerned with the design of the physical body and does not address biological or psychological imperfections that may have been necessary during the evolutionary past but detrimental to contemporary Homo sapiens.

We are the successful evolved descendants of mammals and other animals that evolved from the first multi cellular creatures into the Order *primates*. The human design is effective in most aspects. It has served us well, and our brains have allowed us to overcome many of its limitations and problems. Most of the design remains valid and will not require revision. However, through evolution, certain design features were retained that were advantageous to fish, reptiles, or other mammals but are disadvantageous to *Homo sapiens.*

Life began with cells that formed a flat disc, which then rolled over to create a tubular structure. The tube eventually divided into two openings: one for energy intake from food and waste elimination, and the other for air intake and exhalation.

Throughout much of evolution, animals resembled horizontal tubes with a central processing area located in the front. This area included inputs for vision, sound, food, and air, attached to the front of a central body structure. Early fins, wings, or legs were attached to the backbone to support the animal. Organs were protected by a rib cage made of bones suspended from the backbone. Offspring were released directly from the rear of the body. Along the course of evolution, animals diversified into distinct species that developed features aiding survival in their specific niches. These features and their mutations were passed down through generations. The lineage that gave rise to primates and eventually hominins evolved to become vertically oriented.

Numerous studies have addressed design flaws in humans. These studies often focus on errors that persisted throughout evolution but are now either useless or detrimental to our species' functionality. Some examples include:

Inefficient respiratory system: The trachea serves both as the intake and exhaust pathway for air to the lungs, sharing an entrance at the pharynx with the esophagus, separated by only a thin membrane. This can result in choking when attempting to swallow and breathe simultaneously. While the epiglottis aims to prevent this interchange, it is not infallible, requiring coordination between five cranial nerves and twenty muscles. Stomach acids can flow back through the esophagus into the lungs, triggering coughing and gagging to expel the foreign substance. A pneumonia-causing strain of bacteria resides in the back of the throat, just above the airway. Although human lungs can hold up to 6 liters of air, only about 0.5 liters are useful for normal breathing due to CO_2 buildup.

Location of the brain: The most vital organ, responsible for thought, memory, reason, and control over the entire body, is situated in a highly vulnerable location prone to damage, thereby reducing capabilities or resulting in death.

Eye: Photoreceptors are located on the front of the eye, facing away from incoming light. Neurons collected on the retina exit the eye, leading to blind spots.

Birth canal: In horizontal animals, birth occurs in a straight line through the pelvis. However, being bipedal requires a delivery process that makes a right angle around the pubic bone, exerting extra pressure on both the baby and mother, which can lead to brain damage or death for both parties. Although the close-in legs are necessary for running, they result in narrow hips that are challenging for a human baby, particularly one with a large brain in a proportionately large head.

The proximity of the birth canal to the rectum and urinary bladder: The closeness of the bacterial-sensitive opening to the waste discharge outlets allows for potential infections. The tissues between these two systems are prone to failure during the exertions of childbirth, resulting in a permanent connection between waste discharge and the vagina, a condition known as Obstetric fistula.

Recurrent laryngeal nerve: The nerve connecting the brain to the larynx is unnecessarily complex and lengthy for its relatively simple function.

Spine: The spine in quadruped ancestors served as a bow from which the rib cage and organs were suspended. Transitioning to a bipedal posture placed the spine in a vertical load-bearing role under constant compression. The spine arched backward to center the weight and maintain head posture.

Inflexible knee: Knee movement is limited to a single front-back plane, whereas our actions involve multidirectional motion.

Excessive number of teeth: As our diet evolved to become softer and to accommodate a larger brain, the jaw shortened, but the number of teeth remained constant. This results in retaining the same set of adult teeth for life, leading to the accumulation of cavity-causing bacteria and subsequent tooth loss. Other animals have naturally replaceable teeth.

Excessive number of bones in the feet: As bipedal beings, we do not require the same 26 bones found in tree-dwelling primates.

Limited knee flexibility: Our knee joints evolved from four-legged animals that did not require the range of flexion needed for running and turning, which led to the development of ligaments that align the upper and lower leg bones. These ligaments are susceptible to wear and tear, with the anterior cruciate ligament (ACL) being particularly vulnerable.

Inability to produce vitamin C: Unlike most mammals, primates lack the ability to produce vitamin C. While this was not an issue for primates living in vitamin C-rich tropical environments, it became problematic as hominins migrated to colder climates or embarked on extended journeys without access to vitamin C sources.

Fixed ear lobes: In arboreal habitats, precise sight was crucial, whereas acute hearing was only necessary for general awareness.

Adaptation to vertical orientation: While horizontal body structures are well-suited for activities like grazing, human verticality, while advantageous for most actions, is stressful when leaning over for tasks such as cleaning floors, planting, or picking berries. Verticality compresses the chest, reducing lung capacity.

Vestigial organs: The appendix and tonsils no longer serve a function, yet they remain part of the human body. Similarly, the coccyx has lost its original purpose. Arteries are prone to flow-limiting buildup, and male embryos develop nipples that become nonfunctional after birth.

While many other issues could be identified, this represents what an intelligently designed human might look like with a "clean slate." *Homo designus* is not a transhuman version of *Homo sapiens*, as it is not linked to mechanical or computer-based enhancements. There is no intention to "supersize" *Homo designus* by making them stronger or faster. The focus is solely on improving design within the constraints of known biology.

So, what might an intelligently designed human look like? Homo designus is free from evolutionary constraints and compromises inherited from ancestors. The design objective is to maximize human efficiency.

Homo designus

Move the brain: The brain, being the most crucial organ, is also the most vulnerable. A significant change involves relocating the brain within the chest cavity, near the lungs and heart. The shortened communication pathways between these major organs will enhance efficiency and minimize potential disruptions. This new position keeps the brain warm, reducing its energy requirements. The soft tissues between the brain and protective chest bones allow for expansion. Eyes and ears remain in the head, along with air and food entrances. A movable lower jaw facilitates food input and speech. Analogous to ship design, control systems are internal, while input devices (such as the bridge, radar, and antennas) are placed externally. Visual and auditory inputs are located at the top, with the CPU internal within the chest.

Brain temperature control benefits from proximity to the lungs, which act as radiators providing cooling and dissipating excess heat to maintain an ideal operating temperature.

The head, unburdened by the weight of the brain, becomes lighter, reducing stress on the vertical column and spinal cord.

Three-unit piping: The head will feature two separate tracheas – one for air intake and another for air exhaust. Simple flapper valves will ensure proper air flow direction through the lungs, facilitating CO_2 removal and allowing the air sacs to efficiently utilize remaining air. The elongated nasal channel, no longer constrained by brain placement, can regulate air temperature and humidity on the way to the lungs, and an increased number of olfactory receptors will enhance smell efficiency. The exit orifice, coordinated with the tongue and lips, will enable speech, a proven means of communication. An exclusive esophagus for food entrance eliminates the risk of choking by keeping food and air in separate passages.

The food entrance is located lower to allow lateral movement for chewing. All three openings are situated at the front of the head. Although the tracheas and esophagus will still bend at a 90-degree angle, their paths will no longer intersect.

An optimized breathing system permits smaller lungs, easily positioned on the sides of the torso with reduced compression during bending.

The head houses audio and visual inputs, both oriented forward for directional sensing. Eyes are recessed beneath a protective brow, and ear inlets on the head's sides allow basic sound localization, requiring the head to be turned towards the sound source.

Sensory inputs, along with air and food passages, are enclosed by a protective head shell, featuring a base opening for passage to the torso. The top and back of the skull can convert light into energy directly for the body. The lower jawbone and activating muscles can be positioned further back in the head.

Redesigned eye: The eye will be modeled after the cephalopod eyes of squids and octopi, with wiring positioned behind the receptors to eliminate blind spots. Expanded wavelength perception into ultraviolet and improved low-light vision would enhance Homo designus's visual capabilities.

Organ and bone structure relocation: Primary organs will be positioned within rib cages for protection. The digestive system, including support organs like the pancreas, liver, and kidneys, will be situated along with the elimination point at the torso base. Organs can be anchored to the ribs for alignment.

A central support column, maintaining front-to-back and side-to-side balance, reduces the risk of back pain. Symmetrical rib sets will attach to the central column, directing head weight to the legs and feet. The flexible central support is shielded by the rib cages, skin, and attached muscles.

A flexible spinal cord adjacent to the central column enhances protection and minimizes injury potential. With an internal brain, the spinal cord becomes less vulnerable to neck injuries. A bone plate loosely connected to the rib cage shields the brain, complementing the protective design of the skull.

Arms are affixed to upper ribs with rotational mobility. The thumb and finger arrangement, contributing to manual dexterity, remains preserved.

Hip bones support internal organs and also provide support for upper leg bones at the back and sides.

The reproductive system is located at the lower front of the torso. Childbirth aligns more closely with a Caesarean birth, where the uterus rests atop the pelvis and remains above the leg separation, allowing unobstructed birthing without pubic bone interference. With the front exit system, the birth canal avoids conflict with the pelvis's leg-supporting functions. The lower pelvis is open, facilitating rear waste elimination, physically separate from the birth canal. Alternatively, brain development and mother-child interaction could continue post-birth, similar to kangaroos, making childbirth a midpoint in embryo-to-child development.

A simple cylinder-and-cup hinge, akin to ball-and-socket joints in hips and shoulders, would offer superior knee functionality.

Enhancements will also address attributes like hemoglobin, increasing oxygen carrying capacity, and reintroducing the ability to produce vitamin C.

A more efficient eye design inspired by cephalopods, such as octopuses and squids, wires photoreceptors directly to the optic nerve, eliminating blind spots. While color vision may be limited, a superior design could combine both functionalities.

Several superior design features found in other creatures were not part of the primate evolutionary path. Nonetheless, due to compatibility with the same DNA ancestor, these features could potentially be incorporated into human DNA through modification.

An intelligent being (**IB**) could have incorporated these features into a superior, completely new design, but evolution either discarded them or didn't include them in the human evolutionary path. Birds effectively utilize continuous breathing to fuel flight, with air moving through a single pipe, passing through the lungs, and then exiting through another.

Self-contained fluids: Water, in its various forms, enters the body, serves its purpose, and is subsequently expelled. Some water is stored in blood and organs, aiding temperature regulation through evaporation under stress or heat. Water also eliminates impurities through urine. While this system works effectively in environments with sufficient fresh water, it becomes inefficient during water scarcity.

Part of the water system operates like a car's cooling system, circulating through the body to transfer heat to a cooling organ. The system collects contaminants, transporting them to the bowels for elimination as fecal discharge. Though some moisture loss occurs, most water remains within the body, reducing dehydration. In periods of water shortage, eliminating water through urine becomes wasteful.

Teeth and body part replacement: Sharks continually regenerate their teeth, often as frequently as every few months, maintaining sharpness and minimal bacteria buildup. While humans may not require replacement every few weeks like some shark species, periodic replacement every few years or even decades could be advantageous, especially given the increasing human lifespan. Certain creatures like sea stars, alligators, and certain lizards can regrow entire limbs, deer can regrow antlers, and the African Spiny Mouse can regenerate patches of lost skin. The genetic program for recreating a body part already exists; it only needs to be reactivated.

Insects possess vision beyond our visible light range, allowing them to perceive what we are missing. Most mammals can internally produce Vitamin C, a trait lost in primate evolution.

Asymmetrical Esophagus: Food/liquid entry through the esophagus has to make an abrupt downward turn. It has to be located in front of the spinal column. By moving the throat to either side of the column to come down behind the column the radius is greatly increased reducing potential for choking.

Additionally, what if attributes from the plant world were incorporated? Photosynthesis enables plants to directly harness energy from light, a more efficient process than the energy transformation from plant to herbivore to protein for our consumption. Consider skin capable of directly absorbing energy.

Homo designus might not be aesthetically appealing to *Homo sapiens*. Their appearance will likely differ greatly from ours. However, species have historically found attraction within their own unique attributes. A male warthog, for example, is attracted to a female warthog because she embodies the characteristics of an ideal mate. Similarly, male and female Homo designus may perceive *Homo sapiens* as deformed and unsuitable for partnership. Yet, there's hope for communication and friendship to bridge this gap.

Homo avian

A bipedal structure provides numerous survival advantages: heightened vision above grasses, liberated upper limbs for tool use and holding infants, and efficient movement. However, it also gives rise to issues when contracting with lowering actions, such as bending over. Bending the back to reach objects on the ground during tasks like planting, harvesting, lifting, or desk work creates back problems resulting from this unnatural posture, a universal concern across human cultures.

While human evolution followed the primate lineage, an alternative architectural blueprint was modeled on dromaeosaurid bipedal dinosaurs that eventually gave rise to birds. This design features an organ-supporting rib cage upheld by two central legs. The torso and limbs are balanced atop these central supports. This configuration allows *Homo avian* to be bipedal while retaining a straight-through digestive system. Positioned externally to the rib cage, *Homo avian* can move swiftly without the oscillations observed in wide-pelvis humans and ducks. The birth canal adheres to a straight-line arrangement, with the uterus located at the rear of the legs, thus avoiding any conflict between swift leg pivots and spacious openings for easy childbirth. Various bird beak designs evolved from the T-Rex type mouth and teeth, indicating the presence of DNA for similarities to the side-moving jaw and flexible lips of mammalian herbivores.

The swift-moving raptor-like front legs/arms evolved into avian wings, but they could have equally transformed into grasping hands situated at the ends of extended arms adorned with fingers instead of claws. Employing a pivot mechanism on the central leg-supporting pelvis facilitates bodily rotation from horizontal to vertical. Balancing demands less cognitive effort compared to full-time vertical orientation, a characteristic inherited from *Homo erectus*.

Homo avian incorporates the features of relocated brain, separate air/food entry/exit, vitamin C production, water retention, and regenerative teeth and body parts from Homo designus. The lighter head will necessitate fewer substantial neck muscles.

One advantage of *Homo avian* over fully vertical *Homo designus* lies in the fact that during bending over, as in picking up objects from the ground, the chest and lungs experience reduced compression, thereby preserving lung capacity.

Homo avian and *Homo designus* represent my envisioned life forms that emulate *Homo sapiens* in functionality while mitigating the design flaws inherent in our evolutionary history.

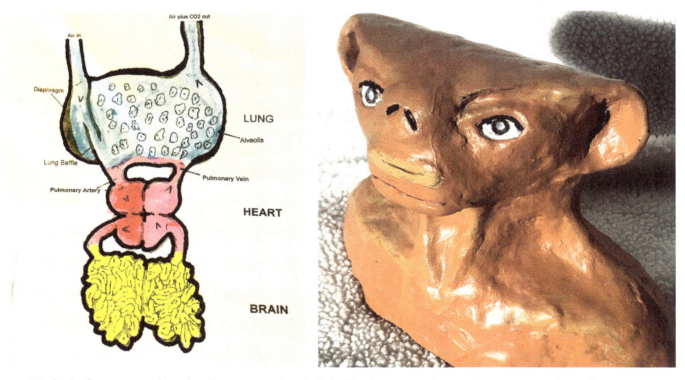

With the brain moved to the chest cavity the skull holds the eyes and ears. Air comes in through an upper opening leading down through an entrance tube to the single lung where the flowing air is mixed with the blood. CO2 air is pushed into the exit tube where pushed up and out. The exit has a tongue teeth and malleable lips for speech. The lower opening is input for food and liquids. The lung is above the heart that is above the brain all within the central chest cavity connected by arteries.

sculpture and design credit: James Martin

Epilogue

So what is the thing we learned that made us the Intelligent Designers?

We are an extraordinary species. We have achieved dominance through our superior brain capacity and the means to apply it through bipedalism, language, an opposing thumb, and an omnivorous diet.

In the realm of all other life forms, symbiotic relationships prevail—between predator and prey, herbivores and plants, and life forms and their environments. When any element changes, the life form either adapts, transforms, or faces extinction. However, humans exist outside of these macro symbiotic relationships. When a food source or environment shifts, we transition to an alternative, preserving the human design with minimal alteration. We possess the unique capability to mold the environment to our needs, ensuring our survival.

Our capacity for abstract creation and understanding is unparalleled. We have initiated conflicts—even resulting in violence and death—over abstract values such as love and hate, which lack physical existence. We engage in battles over meanings of imagined words, the significance of symbols, religious interpretations, and territorial borders that only exist within collective imagination. Conflicts arise when we fail to agree on interpretations.

We inhabit the most resplendent celestial body known to us in the universe. While other planets and moons possess features like mountains, oceans, volcanoes, atmospheric clouds, and ice, Earth encompasses all of these, in addition to being the sole known habitat for an array of life forms, many of which remain unseen, yet they coexist with us.

Our minimum standard of stewardship for our home should be: *"Do not disrupt it."* Nevertheless, despite our superior intelligence and analytical skills, we seem unable to set aside personal and group egos to even meet this minimal standard. This failing casts doubt on the legacy we leave for our descendants.

British astrophysicist Martin Rees once stated, *"This century is special: it's the first in which one species has the power to determine the future of life on Earth."*

We remain uncertain about the natural events beyond our control. An asteroid could be hurtling towards us before we can mount a proper defense. Poles may shift again, or a catastrophic pandemic may emerge without a defense in place. A massive volcanic eruption could trigger a global cloud. After each such event, not all life or humanity may be eradicated, but our familiar planet will be forever altered.

Nick Bostrom, director of Oxford's Future of Humanity Institute, pointed out that *"All of the biggest risks, the existential risks, are seen to be anthropogenic, that is, they originate from human beings."* These encompass nuclear war, biotech plagues, climate change leading to biodiversity loss, runaway AI, and a nanotechnology arms race.

E. O. Wilson remarked, *"We have created a Star Wars civilization with Stone Age emotions, medieval institutions, and god-like technology. Are we cavemen with lasers?"*

Despite our inherent sense of self-importance, we are not as significant in the grand scheme of things.

Earth will endure regardless of our actions. Life will persist, possibly taking unfamiliar forms that we cannot fathom, as these forms best adapt to the altered world and serve as the foundation for Earthly life.

However, these forces won't be able to revert the planet to its state before our impact. The atmosphere and oceans still retain particles of matter we've introduced, and the scars we've left on the surface will only be smoothed by wind and sand, never restoring the original contours. It will take centuries for ice sheets to regain a natural equilibrium. Extinct flora and fauna will not be resurrected. We have irrevocably transformed the world, and there's no turning back from the Anthropocene.

In 2023, the "Doomsday Clock" was adjusted to ninety seconds from midnight, symbolizing the closeness of human time to its end. Created in 1947 to highlight the risk of self-destruction due to nuclear annihilation during the Cold War, the most recent concern added was unchecked climate change. The Bulletin of the Atomic Scientists noted that 2015 marked the warmest year on record, and subsequent years such as 2016 and 2022 were even warmer, pushing us past a tipping point in ice loss, rendering the melt inexorable.

Sir Crispin Tickell marked the Anthropocene's inception as the emergence of farming and domestication. His second marker, the Industrial Revolution, commenced with harnessing natural wind and water power. Dependence on these sources was contingent on quantity, location, and timing until the advent of the steam engine. The Renaissance and Enlightenment broadened our intellectual horizons, fostering advancements in art, philosophy, and exploration. The Age of Exploration expanded our physical domain, revealing new resources and potential.

Humans possess the longest temporal awareness of any species, projecting both forward and backward to infinity. Our memories are supplemented by writing and data storage. We comprehend the timelines of the age of dinosaurs and the big bang, and can predict the probable future of the universe. We study history to trace our origins and seek understanding.

Our capacity for foresight extends beyond the present. We design space missions destined to reach their objectives long after their creators have passed away. Science fiction authors, futurists, and political analysts endeavor to predict what lies ahead. Jules Verne envisioned submarines, atomic energy, and moon missions. Arthur C. Clarke, in 1947, foresaw satellites orbiting Earth. In *1984*, George Orwell envisioned a dystopian future marked by constant surveillance through omnipresent cameras.

Occasionally, they make mistakes. In 1950, Aldous Huxley, failing to anticipate the "green revolution," predicted that due to limited available food, the global population would peak at around 3 billion by the year 2000. Irregular outcomes stem from events that don't adhere to linear extrapolation. Fractal occurrences wield significant consequences and changes, particularly in the realm of technologies that don't uniformly evolve.

Hominins gained a survival advantage by being generalists. In contrast to other species that flourished through specialization, hominins secured an edge by being versatile. As omnivores, our diet carried few limitations. Aided by clothing and shelter, humans spread across all corners of the planet.

As society evolved into greater civilization, particularly with the advent of industrialization, human endeavors grew more specialized. Individuals, much like animals, acquired specific skills that integrated into the broader culture.

While our food options have diversified, our range of habitats has narrowed. We possess the capability to inhabit various environments, yet for efficiency, we've concentrated populations in ever-expanding cities. Globalization has accelerated international trade, but simultaneously, it has transformed localized diseases into worldwide, civilization-halting pandemics.

Perhaps the gravest peril lies in global warming, resulting in the thawing of permafrost, the Greenland ice sheet, and West Antarctica. Characteristics that have developed over ten millennia, upon which natural equilibrium and our societies are founded, are now destabilized.

Global consensus among scientists, after rigorous peer review, affirms that Anthropogenic Global

Warming (AGW) is inducing unprecedented alterations to the world. Human influence over the planet's design extends beyond global warming. Decreasing crop variety heightens vulnerability to diseases or evolved pesticide-resistant insect swarms capable of annihilating entire crop species. Even if the human population eventually stabilizes, the sheer number of individuals could strain numerous resources.

Apart from atmospheric changes resulting from burning fossil fuels and the persistence of nuclear fallout detectable for millennia, alterations caused by dams and canals are disrupting the natural flow of sediment. Half the planet's surface is now shaped by some form of human intervention, akin to "techno fossils."

Over the past five centuries, the developed world, buoyed by seemingly limitless energy access, has enjoyed an unprecedented lifestyle of growth fostered by exploiting nature. However, this lifestyle can't indefinitely expand or persist.

Much of the prosperity experienced by many and coveted by all stems from the depletion and devastation of the planet. Entire economies hinge on resource consumption. The pursuit of sustainable alternatives will necessitate paradigm shifts.

Corporations and coalitions have amassed financial and political power to ensure the perpetuation of their enterprises. A complete transition to renewable energy sources will result in job losses and profit reductions for fossil fuel industries, impacting workers both directly and indirectly reliant on them. Even the most agreeable meat and egg substitutes would imperil cattle and poultry businesses, affecting everyone from ranchers to processing plants. These products have facilitated a lifestyle that may prove challenging to relinquish, even when we acknowledge their harm.

Meeting the universally recognized goal of carbon reduction entails change. Established industries (fossil fuels, concrete construction, and livestock) must yield to emerging sustainable industries (solar energy, plant-based solutions) to supply equivalent energy. The greatest hurdle will not lie in technological advancement, but rather in financial models and resistance to change.

Earth's circumference spans a mere 25,000 miles, with seventy-four percent covered by water, and much of the land comprises deserts, mountains, and regions with limited habitability. The land available for food production is inherently finite.

An aerial view of Earth is unlike that of any other planet. The illuminated side reveals cities, roads, and shifts in the landscape. However, it's the night side that offers a distinct perspective. The network of lights outlines our geography and civilizations.

Pessimists make a valid critique that *Homo sapiens* resemble a cancer on the planet. This "virus" persists by consuming its host—the Earth. Our actions have degraded the atmosphere, landscape, and oceans, elevating planetary temperatures and decreasing biodiversity.

Nonetheless, we have instigated improvements. We've achieved a better balance between wet and arid terrain. Our concerted efforts have yielded disease-resistant measures that benefit diverse species in both flora and fauna, enhancing living conditions.

Regardless of whether a natural or human-induced catastrophe transpires, the Earth we inherit will not be as resource-abundant as what we presently possess. Lord Martin Rees, in "Our Final Hour," projects a mere 50% chance of our civilization surviving past 2100. Access to recovery resources in a post-new-Dark-Ages era might elude us for centuries. Easily accessible minerals such as coal, oil, and iron have already been extracted, necessitating deeper excavation.

Humans possess the power to transcend the natural forces that have shaped all preceding evolutionary steps. Unlike the dinosaurs, we can identify potentially hazardous asteroids and avert the threat. We can recognize and prepare defenses against diseases, even eradicating some or altering the conditions that support their existence.

We possess the choice to continually build upon our accomplishments in a deliberate manner immune to natural evolutionary forces. We can design, comprehend, and construct, or rectify errors and build better. Our cultural evolution has been guided by a desire to harness nature and each other. We recognize that numerous plant and animal species have succumbed to direct and indirect human influence.

We understand that various conditions, whether natural or man-made, can lead to the loss of plant diversity. To ensure survival, a multitude of plant seed banks have been established worldwide. These banks function as Noah's Arks for seeds, preserving a wide array of species that can adapt and be cultivated in a changing world.

However, we must acknowledge the premise stated in the EcoModernist Manifesto: *"Humans are as likely to spare nature because it is not needed to meet their needs as they are to spare it for explicit aesthetic and spiritual reasons…have been spared because they have not yet found an economic use for them."*

We can set aside the escalating demand for fossil fuels and excessive land consumption in acknowledgment of our survival imperative. Moreover, we can forego personal accumulation of resources and materials to promote the collective welfare.

But can we? We've demonstrated intelligence; do we possess the wisdom?

An enduring awareness must persist that when the future clashes with the present, the present will inevitably prevail. When choosing between feeding the family today or preserving pristine streams for future generations, the immediate need for sustenance often takes precedence, as without immediate fulfillment, the future becomes uncertain.

Past actions have not provided an encouraging precedent. Resistance arises from the belief that sacrifices are unjust when others aren't making them, or that denial of what others already possess is unjust. Particularly in highly individualistic societies, accepting sacrifices for the greater good (of nature, the planet, and humanity) proves challenging without a significant shift in perspective.

However, such shifts have occurred before. Recycling has moved from environmental extremism to mainstream practice. The use of lead paint and asbestos in construction is now prohibited, and smoking rates have significantly declined.

Over the last two centuries, human technology has diminished diseases for humans, plants, and animals alike. Despite sensationalized news accounts and geopolitical events like the Russian invasion of Ukraine, interpersonal violence has decreased, large-scale genocides no longer obliterate entire civilizations, and the proportion of human casualties is steadily diminishing. Our resilience to weather effects has improved as climate conditions grow more extreme. More people are enjoying longer, healthier lives. Food production has increased while the land used for agriculture has decreased. We are consciously safeguarding species incapable of fending off anthropogenic threats. Advances in human medical knowledge have enhanced animal health, be it for pets or livestock.

Given our understanding of consequences and demonstrated capacity for change, why haven't we acted more decisively? Are so many individuals so shortsighted as to overlook their own peril? Are the powerful so intent on retaining control that they'd allow destruction before setting aside their egos?

What will humans be like in fifty or a hundred years? With advancements in artificial intelligence and brain-computer interfaces, humans will possess biological access to virtually limitless data and processing power. If Artificial Intelligence (AI), as predicted, achieves comparable data processing capabilities to humans by around 2040, what will the relationship between humans and AI be like in 2050 or 2100? It may be beyond present human comprehension. Human perfection (defined by the standards of that era) may become the norm. Although biologically Homo sapien, they may not resemble us physically.

Threats from our own technologies extend beyond just runaway robots, encompassing software programs reading barcodes at checkout lines and assembly line robots (SPR) replacing human workers. Algorithms can now, with basic input, prepare taxes and draft legal documents, rendering thousands of human workers obsolete. Post this, AI may initiate a "runaway reaction" of self-improvement, in line with the Law of Accelerating Returns, as each successive, more intelligent generation emerges, potentially resulting in a superintelligence qualitatively surpassing human intelligence.

While many carnivores sleep most of the day, humans think and seek understanding of our environment. Our brains don't tolerate prolonged idle periods, often leading to boredom. We create beyond mere necessity. Work contributes significantly to our self-esteem, and replacement by robots can lead to diminished self-worth. How will we redirect our efforts toward activities that bolster self-esteem?

As AI computing power continues to surge, biological/synthetic interfaces will become commonplace as humans leverage complementary strengths. How we shape this partnership, given that humans design it, will hinge not only on technological considerations but also on social and ethical parameters.

This juncture may be pivotal in hominin evolution. The question may transcend the differences between those like Ray Kurzweil, who welcome AI as a valuable tool, and individuals like Elon Musk, who harbor concerns about AI replacing humans. The crux will lie in how AI is employed.

The integration of AI with biological humans could enhance human intelligence, riding on the wave of ever-increasing computing power. Cyborgs may become ubiquitous, integrated into humans as seamlessly as any assistive device.

Will everyone access this partnership? Initial technological inventions tend to be costly, granting the wealthy a "smart" advantage. Some segments of society may remain excluded due to cost, accessibility, or reluctance, creating an intelligence-based caste system, as intelligence equates to power. Will control over data input consolidate benefits for a privileged few?

Artificial Intelligence (AI) relies on data accumulation. The more data processed, the greater the information generated. Will this information serve as a tool for problem-solving and informed decision-making? What decisions will an informed population make in the context of an ultimate democracy? Or will programmers exploit data accumulation to amass comprehensive knowledge about everyone?

Can the data be trusted? Software like Photoshop and ChatGPT can manipulate images, altering media context. Faces, voices, environments, and actions can be distorted, creating scenarios detached from reality. Instead of enhancing information, altered data can foster false information that may be misconstrued as knowledge. Programmers will wield control over facts. Could skewed data diminish knowledge? Will programmers and their controllers exploit data accumulation to scrutinize individuals? Will facial recognition lead to constant surveillance and the death of privacy? Will algorithms dictate all aspects of society? What about conflicting algorithms in news, entertainment, and warfare? Can programmers comprehend output reliability?

Deep fakes blur the line between reality and fiction. Moreover, how will we relate to reality? Virtual Reality (VR) immerses users in a digital realm.

Addressing interconnected issues beyond human capacity—population, income inequality, species extinction, waste, and pollution—demands augmented AI processing power. Accommodating additional data servers necessitates more energy suppliers. Much of this energy generation relies on non-renewable sources, contributing to global warming and climate change, which exacerbate existing problems. Are we trapped in an AI/energy spiral?

Strong financial and political incentives propel AI development. Billions of dollars and numerous technicians drive its advancement despite lingering concerns. Yet, fewer than 400 people worldwide are addressing AI threats.

Evolution has followed an uneven path from energy to matter, life, and thought, culminating in the human cortex, capable of surpassing biological systems through faster, more accurate synthetic evolution.

Forecasting the next step in our evolution remains educated guesswork. Just as Australopithecus afarensis "Lucy" might not have comprehended *Homo habilis,* we may struggle to grasp the implications of synthetic intelligence. Will *Homo sapiens* resist synthetic intelligence as Neanderthals did when faced with encroaching *sapiens*, leading to a similar outcome? If *sapiens* can't adapt rapidly, will we become another former species in the evolutionary chain? Is technology's logarithmic evolution outpacing linear evolution in hominins?

Could the Anthropocene be fleeting? Its full impact might span just a couple of centuries, with synths potentially becoming the dominant influencers in the Synthocene by the late 21st century.

The 2030s could be pivotal for human history. The IPCC warns that with current CO_2 emissions, we'll breach the 1.5°C limit (currently at about 1°C) by 2030, irreparably damaging numerous natural features. Will our consumer-driven products deplete resources and unwittingly destroy critical, unnoticed animal species? What will life be like beyond 2050, with accumulating ocean plastics? What lies ahead post-2030? How will we manage AI post-Singularity, post-2040? Will the planet's rising heat render our blue marble uninhabitable?

How many tipping points must we cross? Arctic, Antarctic, and glacier ice are melting at alarming rates. Regions are becoming uninhabitable. Ocean currents are shifting. Amazon forests and coral reefs are vanishing. Wildfires are transforming frozen tundras into methane-releasing grasslands. Prolonged drought renders soil incapable of retaining moisture.

Can we craft a sustainable world into the 22nd century? Will humans find a compromise between competing priorities? Nature does not compromise, and ultimately, nature prevails. It falls on us to utilize our advanced intellect to design a symbiotic relationship maximizing survival for both us and nature.

Throughout history, *sapiens* have shaped nature to suit our designs. Yet nature reacts, necessitating our adaptation. Land inhabited for 10,000 years may soon become inhospitable for us and our animals. The far-reaching effects of climate change might answer Fermi's Paradox, explaining the "great silence" from other worlds. Perhaps their unchecked technology and resource depletion led to overdesigning their worlds, resulting in catastrophe.

Handling runaway consumerism, climate crises, and viruses shouldn't foster disagreement. These issues can be tackled through data-driven responses. Still, the internal struggle between individuality and collective action remains intrinsic to hominin nature. At critical junctures, both sides have served us well, from challenging orthodoxy (individuality) to embracing collective agricultural advancements.

We refuse to accept conditions as they are; our imaginations foresee better possibilities.

While we exhibit empathy and strive for the betterment of our tribe, this attachment weakens as individuals distance themselves from the broader world. With nine billion people across the planet, building a strong attachment for universal improvement proves challenging. Our species is incredibly diverse—physically, culturally, religiously, and financially—making it difficult to envision common functions, let alone create a common design.

Yet, how will we navigate changing demographic disruptions? Environmental, economic, and political forces are pushing entire groups beyond their traditional homelands. This influx, coupled with declining local Total Fertility Rates, strains cultural identities. Native populations may feel threatened by demographic shifts' power dynamics. Will racial, cultural, or ethnic differences lead to conflicts and dominance struggles by original inhabitants, or will new inclusive identities emerge?

The mere existence of the "Doomsday Clock" indicates an awareness that humanity is jeopardizing itself. While humans possess advanced logical faculties, primal instincts persist. At this juncture of *sapien* evolution, these two aspects perpetually clash, with individuals deciding which prevails in a given situation.

The average mammal species longevity is estimated at about four million years. From the emergence of Homo *sapiens* as a distinct species around 200,000 years ago, we have had time to maximize our potential.

If extraterrestrials had visited Earth roughly 100,000 years ago, they might not have considered the potential of skinny, almost hairless bipedal primates. Our ancestors were inferior competitors in nearly every category against the environment.

We can't outrun cheetahs, but we exceed the speed of sound. We can't match falcons in skyward flight, but we transcend the atmosphere and escape gravity's pull. We're dwarfed by elephants, yet construct mighty dams. We've walked on other worlds and dispatched probes into the unknown. Armed with tools, particularly our exceptional brains, we possess an understanding that spans the universe's origin down to individual particles. We've created machines that solve problems beyond our own capabilities.

Humans have achieved feats nature couldn't replicate. We've developed rotary mechanisms. We've crafted unnatural alloys like brass. We've engineered stronger cross-directional materials like plywood. We record and reproduce sounds and capture light for storage, producing pictures and data transmitted across space.

We've conceived monumental structures—dams, buildings, and ships—far exceeding our scale. Through human-designed applications, we wield immense forces.

Our ancestors were unaware of the environmental harm and potential endangerment of both us and the planet, but we are. Can we learn and reshape our lifestyles to sustain human life on Earth? The Anthropocene is a **When** framework that will extend as long as there are some forms of humans. The "**What**" and "**How**" rests in our hands. To paraphrase *Shrek 2*, " we have the challenge to learn, what we lack may be the capacity."

Designing a sustainable world for future generations is attainable, necessitating a shift from relentless resource exploitation for increased production. We acknowledge limitations, but faith in new technologies to facilitate continuity persists. The necessary technologies exist; it's the will to replace them that clashes with existing institutions.

We stand in awe of Earth, life, and the universe's inexplicable wonder. We perceive with admiration, marveling at the beauty in sunsets, babbling brooks, and starlit skies. We sense beauty and order.

Furthermore, we possess the power to create beauty. Whether in the mechanized beauty of the Cord 810, utilitarian tools like the Stanley 20-001 hacksaw, Calder's spatial art, Michelangelo's Pieta, Monet's Lily Pond, or humans manifest joy through sensory harmony of the grand cathedrals.

Cord 810
photo credit: James Martin

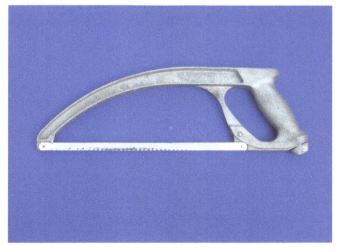

Stanley 20-001
Design creation and photo: James Martin

Alexander Calder
photo credit: James Martin

Pieta, Michelangelo
photo credit: James Martin

Lily Pond, Claude Monet
photo credit: James Martin

LeMans Cathedral
photo credit: James Martin

We are innate explorers, driven by the pursuit of answers. We've ventured into every corner, height, and depth of our planet, and even beyond into space, all in our quest for understanding. We've delved into the fundamental elements of life and matter, a feat no other species could accomplish. We've journeyed into the depths of our minds to decipher the origins of our capabilities. Our thirst for knowledge is insatiable. Questions abound: What constitutes the universe? What defines life and our role as individuals and as a species? What underpins consciousness?

From the time of Democritus, who theorized that all matter is comprised of atoms, we've scrutinized the universe's nature to comprehend its mechanisms. Sir Isaac Newton formulated the laws of motion and gravity, underpinning the Industrial Revolution. William Harvey delved into the body's inner workings to explain its functioning. We've unlocked DNA's secrets, the twin helix of life, and gained the power to manipulate its code.

Who are we destined to become? As we grapple with the question of whether AI can possess consciousness, we might uncover the very essence of our own awareness. Will we fathom the nature of our descendants, or will they comprehend our present state? Will the boundary between organic and synthetic even hold meaning?

Elusive phenomena like "Dark Matter," theoretically comprising 85% of the universe's matter, continue to baffle us. Something influences known matter, but what is it? Then there's "Dark Energy," a term employed to explain unexplained gravitational anomalies. Perhaps these concepts are beyond our perceptual scope, akin to perceiving ultraviolet light unaided.

Unlike our ancient forebears, our lack of understanding doesn't serve as proof of the unseen, any more than ignorance of lightning substantiates a god of thunder. Acknowledged gaps only amplify our curiosity. More significant than our opposable thumbs and bipedal locomotion is our inherent ability to question, even while aware that answers might remain elusive. As humans, we embrace the idea that we don't know.

The Anthropocene epoch is our handiwork—a blueprint incorporating human actions aligned with natural laws to achieve a goal. It's a macro plan comprised of countless micro designs, encompassing all facets of human society, even when these facets conflict with each other. We decide which aspects take precedence and which recede; we define the intended function. Sometimes, the plan aligns with nature, resulting in success. In other instances, it clashes, leading to suffering. We, the designers, conceive and execute these plans, then live with the outcomes—be they intended goals or unforeseen consequences.

This design encompasses all societal components: agriculture, energy, environment, education, emotion, science, politics, economics, arts, and the entirety of the products we generate. This design must account for how these components interplay, for the betterment of the planetary system and all its present and future inhabitants. Regrettably, many, especially those in power, resist acknowledging limits and the need for degrowth.

We possess the means to create a sustainable ecosystem, facilitating growth without straining the planet beyond its capacity. Our inherent nature drives us to seek answers about "**How**" and "**Why**." Stagnation isn't part of our makeup; we're compelled to learn and advance.

However, achieving this will necessitate paradigm shifts. We must find ways to harmonize human needs with the planet's ecosystem, allowing natural forces to keep pace with our human-driven designs. Snow cannot reconstruct glaciers swiftly enough to stabilize water usage. Creatures, especially larger species, cannot evolve rapidly enough to match our swift environmental transformations. Only by regulating the human element can we achieve balance within the planetary equation.

Unless we strike a balance between economic and scientific growth, a fully stable, sustainable global society may remain elusive—and perhaps even undesirable.

Human design represents the next evolutionary stride, poised to carry life to the stars. We stand as the potential birth seed of a universe intelligently crafted to perpetuate growth for eternity. As humans, we occupy the pivotal role in transitioning from primitive life on Earth to a universe teeming with life and intelligence across galaxies. Among all the species that have graced Earth's surface, only humanity has mustered the means and determination to surpass our planetary cradle and venture into the limitless expanse of the cosmos.

In this cosmic voyage, hominins are akin to the Columbuses of the stars. The moon, planets, and eventually star-clustered worlds could become the dominion of human creations, be they biological or synthetic, marked by intelligence and consciousness. Perhaps this pursuit encapsulates the ultimate mission of our species.

Our machines have already conferred upon us a form of immortality. Long after both Earth and ourselves have departed, the Pioneers, Voyagers, New Horizons, and their progeny shall linger as embodiments of human endeavor, transcending our terrestrial limitations to join the eternal legacy of the heavens. Although the same raw materials were accessible to all species, only hominins, spurred by curiosity and inquisitiveness, forged vessels that departed the comfort of our home planet to traverse the cosmos.

Our existence is entrenched in a perpetual dichotomy between self-destruction and self-actualization.

Slaves were transported to the New World during the early 16th century, coinciding with the Renaissance flourishing in Florence. Similarly, in the 1960s, as humans embarked on lunar explorations, the Vietnam War raged, and the development of a measles vaccine marked our simultaneous triumphs and struggles.

Contrary to our anthropocentric impulses, we aren't the universe's focal point, nor the apex of Earth's life forms. As Neil Armstrong, gazing back at Earth en route to the moon, mused, *"It suddenly struck me that that tiny pea, pretty and blue, was the Earth. I put up my thumb and shut one eye, and my thumb blotted out the planet Earth. I didn't feel like a giant. I felt very, very small."*

This planet is our sole abode, our only haven. We are tasked with the astute design of its destiny. While we've achieved remarkable feats and harbor boundless potential, we also harbor the seeds of our own destruction, capable of unraveling not only ourselves but also the planet—the exclusive harbor of known life in the universe. The onus of shaping this design rests with us. The responsibility lies upon our shoulders to demonstrate that **We are the Intelligent Designers**.

We are the Intelligent Designer

James A Martin

"Answer all the questions, but question all the answers"

P. S.

Any writing is made at a point in time. Once written it is set to that time. But history and events move on and new facts replace previous "truths." Projections of the future will be considered incomplete as long as advancements do not occur, or are altered by an unforeseen or under recognized technology Fractal events can cause macro changes. History is never linear.

Despite my best efforts, some projections and perspectives are probably already out of date. So be it.

Bibliography

CHILDREN OF THE TREES

Siegel, Lee S. *"The Rise of Oxygen"* Astronomy Magazine, 30 July 2003

http://en.wikipedia.org/wiki/History_of_the_Earth

Newman, William L. *"Age of the Earth"* Publications Services, USGS. 2007

http://en.wikipedia.org/wiki/Human_evolution

"The First Primates" antrho-palomar.edu

http://en.wikipedia.org/wiki/Bipedal

Morgan, Elaine *"The Aquatic Ape Hypothesis"* Souvenir Press 1997

Gibbons, Ann *"Oldest Members of Homo sapiens Discovered in Africa"* Science 2003

Marshall, Charles R.; Will, Oliver; et al. *"Using the fossil record to estimate the age of the last common ancestor of extant primates"* Nature, Nature Publishing Group 18 April 2002

Beard, K.C. *"The oldest North American primate and mammalian biogeography during the Paleocene-eocene Themal Maximum"* Proceedings of the National Academy of Sciences 2008

Stringer, C.B.. *"Evolution of Early Humans"* The Cambridge Encyclopedia of Human Evolution. Cambridge University Press 1994

Bryson, Bill *"The Mysterious Biped ;A Short History of Nearly Everything."* Random House 2004

Bittman, Mark *"Animal, Vegetable, Junk"* Houghton Mifflin Harcourt 2021

Diamond, Jared *"The Third Chimpanzee"* Harper Perennial 1992

http://en.wikipedia.org/wiki/Origin_of_speech

Zorich, Zach *'Born to Be Mild, Are human beings evolution's most successful story of self-domestication?'* Discover 28 May 2015

Darwin. Charles. *"The Expression of the Emotions in Man and Animals"* London, Murray. 187202

Fitch, W. T. *"The evolution of speech: a comparative review."* Trends in Cognitive Science 2000

MacLarnon, A. M. and Hewitt, G. P *"The evolution of human speech: The role of enhanced breathing control"* American Journal of Physical Anthropology 109: 341–363. 1993

Lieberman, P. *"The evolution of speech: Its anatomical and neural bases"* Current Anthropology 2007

"What Darwin Didn't Know" Nature, PBS 2014

Hanks, John *"Still Evolving (after all these years)"* Scientific American September 2014

Shield, Peter *"Uncommon Sense, Shortcomings of the Human Mind for Handling Big-Picture, Long-Term Challenges"* Steady State Press 2021

Wilson, Edward O. *"The Meaning of Human Existance"* Liveright Publishing 2014

Smith M. D., Craig R. *"A Perfect Threat"* AmJenn Publishing 2022

WE DESIGN US

Fry, Tony *"Design as Politics"* Berg 2011

Price, David. *"Energy and Human Evolution"* 12 November 2007

James, Steven R.. *"Hominid Use of Fire in the Lower and Middle Pleistocene: A Review of the Evidence"* Current Anthropology University of Chicago Press February 1989

http://www.psychologytoday.com/blog/lives-the-brain/201001/was-seafood-brain-food-in-human-evolution

Weiner, S.; Q. Xu, P. Goldberg, J. Liu, O. Bar-Yosef. *"Evidence for the Use of Fire at Zhoukoudian, China"* Science 281 1998

"Meat-eating was essential for human evolution, says UC Berkeley anthropologist specializing in diet" 14 June 1999

Mann, Neil. *"Meat in the human diet: An anthropological perspective"* Nutrition & Dietetics 15 August 2007

http://www.earthhistory.org.uk/recolonisation/first-plants

Types of Wasps' Nests | eHow.com http://www.ehow.com/list_6360633_types-wasps_-nests.html#ixzz2S9XQVnFs
http://en.wikipedia.org/wiki/Bird_nest
Simon JE & Pacheco S *"On the standardization of nest descriptions of neotropical birds"* 2005
http://en.wikipedia.org/wiki/Tool_use_by_animals
Heinrich, B. *"Mind of the Raven: Investigations and Adventures with Wolf-Birds"* New York: Cliff Street Books 1999
Ottoni EB, Izar P, "Capuchin monkey tool use: Overview and implications" Evolutionary Anthropology 2008
"Ingenious fishing method may be spreading through dolphins" Murdoch University. 24 August 2011.
Lilley, Sam, *"Men, Machines and History: The Story of Tools and Machines in Relation to Social Progress"* Cobbett Press 1948
Semaw, S., M. J. Rogers, J. Quade, P. R. Renne, R. F. Butler, M. Domínguez-Rodrigo, D. Stout, W. S. Hart, T. Pickering, and S. W. Simpson.
"2.6-Million-year-old stone tools and associated bones from OGS-6 and OGS-7, Gona," Afar, Ethiopia" Journal of Human Evolution 2003.
http://inventors.about.com/od/gstartinventions/a/glass_3.htm
Tattersall, Ian, *"If I had a Hammer"* Scientific American September 2014
Marlowe, F. W. *"Hunter-gatherers and human evolution"* Evolutionary Anthropology: Issues, News, and Reviews 14 (2): 2005
Ghose, Tia *"Earliest Evidence of Human Hunting Found"* LiveScience May 2013
Turkle, Sherry *"Reclaiming Conversation: The Power of Talk in a Digital Age"* 6 October 2015
Schaffer, Juliann *"Evolutionary Eating - What We Can Learn From Our Primitive Past"* Today's Dietitian April 2009
"Mortality Salience and The Desire for Offspring" ScienceDirect
George, Stephen C. *"5 Animals that Changed Humanity Forever, Domestication was a game-changer for us, and the creatures we took into our care"* Discover 26 November 2017
Hermanussen, Michael; Poustka, Fritz *"Stature of early Europeans"*. Hormones (Athens) July–September 2003
Walchover, Natalie *"Why can't all animals be domesticated?"* Life Science 30 April 2012
Diamond, Jared *"Guns, Germs and Steel"* W W Norton 1997
http://en.wikipedia.org/wiki/Origin_of_speech
http://en.wikipedia.org/wiki/Origin_of_language
Müller, F. M. *"The theoretical stage, and the origin of language"* The Origin of Language. Bristol: Thoemmes Press 1996
Marean, Chris *"The Most Invasive Species of All"* Scientific American August 2015
http://en.wikipedia.org/wiki/History_of_writing
Daniels,Peter T. *"The Study of Writing Systems", in The World's Writing Systems"* ed. Bright and Daniels,
New Analysis Of "Cave Signs" Shows Prehistoric Language Use
(http://humanorigins.si.edu/evidence/behavior/blombos-ocher-plaque
http://www.historyofinformation.com/index.php?
Houston, Stephen D. *"The First Writing: Script Invention as History and Process"* Cambridge University Press 2004
Stroud, Kevin *"The History of English"* Podcast 2019
Atkinson, Quentin D. *"Phonemic Diversity Supports a Serial Founder Effect Model of Language Expansion from Africa"* Science 15 April 2011
Varki, Ajit and Brower, Danny, Denial: "Self-Deception, False Beliefs, and the origins of the Human Mind" Twelve, 2013
http://www.historyworld.net/wrldhis/PlainTextHistories.asp?historyid=ab33
http://en.wikipedia.org/wiki/History_of_money
Kiney, D Money *"A Study of the Theory of the Medium of Exchange"* Simon Publications, September 2003
Graeber, David, Debt: *"The First 5,000 Years"* 12 July 2011
Dow Shelia C, *"Axioms and Babylonian thought: a reply"* Journal of Post Keynesian Economics 2005
Aceri, Elisa *"A Pivotal Time in History: Spiritual Traditions in "The Axial Age"* John Cabot University 27 November 2019
http://www.allpetnews.com/dog-saliva-has-healing-properties
Sumner, Judith. *"The Natural History of Medicinal Plants"* Timber Press 2000
Tapsell LC, Hemphill I, Cobiac L, et al. *"Health benefits of herbs and spices: the past, the present, the future"* The Medical Journal of Australia August 2006.
http://en.wikipedia.org/wiki/Human_evolution
Heng HH *"The genome-centric concept: resynthesis of evolutionary theory"*. May 2009
Stringer, C.B, Jones, Steven, Martin, Robert & Pibeam, David *"Evolution of Early Humans"*. The Cambridge Encyclopedia of Human Evolution. Cambridge University Press 1994
Bryson, Bill. *"28 The Mysterious Biped. A Short History of Nearly Everything"* 2004 Random House
Max, D. T. *"How Humans are shaping our own evolution"* National Geographics April 2017
http://www.medicalnewstoday.com/info/medicine/prehistoric-medicine.php
Dawkins, Richard. *"The Ancestor's Tale: A Pilgrimage to the Dawn of Evolution"* Houghton Mifflin Harcourt 2005
Wilson, Edward O *"The Social Conquest of Earth"* Liveright 2012
Kaufman, Whitley "The Evolutionary Ethics of E. O. Wilson" The New Atlantis 2022
http://fubini.swarthmore.edu/~ENVS2/S2003/Emma/firstessay.html
http://www.beyondveg.com/billings-t/comp-anat/comp-anat-4b.shtml
Livio, Mario *"Why"* Simon & Schuster 2017
Marean, Curtiss W *"The Most Invasive Species of All"* Scientific American August 2015

Adler, Jerry *"A World Without Mosquitoes"* Smithsonian June 2016

"Scientific method" Oxford Dictionaries: British and World English, 2016,

Longrich, Nicholas R. *"When did we become fully human? What fossils and DNA tell us about the evolution of modern intelligence"* The Conversation 9 September 2020

Ellis, Erle C. *"Humans, The Species that Changed Earth"* 2015

Diamond, Jared *"The Worst Mistake in the History of the Human Race, The advent of agriculture was a watershed moment for the human race. It may also have been our greatest blunder"* Discover May 1999

"Was agriculture the greatest blunder in human history?" The Conversation 18 October 2017

NINE BILLION OF OUR CLOSESTS RELATIVES

Krulwich, Robert *"How Human Beings Almost Vanished From Earth In 70,000 B.C."* NPR 22 October 2012

http://www.prb.org/Publications/Articles/2006/Lifestyle Choices Affect US, Impact on the Environment.aspx

United Nations Population Fund

"West Nile Virus: What You Need to Know CDC Fact Sheet" www.CDC.gov.

Andrews, Evans *"Six Devastating Plagues"* History 22 August 2018

Villareal, Luis P. *"Are viruses alive?"* Scientific American August 2008

Panetta, Grace *"The Trump administration declined to use an Obama-era pandemic preparedness playbook, Politico reports"* Business Insider 26 March 2020

http://www.un.org/esa/population/publications/longrange2/WorldPop2300final.pdf

Malthus T.R. *"An essay on the principle of population"* Chapter VII, 1798

"The Debate Over World Population: Was Malthus Right?" CRF Winter 2010

Bellis, Mary *"History of American Agriculture, American Agriculture 1776–1990"* ThoughtCo. 27 August 2021

http://www.imminst.org/

Kadlec, Dan *"Your Longevity is good for business"* Time, 14 March 2016

Blackstone, Andrew *"10 Animals That Practice Homosexuality"* http://listverse.com/2013/04/20/10-animals-that-practice-homosexuality/ April 20, 2013

"Why Is Same-Sex Sexual Behavior So Common in Animals?" Scientific American 20 November 2019

Smith M. D., Craig R. *"A Perfect Threat, Population growth, climate change, and natural resource depletion in the 21st century"* AmJenn Publishing 2021

"Hungary tries for baby boom with tax breaks and loan forgiveness" BBC News 11 February 2019

"World Population Prospects 2019, Population Data, File: Total Population Both Sexes, Medium Variant" United Nations Population Division. 2019.

Moen, OM *"The case for cryonics"* Journal of Medical Ethics August 2015

Hvistendahl, Mara *"Who will prosper and who will fall behind"* Scientific American September 2016

http://en.wikipedia.org/wiki/Doomsday_argument

Harah, Yuval Noah *"Sapiens"* Harper Collins Publishers 2015

Hughes, James *"Citizen Cyborg, Why Democratic Societies must respond to the redesigned human of the Future"* Westview Press 2004

Jozuka, Emiko *"Japan suffers biggest natural population decline ever in 2018"* CNN 23 December 2018

N K, Sanders, *"The Epic of Gilgamesh"* Penguin, London 1972

Sokar, Andrew *"The Gilgamesh Project"* Nexus Magazine June-July 2005

Ellis, Erle C. *"Over Population is not the Problem"* New York Times 13 September 2013

Fitzsimons, Tim *"Colorado lays to rest first legally composted human remains"* NBC News 21 March 2022,

Harari, Yuval Noah *"Homo Deux"* Harper Collins Publishers 2017

Culpepper, John *"What is Natural Organic Reduction?"* AdkAction 4 January 2022

Easterbrook, Gregg "What Happens when we all Live to 100?" The Atlantic October 2014

THIS LAND IS OUR LAND

Slavikova, Sara "Causes and Effects of Desertification on People and the Environment" Greentumble 29 April 2019

"Awakening, Age of Nature" PBS October 2020 http://greenanswers.com/q/2130/water-oceans-ice/dams-infrastructure/what-happens-dam-after-reservoir-beh#ixzz2Mh1XDYKg

www.internationalrivers.org/sedimentation-problems-with-dams

Minh, Ho Binh *"Delta drought gives glimpse into bleak future for mighty Mekong"* Reuters 17 April 2016

Sarah C. Aird, *China's Three Gorges: The Impact of Dam Construction on Emerging Human Rights* Washington College of Law American University

Leeming, David *"Flood, The Oxford Companion to World Mythology"* Oxfordreference.com. 2004 *004*http://www.oxfordreference.com/views/ENTRY.html?subview=Main&entry=t208.e567. *Retrieved 17 September 2010.*

Ulam, Alex, *"Holding Back the Flood",* Discover, November 2013

S.W. Helms: *"Jawa Excavations 1975. Third Preliminary Report",* Levant 1977

Govindasamy Agoramoorthy, Sunitha Chaudhary & Minna J. HSU. *"The Check-Dam route to Mitigate India's Water Shortages".* Law library – University of New Mexico. 2008

Arasu, Sibi *"Himalayan glaciers could lose 80% of their volume if global warming not controlled, study finds"* Associated Press 19 June 2023

http://lawlibrary.unm.edu/nrj/48/3/03_agoramoorthy_indian.pdf. Retrieved 8 November 2011.

Heloisa Yang, Matt Haynes, Stephen Winzenread, and Kevin Okada *"The History of Dams"* 1999

http://en.wikipedia.org/wiki/River_dam

"World Commission on Dams Report". Internationalrivers.org. 29 February 2008.

http://internationalrivers.org/en/way-forward/world-commission-dams/world-commission-dams-framework-brief-introduction.

Kemp, Katherine *"The Mississippi Levee System and the Old River Control Structure"* The Louisiana Environment 2000

Donald Langmead. *"Encyclopedia of Architectural and Engineering Feats"*

"Storm Events Database" National Climatic Data Center. National Oceanic and Atmospheric Administration

http://www.ncdc.noaa.gov/stormevents/eventdetails.jsp?id=417027$5 *28 February 28, 2013.*

http://www.crimesofwar.org/a-z-guide/dangerous-forces-dams-dikes-and-nuclear-stations/

http://en.wikipedia.org/wiki/Dam_failiure

Harden, Blaine *"A River Lost: The Life and Death of the Columbia"* W.W. Norton and Company. 1996

Goldwen, Fredrick "Making Rivers Run Backward" Time June 14, 1982

"Vanishing waters of the world" Time February 8, 2016

Hadfield, Charles *"The Canal Age".* David & Charles. 1981

Cho Renee *"How China is dealing with its water crisis"* State of the Planet, Columbia University 5 May 2011

Musson; Robinson . *Science and Technology in the Industrial Revolution.* University of Toronto Press 1969

Robert, Friedel, *"A Culture of Improvement."* MIT Press 2007

Needham, Joseph *"Science and Civilization in China: Volume 4, Physics and Physical Technology, Part 2,"* Mechanical Engineering. Taipei: Caves Books Ltd. 1986

Chartres, C. and Varma, S. *"Out of water. From Abundance to Scarcity and How to Solve the World's Water Problems"* FT Press 2010

"The Wealth of Waste: The Economics of Wastewater Use in Agriculture" Food and Agriculture Organization September 2010

Ward, C *"Reengaging in Agricultural Water Management: Challenges and Options"* 2006

http://water.worldbank.org/water/publications/reengaging-agricultural-water-management-challenges-and-options.

http://www.un.org/waterforlifedecade/scarcity.shtml

"History of Hydropower". U.S. Department of Energy.

Industrial Archeology Review, Oxford University Press. 1987.

http://www1.eere.energy.gov/windandhydro/hydro_history.html.

Hydropower – A Way of Becoming Independent of Fossil Energy?

Assessment of Stream Ecosystem Structure and Function Under Clean Water Act Section 404 Associated With Review of Permits for Appalachian Surface Coal Mining, July 30, 2010 (PDF)

U. S. Geological Survey Geographic Names Information System: New River

D.H. Cardwell, *" Geologic History of West Virginia"* West Virginia Geologic and Economic Survey 1975

"Appalachian Regional Reforestation Initiative Forest Reclamation" Advisory Office of Surface Mining and Reclamation 11 July 2007.

http://wvcommerce.org/App_Media/assets/doc/travelandrec/industry/marketing/2010%20Economic%20Impact.pd

http://serendip.brynmawr.edu/local/scisoc/environment/seniorsem03/mtr.pdf

http://www.wvminesafety.org/wvcoalfacts.htm

International Energy Annual 2006, Energy Information Administration, 2008,

http://search.aol.com/aol/search?enabled_terms=&s_it=comsearch51&q=mining%2C+history

Roberts, Chalmers *'Subduing the Nile"* December 1902

Ahnert, A.; Borowski, C. *"Environmental risk assessment of anthropogenic activity in the deep-sea"* Journal of Aquatic Ecosystem Stress and Recovery 2000

Sharma, B. N. N. R. *"Environment and Deep-Sea Mining: A Perspective"* Marine Georesources and Geotechnology. 2000

Levit, Tom *" Bottom of Form, How deep-sea mining could destroy the 'cradle of life on earth'* " 28 October, 2010

Beiser, Vince *"Depth Charge"* Wired April 2023

Mack, Eric *"Commercial Asteroid Mining Now Has A 2023 Launch Date To Scout Its First Target"* Forbes 24 January 2023

Fischetti, Mark *"Fresh from the Sea"* Scientific American September 2007

B.M. Misra and J. Kupitz *"The role of nuclear desalination in meeting potable water needs in water scarce areas in the next decades"* Desalination 2004.

Sumner, Thomas *"Quenching Society's Thirst"* Science News 20 August 2016

http://en.wikipedia.org/wiki/Aswan_Dam

"Cultural Resources - Malolotja Archaeology, Lion Cavern" Swaziland Natural Trust Commission,

Heaton, Herbert *"Economic History of Europe"* Harper International Edition. February 1968

http://en.wikipedia.org/wiki/Hydraulic_mining

Kolars, John F., Mitchell, William *"The Euphrates River and the Southeast Anatolia Development Project"* Southern Illinois University Press, 1991

http://en.wikipedia.org/wiki/Great_Flood_of_1993

http://www.nwrfc.noaa.gov/floods/papers/oh_2/great.htm

Pultarova, Tereza *"Humans are pumping out so much groundwater that it's changing Earth's tilt"* Yahoo News

Barker, Aryn and Beishangul-Gumuz *" Ethiopia aims to lift itself out of poverty by damming the Blue Nile"* Time 13 June 2016

MacMath, Jillian *"Are Sinkholes Occurring More Often Than They Once Were?" AccuWeather.* com 4 Sep 2013

O'Hanlon, L. *"The looming crisis of sinking ground in Mexico City"* Eos 102 22 April 2021

Markus, Frank *"A shortcut to self-driving cars: Build a smart-city utopia"* Motor Trend December 2022

Donald Langmead. ABC-CLIO. *"the world's largest artificial waterway and oldest canal still in existence"* Encyclopedia of Architectural and Engineering Feats February 2015

http://www.internationalrivers.org/sedimentation-problems-with-dams

The International Canal Monuments List, http://www.icomos.org/studies/canals.pdf, retrieved 2008-10-08

McCululy, Patrick *"Sedimentation Problems with Dams,* Silenced Rivers: The Ecology and Politics of Large Dams" Zed Books, 1996

"Agua Zarca: indigenous fight against dam costs lives" Both Ends July 2020

Michael McCarthy, *"Water Scarcity Could Affect Billions: is this the biggest crisis of all?"* CommonDreams, 18 March 2013

http://www.csmonitor.com/World/Making-a-difference/Change-Agent/2013/0315 water-wheels-power-India-s-rural-mountain-economy

Marq de Villiers, *"Water Wars of the Near Future"* ITT Industries Guidebook to Global Water *Issues, 1999.*

"Geology of the Sideling Hill Road Cut" Maryland Geological Survey, 2009.

Williams, Jeff. "USGS Research Contributes to Assateague Island Restoration—' *"Mitigating 70 Years of Coastal Erosion Due to Ocean City Inlet Jetties".* Sound Waves November, 2002.

http://www.popularmechanics.com/technology/engineering/gonzo/the-worlds-18-strangest-man-made-islands

"U. S. Engineering Society names Kansai International Airport a Civil Engineering Monument of the Millennium" American Society of Civil Engineers 2001

"Sinking feeling at Hong Kong Airport" International Herald Tribune, 22 January 1982.

http://en.wikipedia.org/wiki/Tunnel

Rogoway, Tyler *"Look How Quickly China is Building its Island Bases out of Nothing",* Foxtrot Alpha *16 March 2015*

"Yellowstone, History and Culture" National Park Service.

"Dutch draw up drastic measures to defend coast against rising seas" New York Times. 3 August 2008

McGeehan, Patrick *"Making a Pitch, Again, for Barriers to Block Storm Surges"* New York Times, 11 October 2017.

O'Sullivan, Feargus *"Venice's Vast New Flood Barrier is Almost Here"* Citylab September 2016.

"Coals costs outweigh benefits, WVU study finds" Charleston Gazette June 2009

http://www.sourcewatch.org/index.php?title=Mountaintop_removal

"Self-Reported Cancer Rates in Two Rural Areas of West Virginia with and Without Mountaintop Coal Mining" Journal of Community Health, July 2011

Schmidt-Nielsen PhD, Knut *"The Salt Secreting Glands of Marine Birds",* Circulation May 1960

Dr. Sues *"The Lorax"* Penguin Random House LLC. 1971

"Who sues for the trees—and the air that we breathe?" Anthropocene 8 July 2021

Stone. Christopher D. *"Should Trees Have Standing?: Law, Morality, and the Environment"* Oxford Press 1972

Zalasiewicz, Jan *"What mark will we leave on the Planet?"* Scientific American September 2016

Emily Elhacham, Liad Ben-Uri, Jonathan Grozovski, Yinon M. Bar-On & Ron Milo *"Global human-made mass exceeds all living biomass"* Nature 9 December 2020

THE CULTURE OF AGRONOMY

Sample, Ian *"Neanderthals may have feasted on meat and two veg diet"* The Guardian 27 December 2010

Peters, Adele *"Against the Grain"* Fast Company May 2016

Hawkins, Paul (editor) *"Drawdown"* Penguin Press 2017

Wessel, T. *"The Agricultural Foundations of Civilization"* Journal of Agriculture and Human Values 1984

"ChoosemyPlate.gov U S Department of Agriculture

"Sugar: World Markets and Trade" United States Department of Agriculture Foreign Agricultural Service. May 2012.

Blackburn, Robin *"Enslavement and Industrialization"* History BBC 2 November *2017*

"Grain" National Geographic Society entry.

Martineau, Belinda. *"First Fruit: The Creation of the Flavr Savr Tomato and the Birth of Biotech Food."* McGraw-Hill 2001.

"Supreme Court hands Monsanto victory over farmers on GMO seed patents, ability to sue" Reuters January 13, 2014

"Colony Collapse Disorder" U S Environmental Protection Agency 16 September 2016

"Palm oil threatening endangered species" Center for Science in the Public Interest May 2005

Spinks, Rosie J *"Why does palm oil still dominate the supermarket shelves?"* The Guardian, UK 17 December 2014

King, Thomas *"Palm Oil"* Say No to Palm Oil" January 2017

Koeppel, Dan *"Banana: the fate of the fruit that changed the world"* Hudson Press 2008

Holmes, Bob *"Go Bananas"* New Scientist. 20 April 2013

Siddle, Julian & Venema, Vibeke *"Saving Coffee from Extinction"* BBC World Service 24 May 2015

Douglas, David & Blomqvist, Linus *"Is Precision Agriculture the way to Peak Cropland?"* Breakthrough 7 December 2016

"How much have US bee populations fallen, and why?" USA Facts 26 April 2023

Saber, Ariel *"The Sheltering Sky"* Smithsonian May 2015

Lombardo, Crystal *"14 Foremost Pros and cons of the Green Revolution"* Green Garbage 2018

Fisk, Susan V *"The brown revolution: A sustainable response to the global food crisis"* American Society of Argonomy 2 October 2013

Lawson, Kurt *" Think Different: Why The Brown Revolution?"* Corn + Soybean Digest 18 January 2013

S. Shephard, *"Pickled, Potted, and Canned: How the Art and Science of Food Preserving Changed the World."* Simon & Schuster. 2001

Smith, K Annabelle, *"The Strange History of Frozen Foods; From Clarence Birdseye to the Distinguished Order of Zerocrats"* Eater 21 August 2014

Bloom, Jonathan *"American Wasteland"* 2010

Shephard, S. *"Pickled, Potted, and Canned: How the Art and Science of Food Preserving Changed the World"* Simon & Schuster. 2001

Gorshkov V.G., Makarieva A.M. *"Biotic pump of atmospheric moisture as driver of the hydrological cycle on land"* Hydrology and Earth System Sciences, November 2007

Wiener-Bronner, Danielle *"The truth, and strategy, of food expiration dates"* CNN Business 17 July 2022

Jean-Pierre Bocquet-Appel *"When the World's Population Took Off: The Springboard of the Neolithic Demographic Transition"* Science 29 July 2011

Graeme Barker, *"The Agricultural Revolution in Prehistory: Why did the Foragers become Farmers?"* Oxford University Press 25 March 2009.

Whipps, Heather *"How the Spice Trade Changed the World* Live Science 12 May 2008

Cohen, Robert *"Sugar Love"* National Geographic August 2013

"Carbon Footprint across the Coffee Supply Chain: The Case of Costa Rican Coffee" Journal of Agricultural Science and Technology. 2012

Peters, Adele *"Against the Grain"* Fast Company May 2016

Corliss, Julie *"Eating too much added sugar increases the risk of dying with heart disease"* Harvard Heart Letter 6 February 2014

"Sweet sorghum for food, feed and fuel" New Agriculturalist, January 2008.

Gaud, William S. *"The Green Revolution, 3 Accomplishments and Apprehensions"* AgBioWorld. 8 March 1968

"How the World Wastes Food " Popular Science, September 2014

"Global response to Amazon forest fire" Preferred by Nature 12 September 2019

Roberts, David *"This company wants to build a giant indoor farm next to every major city in the world"* Vox 11 April 2018

Federman, Sarah *"Vertical Farming for the Future"* USDA 25 October 2021

Foley, Dr Jonathan, *"No, Vertical farms won't Feed the World"* blog 2015

Flannery, Tim *"How farming giant seaweed can feed fish and fix the climate"* 31 July 2017

Lidz, Franz *"Welcome to Farmitopia"* Smithsonian 2015

Marchant, Gabriella *"Australian 'super seaweed' supplement to reduce cattle gas emissions wins $1m international prize"* ABC News. 19 December 2020

MAN'S BEST FRIEND, AND DINNER

Robert W. Shumaker, Kristina R. Walkup, and Benjamin B. Beck *"Animal Tool Behavior, The Use and Manufacture of Tools by Animals"* 2011, Johns Hopkins University Press

Kluger, Jeffery " The War on Delicious" Time 9 November 2015

Chief Luther Standing Bear *"Land of the Spotted Eagle"* Houghton Mifflin, *Boston & New York 1933*

"Nepals Killing Fields" The Daily Mail 12 November 2015

Stringer, Martin D. *"Rethinking Animism: Thoughts from the Infancy of our Discipline"* Journal of the Royal Anthropological Institute 1999

Aris & Phillips *"Dogs in Antiquity, Anubis to Cerberus: The Origins of the Domestic Dog"* Aris and Philips March 2002

Viegas, Jennifer *"World's first dog lived 31,700 years ago, ate big "* Discovery News 16 October 2008

Hunt, Donna & Sussman, Robert "Man the Hunted: Primates, Predators, and the Human Evolution" Westview Press, Boulder, CO 2005

Sinclair, Upton *"The Jungle"* Tucson, AZ: 1905

Roosevelt, Theodore *"Conditions in Chicago Stockyards"* 1906

Kenner, Robert *"Food Inc"* documentary

Swain, Marian *"The Future of Meat"* Breakthrough December 14, 2016

Simon, David Robinson *"Meatonomics, How the Rigged Economics of Meat and Dairy Make You Consume too Much-and-How to Eat Better, Live Longer, and Spend Smarter"* Conari Press San Francisco 2015

Merrit Frey, Rachel Hopper, Amy *Fredregill "Spills and Kills: Manure Pollution and America's Livestock Feedlot"* Washington DC: Clean Water Network, 2000

L A Harper *"Direct Measurements of Methane Emissions from Grazing and Feedlot Cattle"*

Before the Flood Documentary 2016

Journal of Animal Science 77 No 6 1999

Cook, Rob *"World Beef Production: Ranking Of Countries"* Beef2Live 2014

Hoffman Austin D *"A Brief History of Wild Wolves"* Mission Wolves 2021

Nuwer, Rachel *"When lions eat livestock, relocation is common—but often deadly"* National Geographic 2020

Robbins, John *"Diet for a New America"* StillPoint Publishing 1987

Deborah, White *"What Are U.S. Farm Subsidies? Some Say Corporate Welfare, Others Say National Necessities"*

Jacobson, Michael F. *"More and Cleaner Water"* In Six Arguments for a Greener Diet: How a Plant-based Diet Could save your Health and the Environment" Center for Science in the Public Interest, 2006

Harari, Yuval Noah *"Homo Deux "* Harper Collins Publisher 2017

Luna, *Jenny "Americans Are Gorging Themselves on Cheap Meat"* Mother Jones March 30,

Frey, Merrit, Hopper, Rachel Fredregill, Amy *"Spills and Kills: Manure Pollution and America's Feedlot"* Clean Water Network 2000

Harper, L. A. *"Direct Measurement of Methane Emissions From Grazing and Feedlot Cattle"* Journal of Animal Science No 6 1999

Kuhn, Keegan & Anderson, Kip *"Cowspiracy, The Sustainability Secret"* documentary 2014

Webb, Amy *"Welcome to (Synthetic) Meatspace"* Wired 2021

Gans, Jared *"First 'lab-grown' meat approved by regulators in US"* The Hill 21 June 2023

Jones,Nicola *"Fungi bacon and insect burgers: a guide to the proteins of the future"* Nature 4 July 2023

Shindell, D. T.; Faluvegi, G.; Koch, D. M.; Schmidt, G. A.; Unger, N.; Bauer, S. E *"Improved Attribution of Climate Forcing to Emissions"* Science 2009

"Draft U.S. Greenhouse Gas Inventory Report:" 1990-2014, United States Environmental Protection Agency 2016

Brown, Claire H, Fu, Jessica *"Covid-19 has closed meat plants across the U. S. What happens to framers, livestock, prices, and supply?"* Counter 17 April 2020

Lockett, Jon *"BATS OUT OF HELL Wuhan finally bans sale of bat meat and other wild animals becoming forth Chinese city to outlaw dangerous practice"* The Sun, UK 20 May 2020

"Wuhan food markets are selling wild animals, again" NEW DELHI 31 August 2020

Bourne, Joel K Jr. *"How to Farm a Better Fish"* National Geographic June 2014

Herminio R. Rabanal *"History of Aquaculture"* Fisheries and Aquatic Department 2015

Pike, Lili *"The surprise catch of seafood trawling: Massive greenhouse gas emissions"* VOX 18 March 2021,

FAO: *"Cultured Aquatic Species Information Programme"* May 8, 2009

Kwok, Robert *"Runaway Fish"* Science News August 20, 2016

Hinrichsen D *"Coastal Waters of the World: Trends, Threats, and Strategies"* Island Press

Azier, Ian *"Environmental impacts of shellfish aquiculture"* Outside November 2015

World Bank and United Nations Food and Agriculture Organization, *"The Sunken Billions: The Economic Justification for Fisheries Reform"* 2009

"US Domestic Seafood Landings and Values Increase in 2010" NOAA 2011

Casey, Susan *"Voices in the Ocean"* Doubleday 2015

Mariani, Gael et.al *"Let more big fish sink: Fisheries prevent blue carbon sequestration—half in unprofitable areas"* Science Advances. 2020

Ashton, Gail et.al *"Predator control of marine communities increases with temperature across 115 degrees of latitude"* Science, 9 June 2022

Lovgren, Stefan *"Chimps, Humans 96 Percent the Same, Gene Study Finds"* National Geographic News August 31, 2005

Datar, M. Betti *"Possibilities for an in Vitro meat production system, Innovative Food,"* Science and Engineering Technologies April 2010

Siegelbaum, D. J. *"In Search of a Test-Tube Hamburger"* Time April 2009

Abbasi, Tasneem; Abbasi, Tabassum; Abbasi, S.A. *"Energy-efficient food production to reduce global warming and ecodegradation: The use of edible insects"* Renewable and Sustainable Energy Reviews 2011

"Six-legged Livestock: Edible insect farming, collection and marketing in Thailand" Bangkok: Food and Agriculture Organization of the United Nations. 2013.

Hansman, Heather *"The Synthetic Butcher Shop"* Popular Science May/June 2016

Watson, Elaine *"Keep calm and carry on: Navigating the trough of disillusionment for plant-based meat"* AgFunder 8 February 2023

"The Science of Cultivated Meats" Good Food Institute 2023

Ringen, Jonathan "The Great Scramble Fast Company" September 2016

National Agricultural Statistics "Service (NASS), Agricultural Statistics Board," U.S. Department of Agriculture, 30 March 2012

Shahbandeh, M. *"Honey market worldwide and in the U.S. - statistics & facts"* Statista 9 December 2022

"Ballast Water Management" imo.org

Fasola, Laura and Pietrek, Alejandro *"Origin and history of the beaver introduction in South America"* Mastozool.neotropical 16 May 16, 2014

"History of the Saint Lawrence Seaway" Infrastructure Canada. www.infrastructure.gc.ca.

"Ailanthus altissima distribution in Europe" ISSG Global Invasive Species Database. 2009-03-03.

MacKinnon, John R *"Invasive alien species in Southeast Asia"* Asian Biodiversity, October–December 2002

http://www.invasiveplants.net/invasiveplants/phragmites/natint.htm

Solomon, Christopher *"How Kitty is Killing the Dolphins"* Scientific American May 2013

Sterba, Jim *"Nature Wars, The Incredible Story of how Wildlife Comebacks turned Backyards into Battlegrounds"* Crown Publishers, NY, NY 2013

Goldman, Jason G *"Can trophy hunting actually help conservation?"* Conservation this week, 15 January 2014

Jenkins, Mark *"The Fate of the King"* Smithsonian February 2023

"Extinction continues apace," International Union for Conservation, 3 November 2009

"How Starfish Changed Modern Ecology" PBS 38, episode 2 2023

http://www.nwf.org/Wildlife/Wildlife-Conservation/Endangered-Species-Act.aspxeasuring Extinction, species by species" The Economic Times 2008-11-06

Betsey Mason, *"Man has been changing climate for 8,000 Years"* Nature 10 December 2003

http://www.britannica.com/EBchecked/topic/550274/snail-darter

www.procon.org

http://www.worldwildlife.org/species/

Stromberg, Joseph and Zielinski, Sarah, *"Ten Threatened and Endangered Species Used in Traditional Medicine"* Smithsonian October 18, 2011

S L Pimm, G J Russel, J L Gittleman, T M Brooks "The Future of Biodiversity" Science 1995 http://www.globalanimal.org/tag/wildlife-protection/page/9/

Kennedy, C. H. *"State of the Climate in 2011"* NOAA 10 July 2012

Wilson, E. O. *"The Future of Life"* Harvard Press 2002

Kaufman, Marc *"Increased Demand for Ivory Threatens Elephant Survival"*.Washingtonpost.com. 27 February 2007

Chinhuru, Wonder *"Poachers outgun Africa's vulnerable wildlife rangers"* Equal times 8 January 2016

Hogenboom, Melissa *"The woman who gave her life to save Gorillas"* BBC Earth 26 December 2015

Kramer, Andrew E *"Trade in mammoth ivory, helped by global thaw, flourishes in Russia"* New York Times 25 March 2008

Hance, Jeremy *"Over a million pangolins slaughtered in the last decade"* Mongabay 29 July 2014

http://advocacy.britannica.com/blog/advocacy/2007/10/traditional-chinese-medicine-and-endangered-animals/

"The US Pet Monkey Trade" International Primate Protection League IPPL News 2003

http://www.wildvolunteer.com/worldwide-wildlife-protection/

"26 more elephants killed with cyanide in Zimbabwe"

"Impacts of tourism and recreation in Africa" United Nations Environment Programme 15 August 2011

http://www.primate-sg.org/red_list_threat_status/

http://www.nps.gov/yell/naturescience/wolves.htm

www.actionbioscience.org › biodiversity/johnson.html

Lin, Doris *"Arguments For and Against Hunting"* About News 2015

Diamond, Jared *"the Third Chimpanze"* Harper Perrenial 1992

Resnik, Brian *"A million species are at risk of extinction. Humans are to blame"* Vox May 2019

Slezak, Michael *"Revealed: first mammal species wiped out by human-induced climate change"* The Guardian 15 June 2016

Adler, Jerry *"A World Without Mosquitoes"* Smithsonian June 2016

Love, Jennifer *"The Role of Zoos in Endangered Species Conservation"* About Education 2015

Worland, Justin *"The Future of Zoos"* Time 6 March 2017

STICKS AND STONES, AND NANOS

Ball, P. *"The Elements: A Very Short Introduction"* OUP Oxford. 2004

Kaku, Michio *"the God Equation"* Doubleday 2021

"Timeline of chemical element discoveries" Wikipedia

"The Historical Evolution of Concrete" Liatec 2016

Freinkel, Susan *"Plastic's : A Toxic Love Story"* Houghton Mifflin Harcourt 2011

Alter, Lloyd *"Are Wooden Skyscrapers in Our Future?"* Design/Green Architecture March 30, 2011

Knoblauch, Jessica A. *"Plastic Not-So-Fantastic: How the Versatile Material Harms the Environment and Human Health"* Scientific American July 2, 2009

Buranyi, Stephen *"The plastic backlash: what's behind our sudden rage-and will it make a difference?"* The Guardian, 13 November 2018

"The Search for a cleaner, greener plastic. Finding solutions to prevent harmful plastic waste is far from simple" Wyss Institute Communications

"Promising solution to plastic pollution" Harvard Gazette, Harvard University, Boston, MA 23 May 2014

Patel, Prachi *"Transparent wood product could give windows an insulation boost"* March 23, 2023

"Starch can replace normal plastic in food packaging" Phys.Org. 12 June 2018.

"Biodegradable plastic made from plants, not oil, is emerging" abcnews.go.com. 29 December 2008

Klein, Alice *"A new type of plastic may be the first that is infinitely recyclable"* NewScientist 19 August 2020

Song, J. H.; Murphy, R. J.; Narayan, R.; Davies, G. B. H. *"Biodegradable and compostable alternatives to conventional plastics"* Philosophical Transactions of the Royal Society: Biological Sciences. July 2009

Wei Zhang et al. *"Low-temperature upcycling of polyolefins into liquid alkanes via tandem cracking-alkylation"* Science, 2023.

Sanderson, Katharine *"Endlessly recyclable materials could fix our plastic waste crisis"* New Scientist 2 March 2022

Rosengren, Cole *"The strongest have survived: Anaerobic digestion companies see clear path to scaling up"* Waste Dive 12 July 2021

Pandey, Avaneesh *"Scientists Use Bacteria To Forge Silicon-Carbon Bonds"* IB Times November 25, 2016

Storey, Will and Molloy, Claire, and Abadi, Marki *"This fungus-based material is being used to imitate Styrofoam, leather and even bacon"* Business Insider 12 March 2020

Conover, Emily *"Chasing a Devious Metal"* Science News August 20, 2016

Drexler, K. Eric . *"Nanosystems: Molecular Machinery, Manufacturing, and Computation"* New York: John Wiley & Sons 1992

Coghlan, Andy *"Eco-friendly nanowood is a super strong and recyclable Styrofoam"* NewScientist 9 March 2018

Heil, Martha, Tune, Lee *"Wood Windows are Cooler than Glass"* UMD Right Now, August 2016

"'Vegan spider silk' provides sustainable alternative to single-use plastics" University of Cambridge 10 June 2021

Heil, Martha *"A Battery of Wood"* UMD Right Now June 2013

Jong, J. Et al *"Super Wood Could Replace Steel"* Nature 2018

Soumyabrata Roy, et al. *"Functional wood for carbon dioxide capture"* Cell Reports Physical Science, 2023

Drexler, Eric *"Transforming the Material Basis of Civilization"* TEDxIST Alameda 16 November 2015

Zhang, Liang and Marcos, Vanesa and Leigh, David A. *"Molecular machines with bio-inspired mechanisms"* PNAS 26 February 2018

Kile, Meredith *"How to replace foam and plastic packaging with mushroom experiments"* Al Jazeera America. 13 November 2013
"Super Molecules from Superatoms" Scientific American December 2016
"Clean Energy Challenge" 2017-2018

WE HAVE THE POWER

"Annual Mean Carbon Dioxide Data" NOAA/ESRL.
"A Blast from the Past: The Creation of Dynamite" WordPress March 2011
Hill, Donald Routledge, "A history of engineering in classical and medieval times," Routledge 1996
Hirst, K. Kris *"Bitumen-A Smelly but Useful Material of Interest"* Archaeology. 23 October 2009.
Swan, Keely *"Linking energy and wastewater infrastructure a triple win for climate, water, and operating costs"* Princeton University 3 November 2022
Forbes, Robert James *"Studies in Early Petroleum History"* 1958
Frosch, Dan; Gold, Russell *"How 'Orphan' Wells Leave States Holding the Cleanup Bag"* 26 February 2015
Lee, Yong Gyo; Garza-Gomez, Xavier; Lee, Rose M. *"Ultimate Costs of the Disaster: Seven Years After the Deepwater Horizon Oil Spill"* Journal of Corporate Accounting & Finance. 8 January 2018
Smith M. D., Craig R. *"A Perfect Threat, Population growth, climate change, and natural resource depletion in the 21st century"* AmJenn Publishing 2021
King, George E *"Hydraulic fracturing 101"* Society of Petroleum Engineers, 2012
"Alberta proposes limit on oil sands emissions" Kallanish Energy
Sanburn, Josh *"Greed, Politics and the biggest oil boom in decades"* Time 21 March 2016
Zimov, Sa; Schuur, Ea; Chapin, Fs. *"Climate change. Permafrost and the global carbon budget"* Science. June 2006
"Methane Releases from Arctic Shelf may be much Larger and Faster than Anticipated" National Science Foundation. 10 March 2010.
"Oklahoma earthquakes linked to oil and gas drilling, study shows" Phys.org 18 June 2015
REN 21 *"Renewables 2011"* Global Status Report 2011 2011
Darzins, Al; Pienkos, Philip; Edye, Les *"Current status and potential for algal biofuels production"* IEA Bioenergy Task 39. 2010
Aleander, Dr Samuel *"Ecological Civilization, Beyond Consumerism and the Growth Economy"* Sustainability Institute 2021
"NNFCC Renewable Fuels and Energy Factsheet: Anaerobic Digestion" National Non-Food Crops Centre. February 2011
"Tide is slowly rising in interest in ocean power" Mass High Tech: The Journal of New England Technology. 1 August 2008
http://www.alternative-energy-news.info/european-marine-energy-test-tidal-power/
Margonelli, Lisa *"An Inconvenient Ice"* Scientific American October 2014
Kadish, Seth *"On With Wind"* Wired February 2015
Kiesecker, Joseph *"Energy Sprawl"* Nature Conservancy Fall 2017
"Surfing Energy's New Wave" Time International 16 June 2003
"Orbital Marine Power Launches O2: World's Most Powerful Tidal Turbine" Orbital Marine. 22 April 2021.
A.G. Drachmann *"Heron's Windmill"* Centaurus, 7 1961Lucas, Adam (2006).
"Wind, Water, Work: Ancient and Medieval Milling Technology" Brill Publishers.
Price, Trevor J. *"James Blyth-Britain's First Modern Wind Power Engineer"* Wind Engineering 3 May 2005
"Global Wind Report Annual Market Update 2013" Global Wind Energy Council. 23 April 2013.
Shivaram, Deepa *"For the first time, wind power eclipsed both coal and nuclear in the U.S"* NPR 14 April 2022
Sutton, Joe & McCleary, Kelly *"Lake Mead at the Hoover Dam to reach lowest water level in decades"* CNN 9 June 2021
Ottó Bláthy, Miksa Déri, Károly Zipernowsky" IEC Techline. 6 December 2010.
"Energy Consumption Characteristics of Commercial Building HVAC Systems Volume III: Energy Savings Potential" United States Department of Energy
'Transparent solar cells' can take us towards a new era of personalized energy" EurekAlert! 2 November 2020
"2008 Energy Balance for World" International Energy Agency, 2011.
Nix, Elizabeth *"How Edison, Tesla and Westinghouse Battled to Electrify America"* History 30 January 2015
Lambrecht, Andrew *"The Simplified History Of The Electric Car"* InsideEVs 2022
"Hello sunshine: solar-powered carmaker gets £69m boost to rollout first model in 2022" Evening Standard 6 September 2022
Fincher, Jonathan *"EWICON bladeless wind turbine generates electricity using charged water droplets"* New Atlas 3 April 2013
Chabra, Esha. *"Bill Gates Rallies With Tech Leaders To Launch A Multi-Billion Dollar Energy Fund"* Forbes. 30 November 2015
Gates, Bill *"How to Avoid a Climate Crisis"* Alfred Knopf Publishing, 2021
"Natural Gas vs Coal-Environmental Impacts" MetGroup 20 November 2020
Patel, Prachi *"Could nuclear power be a bridge to a zero-emissions world?"* Daily Science 17 February 2022
Wald, Matt *"With Natrium, Nuclear can pair perfectly with Energy Storage and Renewables"* NEI, 3 November 2020
Shende, Rajendra *"At 70, UN sets 17 goals: To be achieved in less than 17 years"* The Economic Times October 2015
"Google Shoots for the Moon" Fast Company Dec 2015
Lomborg, Bjorn *"Cool It, The Skeptical Environmentalist Guide to Global Warming"* Alfred Knopf Publishing 2010
https://arpa-e.energy.gov/?q=arpa-e-site-page/projects

Newman, Rick *"Biden's climate plan depends on one huge change"* Yahoo News 23 April 2021
Orwig, Jessica *"Germany just fired up a monster machine that could revolutionize the way we use energy"* Business Insider 10 December 2015
Davidson, Osha Gray *"Germany's Bright Idea"* Discover July/August 2015
Gibbs, Jeff *"Planet of the Humans"* Huron Mountain Films 2021
Zehner, Ozzie *"Green Illusions"* 2012
Koppel, Ted *"Lights Out: A Cyberattack, a Nation Unprepared, Surviving the Aftermath"* Penguin Random House 2016
Kaku, Michio *"The God Equation"* Doubleday 2021
Crownhart, Casey *"What fusion's breakthrough means for clean energy"* MIT Technology Review 13 December 2022
Achen, Joel *"The 21st Century Grid"* Smithsonian July 2010
Knight, Laurence *"Vanadium: The metal that may soon be powering your neighborhood"* BBC. 14 June 2014
Larson, Aaron *"Benefits of High-Voltage Direct Current Transmission Systems"* Power 1 August 2018
"STARSHIP CENTURY SYMPOSIUM" 21-23 May 2013
Fuller, Buckminster *"Operating Manual for Starship Earth"* Southern Illinois University Press 1969

THE MARKET FOR SELF-DESTRUCTION

Harah, Yuval Noah *"Sapiens, A brief history of humankind"* Harper Collins Publishers NY 2015
Wilson, Edward O. *"The Meaning of Human Existance"* Liveright Publishing 2014
Shelagh Heffernan *"Modern Banking"* John Wiley & Sons 5 May 2005
Popova, Maria *"Adam Smith's Underappreciated Wisdom on Benevolence, Happiness, and Kindness"* The Marginalian 2022
Butler, Eamonn *"The Theory of Moral Sentiments"* The Adam Smith Institute
Saad, Gad *"The Consumer Instinct"* Prometheus Books 2011
Lebow, Victor *"The Real Meaning of Consumer Demand"* 1955
Florida, Richard *"The Rise of the Creative Class"* Basic Books 2002
G Davies, J H Bank *"A History of Money: from ancient Times to the Present Day"* University of Wales Press, 2002
Fry, Tony *"Design as Politics"* Bloomberg 2011
Blackburn, Robin *"Enslavement and Industrialisation"* BBC History 17 February 2011
Smith, Adam *"An Inquiry into the Nature and Causes of the Wealth of Nations"* 1776
Wasson, Elizabeth *"Introduction to 19th-Century Socialism"* 12 October 2016
McNamara, Robert *"Labor History of the 19th Century"* 4 April 2017
Conniff, Richard *"What the Ludites Really Fought Against"* Smithsonian October 19, 2016
Steffen, Alex (editor) *"World Changing"* Abrams, NY 2011
Veblen, Thorstein *"The Theory of the Leisure Class: an economic study of institutions"* 1899
Stromberg, Peter Ph.D. *"Freud's Nephew and Public Relations, The Strange History of Edward Bernays"* Psychology Today 12 February 2010
Calkins, Earnest Elmo *What Consumer Engineering Really is"* Consumer Engineering, Harper and Brothers 1932
Zilber, Ariel *"BlackRock CEO Larry Fink says Ukraine war spells end of globalization"* New York Post 24 March 2022
Drucker, Peter *"The Practice of Management"* 1954
Butler, Rhett A *"Amazon deforestation rises to 11 year high in Brazil"* Mongabay, 14 November 2019
"Amazon near tipping point of switching from rainforest to savannah-study" The Weekly Investor 5 October 2020
Coghlan, Andy *"Consumerism is 'eating the future"* New Scientist, August 2009
Becker, Joshua "21 Surprising Statistics That Reveal How Much Stuff We Actually Own" Becoming Mminimalist
Czech, Brian *"Supply Shock, Economic Growth at the Crossroads and the Steady State Solution"* New Society Publishers, May 2013
Kerschner, Edward, *"Asia Affluence, The Emerging 21st Century Middle Class"* Morgan Stanley Smith Barney 2011
Shaer, Matthew *"The Archeology of Wealth"* Smithsonian March 2018
Suzuki, David *"Consumer society no longer serves our needs"* Science Matters 11 January 2018
Lebow, Victor *"The Real Meaning of Consumer Demand"* 1955
Trentmann, Frank *"Empire of things"* HarperCollins 2016
McFibben, Bill *"Falter Has the human game begun to play itself out?"* Henry Holt & Co. 2019
"World's Happiest Country 2019 Finland comes top ahead of Nordic neighbours" The Independent 20 March 2019
Daly, Herman *"Economics for a Full World"* essay June 2015
Smith, Adam *"The Theory of Moral Sentiments"* 1759
Bremner, Robert H *"American philanthropy"* University of Chicago Press, 1988
Clifford, Catherine *"Billionaire Marc Benioff: Capitalism has 'led to horrifying inequality' and must be fixed"* CNBC Make It October 2014
Brown, Kaleb *"Patagonia's founder has given away the company to fight climate change —7 clothing brands dedicated to going green"* USA Today 15 September 2022
Napoletano, E. *"Environmental, Social And Governance: What Is ESG Investing?"* Forbes Advisor 22 June 2023

BIBLIOGRAPHY

THE TRASH MINES OF MUMBAI

Simmons, Ann M. *"The world's trash crisis, and why many Americans are oblivious"* L A Times 22 April 2016

Khan, Laura Nolan *"Trash, Trash, Everywhere: Unregistered Slum Life in Mumbai, India"* Harvard College, Global Health Review 24 March 2011

Sickler, Lillian *"Mounting Anger over Trash Build-up in Beirut"* The Borgen Project August 2015

Hume, Tim and Mohammed Tawfeeq, *"Lebanon: 'River of trash' chokes Beirut suburb as city's garbage crisis continues"* CNN 25 February 2016

Godoy, Emilio *"The waste mountain engulfing Mexico City"* The Guardian 9 January 2012

Hallman, Carly *"The trash one person produces in one year"* TitleMax Lifestyle 2020

"A Small Plastic Package is a big Culprit of the Waste Filling Oceans" NPR 15 January 2019

Buranyi, Stephen *"The plastic backlash: what's behind our sudden rage-and will it make a difference?"* Guardian 13 November 2018

Dutta, Taniya *"The pandemic is generating tons of discarded PPE. This entrepreneur is turning them into bricks"* Washington Post 24 November 2020

Mehouenou, Josue *"'Trash is gold' as Benin community turns waste in biogas"* phys.org August 2018

Beck, Eckardt C. *"The Love Canal Tragedy"* EPA Journal. January 1979

Brown, Michael H. *"Love Canal and the Poisoning of America"* The Atlantic. December 1979

Choate, Anne, Pederson, Lauren, Scharfenberg, Ferland, Henry *"Waste Management and Energy Savings: Benefits By The Numbers"* U.S. Environmental *Protection Agency 4 September 2005*

Bilikiss Adeblyi-Abiola *"Turning Trash Into Treasure"* Fast Company February 2015

Royte, Elizabeth *"Plastic Planet"* Smithsonian 2015

Osborne, Hannah *"Plastic-eating caterpillar have gut bacteria that can live on polyethylene for over a year"* Newsweek 5 March 2020

Ulrich Eberl, *"Life in 2050: How We Create the Future Today:"* United Nations Food and Agriculture Organization 2015

"Greenhouse Gas Inventory Report: 1990-2014" United States Environmental Protection Agency 2015

Carroll, Chris *"High-Tech Trash National Geographic"* January 2008

Silverman, Jacob *"Why is the world's biggest landfill in the Pacific Ocean?"* Science 2019

Gammon, Katharine *"Groundbreaking study finds 13.3 quadrillion plastic fibers in California's environment"* The Guardian 16 October 2020

Corder, Mike, *"Dutch inventor unveils device to scoop plastic out of rivers"* Associated Press October 2019

Plumer, Brad, *"Space trash is a big problem, These economist have a solution"* Washington Post, October 24, 2013

Zeller, Tom Jr. *"Recycling, The Big Picture"* National Geographic January 2008

"Fact Sheet: Extended Producer Responsibility" OCED

"Ecological Design" teNeues Publishing Group 2008

Dasgupta, Neha & bhardwaj, Mayank *"India set to outlaw six single-use plastic* products on October 2" Reuters 28 August 2019

"G7 leaders depicted in Mount Recyclemore e-waste sculpture" The Guardian 10 June 2021

"Technical guidelines for the environmentally sound management of the full and partial dismantling of ships" Basel Convention series/SBC.

Schuiling, Jacqueline *"End of life ships, the Human Cost of Breaking Ships"* Greenpeace International & FIDH in Cooperation With YPSA. December 2005

Sarraf, Maria *"Ship Breaking and Recycling Industry in Bangladesh and Pakistan"* siteresources.worldbank.org. International Bank for Reconstruction and Development 1 December 2010

Rosengren, Cole *"The strongest have survived: Anaerobic digestion companies see clear path to scaling up"* Waste Dive 12 July 2021

CHANGING THE ENVIRONMENT

https://ucmp.berkley.edu/bacteria/cyanointro.html "Introduction to the Cyanobacteria, Architects of earth's atmosphere"

Lim, Clarissa-*Jan "Uh-Oh, The End Is Nigh"* Bustle 22 January 2015

Stollarz, Patrik *"Climate change brings world closer to 'doomsday' say scientists"* AFP 21 January 2015

Kasting, James F.; Catling, David *"Evolution of a habitable planet"* Annual Review of Astronomy and Astrophysics 2003

Sagan, Carl; Mullen, George *"Earth and Mars: Evolution of Atmospheres and Surface Temperatures"* Science 7 July 1972

Veal, Robyn & Leitch, Victoria (editors) *"Fuel and Fire in the Ancient Roman World"* McDonald Institute Concersations 2019

"We've Been Talking About Climate Change for a Hundred Years" Popular Mechanics January/February 2018

"World Coal Production, Most recent estimates 1980-2007" U.S. Energy Information Administration. 2008.

http://www.ehow.com/info_12322581_difference-formation-oil-coal.html

Marden, Carrie, *"Where No Tree Has Gone Before"* Scientific American February 2013

"Smog kills thousands in England" History Channel, This Day in History

Adler, Jerry *"Hot Enough for You?"* Smithsonian May 2014

Veal, Robyn & Leitch, Victoria (editors) *"Fuel and Fire in the Ancient Roman World"* McDonald Institute Conversations 2019

Reomann, Nicholas *"Major Atlantic Current May Be On The Verge Of Collapse, Scientists Warn"* Forbes 5 August 2021

Broadway, Stephen *"Accounting for the Great Divergence: Recent findings from historical national accounting"* VOX CEPR 20 April 2021

Boissoneault, Lorraine *"The Deadly Donora Smog of 1948 Spurred Environmental Protection—But Have We Forgotten the Lesson?"* SmithsonianMag.com 26 October 2018

"Average American Carbon Footprint" Inspire 21 July 2020

Hamilton, Clive & Grinevald, Jacques *"Was the Anthropocene anticipated?"* The Anthropocene Review 2015

Hickman. Leo *"The 1847 lecture that predicted human-induced climate change, a near-forgotten speech made by a US Congressman warned of Global Warming and the mismanagement of natural resources"* Guardian 20 June 2011

Marsh, George Perkins *"Man and Nature: Physical Geography as Modified by Human Action"* Charles Scribner 1864

"How 19th Century Scientists Predicted Global Warming" STOR Daily 17 December 2019

Jarvis, Jacob *"Fact Check: Did a 1912 Newspaper Article Predict Coal-Fueled Climate Change?"* Newsweek 13 August 2021

"The Unchained Goddess" The Bell Telephone Science Hour 1958

Jenkins, Mark *"True Colors, The Changing Face of Greenland"* National Geographic June 2010

Hulac, Benjamin *"Every president since JFK was warned about climate change"* E&E News 6 November 2018

Glass, Andrew *"Reagan seeks to protect fragile ozone layer"* Politico 21 December 2018

'The History of Earth Day' EarthDay.org

Clean Air Act Requirements and History Environmental Protection Agency July 2016

Alter, Jonathan *"Climate Change Was on the Ballot With Jimmy Carter in 1980-Though No One Knew It at the Time"* Yahoo News 29 September 2020

"Planet of the Year" Time Magazine 2 January 1989

"Shell and Exxon's secret 1980s climate change warnings" The Guardian 19 September 2018

"The President's News Conference in Rio de Janeiro" June 1992

"Kyoto Protocol Fast Facts" CNN Editorial Research 18 March 2021

IPCC "3. Projected climate change and its impacts". In Core Writing Team (eds.); et al. Summary for Policymakers. Climate Change 2007: Synthesis Report. Contribution of Working Groups I, II and III to the Fourth Assessment Report of the Intergovernmental Panel on Climate Change (IPCC) Cambridge University Press. 2007

Rayner, Steve *"A Climate Movement at War"* The Breakthrough Institute 31 August 2016

Friedman, Lisa & Plumber, Brad *"E.P.A. Announces Repeal of Major Obama-Era Carbon Emissions Rule"* The New York Times 9 October 2017

"The Supreme Court just narrowed protection for wetlands, leaving many valuable ecosystems at risk" Science 27 May 2023

Taft, Molly *"God Will Help Us Fix Climate Change, so 'Drill Baby Drill' West Virginia Governor Says"* Gizmodo 15 March 2022

Friedman, Lisa & Thrush, Glenn *"U.S. Report Says Humans Cause Climate Change, Contradicting Top Trump Officials"* The New York Times 3 November 2017

Durkin, Martin *"The Great Global Warming Swindle"* Chanel 4 United Kingdom 2007

Firzli, M. Nicolas J. *"Climate Renewed Sense of Urgency in Washington and Beijing"* Analyse Financière. September 2015

Sutter, John D.; Berlinger, Joshua *"Obama: Climate Agreement, 'best chance we have to save the planet'"* CNN Network, December 2015

Watts, Jonathon *"We have 12 years to limit climate change catastrophe, warns UN"* Guardian October 2018

Lieu, Johnny *"Trump tells 60 Minutes that climate change will change back again"* Mashable 14 October 2018

Barboz, Tony *"Climate change will harm the entire nation if the U. S. doesn't act now, federal report warns"* Los Angeles Times 23 November 2018

Lomborg, Bjorn, *"Cool It"* Knopf 2010

Kajplan, Sarah *"Thousands of scientists issue bleak 'second notice to humanity"* Speaking of Science November 2017

Martinez, Julia *"Great Smog of London's environmental disaster, England" United Kingdom [1952]"* Britannica 2019

"Are We Stabilizing Yet?" June 2020 CO2.earth

McCibben, Bill *"The End of Nature"* Anchor 1989

http:republicen.org

Prokop, Andrew *"Don't just blame Trump for quitting the Paris deal-blame the Republican Party, Trump is solidly within The GOP's consensus on climate change"* Vox 21 June 2017

Knowles, David *"Scientists protest as Trump picks climate change skeptic for key NOAA post"* Yahoo News 16 September 2020

Fingerhut, Hannah *"Harassment of TV meteorologists reflects broader anti-science, anti-media trends"* AP 8 July 2023

climateandsecurityfiles.wordpress.com

Costello, M. Abbas, A. Allen, *"Managing the health effects of climate change: Lancet and University College London Institute for Global Health Commission"* Lancet, 2009,

Wilson, Edward O. *"The Meaning of Human Existance"* Liveright Publishing 2014

Hsiang, Soloman M. *"Quantifying the Influence of Climate Change on Human Conflict"* Science September 2013

Wallace-Wells, David *"The Uninhabitable Earth"* Tim Dugan Books 2019

Nubie, Steve *"Off-Grid AC: 9 Forgotten Ways The Ancient Romans (And Everyone Else) Stayed Cool"* OffTheGridNews 2020

McKibben, Bill *"Falter, "Has the Human Game Begun to Play Itself Out"* Henry Holt & Co. 2018

Friedman, Lisa *"What Is the Green New Deal? A Climate Proposal, Explained "* NY Times 21 February 2019

Ocasio-Cortez, Alexandria *(H.Res.109 – 116th Congress (2019–2020): "Recognizing the duty of the Federal Government to create a Green New Deal"* 12 February 2019

Friedman, Lisa *"John Kerry Launches Star-Studded Climate Coalition:"* NY Times 30 November 2019

Howe, Amy *"Supreme Court curtails EPA's authority to fight climate change"* SCOTUSBlog 30 June 2022

O'Malley, Isabella *"'Code red for humanity' IPCC report says about state of the climate"* The Weather Network 9 August 2021

"UN climate report a 'red alert' for the planet: Guterres" UN News 26 February 2021

Nowles, David *"Republicans largely silent on 'code red' climate change report"* YahooNews 10 August 2021

Taylor, Matthew; Watts, Jonathan; Bartlett, John. *"Climate crisis: 6 million people join latest wave of global protests"* The Guardian. 27 September 2019

"Climate Justice = Social Justice: Conversations Exploring the Intersections of People, Planet, and Power" CSULB 22 September 2020

Smith M. D., Craig R. *"A Perfect Threat, Population growth, climate change, and natural resource depletion in the 21st century"* AmJenn Publishing 2021

Moore, Stephen *"Stop scaring the children"* The Washington Times 21 September 2019

Hawken, Paul (editor) *"Drawdown, The most comprehensive plan ever proposed to reverse global warming"* Penguin Books 2017

Porter, Eduardo *"Blueprints for Taming the Climate Crisis"* New York Times 8 July 2014

https://arpa-e.energy.gov/?q=arpa-e-site-page/projects

Sneed, Annie *"Carbon Breathing Batteries"* Scientific American December 2016

Hughes, Clyde *"Water from air? Solar device wrings H2O out of nowhere"* Science April 2017

Sne, Annie *"Carbon Breathing Batteries"* Scientific American December 2016

Wallace-Wells, David *"The Uninhabitable Earth, Life After Warming"* Tim Dugan Books 2019

Harris, Nancy & Gibbs, David *"Forests Absorb Twice As Much Carbon As They Emit Each Year"* World Resource Institute 21 January 2021

Porter, Eduardo *"Blueprints for Taming the Climate Crisis"* New York Times, 8 July 2014

Smit, Bernard: Reimer, Jeffery R. Oldenberg, Curtis M; Bourg, Ian C. *"Introduction to Carbon Capture and Sequestration"* Imperial College Press 2014

"What is Blue Carbon?" NOAA 26 February 2021

"Researchers Build Machine that Turns CO2 into Fuel" Inhabitat-Sustainable Design Innovation, Eco Architecture, Green Building 6 October 2013

Biello, David *"400 PPM: Can Artificial Trees Help Pull CO2 from the Air?"* Scientific American 16 May 2013

"SSE Thermal and Equinor join forces on plans for first-of-a-kind hydrogen and carbon capture projects in the Humber" Equinor 8 April 2021

Breselor, Sara *"Waste Not, New Eco-Wraps"* Wired Nov 2014

Rosen, Ben, *"Scientists invent a way to create CO2 fuel from a solar leaf"* Christian Science Monitor 1 August 2016

" https://arpa-e.energy.gov/?q=arpa-e-site-page/projects"

Sneed, Annie *"Carbon Breathing Batteries"* Scientific American December 2016

Hughes, Clyde "Water from air? Solar device wrings H2O out of nowhere" Science April 2017

Sne, Annie *"Carbon Breathing Batteries"* Scientific American December 2016

Kile, Meredith *"How to replace foam and plastic packaging with mushroom experiments"* Al Jazeera America 13 November 2013

Trimarchi, Maria *"What Caused the Dust Bowl?"* How Stuff works 4 May 2021

Hickey, Hannah *"Pollution in Northern Hemisphere helped cause 1980s African drought"* UW News 6 June 2013

Shin, Judy "What is the Great Green Wall Of China?" Earth.org 8 October 2020

"The Great Green Wall implementation status and the way ahead to 2030" UNCCD 2020

Kleiman, Dr. Jordan *"Love Canal: A Brief History"* Genesco 2020

"Chernobyl Accident 1986" world-nuclear.org/information-library April 2020

Hayes, Thomas C. *"CONFRONTATION IN THE GULF; The Oilfield Lying Below the Iraq-Kuwait Dispute"* The New York Times. 3 September 1990

Taylor, Alan *"Bhopal: The World's Worst Industrial Disaster, 30 Years Later"* 2 December 2014

Prupis, Nadia *"Lack of Oversight, Damaged Tanks Caused West Virginia Chemical Spill"* Common Dreams 28 July 2014

Czech, Brian *"Supply Shock, Economic Growth at the Crossroads and the Steady State Solution"* New Society Publishers 2013

Mooney, Chris *"The next big energy revolution won't be in wind or solar. It will be in our Brains"* Washington Post, January 2015

Von Kaenel, Camille *"Energy Security Drives U.S. Military to Renewables"* Scientific America March 2016

"Navy quietly ends Climate Change Task Force, reversing Obama Initiative" Navy Times August 2019

"U.S. Military Precariously Unprepared for Climate Threats, War College & Retired Brass Warn" December 2019

Thackara, John *"In the Bubble, Designing in a Complex World"* MIT Press February 2006

Strain, Daniel *"Polar Ice Sheets effects on sea levels sends chills down mid-Atlantic Coast "* Bay Journal November 2014

"Early Warning Signs of Global Warming: Glaciers Melting" Union of Concerned Scientist 2018

Casey, Michael *"Glaciers in Antarctica are melting three times faster than previously thought"* CBS News Dec ember 2014

Goodell, Jeff *"Global Warming: Case Closed"* Rolling Stone 26 September 2013

Zalasiewicz, *Jan "What mark will we leave on the Planet?"* Scientific American September 2016

Davenport, Coral and Robertson, Campbell *"Resettling the First American 'Climate Refugees"* New York Times 3 May 2016

Samuels, Gabriel *"Scientists warn of 'global climate emergency over jet stream shift "* The Independent 30 June 2016

Schiffman, Richard *" Reef Stricken"* Newsweek 3 June 2016

McKibben, Bill *"Can China Go Green?"* National Geographic June 2011

Gertner, Jon, *"Clearing the Air"* Fast Company May 2015

"Before the Flood" Documentary 2016

Curwen, Thomas *"The 102 million dead trees in California's forests are turning tree cutters into millionaires"* Los Angeles Times 14 December 2016

Borenstein, Seth *"Intolerable unimaginable heat forecast for Persian Gulf "* AP Science Writer

Goodell, Jeff *"The Pentagon and Climate Change "* Rolling Stone 26 February 2015

Dave Nyczepir *"Norfolk, Home to World's Largest Naval Base, Must Adapt as Waters Rise"* Defense One 31 August 2015

Moyer, Justin *"Climate Change Alert: Global Carbon Dioxide tops 400 ppm for first time"* Washington Post 7 May 2015

http://www.cna.org/reports/climate#sthash.hddyela3.dpuf

Sarkis, Christine *"Disappearing World: 101 of the Earth's Most Extraordinary and Endangered Places"* Smarter Travel 2012

"Draft U.S. Greenhouse Gas Inventory Report: 1990-2014" United States Environmental Protection Agency 2016

"How to fix it" National Geographic November 2015

Carson, Rachel *"Silent Spring"* Houghton Mifflin 1962

"Growing coral larger and faster: micro-colony-fusion as a strategy for accelerating coral cover" 20 October 2015

Gore, Al *"An Inconvenient Truth"* Rosedale Press 2006

Ghose, Tia *"Earth Gets Greener as Globe Gets Hotter "* AFP 29 April 2016

Zaman, Munir Uz *"Workers feeling the heat as climate change slashes productivity"* AFP 29 April 2016

The American Experience: Drought" PBS. Retrieved 2017

"The Green Wall of China" Wired April 2003

Watts, Jonathan "China makes gain in battle against desertification, but has a long fight ahead" The Guardian 4 January 2011

Baker, Aryn *"What man, and climate change, has wrought"* Time 27 March 2017

"Actions At The Love Canal Site" The New York Times. 23 February 1983.

Depalma, Anthony *"Love Canal Declared Clean, Ending Toxic Horror"* The New York Times. 18 March 2004

"Occidental to pay $129 Million in Love Canal Settlement" U.S. Department of Justice 21 December 1995.

Broughton, Edward *"The Bhopal disaster and its aftermath: a review"* Environ Health 10 May 2005

Parker, Laura A *"Century of Controversy, Accidents in West Virgina's Chemical valley in Lead-up to Spill"* National Geographic 16 January 2014

Beard, Mary *"Pompeii: The Life of a Roman Town"* Profile Books. 2008

"NASA-NOAA Satellite Sees Siberian Smoke Reach Alaska" NASA 30 July, 2020

Lomborg, Bjorn *"Cool It"* Knopf Publishing 2010

Fitzgerald, Michael *"New Tech Cities Urban Upgrades"* Wired November 2014

Shende, *Rajendra "At 70, UN sets 17 goals: To be achieved in less than 17 years"* The Economic Times, October 2015

McKibben, Bill *"Racism, Police Violence, and the Climate Are Not Separate Issues"* The New Yorker 4 June 2020

"Address by President Hollande to the UN General Assembly" UNCC 28 September 2015

Pope Francis *"Laudato Si" Encyclical Letter of the Holy Father on Care for Our Common Home"* 24 May 2015

Nazworth, *Napp "Evangelicals and Climate Change: What Does the Future Hold?"* Christian Post Reporter 12 June 2012

Banerjee, *Neela "Southern Baptists Back a Shift on Climate Change"* NY Times *10 March 2008*

"Hindu Declaration on Climate change" UN Climate Statement 23 November 2015

"Islamic Declaration on Climate Change" External Statement UNCC 18 August 2015

"Combating Climate Change" JCPA May 17, 2016

Payutto, Ven. P. A. *"Buddhist Economics - A Middle Way for the Market Place"* Buddhadhamma Foundation, 1994.

"The Time to Act is Now: A Buddhist Declaration on Climate Change" 14 May 2015

Dalai Lama *"The Four Noble Truths"* Thorsons 1998

Rockstrom, Johan *"Bounding the Planetary Future: Why we need a Great Transition"* April 2015

Pearce, Fred *"Geoengineer the Planet? More Scientists Now Say It Must Be an Option"* YaleEnvironment360 29 May 2019

Taft, Molly *"God Will Help Us Fix Climate Change, so 'Drill Baby Drill,' West Virginia Governor Says"* Gizmodo 15 March 2022

Guy, Jack '*Australian bushfires likely to happen again -- and they could be even worse, inquiry warns"* CNN 25 August 2020

Einhorn, Catrin Magdalena, Maria Migliozzi, Balcki and Reinhard, Scott *"The World's Largest Tropical Wetland Has Become an Inferno"* New York Times 13 October 2020

Dahlmam, LuAnn and Lindsey,Rebecca *"Climate Change: Ocean Heat Content"* NOAA Climate.gov 17 August 2020

"Colorado wildfires show "Climate change is here and now'" CBS News 21 October 2020

Vazquez, Maegan *"Trump baselessly questions climate science during California wildfire briefing"* CNN 14 September 2020

Multople authors, *"Mapped: How climate change affects extreme weather around the world"* Attributes Carbon Brief 15 April 2020

Tandon, Ayesha *"West Africa's deadly rainfall in 2022 made '80 times more likely' by climate change"* Carbon Brief 16 November 2022

"Climate change vicious cycle spirals in Latin America and Caribbean" World Meteorological Organization 5 July 2023

"Is extreme weather caused by global warming?" Skeptical Science 2020

Hawkins, Paul, (editor) *"Drawdown, The most comprehensive plan ever proposed to reverse global warming"* Penguin Press 2017

"NASA Map Reveals what pandemic free 2020 would have looked like" UNILD 19 November 2020

McGrath, Matt *"Climate change and coronavirus: Five charts about the biggest carbon crash"* BBC News 2020

"Ark Encounter in Kentucky suing after flooding causes property damage" ABC News WLEX 24 May 2019

Shalal, Andrea "Climate change poses 'profound threat' to global growth - IMF chief" Reuters 12 October 2020

Baskar, Pranav *"Locusts Are A Plague Of Biblical Scope In 2020. Why? And ... What Are They Exactly?"* NPR 14 June 2020

"Joint Business Statement Supporting Global Climate Strike" American sustainable Business Council 2020

Cappucci, Matthew *"Pacific Northwest heat wave was 'virtually impossible' without climate change, scientists find"* Washington Post 7 July 2021

Marsh, Sarah & Menchu, Sofia *"Storms that slammed Central America in 2020 just a preview, climate change experts say"* Reuters 3 December 2020

"Greece, Turkey battle fierce fires as heat wave continues" The Guardian 06 August 2021

Chia, Krystal *"China Warns of More Floods, Extreme Weather after Weeks of Chaos"* Bloomberg Green 28 July 2021,

Crrington, Damien *"Extreme heat in Oceans passed Point of No Return in 2014"* The Guardian 1 February 2022

"Pakistan Floods 'Worst In Country's History', Says PM Sharif" Barron's. Agence France Presse. 30 August 2022

Sistek, Scott *"Atmospheric river turns deadly as it slams California with flooding, mudslides"* Fox Weather 1 January 2023

"A Supercharged Climate: Rain bombs, Flash Flooding and Destruction" Climate Council December 2022

Mogul,Rhea and Mitra, Esha and Suri,Manveena and Saifi, Sophia, *"India and Pakistan heatwave is 'testing the limits of human survivability,'* expert says" CNN 2 May, 2022

"How is the Climate Crisis impacting South America?" The Climate Reality Project 28 April 2021

Vakil, Caroline *"Yellen to lead investigation into climate change risk to financial system"* The Hill 10 July 2021

Chow, Denise and Lederman, Josh *"Biden Commits to cutting U.S. emissions in half by 2030 as part of Paris Climate pact"* NBC News 22 April 2021

"How Companies can Align with Biden's Executive Order on Climate-Related Financial Risk" NewsDirect 12 July 2021

Knowles, David *"Citing grave threat, Scientific American replaces 'climate change' with 'climate emergency',"* Yahoo News 12 April 2021,

Gore, Al *"How to make Radical Climate Action the new Norm"* TED talk 2021

Kelly, Walt *"Pogo"* 1970

"Quotes From Yuri Gagarin Outer Space Speech" 1961

A SUSTAINABLE WORLD

Shield, Peter *"Uncommon Sense, Shortcomings of the Human Mind for Handling Big-Picture, Long-Term Challenges"* Steady State Press 2021

Boulding, Kenneth E. *"The Economics of the Coming Spaceship Earth"* Sixth Resources for the Future Forum on Environmental Quality in a Growing *Economy in Washington, D.C. 8 March 1966*

"economic libertarian" www.the freedictionary.com

Critchley, Dr Peter *"The Stationary State of John Stuart Mill"* Academia 2004

Beavan, Colin *"No Impact Man"* Goodreads 2009

Russell, Bertland *"In Praise of Idleness"* 1932

Daly, Herman E. *"Economics for a Full World"* presentation, Tokyo November 2014

The Club of Rome, the Predicament of Mankind, *"Quest for Structured Responses to Growing World-wide Complexities and Uncertainties"* A Proposal, The Club of Rome 1970

Anderson, Martin *"The Reagan Boom - Greatest Ever"* Opinion, New York Times 17 January 1990

Meadows, Dr Donna, Meadows, D. L. Randers, J. Behrens III, W. W. *"The Limits to Growth"* Universe Books 1972

Meadows, Dennis *"Growing, Growing Gone: Reaching the Limits"* June 2015

Schumacher, E. F. *"Small Is Beautiful: A Study of Economics As If People Mattered"* B londs & Briggs 1973

King, Alexander and Schneider. Bertand *"The First Global Revolution"* Pantheon 1991

"Sustainable Development Goals" United Nations Foundation 2015

Kurzweil, Ray *"The Singularity is Near"* Penguin Press 2005

Kallis, Giorgos *"The Degrowth Alternative Great Transition Initiative"* February 2015

Hardin, Garret *"Tragedy of the Commons Towards a Steady-State Economy"* 1973

Daly, Herman E., ed. *"Toward a Steady-state Economy"* San Francisco: W.H. Freeman 1973

Turner, Graham *"A comparison of the Limits to Growth with thirty years of reality"* Commonwealth Scientific and Industrial Research Organisation (CSIRO) Sustainable Ecosystems 2008

Hann, Chris, *"The Anthropocene and anthropology"* European Journal of Social Theory *23 May 2016*

Knight, Nika "Anthropocene Math in the Age of Trump" Common Dreams February 22, 2017

"About Us, Stockholm Resilience Centre" stockholmresilience.org. 2 December 2007.

Rockstrom, Johan *"Stockholm Resilience Centre"* 2011

Steffen, W.; Richardson, K. et al. *"Planetary boundaries: Guiding human development on a changing planet"*. Science. 2015

Rockström et al. *"Planetary Boundaries: Exploring the Safe Operating Space for Humanity"* 2009.

Raworth, Kate *"A Safe and Just Space for Humanity: Can we live within the doughnut?"* Oxfam Discussion Paper, 2012.

Steffen et al. *"Trajectories of the Earth System in the Anthropocene"* 2018.

Rockstrom, *Johan, TED talk September 2018*

Raworth, Kate *"Doughnut Economics: Seven Ways to Think like a 21st- century Economist"* 2018.

Jarvie, Michelle E. "Brundtland Report" World Commission on Environment and Development 1987

Lovelock, James, *"The Ages of Gaia: A Biography of Our Living Earth"* W.W.Norton & Co 1995

"The cost of clean air" The Economist 17 February 2015

Khan, Amina *"Caterpillar may hold a solution to plastic waste"* Los Angeles Times April 2017

Armstrong, Paul and Ke Feng *"Beijing announces emergency measures amid fog of pollution"* CNN, 23 October 2013

Henry, Devin *"China to close 1,000 coal mines in 2016"* The Hill 22 February 2016

De Freytas-Tamura, Kimiko *"Plastics pile up as China refuses to take wests recycling"* NY Times 11 January 2018

McDonough, William and Braungart *"Cradle to Cradle: Remaking the Way We Make Things"* North Point Press New York, NY 2002

Sullivan, Laura S. *"Plastic Wars: Industries Spent Millions Selling Recycling, To Sell More Plastics"* NPR March 2020

Vaughan, Adam *"Countries agree to end plastic pollution in ambitious global* treaty" 2 March 2022

Rockstrom, Johan *"Bounding the Planetary Boundaries: Why we need a Great Transition"* April 2015

Kallis, *Giorgos "The Degrowth Alternative, The Green Transition Initiative"* February 2015

Sanders, Robert *"In desert trials, next-generation water harvester delivers fresh water from air"* Berkley News June 2018

Datschefski, Edwin *"The Beauty of Sustainable Products"* Rotovision 2001

Scheer, Roddy Moss, Doug *"The Living Building Challenge"* EarthTalk 6 January 2013

"Good Design for a Bad World" Dezeen Conference 2017

Fearson, Amy *"We need designers, not scientists, to show us how to change the world, says Babette Porcelijn"* 22 November 2017

"History of Safer Choice and Design for the Environment" EPA. 2017

Shedroff, Nathan *"Design is the Problem, the Future of Design Must be Sustainable"* 2009

Papanek, Victor *"Design for the Real World, Human Ecology and Social Change"* Bantam Books 1971

"Recycled plastic products-a hierarchy of uses" EcologyCenter.org/plastics 2021

Lanese, Nicoletta *"Microbes in cow stomachs can help recycle plastic"* LiveScience 30 June 2021

Taylor-Smith, Kerry *"Can Chemical Recycling Solve the Plastic Crisis?"* AZO CleanTech 2021

Tullo, Alexander H. *"Plastic has a problem; is chemical recycling the solution?"* Chemical & Engineering News 6 October 2019

Patel,Prachi *"New Technique Converts Plastic Waste to Fuel"* DailyScience 14 February 2019

Krueger, Barbara, Stewart, Nika *"Universal Design"* Globe Peugeot Press 2011

Thackara, John *"In the Bubble: Designing in a Complex World"* MIT Press February *2006*

Weins, Kyle *" You Gotta Fight For Your Right to Repair Your Car"* The Atlantic 13 February 2014

Kelly, Makena *"Elizabeth Warren comes out in support of a national right-to-repair law"* The Verge 27 March 2019

Bedayn, Jesse *"Colorado becomes first to pass 'right to repair' for farmers"* 25 April 2023

Davies, Rachael *"EU proposes law to increase lifespan of smartphones"* Evening Standard 6 September 2022

Van Hinte, Ed *"Eternally Yours: Time in Design"* Eternally Yours Foundation 2004

Fairs, Marcus *"Good Design for a Bad World"* Dezeen Conference 21 February 2018

Hogue, Cheryl *"Recycling is only one part of solution to plastic waste, experts say, Product design and life-cycle assessment are also needed"* Chemical & Engineering News 25 June 2021

Fetner, Hannah & Miller, Shelie A. *"Environmental payback periods of reusable alternatives to single-use plastic kitchenware products"* The International Journal of Life Cycle Assessment, 2021

Aleander, Dr Samuel *"Ecological Civilization, Beyond Consumerism and the Growth Economy"* Sustainability Institute 2021

Moloney, Anastasia *"Is green-hushing the new greenwashing?"* 26 October 2022

Hogue, Cheryl *"Recycling is only one part of solution to plastic waste, experts say, Product design and life-cycle assessments are also needed"* Chemical & Engineering News 25 June 2021

Quinn, Megan *"2021 could be year for packaging EPR, nearly a dozen state bills in play"* DeepDive 11 February. 2021

Dasgupta, Neha & Bhardwaj, Mayank *"India set to outlaw six single-use plastic products on October 2"* Reuters ESG Environment 28 August 2019

Pajda, Aleksandra *"Lego Has Started to Replace Plastic Pieces With a Sustainable, Plant-Based Alternative!"* Our Green Planet 2018

Fairs, Marcus *"Mobile Phones and other industrial products have the 'number one impact" on climate change"* 21 November 2017

Harris, Mark *"Can we balance our carbon budget by using less stuff? Anthropocene 23 September 2022*

Forsythe, Michael *"China Aims to Spend at Least $360 Billion on Renewable Energy by 2020"* New York Times 5 January 2017

Chestney, Nina *"Global energy CO2 emissions could be cut by 70 percent by 2050: IRENA,"* Reuters 20 March 2017

Wallis, Stewart *"Five measures of growth that are better than GDP"* Independent Thinker 2016

Weller, Chris *"8 basic income experiments to watch out for in 2017"* Business Insider 24 January 2017

"A Guidebook to the Green Economy - Issue 1: Green Economy, Green Growth, and Low-Carbon Development" UN-DESA 2012

Hertwich, Edgar *"Is Green Growth Possible?"* Norwegian SciTech News 21 December 2021

Gordon, Noah *"The Conservative Case for a Guaranteed Basic Income"* The Atlantic 6 August 2014

Lebow, Victor *"The Real Meaning of Consumer Demand"* 1955

Suzuki, David *"Consumer society no longer serves our needs"* Science Matters 11 January 2018

Kohan, Susan E. *"Patagonia's Bold Move Shakes Up The Ideas Of Capitalism And Consumerism"* Forbes September 2022

Aleander, Dr Samuel *"Ecological Civilization, Beyond Consumerism and the Growth Economy"* Sustainability Institute 2021

Perry Tod *"Astronaut shares the profound 'big lie' he realized after seeing the Earth from space. This change in perspective could change humanity"* 1 August 2023

EVIL (a formula)

Oxford Language Dictionary

Dante *"The Inferno"*

Baron-Cohen, Simon *"The Science of Evil"* Basic Books, 2011

Gerard, Moeller. *"Antisocial Personality Disorder, Alcohol and Aggression"* National Institute of Health. 2015

Kristof, Nicholas D. *"Unmasking Horror -- A special report; Japan Confronting Gruesome War Atrocity"* NY Times 17 March 1995

"1937: The Rape of Nanking (Nanjing)" Alliance for Human Research Protection 10 December 2014

Weindling, Paul *"The victims of unethical human experiments and coerced research under National Socialism"* Endeavor March 2016

Maksymiuk, Jan; Dratch, Marianna *"Ukraine: Parliament Recognizes Soviet-Era Famine As Genocide"* 29 November 2006

Lorenz, Andreas *"The Chinese Cultural Revolution: Remembering Mao's Victims"* Der Spiegel 15 May 2007

Sharp, Bruce *"Counting Hell: The Death Toll of the Khmer Rouge Regime in Cambodia"* 2 April 2005
Shield, Peter *"Uncommon Sense, Shortcomings of the Human Mind for Handling Big-Picture, Long-Term Challenges"* Steady State Press 2021
Pinker, Steven *"The Better Angels of Our Nature"* Viking, Penguin Group 2011
Baumeister, Roy F. *"Evil, Inside Human Violence and Cruelty"* Henry Holt & Co. 1999
Griffith, Jeremy *"Adam & Eve without the guilt: explaining our battle between instinct and intellect"* Irish Times 30 May 2016,
Peterson, Jordan B. *"12 Rules for Life, An Antidote to Chaos"* Random House Canada 2018
Popova, Maria *"Adam Smith's Underappreciated Wisdom on Benevolence, Happiness, and Kindness"* The Marginalian 2022
DeWaal, Frans *"The Evolution of Empathy"* Greater Good Magazine 1 September 2005

HOW TO NOT MAKE WAR

Horgan, John *"The End of War"* McSweeney's Books, 2012.
Chernow, Ron *"Alexander Hamilton"* Penguin Books 2004
David L. Smith. *"Less Than Human; How we Demean, Enslave, and Exterminate Others"* St. Martin's Press, February 2012
Marean, Curtis W *"The Most Invasive Species of All"* Scientific American August 2015
Hank Davis. *"Caveman Logic; The Persistence of Primitive Thinking in a Modern World"* Prometheus Books 2009
William James *"History is a bath of blood"* Essay 1906
https://faculty.fiu.edu/~harrisk/Notes/Ethics/Aristotle's%20Ethics.htm
Rogers, Russ *"The Generalship of Muhammad"* University of Florida Press, 2012
Edward O Wilson *"The Social Conquest of Earth"* Liveright Books, Harvard University, April 2012
Milgram, Stanley *"Obedience to Authority; an Experimental View"* Harper Collins.1974
Tomasello, Michael *"Why We Cooperate, Tanner Lectures on Human Values at Sanford"* Boston Book Review 2008
"Ludwig von Bertalanffy" The Information Philosopher
Kyrzweil, Ray *"How to Create a Mind"* Viking Press 2012
Gallagher, Louis (translation) *"The Diary of Matthew Ricci, China in the Sixteenth Century"* Random House, 1942,
Zorich, Zak *"Born to be Mild"* Discover July/August 2015
de Waal, Frans *" The Bonobo and the Atheist: In Search of Humanism Among the Primates"* W. W. Norton 2013.
"Evolution of Fairness" Language Research Center 2016
McCullough, Michael *"Beyond Revenge: The Evolution of the Forgiveness Instinct"* Jossey-Bass 2008
Harmon, Katherine *"Does Revenge Serve an Evolutionary Purpose?"* Scientific American 4 May 2011
Pinker, Steven *"The Better Angels of our Nature"* Viking, Penguin Group 2011
Harari, Yuval Noah *"Homo Deux"* Harper Collins Publisher 2017
DeWaal, Frans *"The Evolution of Empathy"* Greater Good Magazine 1 September 2005
Chenwoth, Erica Stephen, Maria *"Why Civil Resistance Works: The Strategic Logic of Nonviolent Conflict"* Columbia University Press, 2011
Pinker, Steven *Enlightenment Now, The case for reason, science, humanism, and progress"* Viking Press 2018

THE UNNATURAL SPECIES, GENES, AI, AND TRANSHUMAN

Fry, Tony *"Design as Politics"* Oxford International Publishers Ltd. 2012
Strauer BE, Schannwell CM, Brehm M *"Therapeutic potentials of stem cells in cardiac diseases"* Minerva Cardioangiol 2009
Steinberg, Douglas *"Stem Cells Tapped to Replenish Organs"* the scientist.com November 2000
Belmonte, Juan Carlos Izpisua *"Human Organs from Animal Bodies"* Scientific American November 2016
Lambert, Jonathan *"What does the first successful test of a pig-to-human kidney transplant mean?"* Science News 20 November 2021
Prather, Randall *"From pigs that glow to lifesaving swine"* Baltimore Sun 23 January 2022
Wilson, Clare *"How a pig heart was transplanted into a human for the first time"* NewScientist 11 January 2022
Stem Cells Basics *"What are the potential uses of human stem cells and the obstacles that must be overcome before these potential uses will be realized?"* In Stem Cell Information World Wide Web site. Bethesda, MD: National Institutes of Health, U.S. Department of Health and Human Services, 2009
"Creation of the President's Council on Bioethics" 28 November 2001,
"Scientists rally around stem cell advocate fired by Bush" USA Today 30 May 2008.
"Edinburgh scientists use 3D printing to produce stem cells" BBC 5 February 2013.
Gabbi, Arik *"Building the New You"* Smithsonian May 2015
"Creation of the President's Council on Bioethics" 28 November 2001,
"Eugenic Ideas, Political Interests and Policy Variance Immigration and Sterilization Policy in Britain and U.S." World Politics 1 January 2001.
Gowen, Annie *"Straight out of the Nazi playbook': Hindu nationalists try to engineer 'genius' babies in India"* The Washington Post 9 May 2017
Miller, Geoffrey *"What 'should' we be worried about?"* Edge 2013
Harah, Yuval Noah *"Sapiens"* Harper Collins Publishers 2015
Maxmen, Amy *"Easy DNA Editing Will Remake the World. Buckle Up"* Wired July 2015
McKibben, Bill *"Falter, Has the human game begun to play itself out?"* Henry Holt & Co. 2019

Hall, Stephen *"Will we control our Genetic Destinies?"* Scientific American September 2016

Sokar, Andrew *"The Gilgamesh Project"* Nexus Magazine June-July 2015

Freitas, Robert A. *"Exploratory Design in medical Nanotechnology: A Mechanical Artificial Red Cell"* Foresight Institute 1996

Kurzweil, Ray *"The Singularity is Near"* Penguin Books, 2005

"Blood Substitues, and Immobil" Biotech 1998

Kotler, Steven *"Evolution Full Tilt"* Discover March 2013

https://mail.google.com/mail/u/0/#inbox/FMfcgxwLsmclTsbXtjhnHqpBDxsBgnn

"The Next Clone" Smithsonian June 2022

Zimmermann, Kim Ann *"History of Computers: A Brief Timeline"* LifeScience 7 September 2017

Copeland, Jack *"The Modern History of Computing"* Stanford Encyclopedia 18 December 2000

Hailey, Daniel Stephen *Charles Babbage, Father of the Computer"* Crowell-Coller Press 1970

Collier, Bruce & Machlan *"Charles Babbage: And the Engines of Perfection"* Oxford University Press 28 December 2000

Fischmann, Josh *"Revolution in Artificial Limbs Brings Feeling Back to Amputees"* National Geographic 22 February 2014

Huxley, Aldous *"Brave New World"* HarperCollins Publishers 1932

Bailey, L. L.; Nehlsen-Cannarella, S. L.; Concepcion, W.; Jolley, W. B. *"Baboon-to-human cardiac xenotransplantation in a neonate"* J AMA: the Journal of the American Medical Association 1985

Delgado, Jose *"Physical Control of the Mind Toward a Psychocivilized Society"* Harper and Row 1986

Olds, James *"Self-Stimulation of the Brain"* Science 1958

Olds, James *"Reward and Drive Neurons, Brain Stimulation Reward"* 1975

Wise, R A , Rompre PP *"Brain Dopamine and Reward "* Annual Review of Psychology 1989

Kennemer, Quentyn *"Elon Musk's Neuralink Reportedly One Step Closer To Testing On Humans"* 28 March 2023

Britt, Robert Roy *"Brain Chip to Stimulate Orgasms"* Live Science 22 December 2008

Sample, Ian *"Scientists use stem cells from frogs to build first living robots"* the Guardian 13 January 2020

http://www.bio.org/articles/xentransplation-benefits-risks-special-organ-transplantation

Hughes, James *"Transhumanist Politics, 1700 to the near future"* Institute for Ethics and Emerging Technologies 10 April 2009

Istvan, Zoltan *"Artificial Wombs Are Coming, but the Controversy Is Already Here"* Motherboard 24 August 2014

Moore, Max *"The Extropian Principle. A Humanist Declaration"* Extropy Institute 1998

Sacks, Oliver *"The Man Who Mistook His Wife for a Hat and Other Clinical Tales"* Summit Books 1985

Eordogh, Fruzsina *"The Russian Billionaire Dmitry plans on becoming immortal by 2045"* Motherboard 7 May 2013

Neal, Meghan *"Those 'Biopunk' Designs are what the future human will look like"* Motherboard 7 October 2013

Lee, Kai-fu *"AI Superpowers, China, Silicone Valley on the New World Order"* Houghton Mifflin Harcourt 2018

Bryk, William *"Artificial Intelligence: The Coming Revolution"* Harvard Science Review December 2015

"Introducing OpenAI" OpenAI Blog. December 12, 2015.

Hern, Alex. *"DeepMind announces ethics group to focus on problems of AI"* The Guardian 4 October 2017

Schwartz, Oscar *"Could 'fake text' be the next global political threat?"* The Guardian. 16 July 2019.

Vincent, James *"ChatGPT proves AI is finally mainstream – and things are only going to get weirder"* The Verge. 8 December 2022

"Meet Sophia, the female humanoid robot and newest SXSW celebrity". PCWorld. 4 January 2018.

DeGrazia, David *"At what point does AI become conscious"* George Washington University 23 April 2023

"We're teaching robots to evolve autonomously – so they can adapt to life alone on distant planets" The Conversation 1 February 2021

"The Rise of A.I. Companions [Documentary]" Youtube 2022

"What It's Like To be a Computer: An Interview with GPT-3" Youtube 2022

Linder, Courtney *"This AI Robot Just Nabbed the Lead Role in a Sci-Fi Movie"* Popular Mechanics 25 June 2020

Pagliery, J. *"Elon Musk and Stephen Hawking warn over "killer robots"* New York Times 28 July 2015

Sainato, Michael *"Stephen Hawking, Elon Musk, and Bill Gates warn about Artificial Intelligence"* The Observer 2015,

Danilak, Dr Rado *"Why Energy Is A Big And Rapidly Growing Problem For Data Centers"* Forbes May 2017

Conniff, Richard *"What the Luddites Really Fought Against"* Smithsonian 19 October 2016

Marsden, Richard *"Cotton Weaving: Its Development, Principles, and Practice"* George Bell & Sons, 1895

Samuel, Sigal *"AI leaders (and Elon Musk) urge all labs to press pause on powerful AI"* Vox 29 March 2023

Dowd, Douglas F *"Robert Owen, British Social Reformer "* Encyclopedia Britannica

Strange, Adario *"Elon Musk Thinks Universal Income is Answer to Automation Taking Human Jobs"* Mashable November 2016

Li, Fei-Fei *"How to Make AI That's Good for People"* New York Times March 2018,

Paine, Thomas and Spence, Thomas *"Two Articles for Basic Income"* 1795

McWilliam J A *"Electrical stimulation of the heart in man"*. British Medical Journal 1899

Vidal, JJ (1973). *"Toward direct brain-computer communication"*. Annual review of biophysics and bioengineering

Asimov, Isaac. *"I, Robot"* 1950

Giamatti, Paul *"Breakthrough"* National Geographic Channel 2015

Harari, Yuval Noah *"Homo Deus"* Harper Collins Publishers 2017

Moravec, Hans. *"The Age of Robots"*, Extro 1, Proceedings of the First Extropy Institute Conference on TransHumanist Thought 1994

Rao, Rajesh P. N., Stocco, Andrea, *"When Two Brains Connect,"* Scientific American Mind, November/December 2014

Shaer, Matthew *"The Body Shop"* Smithsonian May 2015

Adler, Jerry *"Mind Meld"* Smithsonian May 2015

Allen, Robert (editor) *"Bullet Proof Feathers"* University of Chicago Press 2010

Gera, Deborah Levine, *"Ancient Greek Ideas on Speech, Language, and Civilization. Oxford University"* Press 2003

Brundage D. *"Renal Disorders"* Mosby; 1992

Bostrom, Nick *"A History of Transhumanist Thought,"* Journal of Evolution and Technology 2005

Hughes, James *"Citizen Cyborg: Why Democratic Societies Must Respond to the Redesigned Human of the Future"* Westview Press. 2004

DeGrazia, David *"At what point does AI become conscious?"* George Washington University 23 April 2023

Bailey, Ronald *"Transhumanism: the most dangerous idea?"* Reason. 25 August 2004

Huxley, Julian, *"Transhumanism"* 1957

Rutschman, Ana *"Congress takes first steps toward regulating artificial intelligence"* The Conversation 19 October 2018

I.J. Good, *"Speculations Concerning the First Ultraintelligent Machine"* Advances in Computers, vol. 6, 1965.

"The Transhumanist Declaration" World Transhumanist Association 2002

Winner, Langdon *"Resistance is Futile: The Posthuman Condition and Its Advocates"* MIT Press 2005

Casey, Timothy *"Is the Human Nature Obsolete?"* M.I.T. Press. October 2004

Tennison, Michael *"Moral transhumanism: the next step"* J Med Philosophy 2012.

"Transvision: Faith, Transhumanism and Hope Symposium" 2004

Darnovsky, Marcy *"Health and Human rights Leaders call for an international ban on species-altering procedures"* 2001

http://www.oxforddictionaries.com/definition/english/transhumanism

Levine, SP; Huggins, JE; et al. *"A direct brain interface based on event-related potentials"*. IEEE transactions on rehabilitation engineering : IEEE Engineering in Medicine and Biology Society 2000.

Santucci, David M.; Kralik, Jerald D.; Lebedev, Mikhail A.; Nicolelis, Miguel A. L. *"Frontal and parietal cortical ensembles predict single-trial muscle activity during reaching movements in primates"*. European Journal of Neuroscience 2005

Yam, Philip. *"Breakthrough Could Enable Others to Watch Your Dreams and Memories"* Scientific American. September 2011.

Pais-Vieira, Miguel; et al. *"A Brain-Brain Interface for Real –Time Sharing of Sensorimotor Information"* Scientific Reports 25 September 2014

Max, D. T. *"How Humans are shaping our own evolution"* National Geographics April 2017

O'Doherty JE, Lebedev MA, Ifft PJ, Zhuang KZ, Shokur S, Bleuler H, Nicolelis MA *"Active tactile exploration using a brain-machine-brain interface"* Nature. October 2011

Grabianowski, Ed *"How Brain-computer Interfaces Work"* How Stuff Works November 2014

Kurzweil, Ray *"How to Create a Mind, The Secret of Human Thought"* Viking Press 2012

Kelly, Kevin *"What Technology Wants"* Viking Press 2010

Harari, Yuval Noah *"Sapiens"* Harper Collins Publishers 2015

Urban, Tim *"Neuralink and the Brain's Magical Future"* Wait ButWhy April 2017

Boyle, Alan *"How Elon Musk and Neuralink aim to meld minds and machines with a 'Wizard Hat'."* GeekWire April 2017

Koch. Christof *"Will Machines Ever Become Conscious?"* Scientific American December 2019

Christian, Brian *"The Most Human Human"* Google Books May 2011

Hughes, James *"Citizen Cyborg, why Democratic Societies must respond to the Redesigned Human of the Future,"* Westview Press, 2004

"Converging Technologies for Improving Human Performance" U.S. National Science Foundation, U.S. Department of Commerce June 2002

Suskin, Zaev D. and Giordano, James J. *"Body –to-head transplant; a 'capital' crime? Examining the corpus of ethical and legal issues"* BMC 13 July 2018

Floyd, David *"The Long, Weird History of Universal Basic Income—and Why It's Back"* Investopedia 8 May 2020

Pirsig, Robert *"Zen and the Art of Motorcycle Maintenance"* William Morrow, 1974

Owen, James "Future Humans: Four Ways We may, or May Not, Evolve" National Geographic News 24 November 2009

Ruskin, John *"The Nature of Gothic"* Stones of Venice 1853

HOMO ASTRO AND HOMO COSMOS

Overbye, Dennis *" Far-off Planets Like the Earth dot the Galaxy"* New York Times 5 November 2013

Max, D. T. *"How Humans are shaping our own evolution"* National Geographic April 2017

European Space Agency *"Lichen can survive in space: Space station research sheds light on origin of life; potential for better sunscreens"* Science Daily 23 June 2012

"The Hibernator's Guide to the Galaxy" Wired, December 2022

Putzer, Mark *"CES 2022: What Is the Mysterious Sierra Space Corporation?"* Motor Biscuit 6 January 2022

Emmett, Arielle *"The Big Sleep"* Air & Space, Smithsonian May 2017

Chavis, Jason C. *"Effects of Space Travel on the Human Body"* Bright Hub 3 March 2010

THE INTELLIGENTLY DESIGNED HUMAN, HOMO DESIGNUS

Merriam-Webster dictionary
Hafer, Abby *"The Not so Intelligent Designer"* Cascade Books 2015
Saetre, Glenn-Peter *"Evolutionary flaws disprove the theory of intelligent design"* University of Oslo 24 April 2020
Reisman, Jonathan MD *"The Unseen Body, A Doctor's Journey through the Hidden the Human Anatomy"* Flatiron Books 2022
Rowe, Chip *"Top 10 Design Flaws in the Human Body"* Nautilus 14 May 2015
Cranford, Natham *"The Top Ten Imperfections of the Human Body"* NPR 4 February 2014
"6 Animals that Can Regenerate Body Parts" Scitechdaily.com 17 July 2022

EPILOGUE

Shield, Peter *"Uncommon Sense, Shortcomings of the Human Mind for Handling Big-Picture, Long-Term Challenges"* Steady State Press 2021
Bryce, Emma *"What could drive humans to extinction?"* Live Science 25 July 2020
Andrews, Kylie *"Earth's spin axis shifted by melting ice sheets and changes of water on land"* Science Advances 8 April 2016
Santini, Jean-Louis *"Climate Change brings world closer to "doomsday," say scientists"* Business Insider January 2015
Bailey, Roger, *"Will Humanity Survive the 21st Century?"* Oxford Global Catastrophic Risks Conference July 2008
Bellamy, Edward *"Looking Backward 2000-1887"* Ticknor & Co. 1888
Rees, Sir Martin *"Our Final Century: Will the Human Race Survive the 21st Century?"* Conference 2015
Nicholson, Nigel *"How Hardwired Is Human Behavior?"* Harvard Business Review, Behavioral Science July–August 1998
"The Infulenza Epidemic of 1918" Archives.gov. National Archives and Records Administration.
"The Top Ten deadliest earthquakes in history" msnbc.com 2013
Chalmers, David. *"The singularity: A philosophical analysis."* Journal of Consciousness Studies 17 September 2010
DeBrabander, Firmin *"Life After Privacy, Reclaiming democracy in the age of Surveillance"* Cambridge University Press September 2020
"UnReal Engine, The Most Powerful 3-D Creation Tool" 2022
Sumner, Thomas *"Anthropocene has begun, group says"* Science News 15 October 2016
McKibben, Bill *"Falter, has the human game begun to play itself out?"* Henry Holt & Co. 2019
Hartman, Thom *"Welcome To the Anthropocene - The Age Of Human Die-offs"* Daily Kos 27 July 2022
"EcoModernist Manifesto" April 2015
Zalasiewicz, Jan *"What mark will we leave on the Planet?"* Scientific American September 2016
DeGrazia, David *"At what point does AI become conscious"* George Washington University 23 April 2023
Hawks, John, *"Still Evolving (after all these years)"* Scientific American September 2014
Kurzweil, Ray *"How to Create a Mind"* Viking, Penguin Group 2012
Moores, Bob *"Skeptical"* iUniverse Inc. 2011
Shrek 2, Dreamworks 2004
Kaku, Michio *"The God Equation"* Doubleday 2021
"Neil Armstrong quotes"